114 SCIENCE EXPERIMENTS GUARANTEED TO GROSS YOU OUT!

Oh, Ick!

114 SCIENCE EXPERIMENTS GUARANTEED TO GROSS YOU OUT!

Oh, ick!

JOY MASOFF
with Jessica Garrett and Ben Ligon

ILLUSTRATED BY
David DeGrand

WORKMAN PUBLISHING · NEW YORK

> **D**on't be too timid and squeamish about your actions. All life is an experiment. The more experiments you make the better.
>
> —Ralph Waldo Emerson

Library of Congress Cataloging-in-Publication Data is available.

ISBN 978-0-7611-8738-7

Illustrations by David DeGrand
Design by Lisa Hollander
Cover design by James Williamson and Lisa Hollander
Photo research by Bobby Walsh
Cover photo by huronphoto/E+/Getty Images

Workman books are available at special discounts when purchased in bulk for premiums and sales promotions as well as for fund-raising or educational use. Special editions or book excerpts can also be created to specification. For details, contact the Special Sales Director at the address below, or send an email to specialmarkets@workman.com.

Workman Publishing Co., Inc.
225 Varick Street
New York, NY 10014-4381

workman.com

WORKMAN is a registered trademark of Workman Publishing Co., Inc.

Printed in China
First printing October 2016

10 9 8 7 6 5 4 3 2 1

To all the awesome kids who wrote to me
after reading *Oh, Yuck!* and *Oh, Yikes!*
I can't wait to hear what you have to say about *THIS* book.
—Joy Masoff

To Felix—may you always remain curious.
—Jessica Garrett and Ben Ligon

Ick-nowledgments
Thank you, slime, slugs, and snot!

There are so many people who made this book possible! Where to even begin? Well, let's start with my original group of yuck-sters—the varmints of my Boy and Girl Scout troops at Increase Miller School, without whom there would be no *Yuck*, *Yikes*, or *Ick!* Big high fives as always to my kids, Alex and Tish, and dear Obie Kopchak, who was willing to eat bugs to earn my daughter's heart!

Hip, hip, hooray to Dylan and Taylor Reed, who weren't afraid to get their hands good and dirty. And big smooches to Eli and Addy Townley, who like nothing better than manhandling a few squishy frogs.

And then there are the two people who did a ton of "heavy-lifting"—my totally fantastic and amazing partners in slime, Jessica Garrett and Ben Ligon. I'm pretty sure we all now share one giant brain and can, for a fact, complete one another's sentences and communicate telepathically.

—JM

Globs of gratitude to Joy, our fearless leader. You are a true ick-spiration, and we are so thankful that you convinced us to get our hands grubby and join you in investigating all things gross in our wild and wonderful world. Our students have squabbled over who got the chance to read *Oh, Yuck!* for years in our classrooms, so we couldn't believe our luck to get the chance to work on the "how-to" sequel! Our dinner conversations and email subject lines have never been more disgusting or giggle inducing.

A big burp of gratitude to our expert reader, Tom Savadove, our dear friend who is not only a doctor and geologist but is also obsessed with the disgusting parts of life. His help was invaluable.

Oozing oodles of thanks to our friends and neighbors who tested experiments and got their hands mucky: Maddy Zucca, Jyzelle Rose, Harrison Maxwell Mayer, Kam Unninayar, Amit Bajaj, Anyes Trichard, and Juliette and Lena Arany. A technical tip of the hat to our MIT colleagues and friends for their ideas: Alban Cobi, Amy Fitzgerald, Ed Moriarty,

Natalia Guerrero, and Todd Rider. A round of noisy applause goes to Lee Zamir of Bose for patiently explaining sound and giving us a fun analogy. Thanks to Jo Browne, Tania Veldwisch, Dooshima Mngerem, and the Alessandro clan, who reached back into their teen years to be sure we included the full zits experience. To Phyl and Paul Solomon for supporting and feeding us wacky egg creations along the way. To Jasa Porciello and Jon Petruschke for much encouragement and deep friendship during the writing of this book and always. To all our brilliant and dedicated teachers, who inspired us to explore, ask questions, and never stop learning. Only when we became teachers did we realize how much effort and energy it takes! And to all the students we've taught over the years: You stretched our brains and tickled our funny bones.

Infinite gratitude to our parents: Jean Ann, Peter, Barbara, and Ned. We now appreciate why you taught us to wash our hands so long ago. And why snot is not a topic for dinnertime conversation (unless you are writing a book about it). More important, you taught us how to think and ask questions. Thanks especially to Peter for many helpful comments and his special attention to geological and fungal topics.

The biggest hug in the world to our son Felix (age two when we started, age five when we finished). You patiently tolerated slimy experiments being photographed on the kitchen counter, suggested gross topics to add, and bravely helped us test experiments even though sometimes they made you gag.

—JG and BL

None of this would have ever happened without the good folks at Workman Publishing. Cries of "bravo" to our amazing, ever-patient editor, Margot Herrera, and her dogged assistant (who is definitely part bloodhound), Evan Griffith. A special place in art heaven for Lisa Hollander, who found the most revolting illustrations and wrangled a ton of material into an awesome book. Many warm pats on the back to Bobby Walsh— photo researcher extraordinaire. And many thanks to the entire Workman crew, especially Amanda Hong (production editor), Estelle Hallick (publicity maven), and Lauren Southard (social media) for being such great cheerleaders! Finally, this book wouldn't be half as revolting awesome without David DeGrand's illustrations. YAAAAAAAAY ICK!

—JM, JG, and BL

Contents

Introduction

HEY, YOU! YEAH, YOU . . . THE KID WITH THE GIANT BRAIN!

It's time to put that brain to use in the name of SCIENCE! It's also time to get your hands a little dirty . . . okay, maybe a LOT dirty. All kinds of grossness awaits in the pages ahead, from spiders and worms to farts and fungi. But what kind of science will be your domain?

Why not try your hand at chemistry and conjure up all sorts of fizzy, fetid potions? Or, you can become a biologist and probe the mysteries of your (and other animals') insides. No guts, no glory, as we say! Or perhaps you're obsessed with outer space or loop-the-loop roller coasters? Then you'll want some playtime with physics—the study of the way the world works. And what scientist doesn't like a little tinkering and inventing new things? You'll need engineering and math muscles to build the next great gizmo. Whatever your specialty, there's something in this book for you.

Along the way to science stardom, you will go nose to nose with nature's nastiest, meet some slightly gruesome scientists, and best of all, create all sorts of stinky, slimy concoctions! Just remember: When you're world famous for your amazing scientific discoveries a few dozen years from now, thank your grown-ups for being so patient with you (and maybe give us a shout out too!).

YOU *DO* HAVE A GIANT BRAIN, RIGHT?

Were we wrong? Is your brain the size of a gnat's? Is your favorite word *duh*? If you answered yes to any of these questions, drop this book immediately and go bang two rocks together for the next few hours. This is not the book for you.

Okay . . . you're still here reading this—good! You're clearly using your brain. If so, you will no doubt understand the following rules you *must* follow when conducting any of this book's yucky, superfun experiments. So raise your right hand and repeat after us!

1. I will be safe.
You're not a toddler anymore. You know not to stick a fork in an electrical outlet. But if we say "Get a grown-up to help," it means exactly that! Failure to do so will be the equivalent of sticking said fork in yonder outlet!

2. I will use protective gear when told to.
Hey—you want to gamble with your eyeballs? Got a few spares lying around in a drawer somewhere? We didn't think so. Safety glasses are needed for some of the "adventures" that await you. They are totally cool and make you look even cooler! Wear them! Your eyes will thank you! (You can find them in your size at the hardware store or online.)

Protect your eyes!

3. I will not eat or drink my experiments unless I'm expressly told it's okay.
And that goes for drinking out of any "lab ware" (i.e., the dishes you used in an experiment) without carefully washing it with soap and water. Eating an "edible spider" like the one on page 5 is A-OK. Eating a real one plucked raw from a petri dish is just plain dumb.

4. I will not mess with Mother Nature.
When you are out gathering fungi, bugs, rocks, dirt, spiderwebs, worms, or other awesome things, look around very carefully. Stay away from snakes! Do not disturb nests! And for heaven's sake, don't go number two in a patch of poison ivy.

5. I will clean up afterward.
Rub-a-dub-dub. Wash your hands in a tub—or a sink, or SOMEWHERE—ANYWHERE! When you are done with a project, clean up your mess. Your grown-ups are not your servants, and their greatest joy is *not* in picking up the leftover science stuff you have strewn all around the house.

TRIPLE ICK!

Things will get slimy, smelly, and sticky. You're going to brew some fake snot, conduct a body odor tournament, investigate poop, pop a huge pimple, and hang out with some worms, to name just a few of the *ick-speriments*, *ick-tivities*, and *ick-splorations* that are coming up.

Before you dig in, you might be wondering, "What exactly is the difference between an ick-speriment, an ick-tivity, and an ick-sploration?"

If it's an **ICK-SPERIMENT**, you will be doing some real science using the scientific method. You will ask why something happens, come up with a hypothesis, and then investigate and make a conclusion based on the data you collect. Nobel Prize, look out! Your parents will be proud, and your teachers dazzled, and no one will ever guess just how much fun YOU actually had.

If it's an **ICK-TIVITY**, you will be building or making something. Some of it will be tasty, some will test your cleverness, and some of it, like a portable hair ball, will have no use at all other than being hilarious.

If it's an **ICK-SPLORATION**, you'll be playing the role of fearless explorer, braving the wilds in search of critters (or better still—critter poop). Or maybe you'll just be braving the wilds of your house in search of something small but creepy. Sometimes you'll be combining chemicals just to see what will happen. Seek and ye shall find—something stinky, sticky, or slightly weird!

All right, then! Roll up those sleeves! Let's get MESSY!

HOW TO THINK LIKE A NOBEL PRIZE WINNER

What does it take to be a kick-butt scientist? You don't need bushy white hair, a giant moustache, or even a white lab coat to be a smarty-pants. What you DO need is to remember these six little steps.

1. Question
Be curious about the world around you and get comfortable asking questions like: What? Which? How? Why? Think about what you want to learn. Once you have the right question, you can start figuring out how to arrive at an answer.
Example: Why does Uncle Bob fart so much? The last fart bomb that Uncle Bob unleashed nearly knocked me out!

2. Research and Observe
You have eyes, ears, a nose, fingers, and a tongue. Use them! Read about what other folks have found out. Observe what happens around you, even if it's the smell of a nasty butt bomb that makes your eyes water. Anything can be evidence!
Example: Uncle Bob farts constantly. He also eats a lot of baked beans.

3. Hypothesis
Two little words: *if and then*. Based on what you already know, try to predict the answer to your original question.
Example: If Uncle Bob is a nonstop farter, then it could be because he eats baked beans three times a day. If I make my cousin Mo and my pal Bo eat beans, then they will crop-dust like a duo of flatulent elephants!

4. Experiment
This is the fun part! It's time to test the hypothesis.
Example: I'll ask Mo and Bo to eat beans at every meal for one whole day. We'll hang out together and I'll count all the farts. Then we will do a day with no bean eating, count the farts, and compare.

5. Data
These are the facts and numbers you gather and analyze while doing your experiment.
Example: Mo farted 15 times and Bo tooted 12 times on the bean-eating day, but only 5 and 4 times each on the bean-free days.

6. Conclusion
Finally, you're ready to answer to your original question. Was your hypothesis correct?
Example: Uncle Bob farts nonstop because he has a serious baked-bean addiction! The hypothesis was correct!

Do you recognize these six steps? They make up an awesome process called the scientific method. Scientists use this method all the time. It's a great way to organize your thoughts and observations and to pass your findings on to other scientists. It helps you keep track of your experiments so that you don't make the same mistakes next time (i.e., sleeping over at Mo and Bo's house on bean-eating days!).

It might help if you jot down all your questions, observations, hypotheses, data, and findings in a handy notebook. This way, you'll have a record of all your scientific adventures, and it will be easy to share with friends and teachers so they know just how brilliant you are!

Money Maker

Arachnids

The itsy-bitsy spider's not so bad. One or two on a waterspout? No big deal, really. But a giant, hairy-legged creature the size of a dinner plate with inch-long fangs crawling up your leg? That's another story entirely!

I SPY A SPIDER

Remember that skittish tuffet sitter, Little Miss Muffet, from the nursery rhyme? The one who freaked out when a spider sat down beside her? She had *arachnophobia* (uh-<u>rack</u>-nuh-<u>foe</u>-bee-ah) and she has a lot of company. More people are afraid of spiders than any other creature—even snakes. Spiders can be creepy, but most are really harmless. In fact, most spiders have a bad case of human-o-phobia—they are terrified of people. A spider that has somehow landed on you wants off of *you* a whole lot more than you want *it* off. And FYI, when it comes to spiders, flicking the little critter away is a whole lot tidier than smooshing it onto your skin. Safer too, since a panicked spider can sometimes bite. Just remember they're doing it because YOU totally freak them out!

The *Arachnid* (uh-<u>rack</u>-nid) class contains all sorts of nasty crawling creatures, including scorpions, mites, and ticks. All arachnids have eight legs and two body sections. They don't have antennae the way insects do. But only spiders spin webs. They are definitely the stars of the arachnid show, so let's start with them. There are more than 40,000 different species of spider. Compare that to the 35 or so species of cats and you start to see that there is a lot of variety in the spider world. The great majority of spiders are actually very cool!

FORGET SPIDER-MAN. MEET SUPER-SPIDER!

Think of spiders as tiny superheroes. Just a few spiders crawling around your house will nab, and then nibble on, all sorts of really annoying bugs, like roaches and earwigs. Many insects are disease carriers, but spiders keep you safe by capturing and then gobbling up dangerous pests such as mosquitoes, fleas, and filthy flies. Spiders do love their snacks!

Some folks keep tarantulas as pets! Just don't try to take yours for a walk around the block . . .

TASTY TARANTULAS

35 MINUTES

GO FETCH →

One way to become an arachnid expert is to make a model of one of the ickiest—the tarantula. When you are done, go ahead and eat it, just like a triumphant spider after a fight!

You now know that all arachnids have eight legs and two main body parts. One part is a head-and-chest combo called the *cephalothorax* (seff-uh-low-<u>thor</u>-ax). The other (usually bigger) part is the abdomen. Spiders like the tarantula also have fanglike mouthparts and two antennalike "feelers" called *pedipalps* sticking out of the front of the cephalothorax. These feelers can be so long that they almost look like legs, but they are not, so don't try to put tiny sneakers on them. Finally, spiders also have between two and eight *spinnerets*, handy organs that spin spider silk.

1. Thread six raisins onto a toothpick, leaving about half the toothpick bare.

2. When you get to the end of the toothpick, cap it with a bit of black licorice about ¼ of an inch wide. Think of it as a spider knee!

3. Repeat this with seven more toothpicks so you have the start of all eight tarantula legs.

4. Stick a second toothpick into each licorice end and thread raisins onto each one, this time covering the whole toothpick with raisins.

A large box of raisins (you will need about 15 to 18 raisins per leg)

About 26 toothpicks

Black licorice

1 small to medium plum to represent the abdomen, a tarantula's biggest part

1 large prune or fresh black fig to represent the chest (the larger hunk of the cephalothorax)

1 large purple grape to represent the jaw parts of the cephalothorax

Cap them with another small piece of licorice to represent a tiny spider claw. Make eight of these in total.

5. Attach the plum to the prune (or fig) by sticking a toothpick partway into the plum and then pushing the

exposed part of the toothpick into the prune (or fig). You now have a cephalothorax and abdomen.

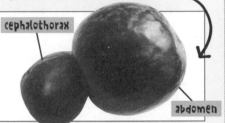

cephalothorax

abdomen

6. Attach each leg to the cephalothorax by sticking the bare part of the toothpick into the prune (or fig). Arrange them with four on each side of the body.

7. Complete the cephalothorax by attaching the jaws—a large purple grape slit about three-quarters of the way through. Use a toothpick to secure it to the rest of the cephalothorax.

8. Every tarantula needs its pedipalps. Thread eight more raisins onto two toothpicks (four raisins each) and stick them in the prune just about at the spot where the grape meets it.

9. Split another toothpick in half and stick the two pieces in the spider's rump. These represent the spinnerets.

10. Leave your tarantula lying around somewhere, then gross out a grown-up by plucking a leg off and nibbling happily. Careful with the toothpicks!

Speaking of edible spiders, the Piaroa peoples of Venezuela are big fans of eating real tarantulas—roasted with a little seasoning. *Mmm!* Folks in Cambodia also think tarantulas are finger-licking good. Fried or oven-baked? So hard to choose!

spinnerets

pedipalps

You can put spiders to use in your garden too. Spider venom is an eco-friendly insecticide, so instead of spraying vile chemicals on your tomato plants, just let your neighborhood spiders spin their webs nearby! No nasty, toxic fluids in your tomato sauce!

Still think spiders are supercreepy? Lucky for you, spiders control their own population growth. When food is scarce, some spiders turn against each other. They pull on eight tiny boxing gloves and FIGHT to the death (just kidding about the gloves!). What does the winner get? No trophy . . . but they do get to EAT the loser. Yum! Spider cannibalism!

WEBMASTERS

Ever walk into a spiderweb? Disgusting! The stuff sticks to you like glue. But stop for a minute and think about this: What if you could spin long steel cables, shoot them out your butt, and link the strands together to create an amazing suspension bridge, with no tools whatsoever? You could if you were a spider. A spiderweb is a total engineering marvel, both in the way it's made and the stuff it's made out of.

Take spider silk. Spiders have special glands that do nothing but produce the liquid that makes web strands. When this liquid is exposed to the air, through the spinnerets, it quickly dries. In this state, it weighs practically nothing. If a spider could somehow crank out a single strand that could circle the Earth (about 25,000 miles, or 40,000 kilometers around), it would weigh only about one pound (450 grams). That strand could then be stretched to go around the Earth a few more times without breaking. Web silk looks fragile, but pound for pound, it's way stronger than steel and even

Kevlar (the material used to make bulletproof vests). That means that if you had a pound of spider silk and a pound of steel next to each other, the spider silk would be way stronger! Useful stuff, but unlike milking a cow, there's no easy way to "silk" a spider, so it would be VERY hard to actually get a pound of it!

When baby sea turtles are born on land they know to head for the ocean. That's called an instinct: No one has to teach them how to do it. It's the same with spinning a web. A spider just knows! Silk can be used to build a house, capture dinner, and protect tender spider eggs. Desert spiders can spin silk that withstands high heat and dryness. Rain forest spiders make strands that resist moisture and won't rot under the dampest conditions. And a spider can produce different kinds of webs—sticky silk to lasso supper, and nonsticky silk to create a path so it can reach its victim.

SPY THESE SPIDERS? Should You Be Scared?

Of the over 40,000 species of spider, fewer than 50 kinds have venom that can be harmful to you, and the most terrible lives in the rain forests of Brazil (see below). So relax! But still—it's best to be spider savvy. Venomous spiders do their damage in two different ways. *Necrotic* (neck-rot-ick) venom eats away at the skin around the bite site. *Neurotoxic* (new-row-tox-ick) venom travels into the nervous system of the victim. Ouch! It's no coincidence that both those words end with "ic" . . . as in "ICK!" Here are a few fearsome foes to be mindful of:

1. Brazilian wandering spiders are residents of the Amazon rain forest and should come with a skull-and-crossbones warning. With legs up to 5 inches long, they are big creepy-crawlers with really toxic venom. They're crazy-aggressive too.

Speak Spider Spiders can't talk or text, but they *can* communicate! When they feel threatened and are about to strike, they often stand up on a few of their hind legs or hop sideways. So don't mess with a spider that's sending that kind of body language. Below, a Goliah bird-eating spider says "back off!"

2. Goliath bird-eating spiders don't usually eat birds, but they can take down a rodent or a frog! With legs up to 11 inches (28 cm) long, they are one of the biggest spiders on the planet. Natives of South America, these enormous creatures have terrible eyesight, so they use their hairy legs to sense motion. Of course, just seeing one of these guys might be enough to give a person a heart attack!

3. Tarantulas are fat, furry, and scary-looking, but in fact their venom is weaker than a honeybee's. A bite might hurt a bit, but it's not really harmful in the long run. What IS annoying is that they can rub those hairy legs together to send little razor-y leg-hair barbs into the air, which land on whomever they think is trying to attack them. It's like getting stuck with a bunch of tiny knives. Most unpleasant!

4. Black widow spiders are considered the most venomous spiders in North America. You can tell if you meet one by its red hourglass marking on the underside of its abdomen. Black widows usually only bite if they are being squashed, but their bites are very venomous and can cause nausea, muscle aches, and difficulty breathing. Ick, indeed! There are also brown and gray widow spiders, among others. An easy-to-remember tip: Stay away from any spider with the word *widow* in it.

SOME SPIDER SAFETY BASICS

If you live in an area with poisonous spiders, here's how to stay safe: Don't stick your hands into piles of wood or leaves. Give a gentle prod with a stick first to send spiders scurrying. And don't leave shoes, boots, or gloves outdoors overnight. To a spider, they look like luxury hotels. If you do leave them out, give them a good bang and shake upside down before putting your tootsies inside!

THE WIDE WORLD OF ARACHNIDS

By now you know that not all arachnids are spiders (you do know that, right?). Here are some of spiders' relatives, all part of the arachnid class.

1. Scorpions live on every continent except Antarctica, so unless you live on that frozen land, keep your eyes out for a critter with a long, curving segmented tail. Of the more than 1,500 species of scorpion, about 25 can kill with one sting! Still, scientists are a creative bunch and have discovered that some scorpion toxins can treat dreadful diseases. And some people in China skewer scorpions on slender sticks, roast them, and crunch away, rather like an arachnid kebab.

2. Ticks

2. Ticks are capable of real mischief. That's because their favorite food is blood. They cut into the skin, insert their feeding tube, and start sucking. Unfortunately, they often carry diseases. Tick-born baddies like Lyme disease and Rocky Mountain spotted fever can make you feel like a pile of rotting garbage. Check for ticks on your skin after playing outside. If you find one, get a grown-up. Never try to pull it off by yourself.

3. Daddy longlegs sure looks like a spider, but he's not (and in fact, many of them are mommy longlegs)! These arachnids, also called *harvestmen*, can't spin a web, and they don't have any venom. They look like an oval brown pill with eight superskinny legs poking out. How to tell the "dads" from the "moms"? Males have longer legs. Like your friendly neighborhood spiders, they eat a ton of pests and other insects and also have a taste for bird poop. Delicious!

Talk about a tree house! This tree is covered in spiderwebs. Millions of spiders in Pakistan took refuge in trees after massive floods displaced them.

ICK-TIVITY

WEAVE A GIANT WEB

GO FETCH

> 3 different colors of yarn or string. One should be 20 feet (6 m) long, the others each about 10 feet (3 m) long.
>
> A large *Y*-shaped stick. Ours made a triangle that was about 3 feet on each side. If you don't live near trees, you can purchase 2 dowels and lash them together to form a *V* shape with some string or pipe cleaners.
>
> A glue stick
>
> A piece of newspaper or other surface that is safe for gluing

Surprisingly, not all spider species spin webs. But those that do make such beautiful ones. You think it's easy to whip up a fly trap out of silk? Try your hand at creating a web the way real spiders do. This won't be any old tiny web either. This web is made for a spider the size of a soccer ball! (If you just want to make an itty-bitty web, you can just choose proportionately smaller amounts of materials.)

1. Pick up your longest piece of yarn. You'll use pieces of this in the next 5 steps. Tie one end to a high point on the left side of your *Y* stick.

2. Pretend you are a spider and release the free end from your spinnerets into the wind. What? You can't shoot strands of silk from your butt? Too bad. You'll have to use your hands to string the yarn across to the other side of the *Y* and tie another knot. Cut the excess string off. A spider would release a thread into the wind and wait for it to catch something—a nearby tree, perhaps—and then they would pull it tight and secure it to whatever they're standing on. This is called a bridge line.

3. Loosely tie another thread of the same color across the *Y* so that it hangs down below the tight bridge thread. Cut the end off.

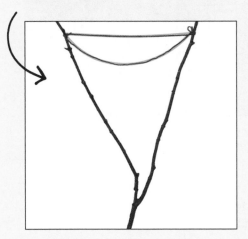

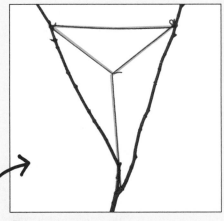

4. Tie another piece of yarn to the center of the loosely hanging thread. This new piece should hang vertically. Secure this piece at the bottom of the *Y* stick, and cut.

5. Create a *V* shape by tying two new pieces of yarn between the bottom of the *Y* stick and the two knots on each end of the bridge line.

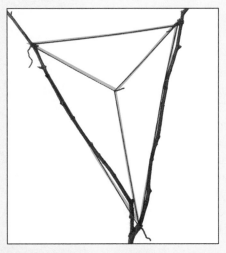

6. A spider would now fill in the gaps with threads that go from the outer edges to the middle. These are called "radius threads." You can make some too. We used eight, but a spider would use as many as necessary for easy travel across the web. Trim all the ends sticking out from the knots.

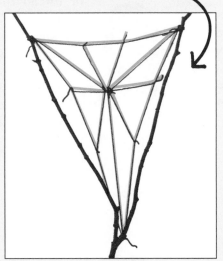

7. Now for the spiral. First, a spider makes a nonsticky spiral that she can walk on. (Otherwise she'd get stuck in her own web! Yikes!) Pick a different color yarn and tie it to the center of the web. Then twist it outward into a spiral. Every time you cross a radius thread, put a dab of glue there to secure it. Keep spiraling until you reach the edge of the web. A spider uses its legs to keep the measurements even.

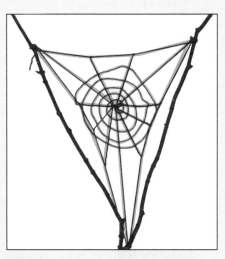

8. Next, a spider would turn around and create a sticky spiral back along the path of the original nonsticky spiral. Take your third color of yarn and rub the glue stick all over it. Get it really sticky!

9. Follow the path of your nonsticky spiral, placing your sticky spider silk just around it and pressing it into the web structure so that both spirals will stay.

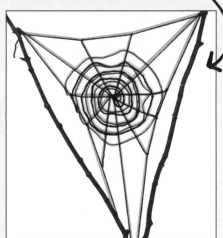

10. Hang your spiderweb in your room and pretend you live on it! Maybe you'll get lucky and catch some yummy flies! Dinner! In fact, before the glue dries, you can play a game called "Spider Suppertime." Use small cotton balls to represent flies (you can color them black with a magic marker) and throw them at the web. Can you catch a fly? Bon appétit!

WHERE, OH "WEAR" IS MY SPIDERWEAR?

Remember the story "The Emperor's New Clothes"? A similar but lesser-known tale involves the French spider lover named François de Saint Hilaire, who in the early 1700s patiently gathered enough spider silk to weave several articles of clothing. Legend has it that the fabulously rich King Louis XIV heard about this amazing fabric and demanded an outfit from Saint Hilaire's spiders. Alas, according to the story, one eyewitness reported that King Louis's suit "tore in all directions," giving his loyal subjects a peek at His Majesty's birthday suit!

Too bad Saint Hilaire did not have silk from the Darwin's bark spider of Madagascar. This orb-weaver spider's silk is the toughest biological material ever studied. The spider can spin strands that are almost 82 feet, or 25 meters, long (that's almost a third of a football field), and their webs are humongous—about 8 feet by 3 feet!

Is spider silk actually suited for clothing? Two ambitious fellows, Simon Peers and Nicholas Godley, decided to find out. Peers and Godley weren't scientists: Godley was a designer and Peers was an art historian. They read about a machine that existed in the 1800s that could extract silk from a spider and turn it into threads, so they decided to build one and put it to work. But first they needed spiders. Lots of them.

So Godley and Peers recruited people to collect Golden-Orb spiders (a relative of the Darwin bark spider). They gathered about 3,000 a day—over a million in all! Then they hired people to patiently pull on the tiny piece

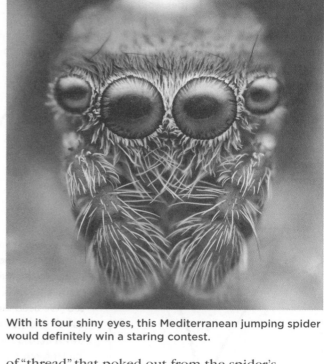

With its four shiny eyes, this Mediterranean jumping spider would definitely win a staring contest.

of "thread" that poked out from the spider's spinneret so that it could be attached to the machine via little pulleys. The spider was put into a little harness along with 23 of its spider buddies so that 24 threads were drawn out at the same time, tugging the contents out of each spider's web sac until there was nothing left. These were all hand-twisted and joined with three more 24-thread strands to make 96-thread strands.

How strong were these strands? Someone compared trying to tear one to trying to rip a bike lock cable. That's pretty strong!

The spiders were returned to the wild, where in about a week their sacs would be full again. The end result was a gorgeous golden-colored piece of fabric. The price tag? It cost over half a million dollars to make, and today it sits in a museum in London.

Haven't learned enough about creepy-crawlies? Scuttle on over to INSECTS (see page 136) for more info on the world of bugs.

This cape made of Golden-Orb spiders' silk took 8 years to make.

Awesome Acids
and Their Buddies, Bases

You're watching a nail-biting mystery on TV. The sneering villain has just dissolved a key piece of evidence by pouring acid on it. Metal is dissolving into thin air in a cloud of hissing, bubbling, sizzling steam! Scary, huh? But relax! There is no reason to fear most acids. In fact, they're really cool.

I'LL HAVE A BOWL OF ACID, PLEASE

Don't let the word *acid* make you freak. After all, you probably eat or drink certain acids every day. Go ahead. Have a big mouthful of carbonic acid. It puts the fizz in soft drinks. Lactic acid forms when milk is turned into yogurt. Ascorbic acid puts the zing in your morning OJ. Acetic acid is the vinegar in your salad dressing.

But what exactly is an acid . . . or a base, for that matter? Well, we humans like to sort things into groups. Long ago—back in ancient Egypt and Greece—curious people (who later became known as chemists) noticed that certain substances had several things in common. So they put them into groups and gave them names, like Bob and Jane. Ha! Just kidding! They called one group acids and the other group bases. They noticed that the acids tasted sour, did wacky things when poured on metals, and could burn through skin. The bases were different.

MOVIE-STAR ACID

One of the scariest and strongest acids is hydrofluoric acid. Exposure to it is very dangerous—it can seriously burn your skin and eyes!—but let's not get confused. There is a scary, totally make-believe version of this acid that got the nickname "Hollywood acid" because TV and movie writers like to pretend it can eat through bathtubs and floors, not to mention people! It doesn't, and it won't. But people who are exposed to superstrong acids like hydrofluoric acid DO need medical attention immediately. Fortunately it's not an acid we come in contact with in day-to-day life.

Bases could also burn through skin, but they tasted bitter and felt slippery. But what *really* made those ancient eyes pop was this: When the acids and bases mixed with one another, crazy things happened—fizzy, bubbling, sometimes violent chemical battles between the two groups!

Acids and bases are really important. They are essential for the chemical reactions that happen in your body, from your stomach right down to each tiny cell. If you've snuck ahead and read about GUTS on page 107, you know a little about hydrochloric acid—the stuff in our stomachs that helps dissolve our food. Our stomach walls are lined with a thick layer of mucus, so the acid can't hurt them, but get that very same acid on the outside of your body and it might irritate your eyes, nose, or throat. If you've ever had the pleasure of vomiting, you'll know how hydrochloric acid can feel as it rises up your throat—no fun! It's a good idea to rinse your mouth with water after upchucking because the acid that came up from your stomach can erode the enamel on your teeth!

Just as there are useful acids and scary acids, the same is true for bases. Your birthday cakes would be pitiful-looking if it weren't for a hardworking base—baking soda—that works alongside acids in cake batter to give it that nice, fluffy texture. And you'd be stinky and definitely dirty if it weren't for that sudsy base, soap.

Sodium hydroxide is a superstrong base that is used to clean clogged sinks. How fierce is this particular base—often known as drain cleaner? Pour sodium hydroxide down a clogged sink and it will eat through a clump of hair the size of a fist along with the other gunk that keeps your dirty bathwater from draining after you bathe. Plumbers hate drain cleaner because if it doesn't manage to get through the whole clog, then when they are called in to fix it, they can get splashed and the sodium hydroxide will burn their skin. This base is no joke!

ELEMENT-ARY SCHOOL

Everything in the universe, including acids and bases, is made up of the same basic building blocks: atoms. Just like a wicked-hard, zillion-piece Lego set, atoms snap together to form things called elements and molecules. Here's a quickie chemistry lesson in case you haven't heard of these little guys or need a mini review before trying some of the experiments that follow.

Atoms—Pretend you are a swashbuckling pirate and you have a chunk of gold (Arrgh!). You also have a mysterious sword that can slice

geek speak!

For all you chemistry geniuses out there, here's how scientists classify acids and bases: Acids always release hydrogen (H) when mixed with water. A base releases hydroxide (OH).

There's nothing quite like a bubbling chemical reaction to bring out your inner mad scientist!

SOMETHING'S GONNA BLOW!

GO FETCH →

Okay, time for some fizzy fun! You might've seen this experiment before, especially if you've ever made a volcano in science class. But some things, especially frothing, messy chemical reactions, never lose their charm. We'll be mixing good ol' vinegar (an acid) with ever-so-useful baking soda (a base), but tasting each first to really get to know these chemicals personally.

NOTE: NEVER TASTE ACIDS THAT ARE STRONGER THAN VINEGAR OR LEMON JUICE! AND NEVER EAT OR TOUCH BASES unless you are sure they are actual foods. Many chemists once *did* taste tests to identify acids and bases, but you should learn from their STUPIDLY SERIOUS and SOMETIMES DEADLY mistakes. Are we yelling loud enough yet? DO NOT MESS AROUND WITH HOUSEHOLD CHEMICALS! Especially bleach and ammonia—avoid these! PROMISE? Good!

1. Place the vinegar and the baking soda into separate bowls. This is one of the few experiments where you have our permission to taste. Dip one spoon in the vinegar and then touch it to your tongue. Now, twy to tawk wit yur mout all puckered up! That's an acid for you. Acids taste sour. They make your mouth get all wrinkly. And vinegar is a very weak acid!

2. Now dip the other spoon in the baking soda and taste. How does it make your mouth feel? Bases taste bitter. Now wet your finger and dip it in the baking soda. Rub your thumb over it. How does it feel? Bases are

- 2 cups white vinegar
- 2 cups baking soda
- 2 small bowls
- 2 spoons
- 1-cup measuring cup
- 1/4-cup measuring cup
- Small cup or glass
- Large bowl (to catch overflow)
- Food coloring (optional)

known to feel slippery. Wash off your fingers and repeat the finger test with the vinegar. Does it feel as slippery?

3. Pour 1/4 cup of your baking soda into the small cup or glass, which you have placed inside the larger bowl to contain any overflow. Then pour 1/4 cup of vinegar in. If you want to add food coloring, you can add it to either chemical first. What happens when you mix them?

4. What would happen if you added more vinegar now? Make a hypothesis and test it. Here's an example (notice the *if, then* words): "*If* I add 1/2 cup more vinegar, *then* I think it will explode over the bowl." Experiment with different proportions of your

reactants (ree-<u>ack</u>-tints) (i.e., the vinegar and baking soda) to see which makes the most foam.

WHAT JUST HAPPENED?

A chemical reaction, that's what! In a chemical reaction, the original molecules swap some of their atoms to make something new and different. The vinegar and baking soda actually exchanged atoms and became three totally new chemicals: sodium acetate, carbon dioxide (CO_2), and a little something we like to call water. (You know *that* molecule pretty well, you brilliant chemist, you!) The water is, well, real water: H_2O. The carbon dioxide gas is what created all that foam. It's also the same gas you exhale every day. And the sodium acetate? It's actually a kind of salt—a "sodium salt of acetic acid," to be extra geeky about it. It's a super-amazing chemical with lots of uses, such as:

● A food additive to make things taste better. Check the ingredient list on different brands of salt-and-vinegar chips. (It may be called sodium diacetate.)

● Creating heat packs for winter sports. When you press on a heat pack, the sodium acetate inside turns into a crystal and releases a ton of heat. Ahh, that feels good.

● An environmentally friendly way to protect concrete against water damage. It seals the concrete so water can't get in and is much safer than the epoxy glue that is often used. So you might just be stepping on it as you skip down the street!

Greetings from the Atomium

The "WRONG" old days. Scientists used to think that atoms looked like this. For more info check out ZAPS!

through metal as if it were room-temperature butter. Now cut that chunk of gold in half. Then cut that half in half. Keep cutting, over and over and over, until you cannot possibly cut one more time. You would need a microscopic knife to actually cut that last bit of gold in half! What you're left with is an atom—a little piece of matter that can't be made into a smaller piece without losing its chemical identity. Any smaller and it simply wouldn't be gold anymore! Atoms are the building blocks of everything we know.

Elements

Elements—You now have a gold atom, but it's so small that it's invisible to the human eye. Not much use if you want to fill up a treasure chest, matey! How do you make a gold coin? You need more atoms of that same element, gold! An element has just one kind of atom in it. It's a pure substance. A solid gold coin is made of zillions of gold atoms that are stuck together. But there are no other kinds of atoms in it. It's just gold. Some other common elements are hydrogen, oxygen, sodium, copper, aluminum, neon, carbon, and silver.

Molecules

Molecules—Two or more atoms that have decided to hang out together. Pretend your name is Oxygen. Now pretend you have an identical twin. When you sit next to each other, the two of you would be the molecule O_2. (The "O" stands for oxygen. The tiny number 2 means that there are two oxygen atoms in this molecule.) You know that weird smell just before a thunderstorm? It's ozone, a gas made from a few bazillion oxygen triplets all hangin' out together—nickname: O_3.

30–40 MINUTES

ICK-SPERIMENT

ROCKIN' ROCKETS

GO FETCH

Safety glasses. Don't argue! These are a must!

An adult to help with the launch

Long, flat area of floor or an outside area that can get wet

Masking tape

A meter stick or yardstick

Several film canisters with lids that snap closed on the inside*

About 10 effervescing (fizzing) antacid tablets

Knife to cut the tablets

Water

Tablespoon

Measuring tape or ruler

Paper towels for cleanup

Your notebook

* Lids that go around the outer edge will leak. You can order them online by searching for "rocket film canisters." You also may be able to get the canisters for free at a local photo-developing location, a camera store, or a drugstore that does film developing.

Why not put the reaction between an acid and a base to good use? That release of gas can launch a little "rocket"! Of course, every rocket needs fuel. You'll use antacid tablets, which grown-ups sometimes take to calm upset tummies. Each tablet is made of citric acid and baking soda (a base)—both just hanging around waiting for the addition of some water to get the party started. When you add water, the acid and base react and release carbon dioxide gas. Now comes the fun. If that gas is released inside a small container, pressure will build up and you can harness that power to launch a rocket skyward.

Let's start by investigating how changing the amounts of "fuel" (the antacid tablets) will affect how far your mini rocket will go. Will a bigger reaction bring more movement or make a mess? What do you think?

1. Set up your runway so that it is 5–6 yards long and 1 yard wide. Tape down your yardstick so that the wide edge faces forward. Your film canister lids will rest against it. You can also just use a nearby wall as the starting point as long as it is completely flat (no curvy baseboard trim). These rockets will travel along the floor or ground so that you can measure how far they go.

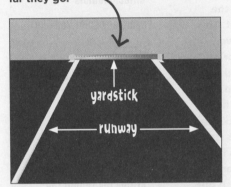

2. Fill each of your film canisters with 1 tablespoon of water (about ⅓ full).

3. Break or cut several of the antacid tablets into quarters and several into halves. Keep one or two whole tablets.

4. Practice pretending to put a piece of tablet in the canister, quickly closing the lid without spilling, and lining the rocket up against your yardstick or wall. Be sure the lid rests against the stick or wall, with the rest of the canister facing forward. After a few practice runs, you are ready to go. IMPORTANT: Once you put a tablet in the canister, hands off!

Wait patiently. Also, be sure that you and your flight crew stand behind the yardstick or off to the side, not in the path of any rockets.

5. Begin with the ¼ piece of tablet. Pop it in a canister. Close the lid. Rest the lid end against the yardstick, or wall, on the runway. Step back.

6. Count down: 10, 9, 8 . . . Blast off! Of course your rocket may launch before your countdown ends, or it may take several countdowns. Rocket scientists are a patient group.

REMEMBER:
DON'T OPEN A LOADED ROCKET AND DON'T LET ANYONE GET IN THE PATH OF THE ROCKET.

7. Enjoy the launch.

lid   rocket

8. Measure how far the rocket went. Record it in your notebook along with the size of the tablet used.

9. Wipe off the runway, then try the experiment again with a different size tablet. Does tablet size affect how far the rocket goes?

NOTE: If the rocket doesn't move after 3 minutes, have your adult helper carefully cover it with their hand and release the lid facing the floor onto some paper towels.

Now, try this:

• Vary the amount of water, but keep the tablet size the same.

• Measure the amount of time it takes each rocket to pop. You can make a

chart comparing the amount of fuel and how long it takes to move. What's your prediction?

• Add a weight of some kind to the canister, such as a small pebble.

• Vary the temperature of the water. Does hot water make it go any farther than cold?

WHAT JUST HAPPENED?

When you dropped your fizzy tablet in water, a chemical reaction occurred. An acid and a base reacted, releasing tiny bubbles full of carbon dioxide. As the reaction continued, more and more carbon dioxide built up in the film canister and began to push against all the sides, a bit like blowing a balloon up with air. But since the film canister can't stretch, the only way the pressure could be released is . . . *KA-BLOO-EY*! The lid popped off and the gas escaped as fast as it could. This pushed the lid of the film canister against the yardstick and sent the canister skimming away across the floor.

A very brilliant scientist named Sir Isaac Newton noticed that this happens all the time in nature, so he made it one of his three laws of motion. He said, "For every action, there is an equal and opposite reaction." In this case, this means that the gas pushes one way (toward the ruler or wall) and the rocket is pushed the other way with an equal and opposite amount of force, causing the rocket to fly across the floor. It's the same science behind a real rocket launch. Rockets burn fuel in engines at their base. The burning fuel pushes down toward the ground, which thrusts the rest of the rocket up in the opposite direction. Blast off!

To test this knowledge, try the ick-tivity on the next page.

Not all molecules are identical twins or triplets like O_2 and O_3. Take best buddies H (hydrogen) and O (oxygen). Bring two hydrogen atoms and one oxygen together and they form H_2O, something you wash with and drink every day: water. CO_2 is carbon dioxide gas—one of the gases you breathe out thousands of times a day. It's made of one carbon atom and two oxygen atoms.

Chemical Formulas—There are millions of other molecule buddies. Baking soda is $NaHCO_3$. (It kind of looks like the word *nacho*, but it isn't nearly as tasty.) These combos of letters and little numbers are called *chemical formulas* and they can tell us a lot about what's in the molecule. In the case of $NaHCO_3$, we know from the little numbers that it must have one atom of sodium (Na), one atom of hydrogen (H), one atom of carbon (C), and three atoms of oxygen (O). (Why Na instead of S for sodium? Well, the letter S was already taken by sulfur, so they used sodium's Latin name: natrium.)

LET'S GET READY TO RUMBLE

What usually happens when someone mixes players from Team Acid with players from Team Base? Generally, three things. For starters, things get a little warm because heat is produced. Meanwhile, acids and bases spew out water molecules when they collide. Finally, parts of the atoms and bases join together to make salts. But don't sprinkle these salts on your fries! Most of them are too acidic or basic, so they taste disgusting and can even be dangerous!

Want to dazzle your neighbor who's always bragging about how smart her grandkid is? Spout out the fact that when acids and bases combine it's called *neutralization* (new-tra-li-<u>za</u>-shun). Neutralization is like the Super Bowl of chemistry. Sometimes it's a blowout with the stronger acid or base doing endless happy dances in the end zone, a chemical touchdown! Other times, if you have just the right amounts, a very strong acid and a very strong base can cancel each other out and end up as a wimpy neutral mix of salty water. Think of it as a football game for chemicals, minus the 350-pound guys in tight shiny pants, that has ended in a tie.

ICK-TIVITY

DO WE HAVE LIFTOFF?

GO FETCH

Did you complete your Rockin' Rockets mission? Good. Your next challenge? Get your rocket to shoot for the moon—or the ceiling at least. This time you'll have passengers—or a "payload." You will need to design some extra parts to help make your rocket go far and fly in a stable manner. If you have several canisters, you can design each one slightly differently (keep notes!) and see which one flies the highest or the straightest.

- Your film canister(s) and lid from Rockin' Rockets
- Effervescing (fizzing) antacid tablets
- Paper (any color you like)
- Scissors
- Round objects, like lids for tracing circles
- Pencil or pen
- Tape
- One small candy, pebble, or tiny toy (about the size of an M&M) for the "payload"
- Plate as a launchpad

Now wouldn't THIS be fun?

1. Have a look at some photos or videos of real rockets. What parts do they all have? At the very least, you will need to build a nose cone and some stabilizing fins. You can also add fun decorations. As you decorate, DO NOT tape the lid shut, and don't tape anything that will get in the way of the lid closing.

2. The nose cone will slice through the air. To make one, draw a circle. It's easy to trace some round containers in your house. You'll want to experiment with different size circles.

Then use your scissors to make two cuts to the center of the circle so that you cut out a ¼ wedge (like a slice of pie).

You can then place one edge over the other edge and pull it around to make a cone. The bigger the circle, the taller the cone.

3. Pop your payload in the cone before you tape it to the end of the film canister without the lid.

4. You can cut a rectangular strip of paper to wrap around the body of the rocket. Just be careful not to tape the lid closed by accident.

5. Make some stabilizing fins. These are usually triangles. You can cut out a rectangle, and then cut that in half along the diagonal. Bend the side a bit and tape them to your rocket. See if your rocket flies better with two versus three or four fins. Do longer or shorter or fatter or thinner fins make a difference? Build several different rocket designs and test each.

6. Set up a launchpad, with a plate on the floor in the middle of a room or outside. Practice pretending to load the fuel, quickly closing the lid, and then placing it lid-side down on a plate. The nose cone should face up to the ceiling or sky.

7. Be sure everyone present is either wearing safety glasses or standing well back. Now load your fuel for real. Begin with small amounts of "fuel"—about a tablespoon of water (so the canister

is about ⅓ full). When you're ready for launch, add ¼ antacid tablet. Close the lid, flip the rocket so that the lid is down on the plate and the nose cone is facing the ceiling, and step back. IMPORTANT: Once you put a tablet in the canister, do not lean down to open it or get in the way. Have patience!

8. Test each rocket that you built, and experiment with different amounts of fuel (½ antacid tablet or a whole one).

WHAT JUST HAPPENED?

Did your payload reach the ceiling? How much fuel was required to get there? What was the best rocket design? All rockets have these basic parts: nose cone, body, fins, and some kind of fuel or way of propelling it up. Hopefully you found that an aerodynamic shape for your nose cone helped it avoid getting slowed down by the air. What nose cone size was best for your rocket? You probably found that adding a little more weight in the nose cone made its flight a little more stable. This is because it moved the rocket's center of gravity to the front. How many fins worked best? What shape or size of fins was ideal? Well-placed fins help the rocket fly straight and be stable. You might have found that your rocket was more stable if your fins were closer to the lid and were fairly large. Can you arrange the fins so that your rocket spins in the air as it flies? Even though these are tiny rockets, the same basic ideas apply to real rockets. To learn more, explore NASA's great website: nasa.gov.

GIVE ME A *p*! GIVE ME AN *H*!

What the heck does little *p*, big *H* stand for in "pH"? The *H* stands for hydrogen. It's the simplest, but also the most important, element on the planet—and in the universe! About 90 percent of the visible universe is made of hydrogen gas. Hydrogen is a busy little element. It's involved in all sorts of chemical reactions. You already know about our awesome buddy H_2O (water). Each itty-bitty drop is made of two hydrogen atoms hanging out with one oxygen atom. And you may remember from Geek Speak on page 12, acids release hydrogen when mixed with water. So, to recap: H = hydrogen. Got it?

What about the little *p*? Nobody knows for sure, but it's commonly thought that the *p* stands for the word *power*. The Power of Hydrogen!

ICK-SPERIMENT

PHINDERS KEEPERS

GO FETCH

- An adult (remember the grown-up rule; boiling water is involved here)
- Red cabbage
- Cutting board and knife
- A cooking pot
- Water
- Strainer
- Bowl
- Spoons
- White bowls, glasses, or paper cups
- Edible liquids, like vinegar, lemon juice, apple juice, and soda, and mild household cleaners, like dish soap, toilet cleaner, shampoo, window cleaner, and hand sanitizer

NOTE: DO NOT test any cleaning agents stronger than these! And be sure to check with your friendly adult before you take any cleaning supplies—they might need that window cleaner! Definitely do not touch bleach or ammonia, and **NEVER** mix them. That can release a really toxic gas.

SEESAW SCIENCE

You probably spent some time on a seesaw when you were younger. Every once in a while the seesaw would be perfectly balanced, with both ends equally off the ground. You could say that acids and bases are on one big seesaw too, but instead of a piece of playground equipment, chemists made up something called the pH scale. And just like the playground, it's tons of pHun! (Aren't chemistry jokes great?)

The pH scale is the way scientists divide the world up into acids and bases using numbers. The pH scale starts at 0 and goes to 14. Anything with a number from 0 to just

Lick a lemon! SOUR!!! That's one way to tell if something is an acid. Remember, acids tend to taste sour and bases taste bitter. But, since many acids and bases are truly ICK-tasting or even poisonous, there's a tongue-free way to find out if something is an acid or base. A pH indicator measures the pH of a liquid and changes color depending on whether it is an acid or a base. You can buy fancy pH paper (also called litmus paper), but you can also save money and rustle up a pot of pH-testing potion in your own home. Then use it to test your hypothesis about which liquids in your house are acids and which are bases! Here's how:

1. Before you start, develop some hypotheses about the liquids you've gathered. Which ones do you think will be acids, and which will be bases? Why?

2. Ask your friendly adult to help chop up about 2 cups of red cabbage leaves. The pieces should be small but not so tiny that they can slip through your strainer.

3. Put the cabbage pieces into the pot and add just enough water to cover the cabbage. Bring the pot to a boil and let simmer for about 20 minutes or until the water is dark purple.

4. Remove the pot from the heat and let it cool.

5. Strain the cooked cabbage juice into a bowl. It's the purple juice that you're after: When it comes to testing pH, this stuff is more valuable than liquid gold. Why? Because red cabbage juice changes color when exposed to acids or bases. (The leftover cabbage pieces are perfectly edible. Eat enough and you can do some cool fart experiments—see page 77!)

6. It's pH test time. Pour two spoonfuls of a household liquid into a white bowl, glass, or paper cup.

7. Mix in one spoonful of your cabbage juice indicator. There's a good chance that it will turn color. The color suggests the pH of your test liquid (though it's not going to be quite as accurate as the pH strips that you can buy).

8. Repeat Step 5 with other liquids you can find using the other white bowls, glasses, or paper cups. Try to assemble an array of different colors to make your own pH scale! Were your hypotheses correct?

ACIDS	BASES
pH 1–2—dark red	pH 8—blue/green
pH 3–4—purple	pH 9–10— green/yellow
pH 5–7—blue	pH 11–12—yellow

WHAT JUST HAPPENED?

The reason that many plants and flowers are red, purple, or blue is because they contain colorful chemicals called *anthocyanins* (an-tho-si-ah-ninz)—the word means "blue flower." Apples, cranberries, blueberries, strawberries, and definitely red cabbage are full of these pigments. When you cooked the cabbage, anthocyanins leached out of the leaves and into the water. Anthocyanins normally look purple but they change when they get near hydrogen. Acids have lots of extra hydrogen floating around. So when you mix an anthocyanin with an acid it turns pinkish. Think of anthocyanin as being embarrassed by acids. It *blushes*! Anthocyanin reacts differently around bases, turning blue, yellow, or green *with envy* (ha-ha), depending on how strong the base is.

under 7 is an acid. Anything more than 7 up to 14 is a base. Pure water is right smack-dab in the middle at 7. Your blood is just a scooch over—around 7.4 on the scale. Different chemicals in your body have different pH numbers—for example, stomach acid has a much lower number (more acidic pH) than your saliva.

So there you have it!
You are now a pH pHenom! pHabulous! Now it's time to leap from the letter *A* to *B* and brave the wild, weird worlds of BACTERIA, BLOOD, BOOGERS, and BURPS. Trust us! It'll be a BLAST.

Bacteria

At this very second there are trillions of microscopic critters crawling around all over your body. They're even **INSIDE** you! They are hanging out on your tongue, nesting in your nose, and frolicking in your intestines. In fact, you have 10 times more bacterial cells in and on your body than actual human cells!

BACTERIA THE BEAUTIFUL!

Bacteria are microorganisms. *Micro* means "teeny-tiny." Seriously, these guys are so small that even though the bacteria cells in your body vastly outnumber your human cells, only about 2 percent of your weight is actually bacteria. In a grown-up, all of them together weigh about 3 pounds—about the same as the human brain.

Not only are your cells loaded with bacteria, these clever critters are in the air around you and on the ground you walk on. Our entire planet is surrounded by a "blanket" of bacteria—they even live six miles high in the Earth's upper atmosphere, where the temperatures are a staggering 60°F below zero!

Though many people are freaked out by bacteria, the truth is that although some bacteria are harmful, the survival of every single creature on our planet depends on these teeny, sometimes terrible, but mostly terrific microorganisms. They perform all sorts of functions, both inside our bodies and in nature. So let's get the scoop on how bacteria can help and occasionally harm.

Remember: wash your filthy paws!

In addition to boatloads of bacteria, your skin can harbor viruses and microscopic mites.

BACTERIA HOTELS

GO FETCH

30 MINUTES

PLUS 1 HOUR COOLING TIME

Bacteria are too tiny to see, unless you have millions of them hanging out in one place. In order to study the Dirty Dozen (see page 23) that are already living rent-free in your home, you need a cozy place to grow lots of them. You can order petri dishes already filled with agar (a gel that's hospitable to many bacteria) online.

Or you can make your own "bacteria hotels" at home. They may not grow all the types of bacteria that are hanging around your house, but you should get to see quite a few. If you opt for making your own, read on!

1. Put the 2 cups of clear broth in the cooking pot.

2. Measure 2 tablespoons of agar and dump into the cooking pot.

3. With your friendly adult's help, turn your stove on to low heat.

4. Stir and gradually raise the heat every few minutes until the liquid boils. Stir the WHOLE time because the agar can easily burn. You will know when the liquid boils because little bubbles will form around the edge of the pot.

5. Every so often, lift your spoon out and look for any of the agar flakes. If you still see some agar on your spoon, keep stirring. When you don't see any more, remove the pot from the heat and let it cool.

6. Place the foil baking cups into the tray. If they come with little inner paper liners, take those out and save them for making zit cupcakes (see page 270).

7. After the agar mixture has cooled a little, ask your grown-up helper to

An adult to handle hot liquids

2 cups of clear beef or chicken broth (canned or cubes)

Cooking pot

2 tablespoons agar (can be found in some supermarkets or online)

Spoon

12 foil baking cups

12-cup muffin tray

Plastic wrap or aluminum foil

12 plastic ziplock bags

pour it into the cups so each is about ⅓ to ½ full.

8. Using a spoon, scoop out and throw away any odd-looking bubbles or blobs that may have formed on the top.

9. Let the mixture in the muffin tray cool even more, and then cover with plastic wrap or aluminum foil.

10. Put the tray in the refrigerator until the mixture cools into a solid (about an hour).

11. When they are solid, take the bacteria hotels out of the tray and put each one into its own personal ziplock bag. Be careful not touch the hotels' gelatin with your fingers.

12. Seal the bags and store in the refrigerator until you are ready for "Check-in Time" (see next page). You will want to use them within three days.

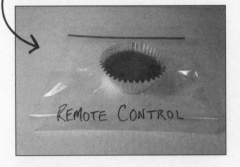

REMOTE CONTROL

WHAT JUST HAPPENED?

You have created a cozy home for bacteria, which tend to grow really quickly if given enough food (bouillon) and a semisolid environment (agar) to grow on. The part of agar that turns into a gel comes from the cell walls of red algae, and, for all you chemists out there, it is actually a polymer made of a kind of sugar. (Dying to play with polymers? Make some "Slimy Snot" on page 208.)

Because you have created a fairly sterile hotel by locking it in a bag, the bacteria you are about to add likely won't have to compete with other microbes (super-tiny critters) that might float by in the air. They can relax and enjoy the whole place to themselves.

CHECK-IN TIME AT THE BACTERIA HOTEL

GO FETCH

Bacteria hotels (page 21)

12 cotton swabs

Permanent marker

Now that you've prepared your bacteria hotels (and put tiny mints on the pillows . . . just kidding), you'll need to get some customers. Bacteria aren't going to ring the door to your refrigerator and ask to rent a room—you'll have to go find them! First make a hypothesis about which place in your house will grow the most organisms. Then test it! These same bacteria hotels can be used for the halitosis ick-speriment (see page 126), so you might want to read that now and do both at once.

1. Take your bacteria hotels out of the refrigerator one hour before you go to round up "guests."

2. Decide where you will swab for bacteria—toilet seat, computer keyboard, toothbrush, kitchen sponge, etc. (See the Dirty Dozen list on the next page for inspiration.)

3. Slightly dampen one end of a cotton swab under the faucet and rub that moist end on the place you think might have bacteria.

4. Unzip a bag, rub the swab on the gelatin in a zigzag pattern, throw the swab in the trash, and then zip the bag tightly shut.

5. Write where the sample came from on the bag in marker and then promise to never open up the bag again: You might be growing some

dangerous bacteria—called *pathogens* (<u>path</u>-oh-jinz)! SERIOUSLY. Now say it out loud, "I will not open this bag again. I promise!" Pinky swear!

6. Repeat steps 2 to 4 with the other items on your Dirty Dozen list, or have fun coming up with your own places.

7. Store your bacteria hotels in a warm, dark place in your home, out of reach of your curious younger brother or sister, your dog or cat, or pet boa constrictor.

8. In a few days, your quiet bacteria bed-and-breakfasts should

transform into bustling megahotels full of colonies of multiplying microorganisms. Take photos or draw pictures of your visitors, but remember your sacred vow: NEVER, EVER OPEN THE BAGS!

9. When you are finished, put the bacteria hotels and baggies in the trash can.

10. Be extra-helpful next time your grown-ups ask you to clean up around the house, because now you know what lives there!

WHAT JUST HAPPENED?

You probably grew some interesting critters in your hotels. Bacteria tend to be white, clear, or yellow. If something is darker, multicolored, and fuzzier, it's probably some type of mold or fungus. (See FUNGI on page 91 for more on those guys!) But no matter what you have growing, odds are it looks completely revolting—and totally cool, of course! Now, don't look at one of the little blobs growing in your hotel and think that it is just one bacterium. It's actually several thousand of them! You can't see a single individual bacterium without a microscope.

Just because you grew some microorganisms doesn't mean that

you grew ALL the kinds that were actually lurking on your cotton swabs. Bacteria are everywhere but, just like people, bacteria are picky-picky-picky. Some like sweet foods. Some like chilly temperatures. So you'll find different types on different surfaces. Your germ hotels are a particular environment, with a particular type of food. So even though a bacterial species was living happily in your kitchen sponge, it might not have been able to grow and reproduce in your hotel because it did not provide their preferred food or temperature.

Which has more germs—your smartphone or your toilet seat? The answer might surprise you!

You can't see bacteria until there are thousands in one place— but they're there!

THE DIRTY DOZEN

What spot in your home do *you* think is crawling with the most bacteria? Here's a list (in no particular order) of favorite bacteria vacation spots that might surprise you:

1. carpet. A whopping 4,000 times dirtier than the average toilet seat.

2. computer keyboard. Yep, every time you type, your fingers pick up or deposit a new load of beasties.

3. Kitchen sink. Germier than your bathroom sink, by far.

4. Kitchen sponge. A real stinker! 200,000 times dirtier than your potty!

5. cell phone screens. Covered in bacteria—*way* more than your toilet seat!

6. TV remotes. The hand that controls the channels also carries bacteria.

7. Kitchen cutting boards. Safer to chop up veggies on a toilet seat unless you wash that cutting board really, really well!

8. Doorknob. A mingling place for everyone's germs.

9. Toilet seat. Yep, more bacteria where you sit than where your poop plops. (But this doesn't mean it's safe to drink from the toilet bowl like a dog. Any bacteria floating in the bowl are likely to be harmful—after all, there's a reason your body wanted to get rid of them!)

10. Your mouth. Stinky breath? Blame bacteria.

11. Your unwashed hands. See why grown-ups nag you about washing with soap?

12. Your washed hands. Turns out it's really hard to scrub away those pesky bacteria!

GET TO WORK, BACTERIA!

Some bacteria make us sick, but most bacteria are awesome. Only about 1 percent of the bacteria on Earth cause diseases, while 99 percent are super helpful. For example, at this very moment you have about 100 trillion intestinal microflora (tiny creatures) living inside your guts. Without these little guys, you would barely be able to digest your food. All those diligent gut bacteria help us get the nutrients and energy from our food. Considering that the average American eats almost 2,000 pounds of food a year, the bacteria in our bellies are a dedicated bunch. Breaking down and decomposing a cheeseburger with fries and a small bag of gummy worms is hard work. Scientists are also discovering that bacteria help our immune system. So, though some bacteria make you sick, lots of others are actually fighting to keep you healthy! After all, YOU are their home!

YO, YOGURT!

Eating yogurt helps to boost the supply of good bacteria in your gut. If you see a "Live and Active Cultures" (LAC) seal, there are at least 100 million bacteria in every gram of yogurt. The more bacteria the better! Here are a few more yogurty facts for your enjoyment.

Exactly what kind of bacteria are lurking in your yogurt? *Lactobacillus bulgaricus* and *Streptococcus thermophilus* are two kinds. There might also be *Lactobacillus acidophilus* or *bifidus* hanging around. Store-bought yogurt labels might tell you which bacteria are inside.

You don't need a cow to make yogurt. You can also make it from the milk of water buffalo, goats, ewes, mares, camels, and yaks. Or you can use coconut, almond, or soy milk.

The yellow liquid that often appears when your yogurt sits around is called whey. It is mostly lactic acid, lactose sugar, and water. When people make Greek yogurt, they put the yogurt in a cloth and let the whey drain out. Cows and pigs like to eat whey, and some people like to drink it. Give it a try! It can even be used as an ingredient in an environmentally friendly coating to make wood floors hard and shiny.

ICK-SPERIMENT
BACTERIA BREW

15 MINUTES PREP
PLUS 12–36 HOURS WAITING

GO FETCH →

Try this nifty little experiment to investigate what good bacteria do when they get up close and personal with milk. You *don't* get to eat the results, but it will show you the action of antibiotics, which kill bacteria. (A shout-out to Dr. Todd Rider at MIT for sharing this ick-speriment.)

1. Be sure your little jars or glasses are clean (wash them in the dishwasher if you can on high heat). Decide if you want to test just one antibiotic or test a few. Each jar

- 2 or 3 clean jars. We used empty spice jars. Empty baby food jars or small clear juice glasses will work too.

- Ultra-pasteurized milk. It often comes in individual drink boxes in the powdered or canned milk section of your supermarket.

- Yogurt with live, active cultures

- Triple antibiotic ointment and several other brands or kinds if you wish, such as single antibiotic ointment or natural antiseptic ointments like tea tree oil.

- 2 or 3 spoons or measuring spoons

- Foil or lids for your jars

Wow, food AND a nice floor all from the work of bacteria on milk!

What's the scoop on frozen yogurt? Bacteria simply go dormant while frozen. When you eat the frozen yogurt, it warms up in your body, and the bacteria basically "wake up" and become will get its own antibiotic. Label the jars: Just Yogurt, Antibiotic A, Antibiotic B, etc.

2. Grab your ultra-pasteurized milk. What does "ultra-pasteurized" mean? It means that before you picked it up from the store, the milk was heated so much that all the bacteria inside were killed, and therefore it doesn't even need to be refrigerated. If you have a single-serving box, pop in the straw and squeeze the container so that the milk squirts out into each of your jars. Fill them halfway.

3. Scoop a booger-size blob of yogurt into each jar. If you're the measuring type, that's about ⅛ of a teaspoon.

4. Using a fresh spoon, measure out a similar-size blob of your triple antibiotic ointment. Pop it in the jar labeled "Antibiotic A."

5. If you are going to test another antibiotic, do the same as above,

but use a fresh spoon and pop it into "Antibiotic B."

6. Put the lid on or cover your jars with foil. Shake everything up a little, being careful not to spill.

You can now either:

a. Put the jars in the warmest room in your house and wait 2 to 3 days.

or

b. You can turn the oven on to 200°F, and then turn it off when it has reached that temp. Pop your experiment in there overnight and look in the morning.

Either way, when the time has passed, pick up your jars and tilt them to the side. What has happened? Why is there a difference?

DO NOT eat the yogurt you made in this experiment. You sure as heck do not want to eat milk with antibiotics for your skin in it. Gross! But you can find lots of great recipes for making your own yogurt online!

WHAT JUST HAPPENED?

We hope that you noticed that the "no antibiotic" jar became thick and goopy. That's because when you added a blob of yogurt, you added some nice, juicy bacteria to the milk. Those bacteria were living in your store-bought yogurt and found a cozy home in your jar in which to replicate (make more of themselves). Then they got busy making lots of lactic acid. That caused the milk to get thick and creamy and, well . . . yogurty. Ta-da! New yogurt! The antibiotics you added to the other jar (or jars) killed the yogurt bacteria so no lactic acid was made and therefore the milk stayed . . . well . . . milky.

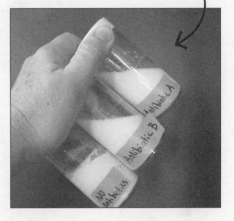

Notice how in our results the stuff in the container on the bottom stayed flat, while the top two still-milky ones flowed to the side. That's because the no-antibiotic one was solid yogurt and didn't flow! No need to sob for those friendly yogurt bacteria! Bacteria are not an endangered species!

active. But be aware: Frozen yogurt, yogurt-covered pretzels, and even some commerical yogurts may not have many or *any* good bacteria in them. Look for the words *live and active cultures*.

So there you have it.

Hope you have a new fondness for all those beautiful bacteria in your body! And speaking of bodies—where would you be without BLOOD? Six feet under! So read on and embrace your inner vampire!

Blood

C alling all vampires. Time to crawl out of that creaky coffin. Don't forget to brush and floss your fangs and grab your cape. You're about to play with your favorite beverage—blood.

BWA-HA-HA!

THE LONGEST RIVERS IN THE WORLD

T here is a network of rivers in your body—rivers of blood vessels. If you could somehow stretch all these arteries and veins out into one long line, it would be somewhere in the vicinity of 60,000 miles long. Your blood vessels would circle the world 2½ times! They are three times longer than the combined length of the world's five longest *actual* rivers. All that packed neatly inside your body.

Just like a busy river, there are "boats" floating along your body's rivers of blood. Red blood cells are the supertankers: They carry oxygen and carbon dioxide. White blood cells are a bit like the Coast Guard or Navy: They're there to protect you from pirates (well, in our case, germs). Then there's plasma—a thick, yellowish fluid. Think of plasma as a fleet of garbage-hauling tugboats. Plasma carts away waste, such as broken-down nutrients, carbon dioxide, and worn-out cells, to keep your river clean. There are also some platelets floating along like life preservers in your arteries and veins. Should you happen to nick yourself, they will clump up and stop all your blood from escaping!

YOU'RE MY TYPE!

J ust as you have a certain eye color and hair color, you also have a specific blood type. There are eight different types. The folks who figured all this out in the early 1900s gave them letter names: A, B, AB, and O. Each blood group has a second part: Rh positive or Rh negative. $4 \times 2 = 8$, right? So four blood groups times two kinds of Rh equals eight different types.

What makes an A an A and a B a B? Did the type A blood study harder to ace the blood test? No! It's just an easy way to name them. There are special substances called *antigens* (ant-uh-jinz) that are a part of each of your blood cells. You can think of them like an ID bracelet: If you are type A, then your body recognizes and allows only type A ID bracelets inside. It says, "Okay, these dudes are cool. Let them through!" If you are type B, your body likes only type B. If you are type AB, your body will recognize both A and B antigens. If you are type O, it's as if you don't wear any kind of ID bracelet, and your body likes only blood with no ID bracelets.

Although people with type O blood can receive only type O blood, they make really awesome blood donors. This is because their blood doesn't have any "ID bracelet" antigens. A person's body with type A, B, or AB will just let that new blood in, no problem. "No ID? Oh, well, come on through." That's why type O is called the universal donor. If you are a type O, people will always be asking you to donate blood. People with type AB are called universal receivers because their blood can receive A, B, AB, or O types.

CUP O' BLOOD

GO FETCH →

10 MINUTES

Wouldn't it be totally cool if you could shrink yourself down and take a ride in a blood vessel? You'd see that blood is made of four components: plasma, red blood cells, white blood cells, and platelets. Assuming you don't have a shrink-ray, here's the next best thing: Head to the kitchen and stir up an edible batch of "blood" with something to represent all four of blood's ingredients.

1. The lemonade will represent your yellowish plasma. Fill up the glass so it's just over half full with lemonade. If you want to be technical, aim for 55 percent, because blood is about 55 percent plasma.

2. The pomegranate seeds or dried cranberries will be your red blood cells. If you are using pomegranate seeds, have a grown-up cut the fruit into quarters. Then hold a fruit quarter in your hand over a bowl so the seedy side is touching your palm and the rind is facing up, and whack the rind repeatedly with a large wooden spoon until all the seeds fall out. Add the seeds or cranberries until the glass is almost completely full. About 45 percent of blood is made of red blood cells.

3. The white flesh of apple or pear will be your white blood cells. Spoon out one piece of apple or pear flesh

Clear drinking glass

Lemonade

Pomegranate seeds or dried cranberries

Apple or pear

Wooden spoon

Knife

Coconut flakes

that is just a little bigger than a cranberry or pomegranate seed and add it to the glass. Less than 1 percent of your blood is made up of white blood cells, so you should only add that one tiny piece. Got a cold? Add another piece (your body creates more white blood cells when you are sick). Feel free to eat the rest of the apple or pear while you contemplate this interesting fact.

4. The coconut flakes will be your colorless platelets. Add a few coconut flakes to the glass. Like white blood cells, platelets make up less than 1 percent of your blood.

5. Stir, and then donate some spoonfuls of your bloody creation to anyone who needs a tasty transfusion.

WHAT JUST HAPPENED?

Although blood contains lots of solid parts, it's mostly a liquid. That's super important, because your heart wouldn't be able to pump red blood cells throughout your body if they weren't suspended in plasma. In case you're wondering how much blood you actually have in your body, about 7 percent of your weight is blood, so grab a calculator and multiply your weight by 0.07 to find out how many pounds of blood you are carrying around. Every drop of your blood has several million red blood cells, along with thousands of platelets and white blood cells—to look at it a little differently, for every one white blood cell, you will find about 40 platelets (they're smaller than white blood cells) and 600 red blood cells.

If you think blood is complicated, check out doggie blood. Dogs have 8 different blood types that have been positively identified, but may even have 13 or more. And cattle? Holy cow! There are 11 major blood group systems— A, B, C, F, J, L, M, R, S, T, and Z.

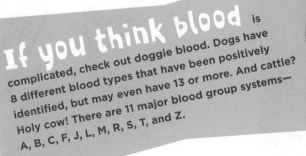

Blood technicians (now *there's* a perfect job for vampires!) know how to test blood to figure out which type is which. Why is this important? When people lose a lot of blood in an accident, or have surgery, they will have to "borrow" blood from someone else. This process is called a *transfusion* (trans-<u>few</u>-zhun). It's an amazing way to save lives. But you can't just give them any old blood. You need to give them the right type. If you give type A blood to a type B person, their body will check the "ID bracelet" antigens and say, "ALERT! ALERT! THIS IS AN INVADER! ATTACK!" Their body will start making antibodies that are like well-trained soldiers, made to pounce on the transfused blood! Fever and chills await the person who gets the wrong blood. In some rare cases, the patient can die. It's a serious business.

MONKEY BUSINESS

So, now that you understand the whole A, B, AB, and O thing, what about Rh? The Rh factor got its name from the totally cute rhesus monkey, in whose blood scientists first discovered it. About 85 percent of the human population has the Rh protein. The rest do not. If you have this special protein, you get to call yourself Rh positive (+). If you don't have it, you are Rh negative (–). Your doc can tell you exactly what type of blood you have. Ask the next time you are there. People with A positive blood like to say they got an A+ at life, but you can tell them "it's just a protein, dude."

Mixing Rh positive and Rh negative blood is another bloody no-no. In fact, if an Rh negative woman is pregnant with an Rh positive baby, the doctors must give her a special shot to keep her body from making antibodies to the Rh protein. If they don't, her baby's blood could be attacked by her blood. That's because our bodies are set up to wage war on anything that doesn't have the right ID bracelet! It's what keeps us safe from all kinds of invading germs.

Under a microscope, blood looks like a funky kind of cereal. The discs are red blood cells, and the things that look like fluffy cotton balls are white blood cells.

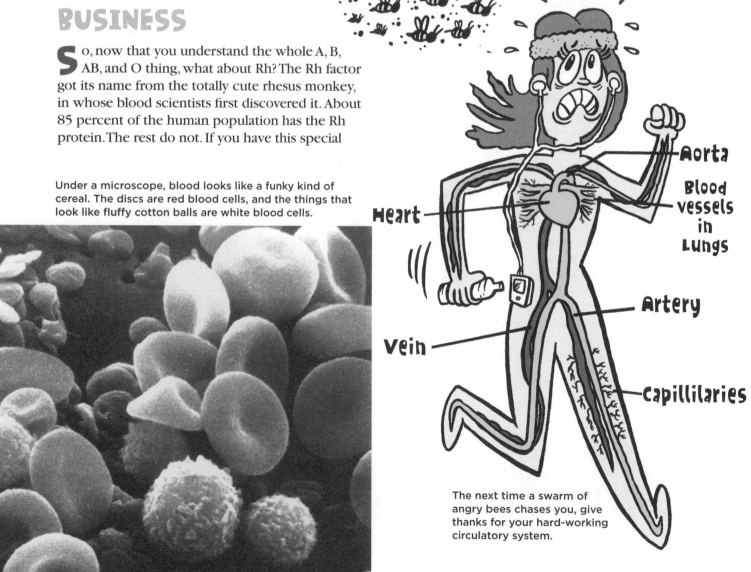

Aorta
Blood vessels in Lungs
Heart
Artery
Vein
Capillilaries

The next time a swarm of angry bees chases you, give thanks for your hard-working circulatory system.

TO THE BATMOBILE!

Bats. Ick. Vampire bats. Double ick! These night-flyers swoop around looking for sleeping animals (all the better to drink your blood, my dear!). Then these crafty critters use heat sensors on the tips of their noses to find a place on their victim where the blood flows close to the surface. Using their razor-sharp teeth they scrape away any fur that might be in the way, bite down, and the ooze-fest begins.

These bats have a special chemical in their saliva that keeps the blood from clotting. It's called draculin (named for Dracula, the most famous bad-dude vampire ever). Another substance in the saliva numbs the skin so the sleeping goat or cow doesn't even know it has become a bat's beverage bar. Vampire bats are pretty small (they only weigh about 2 ounces and are the size of a teacup), so at most they will slurp about a tablespoon of real "red bull."

Do you ever share a pizza with your besties?

Vampire bats are just like you. They share too, but instead of pepperoni, they share blood. Let's say you are a bat who is feeling a little under the weather—just not up to buzzing the fields searching for tonight's goat feast. A kindly pal will go hunt down a critter, tap open a vein, drink up, then fly home and vomit a generous amount into your waiting mouth. What a friend! But bats have manners too. It is expected that you will reciprocate. "Hey, buddy, this next one is on me!"

MY BLOOD IS RED, YOUR BLOOD IS BLUE

We all know blood is red. That's because of a protein in red blood cells called *hemoglobin* (<u>hee</u>-muh-glow-bin) that attracts lots of iron—a reddish mineral. When the iron interacts with the oxygen your blood carries, it produces that lovely red color. With every breath of air you suck in, you send O_2 on a bloody river ride through your entire body as your red blood cells pick up oxygen in the lungs and then carry it everywhere as your blood is pumped out by your "most valuable player" muscle, the heart.

Your heart has two sides. One side pumps blood with low oxygen to the lungs to get "gassed up." The other side pumps out the oxygen-rich blood to every cell in your body, right down to the tips of your pinky toes.

Blood flowing away from the heart travels through tubes called arteries. If you put a finger to your neck or wrist, you can feel blood being pumped through your arteries. Try it! You'll feel a *bump, bump, bump*. It's totally freaky. Almost all arteries carry blood loaded with oxygen. Only one artery—the pulmonary artery—carries blood with low oxygen. This is because it carries blood away from your heart to the lungs to be refilled with more O_2 (and *pulmonary* comes from the Latin word for lungs).

The blood vessels that carry the blood back to your heart are called veins. All of these, except the pulmonary veins, carry deoxygenated blood. (The pulmonary veins move newly oxygenated blood from your lungs back to your heart.) You can see lots of your veins as little blue lines beneath your skin. Veins may look bluish, but the deoxygenated blood within is really a dark red. It's just the way the light hits the thin layer of skin over the veins and then reflects back to your eye that makes them appear blue. Most drawings of your circulatory system show all veins as blue, just to make it easier to see what blood is coming back to the heart versus leaving it. But trust us, your blood isn't blue!

But what about other critters out there? Are they red-blooded too? Take a bite out of an uncooked crab's veins and it will bleed blue. Crab blood has

ICK-TIVITY VAMPIRE'S DELIGHT

GO FETCH →

5 MINUTES

Why do vampires get all the fun? This recipe for fake blood won't make you woozy, but it might make you hungry (and be careful . . . it will stain clothes, couches, and your cat).

- Bowl
- Spoon
- ¼ cup corn syrup
- Red and blue food coloring
- Cocoa powder
- Cornstarch (optional)
- Water (optional)

1. Pour ¼ cup of corn syrup in the bowl and add 50 drops of red and 1 drop of blue food coloring. Enjoy the way the colors slowly ooze through the corn syrup before you mix it with a spoon.

2. Stir in up to 1 teaspoon of cocoa powder (mix in ½ teaspoon at a time and see if you like the color before adding more).

3. You should now have some realistic-looking blood, convincing enough to catch the eye of any vampires in your neighborhood. If the blood seems too runny, mix in a bit of cornstarch to thicken it. If it's too thick, add a little water. You might need to experiment with adding more blue or red food coloring to get the perfect color.

4. Rub some fake blood on your arm and gross out an unsuspecting friend by licking it all off with a devilish grin.

lots of copper in it, which turns blue when exposed to oxygen. And lovely leeches or lizards? Bite into one of those and you will get a gush of green blood thanks to a chemical called chlorocruorin. Some sea creatures have yellow blood and others, like starfish, ooze a clear fluid. Mother Nature likes a bloody rainbow!

"LET" THERE BE BLOOD

Scientific smarties have known for many, many centuries that blood is important to human health. But for 2,000 years, healers all over the world believed that too *much* blood was the problem. Until the mid-1800s, many doctors routinely "bled" people. This means they would actually make a little cut in the skin and let some blood drain out. Or they used leeches to suck some of the blood out. Upset stomach? Chills and fever? Nick a vein and let it drain. A cup here, a pint there—bloodletting was the go-to solution for whatever ailed a person. Not surprisingly, this wasn't the most effective treatment.

Doctors of the past didn't really understand blood as well as we do today, but that didn't stop them from experimenting with it. One of the weirdest blood experiments took place in 1667. Ever heard the expression "gentle as a lamb"? A French doctor, Jean-Baptiste Denis, decided that if he transfused a lamb's blood into the veins of a crazy man he found wandering the streets of Paris, the man would take on the characteristics of the gentle lamb. *Baah-baah*-bad idea. The patient did not survive! The lamb's blood type definitely did not match the poor patient's type.

Now you have the lowdown on the red rivers in your body. But blood isn't the only fascinating substance your body produces. What about those gooey slimeballs you pick out of your nose? Read on and learn how to make a BOOGER that even a food critic would love!

Leeches suck . . . literally!

Boogers

H ey, you! **YES, YOU!** Don't look so innocent. You think we can't see you but we **CAN!** Get that finger out of your nose right this second! But know that you are not alone. The average person dips a digit in his or her nostril about four times a day. So grab a few tissues and let's do a little nosing around.

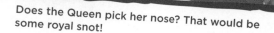

Does the Queen pick her nose? That would be some royal snot!

IT'S SNOT WHAT YOU THINK!

P icture about four to six 8-ounce glasses of water lined up on your kitchen counter. Now imagine that instead of water, those glasses are full of goopy-gloppy *mucus* (<u>mew</u>-kiss)—the stuff that hangs out in your nose parts. That's how much snot your *sinuses* (<u>si</u>-nuss-iz)—your body's mucus factory—shoot out every day. All day long—24/7—your sinuses (two on either side of your upper nose and two above your eyebrows) are busy making this snotty stuff. You don't realize how much is being created because you swallow almost all of it.

Mucus is mostly made of water, but there are a few secret ingredients that

give it its special wonderfulness. Sprinkled in, like biological fairy dust, are certain kinds of proteins, salts, and even sugar. No wonder babies think snot is good enough to eat!

Turns out this slimy mix is great for trapping germs, dirt, and pollen, and for preventing these unwanted visitors from reaching your lungs, where they could cause an infection. Mucus can also destroy bad bacteria and viruses. Much like a welcome mat at your front door, each of your nostrils is lined with zillions of little nose hairs. The mucus slithers down from the sinus snot factory and cozies up in between the hairs. But in the case of your nose, it's an UNWELCOME mat! Intruders, like flu germs, dead skin cells, and floating dandruff flakes, end up stuck in the mucus, where they often form clumps. Soon, any mucus exposed to the air dries up and you are left with a crusty little booger, dangling boldly from your nostril.

BOOGERS FOR BREAKFAST

A ll babies (and plenty of grown-ups) eat their boogers. Why might that be? Dr. Scott Napper, who specializes in biological sciences at the University of Saskatchewan, has a theory about why boogers for breakfast isn't such a bad idea.

A word to kids and grown-ups alike: Just because your snot is green, that does not mean you have a bacterial infection! That's a myth! Your disgustingly drippy nose might just as easily be caused by a virus. Viruses do not respond to antibiotics, and taking antibiotics when you don't need them can actually be harmful!

You can learn a lot about your health from the color and thickness of your nose drippings.

HERE'S WHAT YOU NEED TO KNOW:

Clear and not drippy = normal

Clear and very drippy = early stages of infection. This can last for 1 to 3 days. (If you have allergies, it will last as long as you are exposed to the thing that you are allergic to. Your immune system mistakes the allergen for a germ and attacks it.) Your nose will also run like a faucet on a very cold day because your schnoz tries to warm up the incoming air by increasing blood flow to the vessels in your nostrils. By-product? Yup! Drippy snot!

Whitish yellow = Immune cells (white blood cells) are flooding into your mucus to fight the enemy invasion.

Greenish yellow = Bacteria or dead viral cells are being eliminated from your body and have been added into the mix.

Besides the fact that snot is a little sweet (and humans love sweets!), it's possible that our immune systems—our body's Army, Navy, Air Force, and Marines—can pick up vital information from the bad germs trapped in our snot soup. Know your enemy! Here's how it works: When our bodies are exposed to small amounts of germs, our white blood cells learn how to recognize and deal with the enemy invader. Then, if we are later exposed to a whole bunch of those germs, our white blood cells already know how to handle the germ so they go right to work and prevent us from getting sick. In other words, exposure to small quantities of germs (say, by eating some boogers) can actually strengthen our immune systems. Professor Napper believes that booger-eaters are simply "fulfilling what we're truly meant to do." Explain that to your parents next time they catch you munching on snot!

THE MUCUS ZOO

Noses aren't the only mucus makers. Mucus also lines lots of other parts of your body, like your eyeballs, your throat, your lungs, and your stomach. Other animals depend on mucus to protect themselves from harm. Here are a few mega-mucus makers.

Hagfish—When a sea dweller dies, hagfish get busy! They burrow into dead creatures and nibble their way out. That's disgusting enough, but hagfish have another gross trick to protect themselves from being eaten. They can release over a gallon of slime in one second in much the same way as we sweat. As would-be eaters take a bite of hagfish, they literally almost choke to death on the thick snot coating.

Slugs—Have mucus, will travel. Who needs a well-paved highway when you can create a trail of mucus to slide upon? Thanks to slime, slugs can slide along the edge of a razor without being cut. Slugs also wear a stylish snot coat that keeps their skin nice and moist. They'll die if they dry out.

Opossum—These furry little critters are best known for protecting themselves from larger, hungrier animals by pretending to be dead. Their Academy Award–worthy pretend death scenes include foaming at the mouth AND shooting out a wad of very smelly green mucus from special glands in their butts. This mucus smells like rotting meat. *I'd* leave them alone, wouldn't you?

Parrotfish—No need to own a bed if you are a parrotfish. At sleepy time, these bright blue swimmers simply blow out a soft, cushy mucus sleeping bag. Sweet, snotty dreams . . .

SWEET SNOT SANDWICH

10 MINUTES

The mucus that lines your nose and throat is one of your body's first lines of defense against dust, bacteria, pollen, and other junk you breathe in. Instead of climbing into your friend's nose to see how it all works, make your own boogers and test how they trap airborne invaders!

1. Wash your hands to prep for your debut as a booger chef. Cut two 4-inch-long pieces of bread. Use your fingers to remove the soft inside of the bread. Each piece should be a hollow tube; it's okay if there are still bits of bread stuck inside the tube. The bread will represent a person's nasal cavity.

2. One piece of bread will be someone with a healthy nasal cavity, coated with delicious mucus and a few dried-up boogers. This snot will be extra sweet, because we're going to use honey and butter instead of the real thing. Use a butter knife to smear honey and butter all over the inside of the walls of the healthy nasal cavity bread. The other piece of bread will represent someone whose nasal cavity is sadly lacking in the snot department; leave this piece mucus-free. If the hole in the bread with mucus is larger than the other bread's hole (because smearing honey may have widened it), use a clean butter knife to try to flatten the inside walls of the mucus-free bread until the holes are the same width.

GO FETCH

Loaf of skinny French bread

Bread knife

Butter knife

Honey

Butter

Cinnamon

Sugar

Bowl

Spoon

3. Sprinkle about a teaspoon each of cinnamon and sugar into a bowl and then mix them together with a spoon. These particles will represent the airborne invaders that constantly get sucked into our noses: dust, pollens, spores, bacteria, and viruses.

4. Pour about ½ of the cinnamon and sugar into your hand. Hold the mucus-coated bread in your other

hand over the sink. Put your hands close to your mouth so they are touching and forcefully blow the cinnamon and sugar through the hole in the bread. Repeat this with the remaining cinnamon and sugar and the mucus-free bread. Before you feast on

your snot sandwich, look at how many invaders each nasal cavity caught.

Mucus Free

With Mucus

WHAT JUST HAPPENED?

Although both pieces of bread probably had cinnamon and sugar stuck to their inside walls, the bread with honey and butter probably collected more. Your mucus is sticky to help trap the unwelcome things—everything except air—that we breathe in. It's like lining your nose with glue. Mucus doesn't stay in your nose forever, though. It either works its way out of your nose, when it can officially be called a booger, or works its way down the back of your throat and gets swallowed into your stomach. Think of that as picking your nose and eating it without using your hands!

MY NOSE HAS THE RUNS!

GO FETCH

15 MINUTES

When you are healthy, your nasal secretions are thin and clear, but the mucus thickens up into a nasty snot stew when you get sick. It's time to brew up a batch of fake snot so you can see "mucus" in action. Lucky for you, this glop tastes even better than the real thing.

1. Let's start with a simple recipe for healthy mucus: Pour ½ cup of water and ¼ cup of corn syrup into a pot and stir. Healthy mucus is normally clear and runny.

2. Now let's imagine your body has been invaded by bacteria or a virus that has infiltrated your nasal cavity. Stir a pinch of salt into the pot to simulate these germs.

3. When your body recognizes that it has unwelcome guests, it amps up the production of white blood cells to defend itself. This process thickens and changes the color of your mucus. Add 2 tablespoons of cornstarch and a drop of yellow food coloring to the pot. Turn the heat on and bring the pot to a boil for a few minutes. Continuously stir until the mixture thickens. Play around with the amount

An adult (Remember the grown-up rule. Boiling water is involved!)

Measuring cups

Water

¹/4 cup corn syrup

A pot

Spoon

Salt

2 tablespoons cornstarch

Yellow food coloring

of cornstarch and food coloring until you create some snot you are proud to wear on your upper lip!

4. Feeling theatrical? Hungry? Both? After your fake snot has cooled a bit, dab some beneath your nose, or put some on a tissue, and disgust your friends and family.

WHAT JUST HAPPENED?

When you're healthy, your mucus has a familiar color and texture: somewhat clear and runny. However, once you catch a cold, your body mobilizes millions of white blood cells to combat the infection. The addition of all these tiny troops running around in your mucus thickens it up. Your white blood cells also release colorful enzymes that often give your mucus a yellow or greenish complexion. In other words, your mucus changes color and consistency not because of the germs, but because of the presence of your own body's white blood cells that are protecting you from the germs.

EYE BOOGIES?

Noses aren't the only snot factories. Lots of people also have eye boogers! When you wake up, you just might find those crusty accumulations in the corners of your eyes. These "breakfast" flakes are made of the same stuff as nose boogers—mucus, dust, and dried skin cells. Flick them away, we say!

Now that you have snacked on "snot" and become a mucus master,
let's slide down an inch or so beneath your nostrils and check out your mouth—specifically its job as a broadcaster of the mighty and powerful BURP!

Burps

Imagine a chain saw slicing away at a tree (102 decibels) or a lawn mower attacking the grass (105 decibels). Think of a motorcycle roaring loudly alongside you at a red light (a paltry 90 decibels). Loud, right? Now, ladies and gentlemen, put your hands together for Paul Hunn, a British fellow who burped so loudly that he topped the noise levels of all of these very annoying, very loud things—hitting a whopping 109.9 decibels! (In case you don't know, decibels are the way we measure and compare the loudness of sounds.)

URP!

Right this very second, your body is full of gas. Some of that gas is air that you've swallowed without even realizing it. This happens if you eat or drink too fast, chew gum, or drink from a straw. Even more gas gets produced during digestion. All that food you consume has to be broken down by bacteria in the intestines. As bacteria help your body digest food, they produce gassy by-products like carbon dioxide, nitrogen, and methane. Vegetables like broccoli, cabbage, cauliflower, onions, garlic, and, of course, beans, are particularly good gas producers. All that gas builds up inside our bodies until the pressure is just too much! So how come we don't swell up like a giant parade balloon until we go *kerplooie*? Burps to the rescue! Burping is one good way to squeeze extra air out.

Burping (also known as belching) is officially called *eructation* (er-ruck-<u>tay</u>-shun), a delicious word that even sounds like a belch! *Ehhh-ruuuuuuk-taaaay-shun*. It's the way gas escapes from our digestive tracts via the mouth. The other air expellers are those stink bombs known as farts. And you know what exit *those* use! (More about FARTS on page 77.)

BURP-BLASTING BASICS

If you've peeked ahead to NOXIOUS NOISES (page 160), you know that all sounds are caused by vibrations, but what vibrates when you burp? Here's one popular theory of what's going on. As your stomach does its thing, breaking down the cheese enchilada and chocolate milk you had for lunch, it fills with gas. The pressure builds until the air has to go somewhere. Sometimes it goes up your *esophagus* (eh-<u>sof</u>-uh-gus). Your esophagus is normally kind of flat, like a long, tubular pancake. As the gas rises, it makes the two sides of your esophagus flap together and vibrate, making that *ur-ur-ur-urp* noise we know and love.

STEALTH BELCHING

Feel a real burp brewing, but you're stuck at snooty Aunt Ethel's fancy dinner party?

Here's a tip! Keep your mouth closed and let the burp flee through your nose. The sound is not amplified as much as if you let it rip out of your wide-open trumpet-shaped mouth. You might cover your nostrils as you nose-burp in case you are releasing a smell bomb. If you do let one rip at Aunt Ethel's dinner table, quickly say, "Excuse me," and then tell her that in certain cultures, a burp is a sign of appreciation for a great meal.

STINKY BURP FACTORY

GO FETCH →

Burps are hilarious to hear and sometimes gross to smell but, let's face it, hard to save. When you burp, the air from your stomach escapes, and *poof*—your gift to the world is lost in the wind. In this experiment, you'll use a balloon to trap an artificial burp for safekeeping. What's your hypothesis about which ingredient will make the foulest burp?

- A fun adult
- Balloon
- Empty 2-liter bottle
- Funnel
- Vinegar
- Diced onions or garlic, or orange oil
- Baking soda
- Safety glasses
- Bowl or kitchen sink

BRAP!

1. First, make sure the balloon's opening can fit snugly over the opening of your bottle. Then, remove the balloon from the bottle.

2. Use the funnel to pour ¼ cup of vinegar into the bottle. The bottle is going to be your stomach.

3. Flavor your future burp with different ingredients by adding a tablespoon of finely diced onions or garlic, or perhaps a teaspoon of orange oil, to the bottle. Predict which one will make the foulest burp, and then repeat these steps to test your hypothesis.

4. Rinse out the funnel and dry it with a paper towel. Now use the funnel to add 1 tablespoon of baking soda into the balloon. Shake it down to the bottom of the balloon. The balloon is going to trap a burp from your stomach.

5. Put on your safety glasses.

6. Place the bottle either inside the sink or inside a large mixing bowl. This is just in case anything spills and you make a mess.

7. Attach the opening of the balloon to the opening of the bottle, being careful not to let any baking soda fall into the bottle yet. Keep the balloon folded over with the baking soda inside.

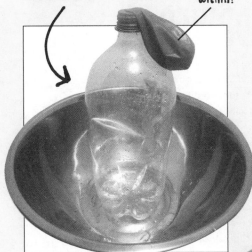

Baking soda within!

8. Lift up the balloon to shake the baking soda into the bottle's vinegar, and then let go of the balloon.

9. Watch the balloon fill up with air as the bottle burps into it!

10. Carefully remove the inflated balloon and smell its contents if you dare.

WHAT JUST HAPPENED?

Carbon dioxide gas is created when baking soda mixes with vinegar. This gas increases the air pressure inside the bottle, so the carbon dioxide rushes out of the bottle into the balloon. As the balloon fills with carbon dioxide, the increased air pressure inside the balloon causes it to expand. Your bottle's burp has been captured! A similar thing happens in your body. Digestion releases carbon dioxide gas, and some of that goes up and out as a burp!

MOOOO-URP! The World's Biggest Belchers

Ahhh, cows. So sweet-looking. Don't you just love to watch them, chomping away on velvety-green grass? But don't get too close. Cows are notorious belch blasters! And every time they burp, they are sending clouds of methane gas into the atmosphere.

You're a smart kid, so you've probably heard of greenhouse gases. They form that thick blanket of gas surrounding the Earth, trapping extra heat and melting the ice caps. NOT a good thing. One thing planet Earth doesn't need is more greenhouse gas. But that's exactly what all those cows are belching. The average cow blasts 250 to 300 liters of methane a DAY. Imagine a 2-liter bottle of soda (that's the big size). Now

HOW TO BURP LIKE A TRUCK DRIVER

1. Head to the kitchen. Eat a meal quickly. The goal is to swallow a lot of air along with your food . . . be careful not to choke, though!

2. Gulp some seltzer or another drink with bubbles. Drinks with fizz will unleash excess carbon dioxide in your belly. Better still, sip that soda through a straw so none of the gas escapes into the air. Best yet—try to quickly guzzle the entire can or bottle. Belch guaranteed.

3. Do some jumping jacks or jump rope soon after eating. Jumping agitates the gases in your stomach (and also causes any soda you drank to fizz and release carbon dioxide gas). Don't be a dolt, though— if you feel like you're going to hurl, stop immediately! While a good, juicy burp is fun, vomit on your shoes is not.

4. Is a burp building up? Tilt your head back and open your mouth. Better acoustics for your belch that way! Now push out your stomach muscles. You are going for that Santa Claus look here. This will help force extra air out.

5. Don't feel like eating or drinking? You can still unleash a biggie by swallowing mouthfuls of air and then letting that air come back up.

Remember: If you dream of someday burping the alphabet, practice makes perfect.

JAILED FOR BURPING!

Careful if you are a schoolkid in Albuquerque, New Mexico. A seventh grader was handcuffed and hauled off to juvenile detention by city police after loudly burping in gym class. After a whole lot of news coverage of the event, "the burp heard 'round-the-city" led to a nasty lawsuit. The charges against the thirteen-year-old were dropped, but wow—being led away in handcuffs just for burping! Maybe it's best to be polite.

line up about 130 more next to it. Now multiply that by every cow on the planet. That's how much bovine burpiness is clouding the air. *Choke! Gasp!*

Argentina is cow country. There are about 51 million head of cattle there, and around 30 percent of that country's greenhouse gases are being burped up by those "*vacas de eruptos*."

So scientists at Argentina's National Institute of Agricultural Technology have a plan! They've been working on a way to trap the burps before they escape by collecting the cows' digestive gases. Their cows wear awesome backpacks with a bunch of valves

Be a belch machine.

Gobble your food too fast and you might burp louder than a cow!

A BELCHING BOTTLE BAND

10 MINUTES
PLUS 1 HOUR WAIT

They may not be as big as Beyoncé or the Beatles, but this rockin' little belch trio *will* give you a better understanding of how burps work.

1. Use the marker to draw a pair of eyes and nose on each bottle. The bottle openings will be their mouths.

2. Put the uncapped bottles in the freezer and wait one hour.

3. Before you remove the bottles from the freezer, put the three quarters in the bowl of water. You only need enough water to get the quarters wet.

4. Remove the bottles from the freezer and immediately place a wet quarter over the opening of each bottle. The quarters will act as the sealed lips over the mouths of the bottles.

 GO FETCH

Permanent marker

3 rinsed-out plastic bottles (similar or different sizes)

Enough space in your freezer to hold the 3 bottles

3 quarters

Bowl of water

5. Wait for your band to warm up—literally! After a few seconds (depending on how warm your kitchen is and the size of the bottles), the bottles will start to burp, causing the quarters to rattle on top of the openings.

6. Each bottle should produce several polite burps. A burp might move the quarter off center, breaking

the seal. If necessary, carefully reposition any quarter that was moved to create a new seal and enjoy a few more burps.

WHAT JUST HAPPENED?

Air is made of gazillions of tiny particles of different gases, such as nitrogen, oxygen, and carbon dioxide. The air inside each bottle chilled when it was in the freezer but warmed up again when outside. When gases get warm, they expand and take up more space. They need to get moving—just like you and your buddies when school lets out for the day. So, the gases tried to escape from the bottle, but the quarter kept them trapped. The water on the quarter created a better seal, completely trapping the air inside. (This "stickiness" property of water is called *adhesion* [add-he-zhun]. Adhesion is why small water droplets can stick to a window instead of falling down.)

As the air inside the bottle continued to warm up, the increasing air pressure eventually became so strong that it overcame the water adhesion and weight of the quarter, breaking the seal and pushing the quarter off. Your bottle has burped, and a rock star is born!

and pumps to suck the digestive gases from cow stomach cavities through a tube and into a holding pouch. That's some pretty impressive cow-engineering!

Speaking of heading off to jail—
get the lowdown on what it takes to solve some unsolved mysteries! The villains await in CRIMES!

crimes

Fingerprints left behind at the scene of a crime? How old-fashioned! In the future, crime solvers may be able to nab bad guys by following the trail of unique bacteria, fungi, and viruses left at the scene. Turns out, there is a *microbiome* (imagine an invisible cloud of microorganisms constantly rising off all our bodies) that is specific to each person. Bacteria escape with every breath and are released off our shedding skin. Even our gut microbes are breaking out of intestine jail! Proof of "whodunit" is literally hovering in the air and the places we've visited. This cloud around us is a new discovery, so it will be some time before it's actually used to catch a crook. Luckily, there are lots of other ways to nab a bad guy in the meantime.

Sometimes the smallest clue solves the crime!

YOU'RE UNDER ARREST!

How DO you catch a criminal? Unless you witness the guilty party in the act, you will likely need some cool crime scene investigation (CSI) skills to make it happen. CSI relies on the fascinating field of *forensics*.

> **FORENSICS** *(for-en-sicks)*—
> a way to investigate crimes using science. Forensic scientists use chemistry, biology, physics, statistics, and pharmacology to find out "whodunit."

Just about anything can be a clue. Was that a blood splatter or did someone's cheeseburger with extra ketchup leak? Testing crime scene evidence (that red splatter, for instance) is one of the best ways to catch a criminal if it turns out to be bodily fluids. Carefully studying objects at the crime scene, such as carpets with weird stains, is another. The surroundings can hold a lot of clues too. A trampled flower bed, footprint, or tire track can reveal where the criminal went after committing the dastardly deed. Even the presence of a flesh-nibbling insect can help solve a crime by pinpointing how long a victim has been dead.

BUILD SOME DNA

GO FETCH →

20 MINUTES

DNA sounds like complicated stuff, but it's really just some basic parts all stuck together. Your own DNA is squishy so let's build a bit of squishy DNA!

1. DNA is shaped like a twisted ladder. The sides of the ladder are made of alternating parts. One part is a sugar called deoxyribose (that's where the "D" comes from in DNA). The other part is called a phosphate group. To represent them, choose two different colors of clay and roll them into skinny snakes. Cut one snake into ten 1-inch pieces to represent sugars. Cut the other into eight ½-inch pieces to be phosphate groups.

2. Now place them into an alternating pattern and squish them together to make 2 long strips. Place the 2 strips about 2 inches apart on a flat surface.

3. Choose four new colors to represent the rungs (or steps) of the ladder. In DNA these are known as nucleotides. (That's what the "N" in DNA comes from.) There are 4 of

GO FETCH

6 different colors of modeling clay

Plastic knife

Plate on which to cut

Flat surface on which to build your DNA strand

Empty paper towel roll

Scissors

them: adenine, thymine, cytosine, and guanine (A, T, C, and G). Make a 6 to 8 inch snake for each color and cut them into 1-inch strips.

4. Each ladder rung is made of two nucleotides stuck together. They will attach to your 1-inch "sugar" pieces on the sides of the ladder. Nucleotides only buddy up in certain ways. Adenine only holds hands with thymine. Cytosine and guanine think everyone else has cooties. Look at the photo for more guidance. You can make a different pattern, as long as you don't break the A-T, C-G rule. (T-A or G-C is fine too.)

5. The model you made is a flat ladder. It helps you see the parts clearly and read the DNA code. But DNA is a twisted ladder called a double helix. That twist helps it wrap up to fit inside each tiny cell in your body. To visualize the double helix, grab a paper towel tube and some scissors. Starting at the bottom of the tube, cut along the spiral seam until you get to the top. You have now created a single helix. To make a double helix, start at the bottom again and cut the single helix strip in half, spiraling up until you get to the top. You are now holding in your hands the two spiral sides of the DNA ladder, or the "sugar-phosphate backbone." You can place colored pieces of tape in the empty spaces to represent the nucleotides if you are a true science geek.

It's practically impossible to commit a crime without leaving some evidence behind. A criminal might *believe* they have thought of every last detail, but all it takes is one teeny little thing overlooked—a drop of sweat, a strand of hair, the brush of a fingertip—and they might as well have left a signed confession at the scene.

THREE LITTLE LETTERS. SIX TEENY CHEMICALS.

When it comes to catching a criminal, what's the most amazing tool a CSI whiz has? Not a computer. Not a fancy microscope. No, it's

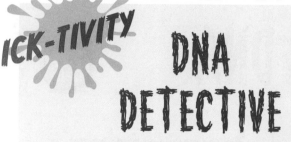

DNA DETECTIVE

3 MINUTES

Time to get to work! You are investigating "The Case of the Stolen Oreos." An entire sleeve of cookies and a quart of milk have vanished. But who did it? There are two suspects—Dolly and Polly—who were both seen lurking in the vicinity of the snacks. Dolly loudly insists she saw Polly with cookie crumbs and a milk mustache on her face.

Luckily you have a clue! A strand of hair has been left stuck to the empty milk jug, but both girls have hair that is similar color and length, so you can't determine the culprit just by looking at them. Back at the crime lab, your CSI team analyzes the strand and makes this DNA profile:

CG-TA-GC-AT-CG

Time to ask each suspect for a strand of hair, then zip back to the lab to analyze the results.

This was Polly's strand: **This was Dolly's strand:**

who stole the cookie from the cookie jar?

WHAT JUST HAPPENED?

Dolly's hair strand matched the strand found at the scene of the cookie crime. Polly might have had the milk mustache, but Dolly is our culprit! So, super sleuths, THAT is how DNA is used to catch criminals OR to prove innocence, which is what happened for Polly. Those chemical DNA ladder rungs tell all. No one wants to spend a lifetime in prison (or in time-out for two weeks for lying) for a crime they did not commit!

---

something really REALLY small that doesn't cost anything and never lies. It's called DNA—short for **d**eoxyribo**n**ucleic **a**cid. Now there's a mouthful! Say it like this: *dee-ox-ee-rye-bow-new-clay-ick* acid. Ha! It even has ICK in its name!

DNA is the reason *you* are you—the reason you have brown eyes, or freckles, or curly hair. It's the reason someone will grow to be 6 feet, 2 inches or have a booming voice, perfect for announcing sports scores: "GOOOOOOOAL!!!" DNA is the blueprint for building YOU and, unless you have an identical twin, no one else has the same blueprint. Every strand of your hair, drop of blood, glob of spit, or flake of your skin has your unique DNA encoded in it.

Think of DNA as a really fantastic story, but instead of being written in words, it's written in patterns of chemicals. There have been cases of people with virtually identical fingerprints, but because DNA is such complex stuff, *everyone* (except identical twins, who have identical DNA) has a unique pattern. CSI scientists LOVE DNA because it can help them identify exactly "whodunit."

THE ABCS OF DNA

Picture a twisted ladder. It's got a strip of wood or metal on each side, and rungs to climb up on. Now shrink that ladder down to an incredibly minuscule size. Instead of being made of wood or metal, this wee ladder is made of molecules. The sides are always made of alternating blocks of a type of sugar called deoxyribose and a substance called a phosphate. The rungs (the things you climb up on a ladder) are made of pairs of chemicals called

Identical twinsies! Same clothes. Same hair. Same DNA.

THE GREAT DNA ROBBERY

30 MINUTES
PLUS SOAKING LENTILS OVERNIGHT BEFOREHAND

GO FETCH

DNA is one of nature's most heavily guarded possessions. Plant and animal cells keep their DNA under lock and key, inside a little sack called a nucleus. But what if you wanted to get into the nucleus and uncover its DNA? We're talking about separating DNA from an organism so you can actually see it and touch it! Read on to find out how to become a DNA scientist-sleuth without leaving your kitchen.

1. Soak the lentils overnight in a bowl of water to soften them up.

2. Blend ½ cup of lentils, 1 cup of cold water, and a pinch of salt in a blender for 30 seconds.

3. Let the slime sit for about 5 minutes so the chunkier pieces sink to the bottom.

4. Gently pour the liquidy "lentil juice" from the blender through the strainer into a small glass until it's about half full. It's okay if some chunks get into the glass, but you mostly want the liquid broth. Discard the chunkier bits.

5. Measure how much lentil juice you have, and then divide this number by six and add that much soap to the juice (for example, if you have 1 cup of lentil juice, add ⅙ cup of soap). It's okay to estimate. Gently stir with a spoon for a few seconds.

6. Pour your soapy lentil juice into a skinny glass or test tube until it's half full (or half empty, if you're feeling grumpy). Wait 10 minutes.

7. Add a pinch of meat tenderizer (or 2 drops of contact lens solution). Tightly cup your hand over the skinny

- An adult
- A generous ½ cup of dried lentils
- Bowl
- Water
- Salt
- Blender
- Strainer
- 2 skinny glasses or test tubes
- Liquid soap
- Spoon
- Meat tenderizer powder (or contact lens solution with enzyme cleaners)
- Isopropyl (rubbing) alcohol

glass or test tube, turn it upside down once to mix things together, and then return to the upright position.

8. Get ready to say "Cool!" Grab your grown-up and slowly add isopropyl alcohol until the glass is ¾ full. Almost instantly, you should see white, wispy strands of DNA float toward the top. Be patient. Over the next few hours, the strands will form a clump of DNA, which should become even more distinct as more separates from the rest of the solution.

WHAT JUST HAPPENED?

You now have a soupy, soapy mess of DNA on top. It had been tangled with other stuff from the cell, including all sorts of proteins. Special chemicals in the meat tenderizer and contact lens solution, called enzymes, removed all the proteins from around the DNA. The lentil's proteins and fats like to hang out in water, but its DNA prefers alcohol. The isopropyl alcohol is less dense than water, so it floats on top, and the DNA floats up there in it.

Don't be too disappointed that you can't see the famous twisted ladder of DNA. You're looking at millions of DNA molecules that are all stuck together, and any individual strand of DNA is far, far, FAR too thin to be visible with the naked eye (or even super-strong microscopes). The folks who figured out the shape of DNA (James Watson, Francis Crick, Maurice Wilkins, and Rosalind Franklin) had to zap it with X-rays and then use math to figure out the pattern of how the molecules scattered the rays. It's amazing that they *could* figure it out without having an actual picture. Electron microscopes have recently captured images of bundles of DNA strands, but even they are still pretty fuzzy.

Now that you know how to find DNA, experiment with some other types of food: spinach, carrots, split peas, chicken nuggets, sunflower seeds, even bacon (usually things with low water content work best). If it was once alive, it has DNA, and now you know how to get it. Forensic scientists use a similar method to separate the DNA found at a crime scene.

nucleotides, or bases: adenine, thymine, guanine, and cytosine. And that's it. That's all there is, folks!

Do you have a best friend? Someone you do *everything* with? In DNA land, adenine will only hang out with thymine. It will never, *ever* be seen with guanine or cytosine. Same for guanine and cytosine. No bit of cytosine would ever be caught playing with some thymine. So the rungs of your ladder are always made of either adenine (A) bonded to thymine (T), or guanine (G) bonded to cytosine (C): A-T and C-G. Hydrogen bonds are what hold the two substance pairs together, a bit like glue.

How amazing (and small) is DNA? If you could somehow lay each single segment of DNA end to end and measure it, one measly cell in your body would have about six feet of DNA. Now, there are somewhere around 37.2 trillion cells in your body. If you laid out all the DNA bits in your body end to end, that strand would stretch 10 to 20 BILLION miles. Considering that the Earth is 93 million miles away from the sun, your DNA would reach to the sun and back between 60 and 120 times! But how does it all fit into your tiny cells? Ask a friend to hold one end of a one-foot piece of string or ribbon. Start twisting the string until it begins to coil on itself. Keep twisting and twisting and it will coil and coil until it is a tiny ball of coils. Your DNA is twisted up kind of like that so a whole bunch can fit in the tiny nucleus of each of your cells. Scientists call DNA's twisted shape a *double helix*.

JOIN THE CRIME-SOLVING TEAM

You can't go out and win a Super Bowl all by yourself. Similarly, it takes a team of crime solvers. But which position to choose? There are so many cool types of forensics!

1. Be a Criminalist—
There's been a jewel heist. A window is smashed and a tray of gold necklaces are missing. Call in the criminalist!

THE CASE OF THE MISSING FLAMINGO

GO FETCH

Someone has stolen your favorite lawn ornament—a pink plastic flamingo—and left a ransom note demanding $1,000,000 for its safe return. You have three suspects—all of whom were recently seen in your front yard: Adam, the gardener; Barbara, the newspaper deliverer; and neighbor Zelda, who was walking Chloe, her highly intelligent dog. The ransom note was written in black ink. Each suspect has been found with a different type of black marker. Forensic *chromatography* (crow-muh-<u>tog</u>-ruh-fee)—the lab techniques used to separate mixtures of chemicals—to the rescue!

3 different black markers or felt-tip pens. Consider using a black permanent marker and two different brands of regular (or "water-soluble") black markers. You can also try dry-erase or wet-erase markers, often used in schools or parents' offices.

A friend (or three)

Coffee filter paper (you can also use a paper towel, but it doesn't work quite as well)

Scissors

Ruler

4 one-inch pieces of tape

4 glasses

Water

SUPER SLEUTH

1. Have your friend (pretending to be the criminal!) write a ransom note on a piece of coffee filter paper with one of the pens. Don't let your friend show you which marker he or she used.

Give me $1,000,000 If you want your Pet back!!!

2. Use the scissors to cut 3 strips of a different coffee filter that are about 1 inch wide and 4 inches long.

3. Draw a black line using the pen found on your first suspect (Adam) across the bottom of one strip of coffee paper, about 1 inch from the end. At the top, write Adam's name. Tape the top of the strip to the marker that you drew the line with so you can hang the strip inside an empty glass. Make sure the end with the black line hangs toward the bottom of the glass. Repeat this for the other two markers and strips, labeling them Barbara and Zelda.

4. Cut a piece of the ransom note into a thin strip that is about 1 inch wide and 4 inches long, tape it to the scissors, and hang it inside the fourth glass just like the other strips.

You've probably heard of Sherlock Holmes—you know, the detective with the silly hat, the weird-looking caped coat, and the pipe in his mouth. Holmes was a great believer in the powers of science and a master of deduction. Even though he was a make-believe character created by the writer Sir Arthur Conan Doyle, he inspired a lot of people to become forensic scientists. So kudos to Sherlock—and his awesome sidekick, Dr. Watson—for making catching criminals cool.

5. Pour water into each glass so the bottom of each strip of paper is barely getting wet. The black line should not be in the water. Lift out the paper as you pour so that it doesn't get splashed.

6. Wait about five minutes. Over time, the pigments in each marker should separate to form a unique pattern. Compare the ransom note's pattern to the three strips. You should be able to identify which marker was used to write the note!

Note: This might not work for all inks because some don't dissolve in water. If the ink does not separate, ask an adult to help you use some rubbing alcohol or nail polish remover instead of water. These stinky chemicals are more powerful at breaking apart the chemicals in some inks.

WHAT JUST HAPPENED?

Water is a sticky chemical. It tends to stick to itself—a force called *cohesion* (co-<u>hee</u>-zhun). Water also tends to stick to other materials—a force called *adhesion* (add-<u>hee</u>-zhun)—which is why your hands stay wet after you dip them in water. On a small scale, the forces of cohesion and adhesion can overcome the force of gravity. This is why the water moved up the paper: Water in the glass was attracted to

water that had soaked into the paper (cohesion), and this water was attracted to the drier paper higher up (adhesion).

Most black markers contain a combination of different-colored pigments or dyes. Some pigments dissolved in the water that slowly climbed up the paper, while other pigments didn't dissolve and never moved. Some dissolved pigments will move easily through the paper, causing their individual colors to separate and climb to different levels.

The ransom plot has been foiled! Pink flamingos sleep well tonight, for science has triumphed again!

THE CASE OF THE DEADLY DUST

30–60 MINUTES

GO FETCH →

You are a crime scene investigator and you have just arrived on the scene of a crime. You see a strange substance sprinkled on the dining room table. Hmmm. Might it be an illegal drug? Or maybe someone was just throwing salt over her shoulder for good luck? How to find out? Chemistry to the rescue!

1. With white chalk or a white crayon, write the name of each substance you are testing at the bottom of a piece of black paper (salt, sugar, baking soda, baking powder, cornstarch, and any optional substances you are testing).

2. Measure out ¼ teaspoon each of your substances and sprinkle them on the appropriate piece of black paper. Wipe your measuring spoon with a paper towel between substances so you don't contaminate the next one and get confusing results.

- 1 piece of white chalk or a white crayon
- A helpful adult
- 2 sheets of black construction paper, each cut into 6 squares
- Measuring spoons
- Salt
- Sugar
- Baking soda
- Baking powder
- Cornstarch (you might also want to gather other white powders or starches, such as cream of tartar or potato starch, that your adult says are safe to use)
- Paper towel
- Magnifying glass
- A toothpick or two
- Your notebook
- Vinegar
- Water
- Tincture of iodine
- Eyedropper
- 9 (or more) small clear plastic cups (paper cups or old take-out containers can work well too)
- Permanent marker for labeling cups (you can also write on a piece of masking tape on the cup)
- Someone to play Watson to your Sherlock Holmes (in other words, a crime-fighting buddy)

Cream of Tartar

Baking Powder

Baking Soda

Salt

Cornstarch

Sugar

3. Study the substances with your magnifying glass. Use a toothpick to separate the grains into individual pieces. Note the shape of the grains. Are they big or small? Round or jagged? Jot down your findings in a notebook by listing each substance on a separate line and making a column called "Looks Like."

4. Now rub a few grains of each substance between your thumb and pointer finger. Describe how each substance feels in a second column called "Feels Like."

5. Sniff time! Get your nosy nose up close, but don't actually inhale the substances! You can do what chemists do and "waft."

That means you wave your hand above it, drawing the smell (but not the substance) toward your nose. Do any of the substances smell? Add your findings in a new column called "Smells Like."

6. Get out three plastic cups. Label them *vinegar*, *water*, and *iodine*. Measure and pour ¼ cup of vinegar in the cup labeled *vinegar*. Put ¼ cup of water in the cup labeled *water* and the same amount in the cup labeled *iodine*. (Don't add the iodine yet.)

7. Get out one plastic cup for each substance you wish to test. Label each

SALT   SUGAR   CORNSTARCH

with the name of the substance you will place in it—salt, sugar, baking soda, baking powder, cornstarch, and any other substances you are testing.

8. Place ½ teaspoon of each substance in the cup marked with its name. Shake the cup gently or tap it on the table to spread out the substance on the bottom of the cup.

9. Imagine that the bottom of each cup is divided into three parts. You will drop water in one part, vinegar in another, and iodine in the third.

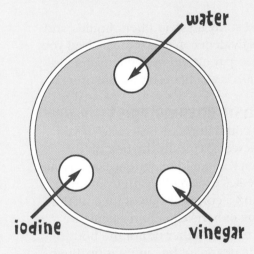

water

iodine

vinegar

10. Place your eyedropper in the cup labeled *water*. Squeeze the rubbery part (the bulb) and release. Then lift up. It should contain some water now. While holding the dropper over the cup labeled *salt*, gently squeeze the bulb to release one drop of water.

11. Look closely as you add the water. Did any of the grains dissolve? Was there any fizzing or a color change? Add one drop of water to each of the other substances, observe, and write down your findings in your notebook in a new column called "Water Reaction."

12. Squeeze out any remaining water from the eyedropper over the

sink. Now grab your cup labeled *vinegar* and add one drop of vinegar to each substance-filled cup (in a different location from where you added the water). Write down what happened in your notebook under the heading "Vinegar Reaction."

13. Rinse out your eyedropper with some water.

14. Ask your adult to help with this step: Find the cup that you labeled *iodine* (it should already have ¼ cup of water in it). Add 10 drops of iodine tincture. (Be careful with this stuff! It stains and is poisonous. Ask an adult for help.) You have just made a dilute solution. (Your bottle of iodine tincture may come with a dropper or it may not. If not, you can use your own eyedropper to transfer those 10 drops.) Wash your hands if any iodine gets on your fingers.

15. Add one drop of your dilute iodine solution to each cup using your eyedropper. What happened? Did some of the substances react differently? Write down what happened in your notebook under the heading "Iodine Reaction."

16. Rinse out your dropper with water. Keep the iodine cup in a safe place so it doesn't get tipped over.

17. You have just created a great chart of observations of these substances. Now you can use that knowledge to figure out an unknown substance!

18. Close your eyes (no peeking!) and have your crime-fighting partner sprinkle a teaspoon of one of the white substances on a piece of black construction paper. Open your eyes and see if you can figure out what it is. Try each of the techniques that you used above to test the substance and compare to your notes. If your unknown substance reacts in the same

way as one of the substances you tested, then you know what it is. Take turns trying to stump each other!

19. When you are all finished, you may rinse out everything in the sink, being careful not to splash the iodine. Don't use these cups again for food, in case any iodine hangs around. You may recycle them, or save them for future experiments.

WHAT JUST HAPPENED?

Different chemicals react to other chemicals in characteristic ways. For example, sugar and salt dissolve easily in water, but baking soda and baking powder do not. When added to the cornstarch, the iodine turned bright purple, but when added to baking soda, it stayed light brown. Sometimes a chemical reaction will occur when you mix two substances, but other chemicals just sit there, not reacting with one another. Amazing color changes indicate that a chemical reaction occurred: Something entirely new was created! With the baking soda and iodine, no reaction occurred, but there was a chemical change when the baking soda was mixed with vinegar: Carbon dioxide gas was created and bubbled away! (Note: Some powders are mixtures of other ones. For example, baking powder is actually a mixture of cream of tartar, baking soda, AND cornstarch! Do the results you got for each of those individual powders still occur when they are all mixed together?)

You created a set of observations and known reactions or "standards," and kept track of them in a notebook just like a real chemist or forensic scientist would. That helped you figure out what an unknown substance was by comparing it to your standards. That's some super substance sleuthing!

You'll need a science background—especially chemistry and biology and forensics—to do this job. You'll go to the scene to search for any physical evidence the villain left behind: the rock that broke the window, fingerprints on a counter, footprints in the dirt outside, maybe even a strand of hair or a piece of thread left where the necklaces once sat.

You will make super careful notes about where you found everything. The hard part is knowing what you are looking for and being patient as you search. Sometimes you'll be looking at a piece of evidence as big as a truck. Other times it might be one teeny carpet thread. You'll bring all your evidence back to the lab and try to figure out what it means.

Forensic entomologists use insects (including flies and larva) to gather information from a crime scene.

2. Be a medical examiner—Gruesome alert!
If you have a VERY strong stomach and find the idea of slicing open a human chest fascinating, this might be the job for you. Turns out, dead bodies tell tales—lots of them. So if someone dies in a suspicious way, the medical examiner steps in. By performing an *autopsy* (*ah*-top-see)—a careful exploration of a body both inside and out—a great deal can be discovered about what happened.

3. Be a forensic lab analyst—Prefer
analysis to evidence-gathering? Be a forensic lab analyst. Your job is to work with all sorts of awesome machines to figure out blood types,

decode DNA, and study mystery fibers, liquids, and powders. All this evidence may eventually lead you to the bad guys. So pay attention in chemistry class, kids, 'cause this job is all chemistry, all the time!

4. Be a forensic entomologist—Bugs!!!!
Who knew they could help solve a crime? If you thought the cops were typically the first on the scene in a murder, you could be wrong. Flies usually are. Hungry blowflies can smell death from up to ten miles away, and a corpse is one of their all-time favorite foods. Bug experts can often calculate the time of death and whether or not the body was moved by the degree of bug infestation. Bugs are also useful in determining if the victim had consumed poison or illegal drugs.

5. Be a digital forensic scientist—Do
you have mad computer skills? Digital forensics may be the field for you! Computer crimes cost us bazillions of dollars every year, and electronic devices like smartphones can "see"

as much as an eyewitness. From an altered photo to a forged e-mail to the retrieval of documents that had been dragged into the "trash," a digital forensics specialist can solve all sorts of crime using nothing but a keyboard and a mouse!

6. Be a forensic engineer—Did you start
taking the family toaster apart when you were a toddler? Does your heart go pitter-patter when you see a screwdriver? Forensic engineering may be the job for you. When a bridge falls down, a plane skids off the runway, or cars collide at an intersection, *these* experts get called in. They will study the wreckage and figure out why and how it all happened. Was it a defective part? Mechanical error? Wicked weather? Someone driving way over the speed limit? These engineering wizards will find the answer.

7. Be a forensic dentist—Forget the tooth
fairy! Turns out, teeth are pretty talkative! Everyone has a different bite and most of us have had X-rays made of our pearly whites. When unknown human remains surface, these tooth-smart dentists are called in to study the teeth left behind and to help ID the dearly departed. Kinda creepy, but necessary when you have no idea who the victim might have been.

8. Be a criminal profiler—Actually
crawling into the head of a criminal isn't possible, but we can learn to understand the way they think. If you like trying to figure out why and how people act the way they do, then you should study psychology—the workings of the human brain—along with criminal justice. Armed with this knowledge, you just

might be able to study a crime scene and say, "The perp is obviously a chubby, nervous baseball fan who loves Joe's Pizza!"

NABBED BY A BUG

One of the earliest crime-solving tales comes from China in the 1200s. A villager had clearly been murdered with a sickle—a curved blade used to harvest crops. The village lawman had an idea. He ordered every person with a sickle to bring their blades to the center of town. He knew some insects are attracted to the smell of blood. Even though the murder weapon had been wiped clean, the odor was still on it. All the blades were gathered and lined up along with their owners.

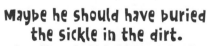

Maybe he should have buried the sickle in the dirt.
Speaking of which, let's get the dirt on DIRT, which is coming up next.

SALE
Deceased body
50% off

Dirt

Do zebra mothers ever march up to their kids and say, "Into the shower with you, right this second. You smell like a zoo!" Do chicken moms squint their little eyes, inspect their chicks, frown, and cluck, "You call those wings clean? Back to the sink this instant. And use soap this time." Not really. The truth is, dirt is a glorious thing. It's even used by certain species to *stay clean*!

SCRUB-A-DUB-DUB, SOME DIRT'S IN THE TUB

Stroll into your bathroom and check out all the stuff on the sink and in the shower. How many soaps, shampoos, and conditioners do you have? How about bubble bath, deodorant, and antibacterial hand sanitizers? We humans are obsessed with staying squeaky clean. But do we really need all that "stuff" to be smell-free and healthy?

EXHIBIT A: ELEPHANTS

Sure, it helps that an elephant is a grayish color—great for hiding filth, right? In fact, elephants are actually clean freaks, but instead of running a bubble bath, they take "dirt showers." Here's how it works: They suck up dust and dried mud with their trunks and then hose themselves—or their little loved ones—with the soil spray. Elephants do not have bath towels. Instead they give a hearty *shake-shake-shake* of their big elephant booties, and as the dried-mud powder flies off, it rubs away dead skin and any uninvited parasites that have been hiding in that crinkly hide. *Ahhhh!* Fresh as a one-ton daisy.

Chickens love dust baths too. A hen in need of a little freshening up will find a stretch of earth, *scratch-scratch-scratch* with her little clawed feet, and when she reaches some dusty earth, will plop down and wallow like a princess in a bathtub. Then she will roll around to work the dirt deep into her feathers—deep enough to reach her skin. When she feels the cool of the earth on the skin's surface, it's time to pop up and do the Chicken Dance (*"I don't want to be a duck, so I shake my butt, quack-quack-quack-quack"*). The dirt not only reduces the oil and moisture in her feathers, it also dislodges any parasites who thought they'd found a finger-lickin' good place to hang out.

Don't forget your armpits! And leave some dirt for your brother and sister!

BUBBLE BONANZA

At the front line of the war on dirt is soap. Soap in itself may seem a little boring. But combine soap and high heat and things get pretty exciting!

1. Observe each bar of soap. What do you notice? How compact or heavy is each one?

2. Ask your adult to help you cut a tiny bit off the end of each bar of soap to examine with your magnifying glass. What do you notice about how it looks and feels? Write down your observations. What do you think will happen when you microwave the bar of soap?

3. Put the bar of Ivory soap in the glass bowl and place it in the microwave.

4. Set your microwave to cook on high for 1 to 2 minutes, but watch through the door and stop every 30 seconds to open the door and observe what is happening. BE CAREFUL! The soap is filled with hot steam, so don't touch until you have waited at least five minutes for it to cool.

5. After about 5 minutes, ask your adult to carefully remove the bowl from the microwave. Let them touch it first. Once they give the temperature "all clear," stick your hands into the mix. Poke away at your

GO FETCH →

A soap-loving adult

3 soap bars of different types. One must be Ivory soap.

Knife

Magnifying glass

Your notebook

3 medium or large glass bowls or other microwave-safe containers

Microwave oven (and permission to use it)

bubbly soufflé, and try to re-form it in a ball or other fun shape to use in your next bath. If it's too crumbly, you can wrap the bits in a facecloth and tie up the ends with a rubber band to make a soapy scrubby for your next bath.

6. Microwave the next bar of soap following the same steps. Repeat with the third bar of soap. REMEMBER: Don't microwave the soap for more than two minutes.

7. Which bar of soap made the biggest pile of bubbles? Which one puffed up the fastest? Why do you think that is? Could you predict which soap would make the best bubbles? Look back at your original observations.

8. Clean up: Soak your bowl in water, then scrub it to remove the rest of the soap. This is not a step for your friendly adult. You've gotta clean up after yourself!

WHAT JUST HAPPENED?

There are a bunch of tiny air pockets trapped inside a bar of soap. Some brands of soap have more air pockets than others. There's a "rule of volumes" in science called Charles's Law, named after Jacques Charles, one of the guys who figured it out. This law states that as the temperature of a gas increases, the volume of that gas also increases. So when you heat the soap, the gas (air) trapped inside it expands. Any water in the soap will also turn into steam (which is water in gas form) and expand. Ivory soap has a lot of air pockets to begin with, so when those gases get hot and expand it really creates a giant bubble bonanza!

SPEAKING OF LICKIN' . . .

Stick out your tongue and lick your finger. Now lick your entire body. And don't forget your ears. What do you mean, you can't get your tongue in your ear? A jackrabbit can! Here's how. Reach your foot behind your head, push your ear forward, and lick. Was that so hard?

Cats, both tame and wild, are big lick fans. Tongues are like pinkish scrub brushes for many felines. If you were a cat, you would spend about half of your awake time cleaning yourself. Can you imagine spending eight hours a day washing up? But cat cleaning is a little more complicated than people cleaning. Are you hot? Lick your entire body to stay cool. Fur a little dry and flyaway? Licking helps distribute a cat's natural oils all over its body. A hungry predator lurking in the bushes? Lick away all traces of the tuna salad you spilled on your fur so you have less of a scent. Cleaning via tongue is a beautiful thing.

PICKY, PICKY!

Lickin' rhymes with pickin', so let's not forget the animals that stay clean by plucking away unwanted "visitors" that have hopped aboard fur or feathers. Many primates, such as chimps and monkeys, use their hands as a combination of comb and tweezers. They pluck away dead skin, insects, or parasites while running their fingers through their fur to sweep away dirt. Grooming is one of the most important events each day for a primate.

Under the sea, where there certainly is plenty of water, fish still manage to get "dirty." Fortunately for some of them, there is a type of creature called a cleaner shrimp that picks off parasites, bacteria, and dead skin. These types of shrimp can also be dental hygienists, cleaning the mouths of moray eels. If you have a fish tank, these little dudes make a great addition. You can buy one at a pet store. Just don't expect them to clean YOUR teeth.

ICK-SPERIMENT
SUPER-BUBBLE

GO FETCH

Who doesn't love to blow bubbles? But what makes some bubbles stick around while others pop right away? Let's see if science can help you make a stronger bubble.

1. Set out several bowls, one for each of the additives you wish to test. Label them with a piece of masking tape and a pen.

2. Put 1 tablespoon of liquid dishwashing soap in each bowl.

3. Add 1 tablespoon of your chosen additive to its bowl and stir. Leave one bowl for just soap, no additives.

Several bowls

Masking tape and pen

Thick liquid dishwashing soap

Several tablespoons

Any or all of the following additives:
- corn syrup
- vegetable oil
- gelatin powder
- glycerin (available from a pharmacy)
- sugar

Several plastic drinking straws

Timer or clock with a second hand

Table or countertop that can get wet, or several cookie trays

Towels for cleaning up

SO? SOAP?

Since *you* can't roll in the dirt and don't have cleaner shrimp to spend hours picking flakes of dirt off your skin, get thee to a shower! And say hello to soap! You use it every day (well, you'd BETTER be using it every day). But what is it?

Well, it's made of fat, water, and something called lye. Fat is kind of gross-looking. Peek in the meat case in your local supermarket and you can see the

4. Add 6 tablespoons of water to each bowl and stir.

5. Put a drinking straw in each of the bowls. (Use a different straw for each bowl. If you have friends over, then each person should get his or her own straw so that you don't swap germs.)

6. Dip your hand into one of the bubble mixes and smear a little bit on a table or countertop (if you are allowed) or other flat surface like a cookie tray. Make a separate area for each mixture, about the size of a small dinner plate.

7. Lift the straw out of that bubble mixture's bowl and put it down on the place where you spread its matching bubble mix on the table or tray.

8. Gently blow a bubble on the table (it will look like a half bubble because the part on the table is flat).

9. If you have friends over, you can each blow a bubble at the same time with different mixes and see which bubble lasts the longest. Or if you are alone, you could blow one bubble and then time how long it takes to burst, then blow another one from a different mix and time that. (Just be sure your bubbles are about the same size.)

10. You can also test which solution allows you to blow the biggest bubbles. When it pops, you can measure the diameter of the damp circle the bubble leaves on the table.

11. Save the bubble solutions overnight so you can use it for the next ick-sploration, as well as try these experiments again tomorrow. With the "older" solution, do the bubbles last longer, or can you make bigger ones? (Hint: We think you'll be surprised.)

WHAT JUST HAPPENED?

Okay, first let's get small. Water is made up of tiny parts called molecules. (To learn more about molecules, see page 14.) As you know, water molecules like to hang out together (scientists say they are

"attracted") and so they actually stick to each other. On the surface of a liquid they get *really* stuck together, and generate a force called surface tension. Think of the molecules as being chained together. If you pull on that chain, you'll put tension on it. Plain water has high surface tension.

But soap lowers the surface tension of water. Remember—soap molecules have a water-loving side and a water-hating side. The soap molecules form a little sandwich around the water. Picture soap as being the bread and the water as being the jelly. The soap forms a thin, flexible "skin" that can stretch when air is blown into it. So the bubble can stretch out, relax, and hang around longer! A bubble will hold together until the water molecules inside the soap "skin" evaporate into the air, or until it touches something dry, like your finger, which rips a hole in the "skin," a bit like bursting a balloon. Can bubbles say "ouch"?

You probably noticed that the soap and water made a nice bubble—better than just water. But it still didn't hang out for too long. When you tested the other additives, especially the corn syrup and the glycerin, they made bigger bubbles that lasted longer. That's because these additives made the bubble stronger by making the soapy liquid thicker. This "thicker skin" keeps the water from evaporating as quickly. Less popping, more oohing and aahing!

---

clumps of white greasy stuff sticking to the slabs of beef. Or stick your hand in a tub of butter. Ugh. But fat does help you stay clean and fresh. Remember bases—especially sodium hydroxide, that super-strong drain cleaner? (If not, back to page 12 with you.) Well, sitting right next to drain cleaner on the dangerous end of bases on the pH scale is something called *lye* (pH 13). We cannot tell a lie—this is really dangerous stuff. But when you mix lye with a fat (like animal lard or coconut or olive oil), something amazing happens. A chemical reaction! All the lye and fat combine to create a new, less scary chemical—soap!

CLEAN FREAKS

Here's how soap works. Water molecules are not the friendliest dudes. They like to stick together with their other H_2O buddies in clumps. As you learned earlier, this property of water is called cohesion. It's the reason you see individual water drops on a window when it rains and not just all-over wetness—each drop is a cluster of water molecules hanging out together. It's the reason water forms little balls when you try to mix oil and water. Soap blasts these clumps of water

You think your grown-ups are picky? How'd you like to sit still while your favorite adult picks nits off your butt?

apart, though, so they can wet everything better. But that's not the only way soap keeps you clean. Soap molecules have one end that likes water and another that likes grease, so they act like a connector between your stinky grime and the water rinsing you. Bits of soap break up that grease and trap it inside little bubbles. When you rinse, the trapped grease goes down the drain along with the water. You can picture your soap as a bunch of cowboys. They have horses that love water and lassos that love grease. Each lasso grabs a piece of grime or grease from your skin. As you keep scrubbing, the bubble cowboys round up all that gunk into little herds. Then they swim off into the sunset (or the drainpipe) on their water-loving horses and your filth goes bye-bye!

Mud, mud, magnificent mud. Thank goodness for soap and water too!

BUBBLE BLAST

ICK-SPLORATION

20 MINUTES

1 HOUR IF YOU TRY LOTS OF IDEAS

GO FETCH →

Now that you've found your ideal bubble solution, become a bubble master! Make 'em big, small, round, and even whip up flat sheets of soap film. Build bubble cities, and bubbles within bubbles!

1. Dip your hand in the bubble solution and spread it over a large area on your table (or a cookie sheet if you need to keep things tidy). This will be your bubble-blowing control center.

- A bowl of your favorite bubble solution from the previous experiment
- 4 plastic drinking straws
- Large flat area where you can spread bubble solution
- 1 or 2 cookie sheets
- Pencil or pen
- Paper or plastic cup
- Funnel
- 3 feet of string
- Scissors
- 1 or 2 wire coat hangers
- Food coloring (optional)
- Plenty of towels

2. Bubble City:

Using a straw, blow some half bubbles on the table (or a cookie sheet).

- How big can you make them? Can you blow a small bubble inside a large bubble?

- Blow a large bubble and a small bubble next to each other. What happens? Will the small one bulge into the bigger one, or the bigger one into the smaller one? Are the walls where they join flat or curved? If you blow a bunch of bubbles, how do they arrange themselves?

- Touch a bubble with your dry finger, then touch another with a wet finger. What's the difference?

3. Cup Bubble Maker: Use your pencil
to pop a hole in the bottom of your cup (you can also use a funnel). Then dip the large cup top in

bubble solution. Blow through the tiny hole toward the table and see if you can make a bubble on the table.

How big can you blow your bubble? Can you separate it from your cup or funnel? If you don't separate it, does air escape through the hole? Can you make a bubble snowman like we did?

4. Bubble Sheet: Pour bubble solution into a cookie sheet. Take 3 feet of string and thread it through two straws. Tie a knot and hide that knot in one of the straws. Now pull the straws apart until the string forms a rectangle with straws on either end. Dip the rectangle in the bubble solution in the cookie sheet. Hold on to the straw rectangle and lift it up and observe the sheet of bubble skin you made. Try to make a bubble by moving your loop quickly through the air. This will take

some practice. You may be able to figure out how to twist the straws to separate the bubble. If you don't have these supplies, just dip a wire coat hanger in the cookie sheet bubble mix. Lift it up and see if you have caught some soap skin.

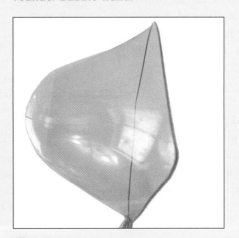

Wave it in the air like you just don't care and see if you can get a bubble to separate from the wire. You can also bend the coat hanger to make a rounder bubble wand.

5. Not tired of bubbles yet? Here are a few more investigations:

● Find other household items that have holes in them, like a window screen or a tea strainer. What happens when you dip these objects in the bubble solution and blow through the tiny holes?

● Observe a bubble from the time you blow it to the time it pops. What colors

do you see? Try this several times. Do you always see the same colors just before it pops?

6. Don't forget to clean up when you are finished! It should be easy! This is soap, after all!

WHAT JUST HAPPENED?

How can a square or triangular bubble wand only make spheres? A sphere is one of nature's most awesome shapes. A bubble wants to hold the most air it can while taking up the least amount of space. Let's imagine a soccer ball and a football that each hold the same amount of air. It will take less material to make the soccer ball, because a sphere is the most efficient shape. Soap bubbles in the air form that way naturally because it takes less soap to do so. You will always get a sphere when you blow a bubble!

Bubbles in the air are always spheres, but what happened when you blew lots of bubbles right next to each other? Those bubbles formed different shapes because they got squished. You may have noticed that when four bubbles came together, one usually broke. That's because three walls coming together are more stable than four. Try popping all the bubbles except one, and you will see that the remaining one will form a sphere (or a half sphere if it's on the table) once it's all alone.

When you blew a large bubble and a small bubble next to each other, what did you notice? The smaller one always bulges into the bigger one. Here's a case of the little guy winning! That's because the smaller bubble actually has more pressure inside. Pressure is a push or pull on a surface. In the large bubble, the pressure of the air you blew is spread over a larger surface, so there is less pressure on its walls. In the smaller bubble, there is more pressure on its walls, so they bulge into the larger bubble. Hooray for the little guy!

THE DIRT ON DIRT

Enough cleanliness! You can't make a decent mud pie from soap, so let's do a quick dig in the dirt. First, show a little respect. Dirt's proper name is *Soil*. And it's not just a brown blob. It's actually made of five different things. Let's line these soil suspects up in size order.

1. ROCKS. Rocks range in size from huge boulders, to stones you can use as slingshot ammo, to the tiniest bits of gravel.

2. SAND. Not just for beaches and building castles. The dirt in your yard or nearest park also has sandy bits in it. Sand grains are made from worn-down rocks and minerals that have been blasted by wind, rain, waves, or other natural forces for a few gajillion years.

3. SILT. Picture one grain of sand. Break off one tiny piece. You now have a grain of silt. When you see a photo of a river that looks very brown, it's because of all the silt floating along in it.

4. CLAY. The tiniest grains of soil. Not only is it good for making little bowls or clay animals, it also helps plant roots get a firm grip on the soil. It's what keeps soil moist, because it has nooks and crannies to hold water, but when packed firmly, it forms a hard layer that will not allow H_2O to pass through.

5. HUMUS. Soil's ickiest—and perhaps its most wonderful! Decayed plant and animal matter make *humus* (<u>hew</u>-miss). Humus is loaded with all sorts of good stuff for growing plants. Just don't confuse it with hummus—chickpea puree—and try to dip a carrot stick in it!

Stir all these components together and you have soil—the perfect thing for making a kick-butt mud pie! In fact, go outside and dig in some dirt and see if you can find any of the parts of dirt that we listed above! But you might also want to marvel at the fact that we make bricks (baked soil), glass (basically melted sand), and dinner dishes (baked clay) from this marvelous muck.

ICK-TIVITY
DIRTY DRINKING

GO FETCH

Dirt belongs in your garden, under your feet, or behind your ears—but not in your water. Here's how you can build a water filtration system that will make dirty water look crystal clear. CAUTION: Even though the dirty water might look clean enough to gulp down, don't drink it!

1. Pour the dirt into one of the soda bottles, and then fill it halfway with water. Add the cap and shake the bottle. Pour a sample of your dirty water into a clear cup and set this cup aside. Later, you'll compare it to your cleaner water.

- ¼ cup of dirt
- 2 empty 2-liter soda bottles
- Water
- 1 clear cup
- 1 teaspoon of alum (available in most grocery stores)
- Scissors
- Rubber band
- 3 x 3 inch square piece of cloth
- ½ cup of gravel
- Fine strainer
- 1 cup of sand

2. Pour the alum into your dirty water bottle. Add the cap and gently shake the bottle for 3 minutes. Let the dirty water sit for 15 minutes. You'll probably be impressed by how much better it looks after it sits. While you wait, it's time to build your water filter. . . .

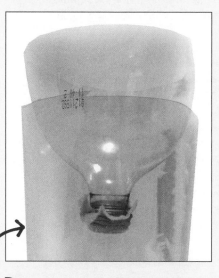

3. Remove the cap of the second bottle and use the rubber band to securely attach the cloth to the top. Have an adult help you cut off the top third of the bottle with the scissors and then turn the top upside down so it nests inside the rest of the bottle.

4. Pour the gravel into a fine strainer and run water over it in the sink until the water runs clear. Transfer this clean gravel into the upside-down bottle top.

Repeat this step with the sand: Rinse it in the strainer and then add it on top of the gravel layer. The cloth should prevent anything from falling out.

5. Slowly pour the dirty water into your new water filter, but do it gently so the bottom layer of sediment doesn't pour out. The water that drips out of the bottom of the filter should look quite clear. Compare how dazzling this water looks with the water in the cup you set aside in Step 1, but remember:

Don't drink it!

6. Now that you're a dirty-water-treatment professional, you can dig even deeper. Repeat the experiment but try eliminating some of the steps to see how important each part of the treatment process really is. For example, what if you don't use alum or sand? How much of a difference does it make in the appearance of the water?

want more dirt?

Soil is even more exciting when it's crawling with earthworms. So wriggle over to the WORMS on page 243 for more fun in the dirt!

WHAT JUST HAPPENED?

Clean water is a must for humans, but most water (even if it's not as filthy as the water you created in Step 1) has debris and microorganisms that need to be removed before we drink it. Water-treatment facilities for cities and towns do exactly what you've just done, but on a much larger scale. One difference is that those facilities may also add chlorine or use ultraviolet light to kill dangerous bacteria. Since you're SURELY not going to drink our filtered water, don't worry about this step.

The tiny pieces of dirt that float around in water instead of sinking to the bottom are called *colloids* (kuhl-loydz). The alum you added makes the colloids stick together, forming clumps, called floc, that become heavy enough to sink. This clumping process is called *flocculation* (flock-you-lay-shun), which is both fun to say and important to do. Flocculation gathers up all the dirt in water for easy removal. Without it, you'd be drinking filth. The sand and gravel act like a gigantic coffee filter, trapping the other bits of dirt that escaped flocculation. The thicker your layer of sand, the cleaner the water gets.

BATHING IN BACTERIA

Highly respected chemical engineer David Whitlock has not taken a bath or shower since 2001—and he's squeaky clean. It's not that he doesn't like a long hot soak, but as he watched a bunch of sweaty horses one summer, he had a bright idea. Horses are dirt bathers, like elephants and hens. Horses also sweat a lot. Dirt baths left the horses decidedly less sweaty. Maybe, he thought, there was some sort of chemical reaction occurring, or, better yet, "good" bacteria in the dirt—bacteria that gobbled up perspiration like we gobble up a hot-fudge sundae. Whitlock gathered some horse-y dirt and headed to his lab, where, sure enough, he was able to isolate a kind of bacteria that ate ammonia—a leftover by-product of sweat that makes you stink.

Your skin is like a city. There are all sorts of "residents" living there—especially bacteria. Lots and lots of different kinds of bacteria. Some of these can make us smell like three-day-old fish or lead to a dreaded ZIT! A good bacteria that can get rid of the stinky ammonia and the bad bacteria doesn't sound too shabby!

Whitlock needed a test subject to try his theory—himself! He mixed the bacteria he had isolated with water and poured it all over his head and body. That's it. Nothing more. Doing anything that would wash the bacteria off would ruin the experiment. Fast-forward 14 years with hardly a shower. Does Whitlock smell like an unwashed sock? Nope! In fact, he now owns a company called AOBiome (AOB stands for ammonia-oxidizing bacteria) that manufactures an awesome bacteria wash.

The spray works by creating a healthy environment (or biome) for all those hardworking, ammonia-eating bacteria. What's a biome? Picture a perfect little park where all the plants and animals get along happily with all their needs met. That's what Whitlock is trying to create on human skin, a lovely playground where bacteria can devour all the foul-smelling ammonia!

BUBBLE BATHS IN SPACE?

Zap! You are an astronaut up on the International Space Station (ISS) and you are feeling a little grimy. A shower sure would feel good, but how? Water + a weightless environment = a disaster. Water droplets would be floating all over the place. To make matters more complicated, water is just about the most valuable thing on the station. So astronauts make do with a swipe of a damp washcloth and special soap and shampoo that need no rinsing.

Astronauts can't blow bubbles on a space walk. That's because there are no air molecules in space, so there wouldn't be anything to push back on the outside of the bubble, holding it together, so it would pop immediately. Fortunately, the space station has air pumped inside it so the astronauts can breathe, do their experiments, and even blow bubbles if they are feeling playful.

Our cave-dwelling ancestors did not have antibacterial soap or bubble baths. All our bathing, especially with bacteria-killing soaps, has upset the balance of our skin microbiome, particularly affecting AOB. By getting AOB levels back up, some folks have seen gnarly skin conditions like acne clear up—plus, they've stayed clean without ever setting foot in a bathtub or shower.

So, feeling a little less than fresh after a sweaty soccer game? Maybe soon you will be able to just mist some N. eutropha, the good-for-your-skin bacteria, all over. No baths or showers necessary!

Speaking of getting clean?
what is that waxy gunk hanging in your ears? Onward, EARS await!

Earwax AND Ear Hair

What exactly is earwax? Why do older guys sprout tufts of ear hair? Why do elephants need such big ears? What exactly are our ears trying to tell us? So many questions! Listen up for the answers.

HEAR YE, HEAR YE!

Let's imagine ears with no wax. For starters, your ears would itch like crazy because they'd be so dry! Wax keeps your ears nice and moisturized.

In fact, a popular how-to magazine from the 1830s offered the following remedy for chapped lips: Insert finger in waxy ear. Dig out a chunk of earwax. Rub that wax on dry lips. Ta-da! Now give us a big smooch!

Second, you would constantly be fighting off ear infections. Big ouch! Earwax has awesome ingredients that ward off germs. One study found at least 10 proteins in earwax that fight microbes such as bacteria and fungi.

Third, you'd have a lot of dirt and dust, and even water, irritating your inner ear. Earwax is a lot like a big wall that keeps all the bad stuff out.

AND LISTEN CLOSELY HERE. Leave your earwax alone! It's there for a reason. Don't poke at it with a cotton swab. Don't stick your fingers in there (not even if you have chapped lips!). Digging around will only make your ears itch, and worse, push some wax farther in, creating a clog. You might even damage your very important eardrum! Ears are basically like self-cleaning ovens—no need to do anything!

What do ears have to do with stinky armpits? Well, the official scientific name for our golden ear globs is *cerumen* (si-<u>roo</u>-min). This waxy stuff is cooked up in two places. The first is your *sebaceous* (suh-<u>bay</u>-shuss) glands, which produce an oily, fatty substance called sebum, just

Resist the urge to scratch an itchy ear. You could end up building a wax dam.

EARWAX SLUMBER PARTY

10 MINUTES

Invite a few friends for a sleepover. You can use a flashlight to make scary shadows in the dark . . . and you can also use it to learn more about earwax! Why sleep when you can snoop around in someone's ears?

Send out invites and remind your friends NOT to clean their ears for a few weeks before the big event. When your guests have assembled, take turns peering in each other's ears and make a chart describing the color and consistency of each guest's ear contents. You might even photograph some of the more impressive globs and paste printouts of them into your notebook for further observations!

> **GO FETCH**
>
> Flashlight
> Camera (optional)
> A few brave friends
> Your notebook

Note: DO NOT stick anything in anyone's ears or you will be sent to the dungeon and never released!

like a fast-food joint. But there are also drier ingredients that come from the apocrine sweat glands— the same glands that produce sweat and can cause stinky armpit BO (see Odious Odors on page 170). Inside your ear canal, the oily and the dry mix, and very slowly, slowly, s-l-o-w-l-y ooze along toward your ear exit. When you wash your hair and water dribbles into your ears, the wax will usually soften, causing the clumps to break up into small bits, fall out of your ear, and then wash down the drain.

WHERE IN THE WORLD DOES YOUR EARWAX COME FROM?

Depending on your ancestors, you will have a distinctive kind of earwax. Some of us (with ancestors from Africa and Europe) have wet wax. This is often the color of honey and feels sticky. Those of us with Asian or Native American ancestors have drier earwax that is white and flaky.

Earwax also smells different depending on where your ancestors are from. What does *yours* smell like?

Unless you want wax oozing out your ears for all to see, give them a daily wipe with a wet washcloth. NO Q-tips!

A WHALE OF A WAD

How often do whales clean their ears? How about never! Recently scientists dug out a 10-inch-long (25-cm) piece of earwax from an unfortunate blue whale that crashed into a ship and died. Whales' earwax, which is made of keratin (the same hard stuff that makes up our fingernails) and lipids (a fancy sci-word for fats), builds up in layers like tree rings, so marine biologists can tell how old a

15 MINUTES

TO SET UP AND 1 DAY OF OBSERVATION

ICK-SPERIMENT
WAX BLASTERS

GO FETCH

What did you just say? Sometimes people with particularly waxy ears find that everything sounds muffled. If that happens to you, get your ears to a doctor, but don't forget to take the rest of you! Drugstores have special potions that soften some of the wax, and doctors have ways to flush out that gunky wax plug. Let's test a couple of these wax busters and compare them to plain water and oil. Which will work the best?

1. Next time you go to the doctor's office, ask if they can clean out your ears. Collect those hunks and bring them home. Your parents might also be able to swipe some wax emerging from your ear with a tissue. DO NOT go digging in anyone's ear. If you push too hard, you might jam the earwax down farther into the ear, or even hurt the eardrum—NOT fun!

If your grown-ups or doctor found some earwax for you, divide the earwax into four equal parts using your stick or fork, and put them in the middle of each piece of tissue.

An adult to help, especially with the hydrogen peroxide . . . it can damage your clothes or bleach your hair

A few small blobs of earwax

Toilet paper or tissue paper (cut into 4 small squares about 1 x 1 inch)

Scissors

Toothpick or the end of a fork

4 small glasses or cups (or test tubes)

Teaspoon

Water

Rubbing alcohol

Hydrogen peroxide

Baby oil (mineral oil)

2. When you have equal amounts of wax on all the tissue pieces, put one tissue into each cup/glass/test tube, with the wax clearly visible through the glass.

3. Label each cup/glass/test tube with the liquid that you will put in it.

4. Put about a teaspoon of

each liquid into the appropriately labeled cup and cover them.

5. See what happens to the wax over the next day or two. What do you notice?

WHAT JUST HAPPENED?

Spoiler alert! Don't read until you have done your own experiment! You probably noticed that the earwax that was in the water and hydrogen peroxide got kind of white and fluffy, while the wax in the baby oil and rubbing alcohol didn't change much. The hydrogen peroxide fizzes when it comes in contact with the wax, which breaks up the wax into smaller bits, making it look fluffy. But that fizzing can be annoying in your ear, and hydrogen peroxide can bleach your hair or clothes if you drip it in the wrong place. Scientists who study this (and yes . . . you *can* study earwax for a living) have found that water is actually the best thing to clean your ears! It's just as effective as store-bought products. So just let a little warm water dribble in your ears when you shower, or gently wipe your ear with a washcloth. But remember, it's healthy to have some wax in your ears!

ICK-TIVITY: LEND ME AN ELEPHANT EAR!

15 MINUTES

GO FETCH →

Materials:
- String
- Pencil
- Cardboard or construction paper
- Ruler
- Scissors

When it comes to ears, no one can top an elephant. Elephants' ears aren't just plain big; they're enormous compared to the size of their bodies. Those wrinkly flappers can be about ⅙ of their body's total surface area. So, how big would your ears be if they grew to elephant-size proportions?

1. First you have to figure out your height (in inches). For example, if you are 4 feet, 8 inches tall, then you are really 56 inches tall (because 4 feet = 48 inches, plus 8 more inches equals 56 inches). You probably already know how many pounds you weigh, but you might want to jump on a bathroom scale just to make sure.

2. Look up your height and weight in the table below to find out the size of your elephant ears. Use numbers that are closest to your actual height and weight. There are four things worth noting about this table. First, it is pretending your elephant ears are circles (because it makes the math easier to do, and circles are easier than actual ear shapes to draw). Second, it shows the radius of your elephant ears; the radius is the distance from a circle's center to its edge. Third, it displays the numbers in centimeters, because decimals are easier to use with centimeters than inches. Finally, it shows some potentially ridiculous combinations: a 6-foot person who is only 50 pounds?!? However, these are just numbers that come out of an equation and are useful for estimating the elephant-ear size for both real and imaginary people.

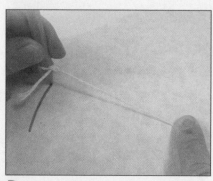

3. Use a string and pencil to draw two circles (one for each ear) on construction paper or cardboard with the appropriate radius for your height and weight from the table below. You do this by tying a piece of string to a pencil. Measure the string so that it matches your elephant ear's radius in centimeters. Then hold the end of the string in the center of your paper, and pick up the pencil. The pencil will draw a circle around your center point if you hold the string carefully. Double-check that your circle is the right size.

4. Cut out your circles and use some more string to attach them to your ears. Feel free to cut them into slightly more elephant-ear shapes. Your ears are now officially wicked big.

WHAT JUST HAPPENED?

That table full of numbers is based on something called the Mosteller formula, which estimates the surface area of your body. Knowing your surface area can be helpful for lots of reasons. For example, besides calculating the size of your ears if you were an elephant, you can also use it to figure out useful things such as how many stamps you'd need to cover your entire body, or how much paint you'd need to paint your gym teacher completely blue. Okay, on second thought, maybe it isn't as useful as we first thought!

RADIUS (in centimeters) OF YOUR ELEPHANT EARS

WEIGHT (in pounds)	YOUR HEIGHT (in inches)														
	44	46	48	50	52	54	56	58	60	62	64	66	68	70	72
50	10.5	10.7	10.8	10.9	11.0	11.1	11.2	11.3	11.4	11.5	11.6	11.7	11.8	11.8	11.9
60	11.0	11.2	11.3	11.4	11.5	11.6	11.7	11.8	11.9	12.0	12.1	12.2	12.3	12.4	12.5
70	11.5	11.6	11.7	11.8	12.0	12.1	12.2	12.3	12.4	12.5	12.6	12.7	12.8	12.9	13.0
80	11.9	12.0	12.1	12.2	12.4	12.5	12.6	12.7	12.8	12.9	13.0	13.1	13.2	13.3	13.4
90	12.2	12.4	12.5	12.6	12.7	12.9	13.0	13.1	13.2	13.3	13.4	13.5	13.6	13.7	13.8
100	12.5	12.7	12.8	12.9	13.1	13.2	13.3	13.4	13.6	13.7	13.8	13.9	14.0	14.1	14.2
110	12.8	13.0	13.1	13.3	13.4	13.5	13.6	13.8	13.9	14.0	14.1	14.2	14.3	14.4	14.5
120	13.1	13.3	13.4	13.6	13.7	13.8	13.9	14.1	14.2	14.3	14.4	14.5	14.6	14.7	14.8
130	13.4	13.5	13.7	13.8	14.0	14.1	14.2	14.4	14.5	14.6	14.7	14.8	14.9	15.0	15.1
140	13.6	13.8	13.9	14.1	14.2	14.4	14.5	14.6	14.7	14.9	15.0	15.1	15.2	15.3	15.4
150	13.9	14.0	14.2	14.3	14.5	14.6	14.7	14.9	15.0	15.1	15.2	15.4	15.5	15.6	15.7
160	14.1	14.3	14.4	14.6	14.7	14.8	15.0	15.1	15.2	15.4	15.5	15.6	15.7	15.8	16.0
170	14.3	14.5	14.6	14.8	14.9	15.1	15.2	15.3	15.5	15.6	15.7	15.8	16.0	16.1	16.2

whale is by studying this foul, fishy-smelling waxy buildup. They can also dissect whale ear goobers to figure out how polluted the Earth's oceans are. For example, the hunk scientists removed from that deceased blue whale had DDT (a really bad pesticide that is now banned in most parts of the world) trapped within.

MY, WHAT BIG EARS YOU HAVE . . .

Listen up! Ears aren't just for hearing. Elephants and other animals also use their ears to keep their bodies cool. Because the blood vessels in the ears are so close to the surface, much of the heat is lost as the blood is pumped through the ears. The bigger the ear, the larger the area for blood to flow through, the more heat loss. As cooler blood returns back toward the heart, it helps cool down the rest of the animal's body. That's important when you are a huge creature living in a very hot climate! In fact, elephants, rabbits, and foxes that live in warm climates have larger ears than their relatives who live in cooler climates. Survival of the coolest!

Basset hound's long ears drag on the ground and pick up scents, enhancing their tracking abilities.

WHEN I GROW UP I WANT TO BE AN EAR CLEANER

The city of Chengdu in China is famous for many things—among them an amazing panda research center, and the city's wandering ear cleaners, who gather in local teahouses, their pockets full of the tools of their trade—knives, tiny scoops, copper spikes, and, best of all, brushes made of goose feathers.

With tools in hand, the ear cleaners get to work. They tickle, probe, and gently scrape as their customers sit back in bamboo chairs. The ear cleaners claim that they can improve a person's health by touching certain pressure points in the ear that link to other bodily organs to increase blood flow and speed healing.

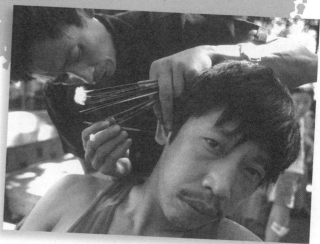

LITTLE EARS, BIG EARS

Big movable ears are awesome. They help the critter attached to them focus on hearing the softest of sounds. You might have noticed how animals such as rabbits and dogs twitch their ears around—this helps them detect sounds coming from different directions, an important tool for survival in the wild! We humans have nine muscles in our ears. That should allow us to move them a bit, but most of us can't. Can you? Find a mirror and try.

It's easy to test if having bigger ears (or perhaps foldable or movable ears) can help you hear better. Go stand across the room and have someone whisper something very softly. Still can't hear them? Try cupping your hands around your ears into a funnel shape. Can you focus on the sound now?

SOUND THE SIRENS!

People do not have elephant-size ears, but that hasn't stopped scientists and engineers from putting hefty ear size to use. In the mid-1900s there was a terrible war—during World War II planes flew overhead carrying deadly bombs, so knowing when they were coming was a very big help. Advance warning gave air wardens time to sound sirens that would send citizens scurrying to safety. If only there was some way to hear the incoming bombers sooner! So engineers got to work. Giant ears to the rescue! Plane spotters across Europe donned all sorts of elephant-shaped headgear. At a time when every second counted, the giant metal ears helped to "catch" the sound waves and amplify them slightly, which, in turn helped save lives. So what if they were totally bizarre-looking!

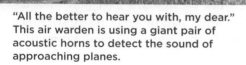

"All the better to hear you with, my dear." This air warden is using a giant pair of acoustic horns to detect the sound of approaching planes.

 **ICK-TIVITY**

EARWAX LOLLIPOPS

 **45 MINUTES**

→ **GO FETCH** →

A grown-up

Bowl or pie plate of packed snow or chipped ice

1-cup measuring cup

Medium saucepan

2 cups real maple syrup

Pat of butter

Wooden spoon or stick

10 or more cotton swabs

Fancy plate for serving

Optional:
- small plate for holding your sticky wooden spoon
- candy thermometer
- several cups for serving "dog pee" slurpees

Admit it: You've always wanted to be able to sculpt amazing figures out of earwax. (We know you have!) Well, you can either delicately collect your earwax over the next 20 years until you have enough, or you can make some fake earwax. This stuff looks like the real thing but is actually delicious—unlike the real thing. Freak out your family and neighbors by serving them a tasty selection of "used" cotton swabs covered in "earwax."

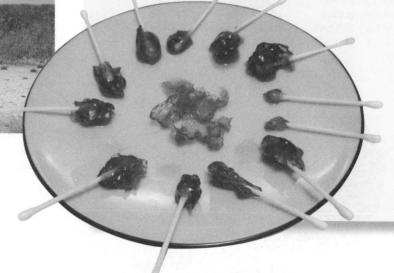

1. If you have long hair, tie it back. Make sure your clothing is not loose. No baggy sleeves here.

2. Go out in the snow and scoop up a big bowlful of clean white stuff. If you don't have any snow, use a hammer to break up a towel-wrapped bag of ice into tiny bits, or go to your local shop that sells shaved ice.

3. Pack the snow or ice into a bowl or pie pan and place it in the freezer.

4. Rub the pat of room-temperature butter in a circle around the inside top edge of a saucepan. The fat in the butter helps keep the maple syrup from bubbling over the top.

5. Pour the maple syrup into the pan and have your adult heat it gradually over medium heat until it comes to a boil (5 to 10 minutes).

6. When the maple syrup gets to a rolling boil, turn the temperature down to low so that it doesn't get too foamy and boil over. About half the surface should be covered in bubbles, both large and small.

7. Cook on low for about 15 to 20 minutes. You've heard the old saying "A watched pot never boils," right? Well, you and your adult helper MUST watch this boiling pot! Be careful! The syrup expands as it boils and can boil over in a second.

8. While you wait, rub butter on your serving dish (otherwise your guests will never be able to pick up their earwax snacks). Also, pull the cotton off one end of each of your cotton swabs (so that your guests don't end up with a bunch of cotton in their mouths! Now that WOULD be gross). Just remember to keep a close eye on your boiling syrup the whole time.

9. After about 15 minutes, the bubbles will change. The large bubbles will get larger and last longer. In a few more seconds, the liquid will look somewhat glassy. (If you are measuring with a candy thermometer, the syrup will be around 234°F/112°C.)

10. Insert your wooden spoon or stick and lift it high above the pan. When the syrup drips harden into threads, it's ready.

Turn off the heat. DON'T stir the syrup, or it will form crystals, which will ruin your "earwax" look. (If it begins to turn dark brown or starts smoking, immediately pour it on the snow. You will then have some burnt-tasting, dark, and crunchy earwax candy. That happened to us the first time, and though we couldn't serve it with the cotton swabs, it was still just as icky and yummy . . . in a crunchy, burnt way.)

11. Remove the pan or bowl of packed snow from the freezer.

12. Have your handy grown-up pour the syrup onto the snow in interesting shapes or long strings. But don't let them pour the syrup back on top of itself! If the syrup runs rather than hardens, it hasn't boiled long enough. Put it back on the stove for a little longer.

13. Wash your hands, put a bit of butter on your fingertips, and pick up a piece of the candy. It will be crisp and cold. Warm it in your fingers for a second and then wrap some around the non-cottony end of a cotton swab. Wrap as much as you want, depending on how big you want to make your earwax lollipop. Be sure to take all the "earwax" candy off the snow within a few minutes, or else it will begin to melt.

14. Place the earwax swabs onto your buttered plate and offer them up for a gross-out dessert. Keep them in the freezer until the magic moment, so that they don't melt all over the plate. If you don't want to use the cotton swabs, you can twist and pull the pieces of candy and form them into interesting sculptures. Then serve very soon (or put in the freezer), with a note calling them "earwax sculptures." (If your snow looks yellow once you've removed the candy, serve a bit of "dog pee" snow on the side!)

WHAT JUST HAPPENED?

Boiling the maple syrup made some of the water molecules evaporate out of the mixture. This "concentrated" the syrup, making it thicker. Pouring the hot syrup on the cold snow causes it to thicken rapidly. Sugar shacks in Canada and the northern part of the United States make maple candy this way. However, they wrap it around ice pop sticks and likely never thought of it as looking like earwax!

The Putrid Past

Gently (and we mean VERY, VERY gently) tickle your ear opening with a clean pointer finger. It feels kind of nice. Turns out ears are loaded with nerve endings and many of these nerve endings are hooked up to other parts of your body—especially your intestinal organs. Back in ancient Rome, a favorite pastime was the food orgy. People would literally stuff themselves to the point where they had to upchuck. A favorite way to bring up the barf was to tickle the ear canal with a feather. Very stuffed tummy + ear tickle = "I'm going to hurl!"

THE EAR BARBERSHOP

Let's take a look at another bit of ear grossness—hairy ears. This is mostly an older-dude phenomenon and no one has really figured out why it happens. We all have tiny hairs all

over our bodies called vellus hair. But sometimes those vellus hairs go over to the dark side and become something known as terminal hairs: the thicker stuff you have on your head and that you'll sprout in other parts of your body thanks to puberty. Biologists who study hair growth think that particular male hormones build up over time to a point where certain kinds of hair get "overfed" and grow crazily, including ear hair. The next time you are at a family gathering, do a secret search for the waxiest and hairiest ears. Who has the biggest tufts of hair sprouting out? Who has visible wax? Is there any correlation between the two?

Take a little off the top and a whole lot off the sides. Former Guinness World Record holder Radhakant Bajpai of India has some of the longest ear hairs in the world! Perhaps he should try braiding it?

What's across from your ears? YOUR EYES!
Up next: Learn how to cross them and drive grown-ups crazy!

Eyeballs

Squishy! Gooey! Slimy! Three of an ick-ster's favorite words, and they can all apply to eyeballs! But bet you didn't know that your baby blues, soulful browns, or gorgeous greens and hazels suck up as much as half of your brain's power when you watch a cartoon. Or that the muscles that control your eyes are the most active muscles in your body. Or that we blink about 15 to 20 times a minute, with each blink lasting between a tenth and a third of a second. Or that we can see up to 10 *million* different colors! What else don't you know about those two little orbs nested in your skull?

EYE, CARAMBA!

Because they are really squishy, eyes need to be protected. Your body does a great job at this. If you carefully feel around the outer edge of your eye socket (starting on your eyebrow), you will feel the "bony sockets" that provide a home for your eyes. These protect your eyes from getting hit by the soccer ball that annoying kid down the street just kicked at you without warning. Your eyebrows are like little sun shades and help prevent your eyes from getting too much light. When you squint, down come the brows. Your eyelids and eyelashes

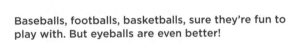

Baseballs, footballs, basketballs, sure they're fun to play with. But eyeballs are even better!

protect your eyes from small bits of flying junk. Surely you don't want airborne dust or the dead skin cells that your body is shedding right this very second to land in your eyes?

If anything does get into your eyes, it's time to blink. Nested above the upper lids of your eyes are the *lacrimal* (<u>lack</u>-rim-ull) *glands*—the place where tears are made. When you blink, tears flow from the glands and wash over your eyes. Tears contain oxygen and nutrients for your peepers too, as well as enzymes that can destroy bacteria. Those tears, and any gunk caught in them, drain into tiny holes called *puncta* that are located in the inner corners of your upper and lower eyelids. The tears eventually drain into your nose, which is why you have a small snot-fest whenever you have a good, long cry. You can see the pinkish puncta in the mirror if you look closely at the inner corner of your eyelids.

Now on to the ooey-gooey jelly bits of the actual eyeball.

HOW TO CROSS YOUR EYES

2 MINUTES

Don't worry . . . your eyes won't get stuck there . . . even though some people will say that they will!

feel very strange because your muscles have to work in ways they are not used to working.

● With your eyes open, hold one finger up about a foot away from your face and then slowly bring it toward your face, keeping your eyes focused on your finger. When your finger is about 3 inches away from your face, hold it there and keep focusing on the finger. Your eyes should be crossed now. Ask a friend or sibling to check for you.

● Another way to cross your eyes is to look at the tip of your nose with both eyes. Now slowly start to look up, while still keeping your eyes angled toward your nose. Your eyes will be unfocused and might

● If your eyes "snap back" into focus, they are no longer crossed. Getting your eyes to cross, even with the above tricks, will take practice. Once you have mastered this feat, you can try the ultimate ick-skill of moving your eyes in different directions. With your eyes crossed, keep one eye focused on your nose, while moving the other eye out to the center or all the way to the other side. Practice enough and you'll be able to gross out people in the blink (or roll) of an eye!

CORNEA ON THE COB?

Just hold the butter and salt! The *cornea* (<u>cor</u>-nee-uh) is a bit like the windows in your house, but dome-shaped. It's the clear part that sits in front of your lens. Its shape is the reason a lot of us need to wear glasses. Together the cornea and the lens help focus light on a part of your eye farther back called the *retina* (<u>ret</u>-in-uh) (more about that part in a bit). But sometimes our lenses and corneas need a little extra help to focus the light correctly onto the retina.

MY, OH MY, OH MYOPIA

If your eyeball is a little too long or your cornea too curved, then the cornea and lens will focus the light a little ahead of your retina but not directly on it. Objects that are far away will look blurry, even though you can read this sentence easily. This is called *myopia* (my-<u>oh</u>-pee-uh)—also known as nearsightedness. If the whiteboard at school looks blurry, you might have myopia. Lots of school-age kids have it.

If you're be able to see faraway objects, but close things are blurry, you might have *hyperopia* (hi-per-<u>oh</u>-pee-uh), or farsightedness. This means your eyeball is too short or your cornea is too flat.

And if your cornea isn't symmetrically round but irregularly shaped, often compared to the shape of a football, EVERYTHING could be a bit blurry. That's called *astigmatism* (uh-<u>stig</u>-muh-tiz-um).

But fret not! Any of these problems can be solved with awesome glasses or contacts, extra lenses that help your cornea and lens focus light onto your retina. Your ordinary human abilities are now enhanced by science! It's like you're bionic!

ROSES ARE RED, EYEBALLS ARE BLUE (OR BROWN OR GREEN)

Light enters your eye through your *pupil*, the black hole in your eye's center that is surrounded by the colorful *iris* (<u>eye</u>-riss). Your iris controls how much light enters through your pupil. When certain muscles in your iris contract, the pupil widens and more light gets in. When your iris relaxes, other muscles can cause the pupil to shrink, letting less light in.

Got blue eyes? Until about 10,000 years ago, all human irises were brown. Blue eyes are a mutation. (A mutation means a change in the DNA that determines eye color. It doesn't mean that blue-eyed people are mutant freaks with two heads.) That mutation was passed on to the children of the original blue-orbed parent, who then passed it on to THEIR kids. This means that all blue-eyed people have a common ancestor. And here's a shocker: Blue eyes might LOOK blue, but just like the blue sky or the blue ocean, that's only because they are reflecting light in a certain way. They aren't really blue at all. Same with green and hazel eyes. Everyone's eyes are

Much of the work the brain does involves processing information from your eyes.

PLAY WITH YOUR FRIEND'S EYES

GO FETCH →

Now don't get too excited! We're not going to teach you how to pop out your friend's eyes and roll them around like marbles. (In fact, you had better treat your eyes and your friend's eyes with EXTREME care). Instead you'll get a chance to watch a pupil expand and contract.

Look deep into your friend's eyes. Avoid the urge to giggle. (Oh, never mind, giggle away.) Notice the color of the irises. Then look at the size of the pupils (the black dot in the center). Now turn on your flashlight and briefly shine it in one eye. What do you notice? Take the flashlight away and see what happens. Shine the flashlight again, but this time look at the other eye (the one that doesn't have the flashlight shining into it). What happens to that eye when you shine the flashlight into the other eye? Ask your friend what it feels like when the light shines into

Flashlight

Somewhat darkened room

Friend (Unless all your friends are busy making scabby spaghetti from page 199 for their families. Then use a mirror and your own eyes.)

an eye. Now let your friend have a turn blinding you with light (uh . . . we mean "observing your eyes for the purposes of science").

WHAT JUST HAPPENED? **T**he muscles in your friend's eyes expanded and contracted depending on how much light was shining on them. More light =

small pupil. Less light = big pupil. Your iris—the colorful part around your pupil—is made of two types of muscle. These muscles move a bit like a camera aperture, opening and closing to allow more or less light into your eye. When the light is bright, a ring of muscles around your pupil, called a sphincter—just like the one that keeps your poop safely inside you until you reach a bathroom—squeezes, making your pupil smaller. Less light enters your eye, which is very handy when you walk outside on a sunny day. Other muscles, called dilator muscles, can pull out to expand your pupil. You know what happens when you walk into a dark room? Just wait a few moments, try not to walk into any furniture, and your pupils will expand to let more light in and allow you to see even when the light is very dim.

KEEP AN EYE ON YOUR EYEBALLS

2 MINUTES

GO FETCH →

1. Close your eyes and GENTLY touch two fingertips to each of your eyelids. They should just rest there, not push at all.

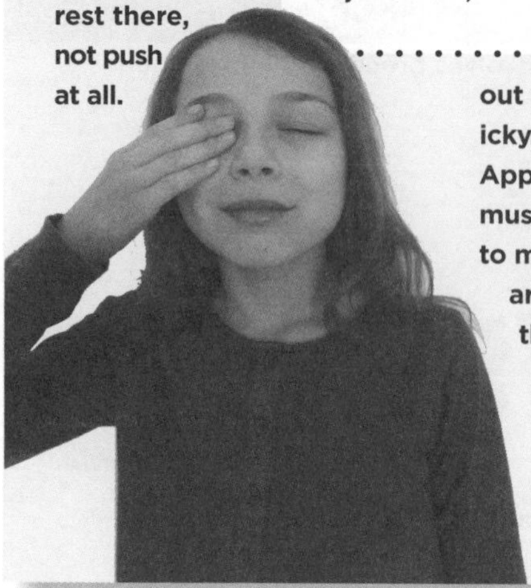

Your CLEAN hands

Your eyeballs (Now, where did you leave them? Oh wait. They're already in your head.)

2. Now wiggle your eyeballs around from side to side and up and down. Are you weirded out yet? It does feel a little icky. But SO interesting! Appreciate all the tiny muscles that must contract to make your eye move around. Can you feel that your eyes are not perfectly round? You may be able to feel your cornea—it's like a raised bump in the middle of your eye.

brown, but your iris has three layers, kind of like an Oreo cookie (but don't try to lick it). There's a thin layer on each end with a spongy layer in the middle. People with "blue" or "green" or "hazel" eyes only have pigment on the bottom layer, and that pigment is indeed brown. But depending on how that middle spongy layer reflects the light, their brown eyes appear blue or green or hazel. So the next time you see someone with beautiful blue eyes, tell them, "What lovely mutated irises you have!"

EYE-HOY, MATEYS!

Pirates may not have known as much as you do about eyes, but they knew enough to wear eye patches, even if they had two perfectly good eyes. The patch not only made them look tough, it kept one eye always ready for the dark. Pirates needed this because they often jumped aboard ships and battled their way into the dark cabins below. Without a patch, they would be totally blind coming from the bright sunlight, but with a patch, they could just flip it up and that eye was ready to go! Avast, ye scurvy beasts!

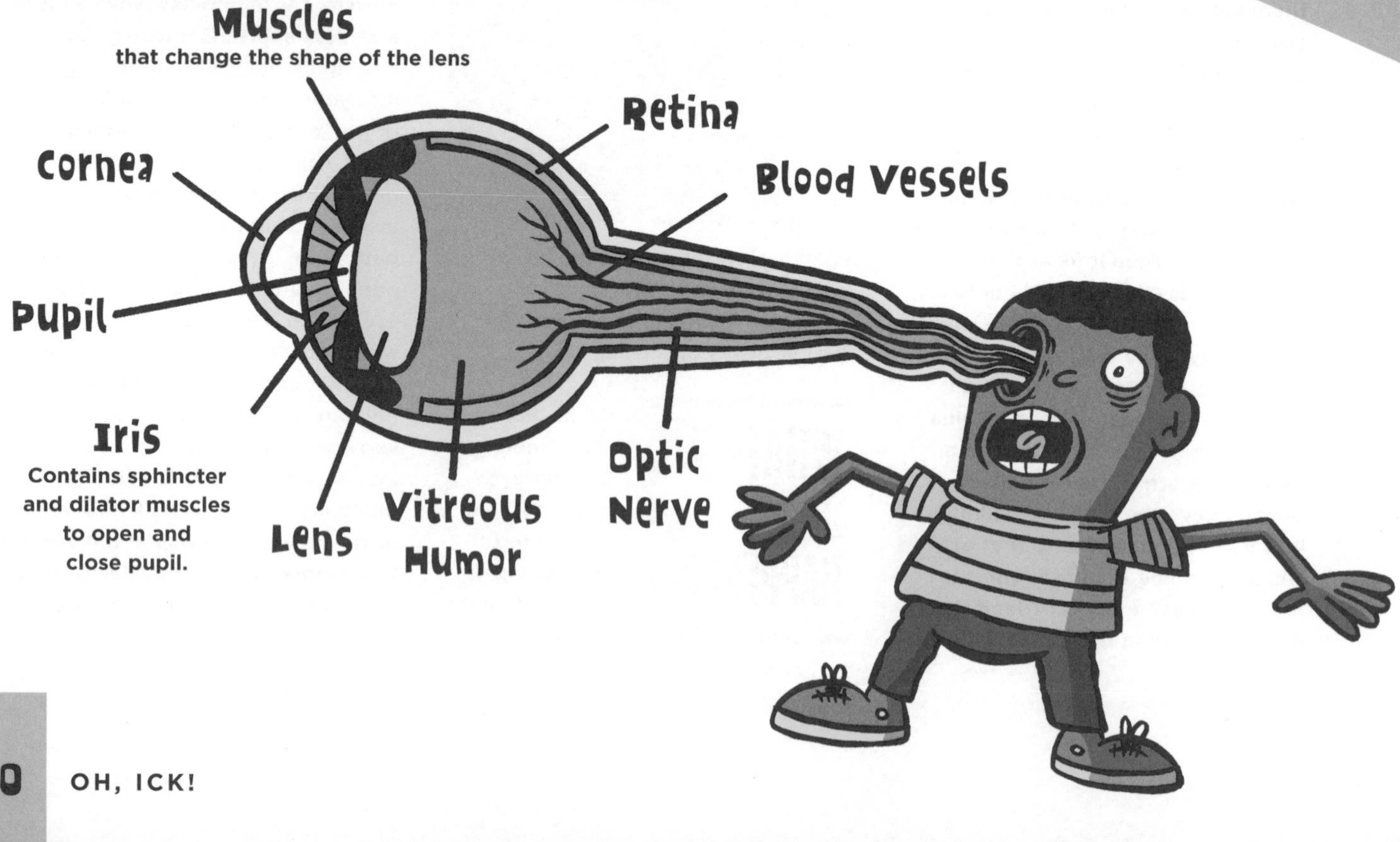

Muscles
that change the shape of the lens

Retina

Cornea

Blood Vessels

Pupil

Iris
Contains sphincter and dilator muscles to open and close pupil.

Lens

Vitreous Humor

Optic Nerve

JUMPING THUMBS

5 MINUTES

GO FETCH →

Because your eyes are in slightly different locations on your head, each eye sees a slightly different scene. Your brain puts the two scenes together to create one clear image. Here's a fun activity to help you understand this concept.

Your eyes

Your thumb

An object in the distance

1. Look at an object in the distance, such as a light switch on the wall.

2. Close your right eye.

3. Hold up your right arm and line up your thumb with whatever object you are looking at.

4. Don't move a muscle other than the ones in your eyes: Open your right eye and close your left. Did your thumb jump?

5. Compare how much it jumps when your thumb is close to your face to how much it jumps when it's as far away as you can reach.

WHAT JUST HAPPENED?

This little activity shows that each eye sees a slightly different image, making your thumb appear to hop as you switch between eyes. The illusion of your thumb moving is called parallax. The word comes from the Greek word *parallaxis*, which means "alteration."

Parallax allows us to see depth— giving us 3D vision! Astronomers can also find out how far

away nearby stars are by using parallax. They take a picture of a star in January (when the Earth is on one side of the sun) and again in July (when the Earth is on the other side). Imagine that those two points of the Earth's orbit are like two giant eyes in the sky. Because we know the distance between those two locations (186 million miles—that's the diameter of the Earth's orbit), astronomers can then compare how far the star "jumped" in relation to stars behind it. And from that they can calculate the distance from the Earth to that star!

SQUISHY BITS

In the space behind the lens and in front of the retina there is clear, Jell-O-like stuff called the *vitreous humor*. It can't tell any knock-knock jokes, but it does help give your eyes their spherical shape. The retina sits at the back of your eyeball. It's basically the big curved movie screen in your eyeball movie theater, minus the popcorn and red velvet seats. It's made of special cells that can detect light. The cells of the retina convert light into electrical signals that travel through your optic nerve to the parts of your brain that process vision. The image that you see hits your retina upside down, but your brilliant brain cells turn the image right side up. It might be hard to walk around if the whole world looked upside down!

EYE LOVE YOU

You know that the iris expands and contracts in response to light, but did you know that it also responds to your emotions? Got a crush on a classmate or a big case of "dislike" going on with the neighbor's pit bull? Love = bigger pupils. Dislike = smaller pupils. Pupil size also changes when you are thinking hard. That last history pop quiz? You just might have had tiny pupils! You could grow up to be a scientist who studies this kind of thing, called *pupillometry*—the size of pupils. How's that for an eye-opening career?

ODDBALL EYEBALLS

As awesome as our eyes are, they are not the most extraordinary in the animal world—not by a long shot. Many animals can see great distances or when it's really dark out. Take eagles, for example. They can spot an innocent bunny munching on a lettuce leaf from almost two miles away. And while you might stumble around in the dark, a lion (or a house cat!) can pick out and pounce on a moving midnight snack with ease. Want more animal eyeball trivia? Read on!

The better to see you with, my dear—

Picture a basketball. Now imagine it in the skull of a colossal squid to get an idea of the size of the largest eyeball on the planet. (The colossal squid is not the same as the giant squid—it's even bigger than that!) "Gigant-ICK" squid eyes come in handy for seeing in dim light. Very useful for a creature that has to find food deep below the ocean's surface, where the sun does not shine.

This giant squid eye is the size of a hand! But colossal squids can have eyes the size of basketballs.

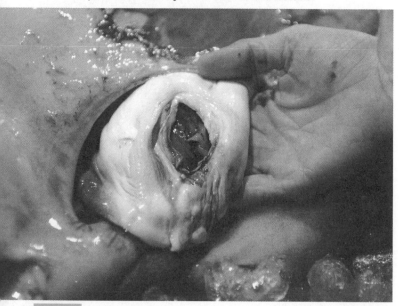

ICK-TIVITY

30 MINUTES · PLUS HOURS OF FUN!!!!

SEEING UPSIDE DOWN
GO FETCH

- 2 paper or plastic cups

- 10 centimeter focal length biconvex lens (38 millimeters diameter). You will have to order these online unless you happen to have one lying around.

- Pencil

- Utility knife and an adult to help with using it

- Clear tape

- Paper tube from the inside of a roll of toilet paper (or a paper-towel tube cut in half)

- Piece of opaque plastic that you can cut (we got ours from a takeout food container) or a piece of wax paper

- Marker or pen that can draw on plastic

- Scissors to cut the plastic

- Glue stick or white glue. You can also use more tape.

Your eyeballs are about the size of a big gumball. The lens part of the eye is about the size of an M&M. Anyone else hungry? You can make a colossal squid-size working model of an eyeball that will show you how your retina sees things.

1. Turn one cup upside down on the table. Place your lens on the end now facing you and use your pencil to trace a circle around it.

2. Get your adult to help you cut a hole slightly SMALLER than the one you traced. It's okay if it's not a perfectly neat circle.

3. Rest the lens on that hole and use a few small pieces of tape to hold it over the hole. Try not to cover the lens with tape, and also try to keep your grubby fingerprints off it. Set that cup aside.

4. Pick up your toilet-paper tube and place it on the bottom of your second cup. Trace a circle around it.

5. Ask your adult to cut a hole that is slightly BIGGER than the circle you traced. Insert the paper tube into the hole and test to see if it can slide back and forth through that hole. If it can't, cut a slightly bigger hole.

6. Take the paper tube out of the cup and place one end on your piece of plastic. Use your pen or marker to trace a circle around it.

7. Cut out the circle in the plastic just slightly larger than your paper tube.

8. Put a little glue on the end of your paper tube and then glue on the plastic disc you just made. Be careful not to get too much glue on the disc. You could also tape it on if you are careful not to cover much of the disc.

9. Put your paper tube with the disc through the mouth of the second

cup and back into the hole you made. Important: The plastic disc should end up inside your cup.

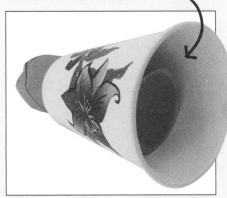

10. Now bring the mouths of both of your cups together and tape them shut. The lens is on one end, the plastic disc is somewhere in the middle, and the open end of your paper tube is at the other end.

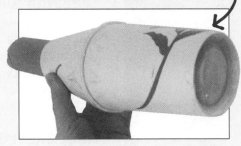

11. You have now made a not-very-round model eye! (You could make a round eye by cutting into a toy ball, but why waste a perfectly good ball?)

12. Hold the lens end up to something (or someone) that is well lit (like a tree outside, or a friend nearby) and look through the open end of the paper tube. You don't have to put your eye right up to it . . . in fact, it may work better if your eye is about 6 inches away from the end of the tube. Move the paper tube away from you or toward you to bring

the image into focus. Enjoy looking at things all over the place . . . upside down. Exactly the way your brain sees them!

WHAT JUST HAPPENED?

Your real lens is a bendy, see-through bunch of tissue that sits right behind your iris and pupil. The lens of your cyber eye worked just like the lens of your real eye. It took in the light that bounced off your friend's face or whatever you were looking at, then it focused that light on the plastic disc representing your retina. Retina cells sense light and convert it into electrical signals that travel up your optic nerve. The optic nerve carries those signals to the parts of your brain in charge of seeing.

You got your model eye to focus by moving the paper tube/plastic disc "retina" closer or farther from the lens. Your real retina doesn't move in and out like that. Instead, tiny muscles (called ciliary muscles) make slight changes to the shape of your lens, and that's how you focus. In fact, at this very second, as you read this page, those tiny muscles are hard at work. Take a moment to look up at something far away. As you did so, the tiny muscles relaxed and your lens flattened a bit. That's why it's good to take a break from reading or video gaming every so often. Relax your eyeballs and look at something in the distance. Your eyes will thank you!

Open wide and never stop—

Frogs never, ever close their eyes. Neither do fish. Guess this means they can't wink at each other.

Hairy eyes—

Some bees have hair sprouting on their eyeballs. These tiny hairs help them figure out wind direction and how fast they are flying. So what do you think? Comb your hair AND your eyes?

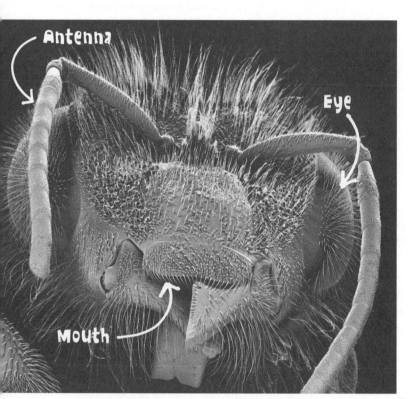

The honeybee has large, hairy eyes. It might be time for a trip to the barber!

Dragon eyes—

The dragonfly is the supreme hunter of the insect world. Why? Its eyes are so big they cover the entire head, like an eye helmet! If you had dragonfly eyes, your entire head would be nothing but eyes! These creatures have a 360-degree field of vision. That means they can actually see what's happening behind them and in front of them at the same time!

Antenn-eyes—

Oh, to be a stalk-eyed fly. Why waste valuable face space when you can just put your eyes on the ends of two antennae that stick out of your head? Male stalk-eyed flies have MUCH longer eye stalks than females and they can even "flex" them to make them bigger. During mating season, the guy flies stand face-to-face comparing eye-stalk size. The bigger the distance from face to eye, the more handsome the fly.

Sleeping with one eye open—

Is something going to attempt to eat you when you try to grab a little shut-eye? Some species (dolphins, iguanas, and many birds) will literally snooze with one eye open. Since the other eye is closed, one part of the brain gets to rest. The eyes and the matching brain parts take turns resting.

Hey, one-eye!—

You've probably tasted a shrimp before. Shrimp belong to a group of animals called *crustaceans* (crust-a-shunz). One member of the crustacean family is a teeny little critter known as *Cyclops*—the only animal on the planet that comes with just one peeper. Cyclops got its name from a character in Greek myths—a fearsome monster with only one eye plastered in the middle

CRY, BABY!

Wah-wah-wah! Newborn babies sure can cry, but their eyes produce no tears. That salty liquid does not start dripping out until those wee wailers are at least a month old. And for the first few days of a baby's life, it is believed that an infant actually sees the world upside down and very blurry. Our brains learn how to flip the image, but it takes a few days to figure it out.

of his forehead. Relax! Cyclops, the copepod (a kind of wee plankton) probably won't scare anyone. They are only about 2 millimeters long—a little more than the thickness of a dime.

Color me Jealous—We might be able to see up to 10 million different colors, but mantis shrimp take the prize for the most complex eyesight of any known animal. Their eyes have 12 color receptors (compared to our pitiful three!). We can see only one kind of light—visible light— but they can see also see ultraviolet and infrared light that's invisible to us.

Mammal master—If you were a tarsier— a squirrel-size, night-loving primate from Southeast Asia— you would have the largest eyes of any mammal, relative to the size of your body. Picture yourself with eyes the size of grapefruits, and you get the idea!

With their ginormous eyes, tarsiers always look surprised!

ICK-SPLORATION

HOLEY HANDS!

5 MINUTES

GO FETCH

Piece of paper (8 1/2 x 11 inches) or an empty paper towel or toilet paper roll

Okay, okay . . . don't get all worked up. We're not going to make you cut a hole in your hand. But (together with your awesome eyeballs and brain) we can give you the ILLUSION of one.

1. Roll up the paper the long way, so that you have a tube that is about a half inch wide.

2. Put the tube up to your left eye, holding it with your left hand.

3. Put your right hand about ¾ of the way down the tube so that the tube rests in the curve between your thumb and pointer finger.

4. Keep both eyes open. With your left eye look through the tube, and with your right eye look at your hand—at the same time. Can you see the hole in your right hand?

5. Slide your right hand up and down the tube. Where can you see the hole best? What happens if you put your right hand far away?

WHAT JUST HAPPENED?

Your brain got two images but couldn't make sense of them. It freaked out, so you saw both at the same time, making it look like you had a hole in your hand!

SEEING DOUBLE

So you can't spot an ant from the top of a skyscraper or see what's going on behind you. Still, your eyes have some awesome features. For example, humans have *binocular* (bin-<u>nock</u>-u-lur) vision. Binocular means that our two eyes work as a team to see. This works because

EINSTEIN'S EYEBALLS

You know Albert Einstein. World's most famous scientist. Bushy head of white hair. Big mustache. $E = MC^2$. Well, now you can feel sorry for him too. Poor Einstein's eyes were stolen during his *autopsy* (<u>aah</u>-top-see)—a medical study of a dead body—in Princeton, New Jersey, in 1955. Scientists really wanted to peer at the brain of the great man to see if there was a physical explanation for his genius. Creepy. But even creepier, during the autopsy his eyeballs were plucked away and given to the guy who checked Einstein's eyesight once a year—an eye doc named Henry Abrams. Abrams walked out of the autopsy room with the great man's eyes, then placed them in a jar in his dresser drawer for safekeeping. He kept them there for many years before moving them to a safe deposit box in a local bank. And you thought keeping a lock of someone's hair was creepy!

Abrams died in 2009. At the time this book was written, the eyeballs were still floating in that very same jar, behind lock and key in a New Jersey bank. Hopefully at some point E's eyes will be allowed to rest in peace!

our eyes are very close to each other—about 2 inches apart. Here's a general rule of thumb, although there are exceptions: Animals that hunt—lions, wolves, and eagles—have close-together eyes, all the better to focus on and chase after some yummy dinner. Animals that are hunted—rabbits, buffalo, and deer—have far-apart eyes so they can see more of the area around them. That way they can keep a lookout for those hungry hunters!

The coolest part about binocular eyes is that they allow us to see things in 3-D. Our two eyes are gathering data about the distances of the objects we are looking at, while our brains are busy using this data to calculate how far away these objects are. The farther away something is, the less depth and detail you will see. Depth perception is very useful if you are a predator like a hungry lion. Just how far is that juicy-looking zebra? The eye-brain connection gives you the answer, so you'll know exactly when to pounce.

Ever been to a 3-D movie? Those totally awesome movies are made using two camera lenses set slightly apart, just like our eyes. When the two resulting images are projected through different filters, it fools our brains, creating the illusion that the actors or objects are actually floating in space—coming right at us! Quick! Duck!

So there you have it! Gushy, squishy eyeballs. But what about the things you can't see, the things you can only smell? FARTS is up next, and you just might want to hold your nose!

Farts

Think of a gorgeous movie star or your favorite sports superhero. Now close your eyes and imagine this amazing person unleashing a giant, stinky, super-noisy *f-f-f-f-ft-ft-fart*. Princesses, priests, professors, principals, poets, presidents—everyone does it!

The average grown-up will toot out about half a liter of gas each and every day. How much is that? Picture a balloon the size of a grapefruit. Now imagine that amount of gas escaping from your rear blowhole. Most adults shoot the breeze about a dozen times a day, but some real gasbags can unload upward of a hundred farts in a 24-hour period!

PEE-UUU!

Here's what you should know about those sneaky stench bouquets.

WHY DO WE FART?

To put it simply, a fart is a little cannonball of gas that gets expelled (often forcefully) from your anus (otherwise known as your butthole). How did that smelly air end up in your body in the first place? Well, you either swallowed it, or it was produced by bacteria in your large intestine. Most of the gas you pass is made up of carbon dioxide, nitrogen, oxygen, and hydrogen, but none of those gases is smelly. The blame lies with sulfur, a chemical present in a lot of the foods you eat. In the body, sulfur joins up with the atoms of other chemicals to make *hydrogen sulfide* gas, which smells like rotten eggs, and *dimethyl sulfide*, which smells like days-old fish. There are other air foulers in the mix, such as *skatole* and *indole*—the chemicals that make poop reek.

STENCH STEW!

The amount you toot is based on the kinds and combinations of food that you eat and how much air you accidentally swallow when you eat. Some foods cause your gut bacteria to go crazy making gas. Others not so much. If you swallow lots of air when you snack (usually because you are eating too fast) or chew gum or drink through a straw, what you don't burp up will go out the other end (see BURPS on page 35 for more on air gobbling). Any which way you look at it, it's all a recipe for *pee-uuuu*!

How smelly can you get? Well, what have you just eaten? Foods with a lot of sulfur in them are a surefire recipe for "hold your nose!" Ironically, some of the foods that are healthiest for us—including beans, cabbage, and broccoli (oh, stop whining and eat the broccoli anyway)—are loaded with sulfur. So too are bananas, pineapple, and watermelon. Meat and dairy? Yup, sulfur! And eggs? That yolk is basically a big ball of sulfur. Even bread! Here's a fun fact: Beans and broccoli are especially bad because they contain a carbohydrate called *raffinose* that will certainly offend *your* nose at some point. It is difficult for your stomach and small intestine to digest this stuff, so it heads on down to hang out in your large intestine. The bacteria that live there get busy trying to digest the raffinose and other undigested carbohydrates, and as they do, *they* release gas—especially hydrogen sulfide. Fruits and artificial sweeteners are another guilty party. If you see the words *sorbitol* or *fructose* on the food label of your most recent snack, be prepared to deliver a master blaster in the not-too-distant future. Those two sugars are super yummy for the bacteria in your large intestine. You guessed it . . . more bacterial gas released into your intestine! So really, when you think about it, *you* aren't farting, the millions of bacteria in your lower gut are. Since they don't have butts, the gas gets released through their membranes and comes out *your* rear. *TOOOOT!*

GRUESOME SCIENCE

THUNDER FROM DOWN UNDER

Kangaroos have some pretty cool abilities. They can jump 25 feet in a single bound! Mama kangas raise their babies in a pouch for the first seven or so months. But one of the *most* amazing things about them is their extra-special butt blasts. Unlike most critters, kangaroos unleash environmentally friendly farts. This was really interesting to Professor Athol Klieve, an Australian who studies the microbes that live in intestines. What a fun thing to be an expert on!

Australia has lots of cows and sheep, and these two animals are big-time wind breakers! They pass so much gas that they are responsible for about 15 percent of the greenhouse gas emissions on that island continent. That's right, they burp and fart methane . . . a gas that is worse for climate change than carbon dioxide. If only there was some way to get cows and sheep to fart like kangaroos! Turns out that kangaroos have a unique bacteria in their stomach linings that zaps methane. Dr. Klieve is studying whether adding kangaroo gut bacteria to cattle feed will stop those smelly heifers from adding warming gases to the atmosphere. Would you eat kangaroo gut bacteria to have Earth-friendly farts? Hmmm. Food for thought!

FARTING SLIME BAG

GO FETCH

15 MINUTES

Fart sounds! So much fun! Slime plus fart sounds? Even better! Here's how to mix up a batch of slime that's not only fun to play with but will also make some pretty distinctive noises as well.

1. Combine ½ cup of glue with ½ cup of warm water in the bowl and stir well with a spoon. If you want your farting slime bag to be a color other than white, add a few drops of food coloring.

2. In the mug, mix 1 teaspoon of borax powder with ¾ cup of warm water.

3. Slowly pour the watery borax into the watery glue, stirring as you pour.

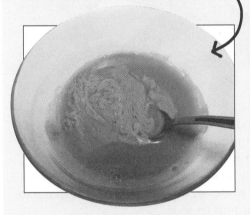

You might not use all of the watery borax. When the mixture gets really gooey and harder to stir, stop pouring and use your hands instead of the spoon to mix everything together until it feels like a ball of slime. You may have some leftover water in the bowl.

4. Remove your slime from the bowl and rinse it and your hands off, because any leftover borax might irritate your skin. Your slime is NOT edible, but now it's totally safe to

- Measuring cup
- White glue
- Water
- Bowl
- Spoon
- Food coloring (optional)
- Mug or other container
- Borax powder (available near the laundry detergent in your supermarket)
- Plastic drinking straw

play with. Enjoy the sheer pleasure of your gooey creation. . . . Stretch it and squeeze it! So icky!

5. The farting fun can now begin! Stick a straw into your slime and blow hard. You'll have better control if you hold the slime in your hands while blowing, and you'll probably get the best results if you stick the straw only about half an inch into the slime. With a little experimenting, you should be able to create a wide variety of dazzling fart noises.

6. Your slime just might become your new best friend. To keep your slimy friend safe and prevent him from drying out, store him in a sealed plastic bag when you're done playing.

WHAT JUST HAPPENED?

All sounds, from twangy banjos to elephant farts, are caused by vibrations. A guitar makes sounds because of vibrating strings. You make sounds when you talk because of vibrating vocal cords in your throat. When you fart (and 'fess up—you DO), intestinal gas rushes out of your rear end, causing noise-producing vibrations of your anal sphincters: the muscles that normally keep the end of your digestive system tightly closed.

Your inflated slime bag makes a farting noise in a similar way. When you blow air into the slime, the air passes by small folds in the slime as it escapes. These folds then vibrate and emit that charming sound we know and love!

Curious about the chemistry of your slime? Head on over to SLIME, page 204.

FUN FACT!

Pumpernickel means "goblin that breaks wind" in Old German.

ICK-TIVITY

HOW TO MAKE FART NOISES

2 MINUTES

GO FETCH →

A straw—bendy straws work best

Want to drive a grown-up crazy? The ability to make realistic fart noises is an important life skill!

1. Tuck the straw in the crook of your elbow.

2. Squeeze your arm tightly so the straw is buried in your flesh.

3. Blow hard through the straw.

4. Ta-da!!! Tooting made simple!

You can also place your lips on the back of your hand and form a tight seal. Blow. Keep practicing until you produce that beautiful sound we all know and love.

THE NAME GAME

Hiney hiccup

Under thunder

crack concerto

Fanny beep

How many different words can you think of for the act of expelling air from between your butt cheeks? Here are 10 to savor:

Booty bomb

Butt sneeze

Poop-Tart

Rump roar

Seam Splitter

Tush trumpet

AND NOW . . . BUTTROLL, PLEASE

There are lots of body parts that can produce putrid smells (think smelly armpits, bad breath . . .), but other than burps, only one comes with magnificent sound effects. Why is a fart so noisy? You might think it's the sound of your butt cheeks flapping, but the musical instrument involved is really your anal sphincters—two tight rings of muscle that keep your poop from emerging until you can park your butt safely on

the toilet. What you are hearing during a fart are the rings vibrating as the air passes through. The more gas, or the greater the pressure, the more musical your toot will be. Sometimes sitting can amplify the noise, so if you're trying not to make a scene, stand up to toot.

MEET DR. FART

Imagine devoting more than 50 years to the study of flatulence. That's exactly what Dr. Michael Levitt—hailed as the world's leading authority on flatus, the official "science" word for tooting—has done. He began with an experiment to discover exactly WHAT smelly gases were being ejected during a fart. He and his two colleagues collected butt blasts from 16 people after feeding them pinto beans and lactulose (a sort of super-sugar). The flatus was collected

SLO-MO STINK RACES

30 MINUTES

GO FETCH

We have all farted in front of friends. With luck, not everyone will notice. Let's investigate how stinky smells move through the air, and see which smells travel the fastest.

1. Make two charts like those below.

2. On your mark! Stand with all the stinky-food bags at one end of a room. Have a friend stand 3 feet away and another friend stand 6 feet away from the food. If you have more friends with you, have them stand farther still.

3. Try to predict which stinky food will be the first to be detected by your friends' noses.

4. Get set! Tell your friends to close their eyes. Ask them to raise a hand as soon as they can smell any of the food.

5. Go! Open the top of the bag of the first food and start the stopwatch. Don't tell them which bag you're opening; let their noses do the work. Write down the time it takes for each friend to detect the smell.

6. Repeat steps 1–3 for each of the other skunky foods and record the results. And yes, if you are feeling particularly gassy, then feel free to substitute a fart for one of the foods. You might want to open a window or

2 or more friends

4 plastic ziplock baggies, each with a different smelly food sealed inside it (examples include pieces of oranges or orange peels, stinky blue cheese, chopped onions, vinegar, vanilla extract)

Stopwatch

Paper

Pencil

Calculator

turn on a fan to clear the air between races.

7. Do the math to learn how fast each smell traveled (see column 3 of each chart below).

WHAT JUST HAPPENED?

Gas molecules, such as the ones that make up air (nitrogen, oxygen, carbon dioxide, and argon), as well as the ones in your farts, are always in motion, zipping around quickly in all directions. The molecules bump into each other and the walls and other objects in your house, quickly

spreading through the whole room. You can smell things because very light and microscopic particles of smelly objects—roses, farts, or wet doggie—evaporate into the air and travel along with the air molecules until they enter your nose. These odor particles aren't trying to enter your nose. Instead, they randomly move and bump their way through the air, moving from areas of high concentration to low concentration. The official scientific name for this is *diffusion* (dif-<u>few</u>-zhun). When you fart, gases from your intestine exit your body through your anus and drift (diffuse) into the air until you (or grossed-out others) can smell them.

The average speed that any particle moves through the air depends on its mass and the temperature of the room. Heavier particles move more slowly than lighter particles at the same temperature. Take a look at your charts and compare your results. The smells that your friends noticed quickly were probably made of lighter particles than the ones that took longer to diffuse across the room. The heavier particles took longer to get to their nose, but the *ugh-roma* is likely to stick around longer, because the particles won't spread out as fast.

FRIEND WHO WAS 3 FEET AWAY		
FOOD	TIME TO SMELL IN SECONDS	FEET PER SECOND (3 ÷ NUMBER OF SECONDS)
Chopped Onions		
Vinegar		
Blue Cheese		
Vanilla		

FRIEND WHO WAS 6 FEET AWAY		
FOOD	TIME TO SMELL IN SECONDS	FEET PER SECOND (6 ÷ NUMBER OF SECONDS)
Chopped Onions		
Vinegar		
Blue Cheese		
Vanilla		

via a tube stuck up each volunteer's butt. Then, two judges, chosen because they had extremely sensitive noses, sniffed the contents of all the collected gas bags, rating them on a scale of 1 to 8—with 8 being "very offensive." These sensitive-nosed scientists could detect tiny differences in the composition of the various gases. As you can probably guess by now, the sulfur compounds ranked highest on the smell scale. Fart sniffing: a handy skill to have, but a terrible job!

There is a type of charcoal that zaps the stench of certain gases, including hydrogen sulfide—the stuff that the foulest flatus is full of. A particularly gassy fellow, who was losing friends left and right because of his awful emissions, invented a "Toot Trapper"—a little pillow stuffed with this special charcoal.

The Musical Fart

The most fart-producing food is baked beans. It truly is the musical "fruit"—the more you eat, the more you toot!

ICK-TIVITY

KEEP A FART JOURNAL

Write down everything you eat over one weekend. Try to include a day with lots of sulfur-rich foods. Pile on the beans! Go to town with broccoli! Wash it back with some sweet apple juice, and polish it all off with a stick of sugarless gum. Then every time you fart, make a hash mark for that date. Note if it smelled fine or foul. Can you see a cause-and-effect relationship between what you shoved in your piehole and what came out the other end? Did you notice that when you ate sulfur-rich foods, your farts smelled worse?

Eat beans or other gas-masters and you just might end up as gas-blaster! Find out which foods make YOU toot!

Dr. Levitt decided to test if this trapper really worked. Eight volunteers pulled on special gas-tight underpants made of Mylar—the stuff they use to make shiny silver balloons. The underpants were sealed at the waist and around the thighs with duct tape and then were pumped full of farty air—much like pumping up a bike tire. Some pants had a piece of Toot Trapper placed in the butt part. Some had a fake Toot Trapper (it looked like one but had no charcoal), and some had nothing. Special machines measured what gasses leaked out.

The Toot Trapper worked! No doubt about it! Thanks to that brilliant experiment, more advances in fart-control undies were developed. Today you can buy underpants with a toot trapper AND a fart muffler in them. No smell AND no telltale noise. There are also chair seat cushions designed to capture gnarly aromas. But unless your emissions are limiting your social activities, why bother? Benjamin Franklin, one of the founders of the United States, was all in support of the "Liberty of Expressing one's Scent-iments." In other words: "Fart Proudly!"

FRIGID FARTS

35 MINUTES

INCLUDING 30-MINUTE WAIT TIME

GO FETCH →

Does temperature affect whether and when your farts are detected? Does farting on a hot summer day cause your nose more pain? Because it's really tricky to trap your farts in a balloon without some serious medical equipment, we'll use a more practical substitute to find out!

1. Put a few drops or dollops of your odorific food inside each balloon. Be careful not to get any of the food on the outside of the balloon. This is easier if you use a funnel or have someone stretch the balloon open while you drop the food inside.

2. Blow up each balloon, knot the end, and put each one in a container. Close each container.

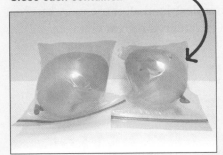

2 small balloons

A fragrant food (vinegar, vanilla, blue cheese, oranges, or finely chopped onions)

Funnel

2 closable containers (sealable plastic bag or plastic container) large enough to hold a blown-up balloon but small enough to fit in your refrigerator

3. Put one container inside the refrigerator (or another very cold place) and another in a warm, preferably sunny place.

4. After 30 minutes, open up each container and compare which container smells stronger.

WHAT JUST HAPPENED?

You already know that air is made of gases that are always moving around. The warmer the air, the faster the gas particles move because they have more kinetic energy (that's the energy of motion). You probably noticed that the colder container smelled less than the warmer container. This is because the odor molecules in the colder container seeped out of the balloon more slowly because they weren't zipping around as fast as those in the warmer container. You might also be wondering how anything could escape from the sealed balloon: Air slowly escapes from balloons because of tiny holes in the rubber, which is why all balloons deflate over time. Diffusion happens more quickly in warm air because the particles of air are bumping more quickly into each other. In other words, your summer farts will fly farther and reach more noses than your winter farts!

POOT!

THE ART OF THE FART

Let's all applaud Bernard Clemmens, a gentleman from England. According to Guinness World Records, he holds the record for the longest butt blast—2 minutes, 42 seconds. The next time you feel a fart brewing, grab your smartphone, hit the stopwatch app, and time your emission. Can you top Bernie's?

And one more fart tidbit . . . Corpses fart! A dead person can still cut the cheese as foods in the intestine continue to decay. Talk about haunting!

Fossils

THE VERY, VERY, VERY DEAD

You can't have a fossil without a dead animal or plant. Sob! When you go to a science museum and see the towering skeleton of a dinosaur peering down at you, you are actually not even looking at bones. What you are seeing is basically rocks that have replaced the bones. Amazing, huh? Those "rocks" began to form when the deceased dino started to decay, millions of years ago.

Let's pretend YOU are a frilly-necked triceratops. You're trotting along on a high ridge, texting your BFF, not paying a lick of attention to where you are going. . . . Oh, wait—no smartphones 66 million years ago. Okay, let's try again. You are a triceratops trotting along, thinking about which ferns to have for lunch, not paying any attention to the fact that there is a cliff just ahead. Over you go, with your life flashing before your eyes, until you crash to the ground far below. To add insult to injury (or in this case, insult to death), a random mudslide comes rumbling down, permanently entombing you. Over time, everything that is soft in your carcass, such as your skin, tender flesh, and all those juicy internal organs, begins to undergo a great change.

HOW TO BECOME A FOSSIL IN 3 NOT-SO-EASY STEPS

1. Die under the right circumstances.
Not every corpse will end up as a fossil. In fact, hardly any do. Usually hungry animals and insects and even bacteria will gnaw away all the squishy parts of the dearly departed, while hard parts, such as bones, teeth, and shells (if the animal was a sea creature) corrode or break apart. In order to become a fossil, the animal must die in a place where all those gnarly predators can't get at it AND in a place where it is covered immediately so its hard parts don't break apart. Falling into a mud hole, a tar pit, or a river bottom sets an animal on the right road to fossil stardom.

2. Decay away. Even sunk deep in the mud and coated with ooze, the hapless animal will slowly rot

Okay, so you might be thinking: What's icky about fossils? They're not gross. In fact, they are awesomely cool. But think about this: How did a living, breathing, drooling T. rex go from ruling the animal kingdom to becoming a big pile of stonelike bones? And let's not forget the awesome discoveries made by the lucky scientists who managed to step on giant piles of fossilized dino poop. Let's zip back through time, say, 66 million years ago, and let the fossil yuckiness commence!

HOT DIG-ITTY

GO FETCH ➤

To some folks, the thought of playing with a pile of petrified bones in the dirt sounds rather disgusting. We're gonna bet you're not one of them! Hunting for fossils is awesome, so let's dig in!

1. You and a friend should each take a rectangular container. These will be the dig sites for the fossils. Without your friend watching, sprinkle some dirt inside the container, place some pretend fossils in the dirt, and then bury them under more dirt. Repeat this process, trying to alternate layers of dirt with fossils. The final layer is just dirt so everything is hidden. Your friend should do the same with their container.

2. Swap containers with your friend.

3. When paleontologists prepare a dig site, they partition it into a grid. Each of you should tape two pieces of string or dental floss on top of your container so it is divided into four equal sections. We'll call the string that goes across the length (the long side) of the container the HORIZONTAL string, and the one that goes across the width (the shorter side) the VERTICAL string. We will refer to your four sections as northeast, northwest, southeast, and southwest.

4. Use your spoon to slowly and carefully start digging in one section.

2 rectangular containers (for example, a deep casserole dish or a shoe box)

4–8 cups dirt or potting soil

Pretend fossils: chicken bones, leaves, seeds, and/or small plastic toys

String or dental floss

Paper and pencil

Tape

Spoon

Ruler

An old toothbrush

Only dig a tiny layer at a time. Dirt that is dug up should be placed in a separate container so that after the experiment you can throw it on your garden or put it back in your mom's favorite potted plant.

5. Eventually you should find the tip of something. You might be excited to pull it out, but first record your discovery in your notebook. Draw six columns labeled object, location, X-distance, Y-distance, depth, and length.

Make all measurements in centimeters (it makes the math much easier). The object is what you found (example: chicken bone). The location is what part of the grid you found it in (example: northwest). X-distance is the HORIZONTAL distance (in centimeters) from the bottom left corner of the grid you found the object in (example: 3.6 centimeters). Y-distance is the VERTICAL distance (in centimeters) from the bottom left corner of the grid you found the object in (example: 5 centimeters). Depth is the height between object and the

string. We'll talk more about length in a moment.

6. Delicately remove the object with your spoon, then clean it up with your toothbrush (paleontologists have lots of soft brushes for removing dust and dirt without hurting the fossil). Measure the length of your fossil and record it in your notebook.

7. Repeat steps 4 through 6 in all sections of your dig site. Let no stone (um . . . soil) go unturned!

WHAT JUST HAPPENED?

You can probably imagine how painstaking the real fossil-finding process is! Paleontologists are very careful when detailing their finds. They make grids at the dig site just like you did, and carefully write down every detail about where they find each bit of fossil. The data they collect is helpful in reassembling the bones of the long-dead critter so its head is not placed where its butt should be.

The deeper you dig, the further back in time you go. Usually, older fossils are buried deeper underground and more recent fossils are closer to the surface. The relative depth of one fossil compared to another gives you clues as to which one is older. For example, you can infer that the banana peel in the middle of your trash can was thrown away after the gum wrapper in the bottom of the trash can but before the dirty tissue on the top. Using the same logic, scientists can make inferences about the ages of the fossils they find by looking at the relative ages of rocks above and beneath their finds.

away. In time, the flesh and internal bits vanish as bacteria and fungi merrily munch them up. All that will remain is a skeleton. The carcass keeps sinking deeper, and the mud surrounding the body gets even more squished and compacted. Mud is made of teeny-tiny bits of rock filled with minerals and chemicals that slowly seep into the hollow spaces of the animal's bones. Over many thousands of years, this mineral soup basically replaces the bones and hardens into rocklike formations that hold the shape of the original bone. In other cases, the bones (or feathers, or leaves) crumble away and leave an empty space in the rock, kind of like a reverse-fossil. Scientists can fill in these holes to get an image of what bone was once there.

3. Get discovered.
The Earth is always changing. A desert today might have once been an ocean. Rivers dry up. Winds howl and wear down mountains. Rushing water gnaws away at rock. What was once buried sometimes finds its way closer to the surface. That's where luck and pluck come into the picture. Someone has to stumble upon or dig for a fossil. That person is a *paleontologist* (pay-lee-un-<u>tall</u>-uh-jist). These are the lucky scientists who dig up and study the bones of creatures that disappeared long ago. But there is more to fossils than just bones.

OH, ICK-NOLOGY!
I MEAN . . . ICHNOLOGY.

Ichnology. What a perfect name for the branch of science that explores the traces of life of creatures of the past—all the stuff people and animals left behind that were not their actual bodies. Ichnologists search for things like footprints, nests, toothmarks, and, coolest of all, bodily excreta! What's that? It's fossilized poop! It's awesome to find a dino thigh, but extra cool to find a 2-foot-long, 6-inch-wide dino doo-doo, like the one ichnologists

Could this be the world's longest fossilized dung? This jumbo jobbie is 40″ in length and dates from the Miocene-Oligocene boundary, which makes it about 20 million years old. It sold for $10,000 at auction.

found in western Canada. You'd need a lot of toilet paper to wipe THAT one away!

Coprolite is the official sci-name for fossilized feces, and there are piles of it all over— for example, the 30-foot-high pile of petrified dinosaur poop that ichnologists found in a cave in southern Chile. That's a dome of doo-doo as tall as a three-story building. Or maybe you'd like to wear a poop pendant? There is a gemstone called *agatized coprolite*, which is made from fossilized poo that has been cut and polished.

If you think only dinosaurs and mastodons left behind petrified poop pies, think again. Scientists found 50,000-year-old Neanderthal feces in Spain in 2014. Another cache of more than 1,000 ancient human poops— some 8,000 years old—was discovered at the back of Hinds Cave in Texas. Clearly it was once home to a prehistoric human latrine. These ancient doo-doos are rock-hard and fossil-like, but in fact are just dried-out, well-preserved poops, thanks to the cave's cool, dry conditions. Ewww? Perhaps. But it's very interesting to science sleuths. By studying what's in feces, folks can figure out what dinosaurs, long-dead deer, or dear old dads (and moms) ate for dinner a very long, long, LONG time ago.

ICK-TIVITY

FAST FOSSIL FACTORY

GO FETCH

30 MINUTES
PLUS ABOUT 1 WEEK OF WAIT TIME

It takes many thousands of years for fossilization to occur. But who's got the time? In this experiment, we will make a pseudo-fossil by reproducing the geological steps in super-fast-forward motion.

1. Get a grown-up to help you use the bread knife to cut the sponge into two thin slices.

2. Use the scissors to cut one sponge into the shape of a prehistoric fish, dinosaur, or other organism.

3. Sprinkle some sand into the container so the bottom isn't visible. Place the sponge inside the container. Your spongy critter just died and sank to the sandy ocean floor to be fossilized.

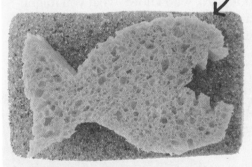

4. In time, sand and other matter sink on top of your creature. Speed this up by covering the sponge until it's completely hidden by a layer of about ¼ inch of sand.

5. Mix 1 cup of very hot water with 4 tablespoons of salt, trying to dissolve as much as possible by stirring with a spoon. Slowly pour the solution on top of the sand. Mineral-rich

Kitchen sponge

Bread knife

Scissors

Container with flat bottom, just large enough to hold the sponge

A cup or 2 of sand

Glass or cup

1 cup of hot water

4 tablespoons of salt

Spoon

groundwater is now seeping into the layers of sediment, causing changes to the remains of your creature. Push the spoon into the sand and sponge to force out air bubbles, creating more spaces for the salty water to fill in. Add additional batches of your liquid brew if you feel your sponge isn't getting fully drenched.

6. Place the container in a warm (and ideally sunny) spot for either about seven days or 70 million years, whichever is more convenient and gives the sand enough time to dry. It's okay if the sand is not totally dry, but you don't want any visible water.

7. After a week, unearth the sponge from the container and gently remove your fake fossil. It will probably still feel a little moist (which wouldn't happen with a real fossil). Let it rest on top of the sand in a warm,

sunny place for another day or two so it really dries out. Congratulations, you're now the proud owner of a crunchy faux fossil.

WHAT JUST HAPPENED?

When a dead animal sinks to the ocean floor, it is normally gobbled up by scavengers or rots away. But sometimes enough sediment can cover the animal before this happens, and it becomes entombed. The sediment surrounding the animal can eventually turn to stone because of the intense pressure above it. The animal now rots much more slowly while groundwater seeps into it. The minerals in the groundwater fill up the spaces where the body parts dissolve away. Eventually, the entire animal skeleton is replaced by minerals and, presto, a fossil has formed!

After you dig up your sponge and let it dry out, you should discover that it has become much more stiff and hard than it was a week ago. The salt was left behind when the water evaporated. Tiny salt crystals formed inside the sponge's holes, making the sponge much more like a solid rock. The groundwater that makes fossils in real life uses different minerals (such as silica, calcium carbonate, and iron ores), but the process, called *permineralization* (per-<u>min</u>-er-a-lie-<u>zay</u>-shun), is the same as your sandy fossil factory.

22 23 24 25 26 27 28 29 30 31 32 33 34 35 36 37 3

87

An ostrich just makin' a future urolite!

Many scientists think that birds are the modern-day descendents of the dinosaurs. Bird bone structure resembles that of certain dinosaurs, and their eggs do too. But ostriches (which do look a wee bit prehistoric) are similar in another way—they unleash a fire-hose-velocity stream of pee. Ichnologists discovered fossilized, dried-up pee ponds that look very much like the ones left by modern-day ostriches. The only difference? A few million years!

THE BONE BRIGADE

Want a fun career? Become a fossil hunter! And no need to wait until you're a grown-up. Mary Anning was 10 or 12 when she helped her family unearth ichthyosaur fossils. Born in 1799, a poor girl with a keen eye and a ferocious curiosity, she scrambled up and down the sometimes dangerous coastal cliffs near her home in England and unearthed all sorts of splendid Jurassic-era fossils. She grew up to become one of the most famous fossil hunters ever. More recently (in 2008), five-year-old Emilia Fawbert unearthed the fossilized vertebra of a giant rhinoceros that roamed Earth 50,000 years ago.

If you look hard, who knows what you might find. There are all sorts of millions-of-years-old fossils still being discovered, and sometimes they reveal

A PREHISTORIC POTTY STOP

Why stop with poop? What about pee? After all, dinosaurs and other extinct species had to tinkle too, didn't they? Some clever ichnologists have found *urolites*—basically holes (one the size of a bathtub) that had been made in the soil by now-extinct, very large creatures taking massive leaks. Based on his findings, one ichnologist has even calculated the possible size of the dinosaur's bladder, as well as how much liquid was piddled onto the ground and from what height. And trust me, you would not have wanted to stand underneath that creature when it let loose.

What if you time-traveled back 66 million years to when the Anzu lived? You'd have to watch out for the "chicken from hell."

A STICKY END

Ah, the charmed life of a mastodon—a huge creature that looked like an elephant covered in cheap shag carpet. It's a bright sunny day 40,000 years ago and romance is in the air. Sadly, one mastodon is so busy crushing on a dreamy, super-cute new mastodon that just moved into the 'hood that he doesn't look where he's going. Suddenly his hooves are caught in thick, gooey, hot, bubbling tar. That's what happened to more than 300,000 creatures at the La Brea Tar Pits, in what is now downtown Los Angeles, California. (Oh, and by the way, La Brea means "The Tar" in Spanish, so saying *The La Brea Tar Pits* is like saying The The Tar Tar Pits.)

La Brea sits atop a small underground lake of crude oil. The oil seeps up along cracks in the Earth's surface, and when it reaches the top, it forms pools of liquid asphalt—the stuff used to pave roads. For tens of thousands of years, the tar has bubbled up. Leaves and other vegetation would blow onto the sticky gunk and make it look just like dry land. All sorts of poor, innocent animals would accidentally stumble into the tar. Mastodons, ground sloths, ancient camels, dire wolves, and fierce saber-toothed cats might have thought they were all-powerful, but even razor-sharp teeth don't cut it when your feet are stuck in gooey tar. For all these creatures, La Brea was the end of the line! Fortunately for us, the fossils found in the tar can now be seen in a museum at La Brea.

In the land of movie stars, this replica mastodon is ready for its close-up!

a kind of dinosaur nobody knew existed—for example, the Anzu, a recently discovered dinosaur that paleontologists nicknamed the "chicken from hell." Picture an almost 8-foot-tall creature covered in feathers, with sharp claws and a beak! Bet those eggs would make one heck of an omelet! Although the area in the Dakotas where the megachicken was found is one of the most picked-over places on Earth for dinosaur fossils, this particular Big Bird had never before been seen. "The fact that this big, distinctive, very weird-looking animal remained effectively hidden in one of the best-explored sets of rocks shows you how much more out there is left to be found," said paleontologist Matthew Lamanna of the Carnegie Museum of Natural History in Pittsburgh.

THE BONE WARS

Dinosaurs have been buried for millions of years. Yet, all the dino fossils we know and love were only discovered about 150 years ago. Why? The completion of a transcontinental railroad that linked the Atlantic side of America with the Pacific made it easy to get out to the American West. Turns out that big chunks of Utah, Colorado, and Montana were the perfect places to find huge dinosaur bones. America's Wild West was the greatest dinosaur graveyard on the planet!

In the years after America's Civil War ended, paleontologists Edward Cope and Othniel Marsh dug and dug and dug some more, all over the American West. And as they dug, they tried to ruin each other's lives. Both Cope and Marsh wanted to be the king of the fossil-finders—to outdo the other in the number of new species they found. To put it simply, they started out friends but ended up hating each other. They became guilty of sloppy science, even using dynamite at dig sites to find bones faster. If it meant spying, stealing, or offering bribes to win the crown of dino king, then why not? When Cope reconstructed an underwater dinosaur and stuck the head on the end of the tail (*whoops!*), Marsh did a thousand happy dances and made sure *everyone* knew about Cope's mistake.

After all was said and done, they both ended up flat broke and with their careers in tatters. But, wow, what they found. The first brontosaurs, stegosaurs, and allosaurs! Triceratops! All sorts of prehistoric beasts! More than a hundred new species of dinosaurs! Too bad they had awful scientific habits. They would find the same bones and give them different names. They would deliberately smash bones to keep them out of the other's hands. They made a big fossil mess, and that's unfortunate, because they were both brilliant, and they lost a lot of good fossils in their efforts to defeat each other. So note to self—always respect the scientific process and play nicely with your colleagues, unless you want to end up as a science joke punch line.

Want to be a paleontologist? Learn patience!

TALES FROM THE DINO GRAVE

Paleontologists are still digging up all sorts of awesome critters. Recently, three almost intact fossils of triceratops were found all in one spot. Since these frilly-necked dinos are very rarely found near each other, scientists were surprised and went happy-crazy with this find. What do *you* think happened? Why would solitary creatures suddenly be hanging out together? Had they formed a rock band? A three-dino bobsled team? It's one thing to find the remains of long-gone creatures, but it's a big leap to figure out how they lived, or how they perished. In the case of those three triceratops, paleontologists think they were unfortunate victims of a hungry party of T. rexes hunting in a pack, who corralled their innocent victims and then had a hefty picnic. Every bone tells a story.

Paleontologists constantly think about why all dinosaurs eventually disappeared from the Earth. Most think that an unfortunate collision with a projectile from outer space had a lot to do with it. Just off Mexico there is a crater that's estimated to be about 110 miles (180 km) wide—a huge hole made 66 million years ago. That's just about the time the dinosaurs suddenly died off. The impact could have warmed the whole Earth so much that it became like a dino-cooking pizza oven. The impact also might have spewed a lot of sun-blocking dust in the air. No sun? Plants die off. Not enough plants to eat? There go the vegetarians. No vegetarians? Meat eaters are out of luck. End result: no food for anyone, including dinosaurs. Other scientists think that global-scale ash-spewing volcanoes were the guilty party.

We could go on, and on, and ON about fossils, but there is still more *fun* waiting. Lurking down in the dirt with all those fossil finds are some other *very* interesting things! So read on!

Fungi

Picture a monster so big that it covers 1,665 football fields. Bet you don't want to meet something **THAT** size in a dark alley! It weighs between 7,000 and 35,000 tons. It's at least 2,400 years old, and some scientists think it might even be pushing 8,600 years old. That's a **LOT** of birthday candles to stick on a cake. And not only that—this thing is a killer, destroying large tracts of trees in parts of the United States and Canada, but it's so well hidden you can rarely see it. What is this strange and bizarre creature? Time to hang out with some fun guys. No! Wait! We mean fungi!

DWELLERS IN THE DIRT

Unless you are one of our cave-dwelling readers, we're pretty sure you live aboveground in a dry, well-lit house, protected from the rain. But there is a different life-form that loves damp, dark places. They are *fungi* (<u>fun</u>-guy)—a whole amazing kingdom of life representing more than 1.5 million different species.

You've probably seen a mushroom sprouting in a damp place. Maybe you've eaten some atop a pizza? Mushrooms are the best-known members of the fungi family. When you see a toadstool sprouting out of the ground, what you are seeing is the "fruiting body" of a fungus. There's a whole lot more going on under the soil. But more about that in a bit.

Without fungi, we would be in BIG trouble. They have a bunch of important jobs to do. Along with their decomposer buddies, bacteria, molds, and other fungi break down things that have died, feasting away until a deceased plant or animal is nothing but a teeny pile of nutrients that other organisms can put to use. They are nature's recyclers. If not for them, the world would be covered with piles of dead animal bodies and dead plants, just lying there. What a mess! Smelly too.

Plus, without fungi there might not be any trees, because fungi hang out in tree roots and supply important nutrients that help trees grow. But, then again, the wrong kind of fungus can spell doom for a forest.

Honey fungi have a sweet-sounding name, but they can suck the life out of a host tree.

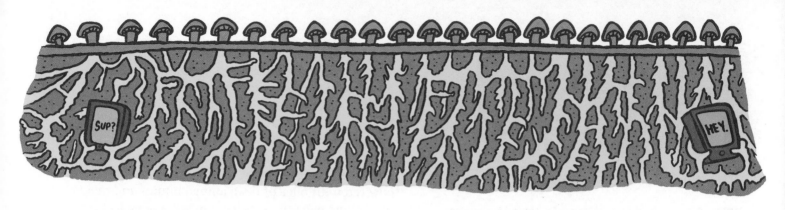

HUMONGOUS FUNGUS

Back to our underground monster! That gigantic organism—the largest living thing on Earth—is called a honey fungus (scientific name: *Armillaria ostoyae*). Ooooh—honey sounds sweet and yummy! But not if you are a fir tree in the Blue Mountains of Oregon. Then it's your worst nightmare. How did the fungus get so humongous? How does it kill? What the heck is it?

To understand what's going on, we need to look under the soil. All fungi send out a bunch of tiny white branching tubes called *hyphae* (hi-fee) into the soil or a rotting log. They use these to find and ingest food. The hyphae hook together to form a delicate network, like lace, called a *mycelium* (my-see-lee-um). The hyphae tubes that make up a mycelium are REALLY tiny. Imagine that you are holding a little cube that measures 1 inch on every side. If you packed it with soil from a fungus-friendly area and then carefully picked out all the tubes and laid them end to end, they would reach 8 miles! But each tube is so thin you'd hardly be

The Putrid Past

FUNGUS TOWERS

Through fossil research, scientists have learned that more than 350 million years ago—tens of millions of years before dinosaurs frolicked on our planet—the biggest living things on Earth were enormous spearlike fungi called *prototaxites* (pro-toe-tax-iteas). Stack three or four NBA basketball players atop one another and you will get a sense of the height of these slender towers of fungus.

able to see one! Next time you step in an area where mushrooms grow, you are treading on miles of mycelium all packed together. You might be able to see some whitish cobweb-looking mycelium if you roll over a dead log or peel the bark away from a rotting stump. (Never peel bark off a living tree. That wounds the tree and may kill it.)

The mycelium makes up the body of the fungus. The mushroom you might eat is the fruit and only appears at certain times of the year, so most of the time you don't know any "fun-guys" are lurking. Some fungi have a tiny mycelium, but some, like the honey fungus, can have huge ones stretching for miles. Every part of the giant Oregon honey fungus mycelium is connected underground, and every part of it is as identical. Scientists have tested different parts of the fungus in the areas where trees are dying in Oregon and found that it is one massive organism extending for miles in every direction! So next time someone asks you what the largest organism is in the world, don't say the blue whale (though that is still the biggest animal), say *Armillaria ostoyae*!

Many fungi are thought to be helpful to plants. Amazingly, just like an army with a zillion walkie-talkies, a mycelium can communicate through the hyphae and help plants communicate through them, kind of like the internet. In fact, scientists have dubbed it "the wood-wide-web." The mycelium has been found to transmit chemical messages and even nutrients between different species of plants! But other fungus mycelium—cue spooky music—can transmit toxins (and many mushrooms are very toxic to humans too, so never eat an unknown mushroom). The honey fungus mycelium kills a tree by climbing up inside the bark and stealing its water and nutrients. When the tree eventually dies, the mushroom decomposes it and grows even bigger. If you're a fir tree, best not to lay down roots near this beast of a

FOAMY FUNGI

GO FETCH

10 MINUTES

Yeast are teeny-tiny fungi, but they can make great big playthings! Here's proof: a glorious, foamy mess, sometimes called elephant's toothpaste, because the amount of foam is—well—rather enormous.

1. Add a packet of yeast and 3 tablespoons of warm water to a bowl. Stir with a spoon.

2. Put on your safety glasses and have an adult use a funnel to pour ½ cup of hydrogen peroxide solution into the plastic bottle. Do this over your cookie sheet or pan.

3. Your turn: Pour ¼ cup of dishwashing soap and a healthy squirt of your favorite food coloring into the bottle. Gently swish the bottle around to mix its ingredients. Place the bottle on the cookie tray.

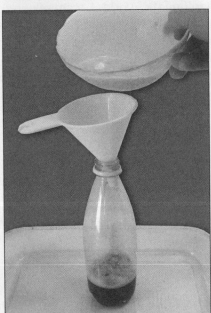

4. Wait four minutes, then pour the yeasty water through the funnel and into the bottle and be prepared to

> Baker's yeast (found in packets in the baking section of your grocery store)
>
> Warm water
>
> Small bowl
>
> Spoon
>
> Safety goggles and an adult
>
> Empty 16- or 20-ounce plastic soda or water bottle
>
> Funnel
>
> 3 percent hydrogen peroxide solution (available at any pharmacy)
>
> Large cookie tray with sides or a large cake pan
>
> Liquid dishwashing soap
>
> Food coloring (slime green is always a fun choice)

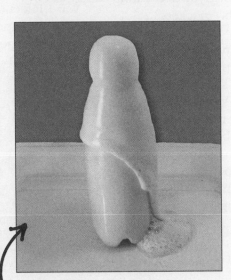

quickly remove the funnel and back up! A frothy foam will come gushing out.

WHAT JUST HAPPENED?

Water's scientific nickname is H_2O, which means it's made of 2 atoms of hydrogen stuck to 1 atom of oxygen. Hydrogen peroxide is also made of hydrogen and oxygen atoms, but because it has a different number of those atoms, it's an entirely different chemical: It's H_2O_2. Biologically speaking, hydrogen peroxide is dangerous because it has the power to rip cells apart. The bad news is that living things naturally create hydrogen peroxide. Yep, your own cells are making it now as they turn your food into usable energy! The good news is that living things also make a chemical called *catalase* (<u>cat</u>-uh-laze), which converts hydrogen peroxide into much safer chemicals—water and oxygen.

Those little grains of baker's yeast are living fungi, and yeast acts like a catalase factory under the right conditions. In their package, the yeasty beasties are dormant—just snoozing away—but warm water wakes them up. After you add them to the hydrogen peroxide, the yeast's catalase speedily converts hydrogen peroxide into oxygen and water. All that oxygen gas gets trapped in the soap, creating tons of bubbles. The reaction is also *exothermic* (ex-oh-<u>thur</u>-mik), meaning it creates heat. If you touch the foam, it will feel warm (but wash your paws after, just in case some hydrogen peroxide remains). Even more of foam can be created with stronger solutions of hydrogen peroxide. If your grown-ups are up for it, try a 6 percent solution (which you may be able to find at a hair salon). Your creation can be safely washed down the drain.

fungus! Interestingly, as they learn more about it, scientists are realizing that the honey fungus may not be a total baddie. Decomposing trees provide lots of nutrients for new and different trees to grow, so in a way, this ancient killer fungus helps the whole forest become more diverse.

FUNGI 'TWEEN YOUR TOES! FUNGI ON YOUR CLOTHES!

Since you are NOT a fir tree in Oregon, let's talk about how fungi affect people. Truth is, we would be a lot worse off in a fungi-free world. Fungi provide us with germ zappers such as penicillin and other antibiotics. And let's not even get started on the food we eat. Never mind cream of mushroom soup or stuffed mushrooms. We wouldn't have bread without yeast, the tiny fungi that make dough rise and give it that nice soft, airy texture. Without yeast, you'd be eating peanut butter and jelly on crumbly crackers.

Alexander Fleming

On the other hand, fungi are not always fun! There are about 300 types of fungi that can make you pretty miserable. These are parasites. Under the right conditions, they cause skin infections like ringworm and itchy athlete's foot. Certain fungi can damage the lungs and bring other icky illnesses. And they are stubborn little critters, not easily killed, so if you get a fungal disease, it can be tough to cure. They can also attack certain plants, stealing their nutrients and laying waste to valuable crops like rye and tomatoes.

What else would you expect from organisms that love dark and dampness? Organisms that are happiest in soil and decaying organic matter like leaves or rotten wood?

A SCIENCE NOT-SO-FAIR

Penicillin is a wonder drug made from mold. The first true *antibiotic* (an-tie-by-<u>ah</u>-tik), it fights bacterial infections. And no doubt about it—it has literally saved millions of lives. But its discovery is a tale of dirty dishes, murdered mice, freeze-dried urine, and one rotten melon from Peoria, Illinois.

You may have heard of Alexander Fleming—the Scotsman who "discovered" penicillin in 1928. Of course, it's never quite as simple as all that. Scientists had been aware of the bacteria-busting powers of certain molds for quite some time but couldn't figure out the hows and whys.

Now, Dr. Fleming was a messy man. He had been away on summer vacation, but before he left he'd been a bit sloppy about washing out his petri dishes. When he got back, he was surprised to see that one dish of bacteria had a blob of mold on it that had definitely not been there before—more important, the mold had destroyed the ring of bacteria around it. How cool was that! There was only one problem. Fleming tried hard but couldn't figure out how to take that mold and turn it into an effective drug that might save a life. He made gallons of "mold juice," but his concoctions were virtually useless, so eventually he moved on.

Fast-forward to 1939. A horrible war—World War II—was engulfing the world. A team of scientists at Oxford University in England had read Fleming's research on penicillin. During World War I, infections had killed more soldiers than enemy weapons had, and they were continuing to ravage the population, so the scientists decided to

Not exactly what you hope to find in your lunch box, eh?

CONTROL SUNNY WINDOW

MOLD ZOO

GO FETCH →

15 MINUTES

PLUS 2–3 WEEKS OF OBSERVATION

6 ziplock plastic bags

Knife and spoon

6 small pieces each: bread, cheese, your choice of fruit (like strawberries, oranges, cut grapes), your choice of veggie (like zucchini, cucumber, bell pepper)

Salt

Sugar

Tape

Permanent marker

You wouldn't want to hang out with a tiger *inside* its habitat in a zoo, but it's really fun to watch from the other side of the fence. The same is true with moldy food—disgusting to eat, but cool to observe from a safe distance. Let's make some mold zoos and investigate how temperature, salt, and sugar affect mold growth.

1. Let a grown-up know what you are up to. You are about to create some moldy food and you don't want to freak out an innocent, unsuspecting adult—or use their new groceries for your moldy experiments!

2. Write *salt* on two of the bags, *sugar* on two, and *control* on the last two.

3. With your grown-up's help, slice up some bread, cheese, and fruit into pieces that will fit in a plastic bag. Each bag will contain all the types of food, so you'll need six pieces of each type of food.

4. Sprinkle some water over the food with a spoon so it is a little damp (mold likes moisture).

5. Add each type of food to each plastic bag. For your salt bags, sprinkle about 1 tablespoon of salt on the food. For your sugar bags, sprinkle about 1 tablespoon of sugar on the

CONTROL SUNNY WINDOW

food. Shake the bags to help distribute the salt and sugar. You won't add anything to the control bags.

6. Seal the bags shut. As an extra precaution, add tape over the seal so it's airtight. Promise never to open up these bags again, in case you grow some dangerous mold!

7. Place one set of control, salt, and sugar bags in the refrigerator. Place the other set of bags in a sunny window. Make a hypothesis for which bag will grow the most mold.

8. Over the next two to three weeks, observe what types of mold start to grow in the bag. Take photos or draw pictures to keep track of the growth. You'll probably start to see some fuzzy white, blue, or green life-forms on the food in your plastic zoos. But do all bags have the same amount or type of molds?

9. After about three weeks, it will be time to say farewell to your moldy friends. Do not open up the bags. Take them outside to the trash can.

WHAT JUST HAPPENED?

Molds are everywhere because they reproduce by creating microscopic spores (tiny seedlike things) that float through the air and randomly land on different surfaces: your clothes, your pillow, your hair, and your food. Spores need three conditions to grow into mold: food, moisture, and warmth. All of your bags had enough food, but the amount of warmth and moisture varied.

Your mold zoos by the sunny window were like spore spas. They had all the right conditions for mold to blossom. You probably noticed that the bags in the refrigerator had slower mold growth than the other bags. Molds don't like cold.

Among the three bags by the window, your sweet and salty bags probably had the least mold. These common chemicals dehydrate the food they touch, making it too dry for mold to grow. In fact, our ancestors used salt and sugar to preserve food in ancient times. Scientists have learned that salt and sugar block mold's ability to produce the chemicals it needs to survive and can even damage the fungi's DNA. The fact that salt and sugar also taste so darned good is just one more reason that we've been adding them to our food for thousands of years!

Different kinds of molds prefer different foods. You might notice a white mold growing on the bread. If you let it sit for a few more days you may see tiny black dots, which are the spores, getting ready to fly free and make more mold—but only if you open the bag, which you won't!

experiment to see if penicillin could cure bacterial infections. Professors Howard Florey and Ernst Chain headed up the team, but it was their younger associate, Norman Heatley, who figured out how to extract and purify penicillin, and how to make lots of it.

England was at war and everything was scarce. With barely any money for their experiments, Heatley began growing penicillin mold in just about anything he could find, from old biscuit tins to battered hospital bedpans. Soon there were containers stacked everywhere. By May 25, 1940, they had enough penicillin to try an experiment. Mice were given injections of a fatal dose of killer bacteria, but half of those furry little fellows were also given injections of penicillin. Within hours, the untreated mice had toppled over and died, but the penicillin-treated mice were still alive.

Time for a test on a human. It took 500 gallons (2,000 liters) of mold culture fluid to get enough pure penicillin to treat one person. (Mentally line up 1,000 large-size soda bottles to get an image of how much mold juice you would need!) Penicillin does its bacteria busting and then is quickly excreted via pee. To conserve their penicillin, they collected the patient's urine, cleaned it, and reinjected it. Yuck! But it seemed to be working! The patient was getting better. Unfortunately they simply did not have enough penicillin to cure him, but they *knew* it could work.

The war was going badly, though, and the scientists were worried that England might fall to the enemy. Their wonder drug MUST be protected! Heatley, always the creative one, had a plan. Should an invasion seem likely, they would burn all their research papers, smear penicillin spores all over their jackets, and simply "wear" their research as they fled the country. Fortunately they didn't have to do this. Nonetheless, with the war raging, there was no money for research. So off to America they went, hoping to continue their penicillin studies overseas. As luck would have it, Mary Hunt, one of Heatley's American colleagues, happened upon a revoltingly moldy melon in a fruit market in Peoria, Illinois. It turns out that the melon was playing host to a superstrong strain of penicillin. Meanwhile, new ways to enhance the spores were discovered: Zapping the mold with X-rays and then ultraviolet rays made it even more potent. Finally it was possible to produce enough penicillin to cure someone of infection. YAY, TEAM!

In time, Fleming, Florey, and Chain all got Nobel prizes—the *biggest* award there is in the sciences. But quiet, creative Norman Heatley, the fellow who actually figured out how to produce the drug, got nothing. That's SO not science-fair! At least he could comfort himself with the fact that his work saved millions of lives. And now you know the story of penicillin and its unsung hero!

IF YOU WERE A FUNGUS

Fungi might seem pretty creepy, but you have more in common with these organisms than you might realize. Prefer warmer weather? You now know that fungi do too. Need to eat? Animals (including you) and fungi are *heterotrophs* (het-uh-ruh-troafs). Unlike plants, which can produce their own food from within, heterotrophs need to actually eat to get nourishment. We do it by putting things into our mouths. But if you were a mold, you would lie atop your food and ooze chemicals to dissolve your dinner, which would then be absorbed into your body in much the same way a dry sponge absorbs water. Sounds like fun. Can you imagine lying on a pizza and having it seep into your skin?

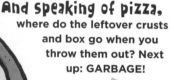

And speaking of pizza, where do the leftover crusts and box go when you throw them out? Next up: GARBAGE!

garbage

When you throw something into a trash can, you probably stop thinking about it. As far as you're concerned, that trash is gone. But the truth is, there really is no "gone" with garbage. Your mucus-smeared nose wiper has simply been moved. But where to?

Hey, you! Yes, you, the kid who just threw that apple core, snotty tissue, and empty juice box into the trash can! (You DID throw it all into the appropriate bin and not on the sidewalk, right?) How much garbage do you think you produce a day?

According to the Environmental Protection Agency (EPA), the average American makes about 4.4 pounds (2 kg) of waste per day. About one third of this gets composted or recycled (more about that later), which means the typical American adds a little more than 1,000 pounds (455 kilograms) to the garbage piles every year. That's a lot of stinky trash being piled atop planet Earth!

TO THE DUMP, TO THE DUMP, TO THE DUMP-DUMP-DUMP!

Let's pretend you are a used baby diaper (*ewww!*) and you've been deposited in the garbage and hauled to the curb. You're sitting there calmly, surrounded by your garbage friends, when suddenly you find yourself roughly heaved into the back of a big, noisy, reeking garbage truck. The inside of a garbage truck is not a place for the faint of heart (or the faint of nose!).

Once you are loaded into the truck, a big blade will pop out and shove you into the back of the waste container. Every so often, as the level of trash grows, a large piece of metal called a compactor will drop down from the truck's top and flatten the growing pile. *OUCH!* The average garbage truck can hold 12 to 14 tons of trash—about 800 to 850 homes' worth. Stick your nose in a week's worth

If we keep polluting the Earth, we might all have to wear gas masks one day!

of garbage and you'll start to get an idea of the aroma inside the truck.

When the truck is full, it will head to a landfill where it might be weighed on a giant scale since there are limits to how much trash a landfill can process (plus the landfill probably charges your town a certain fee for every ton of garbage it deposits). Once you arrive at the landfill, machinery on the underside of the truck will tilt the giant waste container and out you will tumble! But your smelly adventure is far from over.

Dump dining: Trash is a gourmet restaurant for some creatures, including seagulls.

HOW TO BUILD A LANDFILL

A landfill is different from a dump. While a dump is just a big pile of trash, a landfill is a modern engineering feat, full of pipes and linings to keep all the rotting stuff contained.

1. Dig a big hole—You're going to fill it up with lots of trash, so make sure it's a big one!

2. Add a waterproof liner to the bottom—One important goal of a landfill is to keep poisonous chemicals or water containing bacteria from getting into our drinking supply. Landfills protect the groundwater (that's water that flows underground) by laying down about two feet of clay, a plastic liner, and another two feet of sand at the bottom of the big hole. This is to keep any *leachate* (lee-chate)—liquid that leaks out of garbage—from getting into the groundwater. And compressed garbage also leaks fluids on its own. If it does, it could contaminate many towns' drinking water supplies or individual wells. No one wants battery acid, rotten eggs, baby poop, or antifreeze in their drinking water.

3. Make a plan—You want to make the most of the space you have so that you don't cover the whole town with landfills. Make a grid with sections (or cells) for each day's trash. A typical cell might hold 2,500 tons. Once a cell is full, heavy machinery (like bulldozers and rollers) will come and crush the crud to compact it further. Then all that trash will get topped with several inches of soil and compacted even more.

4. Collect all the liquids—Plastic drainage pipes will suck up any rainwater, snowmelt, or leachate and move it into a special pond away from the garbage, where it is treated until it is safe to be disposed in a river.

5. Set up groundwater-monitoring sites—Drill some wells near the landfill to check for toxic waste leaching into groundwater. That way you will know if there's a leak right away before someone turns on a faucet and gets a glass of contaminated water.

6. Collect garbage farts—Bacteria hang out at dumps by the gazillions and are super useful for breaking down the garbage. The by-product is landfill gas—about half methane and half carbon dioxide, with a little nitrogen and oxygen tossed in. The methane gas is collected in a series of pipes, and at some landfills is used for fuel and burned to generate electricity.

7. Cover it up—When the landfill has reached capacity (on average it takes about 30 years), a final covering or cap will be added over the mountain of mess. Many times, it is installed almost the same way as the original liner. This final cover can be made of another clay layer, a plastic liner, and two more feet

TONS O' TRASH

GO FETCH ➤

10 MINUTES

EACH DAY FOR AT LEAST A MONTH

Alert your family! YOU are going to be the trash inspector for the next month. Yup! An entire month! You're going to collect data on the weight of the trash your family tosses. Once you have this data, can you trim down the trash and increase the recycling rate in your own home?

1. Move the bathroom scale near the kitchen trash can to remind you to weigh the household trash for the next month. (A full 30 days will give you better data than just one week of measurements, because you might throw out more trash one week than the next.)

2. Create a chart on a piece of paper with three columns: Trash, Recycling, and Compost. (Don't compost? Time to start! Dig your way over to page 104 to learn how!)

3. Every time you empty out the trash, recycling, or compost, find out its weight first. Just step on the bathroom scale without the trash, and then step on the scale while holding the trash. Subtract your weight without the trash from your weight with the trash. For example, you might weigh 84 pounds without the trash but 90 pounds while holding the trash, so you have 6 pounds of trash. Record this number in your trash column.

4. Make sure you are tracking data for all the trash cans in your house! Don't forget bathrooms, bedrooms, the garage, your antigravity room, or your unicorn stable.

5. Your recycling bin and compost bin weigh something even when empty, so you'll need to find the weights of these containers.

Bathroom scale

Paper

Pencil

Calculator

Your trash, recycling, and compost containers

Step on the scale without your empty recycling bin and then step on the scale with your empty recycling bin. Subtract your weight without the bin from your weight with the bin to find the recycling bin's weight. Repeat this with the compost bin.

6. Every time you empty your recycling or compost bin, remember to subtract the weights of the bins. Keep a record of how much recycling and compost you generate in the recycling and compost columns.

7. Because your weight can change a bit every day, always weigh yourself

first before weighing yourself with the trash, recycling, or compost.

8. At the end of the month, calculate your total pounds of trash, recycling, and compost by adding up each column.

9. Divide each total by the number of days in your month of study (probably 30 or 31). Now you know the average amount of trash your family made each day.

10. Divide these daily averages by the number of people in your family. Don't forget to include yourself. Now you know the average daily amount of each type of waste per person.

11. Add up the three types of waste for each person. This is the total daily amount of all waste per person. How does your family compare to the national average of 4.6 pounds per person?

WHAT JUST HAPPENED?

It takes time and effort to understand your family's waste stream, but you can learn and do a lot with your hard-earned data. You can multiply your total amounts by 12 to estimate how many total pounds of trash, recycling, and compost your family will make in a year! You might have found that your family started to increase its recycling and composting efforts with you as trash inspector. Draw a picture of some watchful eyeballs to hang above your trash can to motivate your family to recycle and compost more and throw away less.

of soil on top, often with native grasses and shrubs planted too. This "lid" seals the waste in and keeps scavenging rats, mice, birds, and flying insects out.

8. Play on the pile—Many towns have turned landfills into parks! That cool little hill you just rode your bike down? It might be covering a smelly pile of chicken bones, soggy used vacuum cleaner bags, and dirty tissues. Hooray for modern engineering! Now, if only we could figure out how to not make any waste at all. . . .

DON'T TRUST RUST

Y ou probably won't see broken washing machines, falling-apart cars, broken bedsprings, and the like in a landfill. Those giant hunks of garbage usually end up in a junkyard.

Every good junkyard worth its salt is a giant chemistry experiment in action. There are all sorts of things just sitting there, slowly breaking down, covered with flaky orange-red patches. That stuff is rust—something that can turn a piece of iron to dust.

Some see a pile of rusting metal. A junkyard owner sees a recycling paradise.

GARBAGE GROUNDWATER

30 MINUTES

GO FETCH →

- Large rectangular glass baking pan (or other see-through waterproof container with a flat bottom)
- 4–8 cups sand (from your local garden or building supply store)
- Small toy figure (optional)
- Plastic wrap, 4 pieces cut into 4-inch squares
- Pencil
- Cotton balls or newspaper
- 3 different colors of food coloring
- Dirt (from your backyard or local gardening store)
- Water
- White paper
- Scissors

W hen rain falls on piles of trash, toxic chemicals can dissolve in the water and seep into the groundwater as leachate. That's why people invented landfills, because dumps (basically just throwing trash in a hole in the ground) were polluting the groundwater. As you read earlier, landfills have ways to keep poisonous chemicals in the trash from getting into our drinking-water supply. There's another kind of storage for hazardous waste and petroleum (oil)—underground storage tanks, which are big containers located underground. They're good because they're out of the way, but they're bad because if they leak (and many of them have), people usually don't know until poisonous chemicals are found in their drinking water. So, let's build and compare these three options (landfill, dump, and a leaky underground storage tank) and find out for ourselves how much they impact drinking wells.

1. Fill the baking pan with about an inch of sand.

2. Hollow out a crater in three of the corners. Each crater will be a different type of trash site: a landfill, a dump, and a storage tank. Stick a small toy figure in the fourth corner to represent a town that hopefully won't be affected by all the neighboring trash.

3. Line one of the craters with a piece of plastic wrap (a 4×4-inch square). This is your landfill. Use your pencil to poke some holes in the other piece of plastic wrap and line the second crater with it. This will be the storage tank. Not all storage tanks are leaky, but history shows that plenty of them have been. The third crater is your dump and has no lining at all.

4. Decide if you will use cotton balls or newspaper for your trash. Place one cotton ball in each trash site. Or, if you use newspaper: Rip it into pieces that are about the size of a Popsicle stick, crumble them up, and use two pieces per trash site.

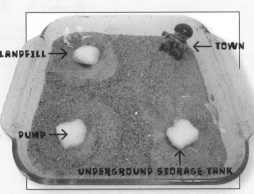

5. The cotton or newspaper for each trash site will get a different color of food coloring. For example, the landfill might get blue food coloring, the dump might get yellow food coloring, and the storage tank might get green food coloring. Squeeze about 5–10 drops of food coloring on each item.

6. Add another 4×4-inch layer of plastic wrap on top of the landfill. Try to fold it over the bottom liner to make a good seal. Poke a few holes in another 4×4 piece of plastic wrap and put it on top of the storage tank.

7. Add a thin layer of dirt onto the top of the landfill and storage tank. Do not add any dirt to the dump.

8. Now it's time to make a rainstorm. Slowly pour about a ¼ cup of water onto each trash location.

9. Use your pencil to "drill" 3 "monitoring wells" between your "town" and each trash location. This means poke 3 holes in the dirt and sand until you reach the bottom of the pan.

10. Cut up some slivers of white paper, about the width of a pencil. Fold them in half lengthwise so they are sturdier and stick one into each sand hole. Remove them after about 30 seconds. Observe if the paper has picked up any of the food coloring from the garbage sites. If your wells are dry, add more water to each trash location and try again.

WHAT JUST HAPPENED?

Odds are that your landfill did not leak any of its color into the wells, but your dump and storage tank probably had some serious leakage. Landfills are built so that they usually don't leak, but just in case, lots of pipes are added to collect and treat any leachate and storm water. There's nothing sanitary about a dump, which is why most towns now use landfills.

Even with landfills, it's still not a good idea to throw dangerous items into the trash. They can hurt the workers who collect your trash and any animals that might sneak in, and they could possibly leak out of a landfill into your town's drinking water. Ask if your town has "hazardous-waste collection days." Bring things like used batteries, which contain toxic chemicals such as mercury and strong acids, to special collection sites. Earth911.com is a great site for learning more about how to dispose of trash in an earth-friendly, animal-friendly, and human-friendly way.

Iron is the fourth-most-common element in the Earth's crust and the sixth-most-common element in the universe. You even have iron in your body—it's the stuff that carries oxygen through your bloodstream via your red blood cells. Iron is also the main ingredient in steel. It is super-strong stuff. But mix iron with two other ingredients—water and oxygen—and it starts to literally crumble. The iron slowly turns into iron oxide, and what was once strong becomes weak and flaky. A massive bridge that can cross a river and hold up 50 tractor trailer trucks can begin to fall apart if it's not covered with rust-repelling paint, all because of a little air and moisture.

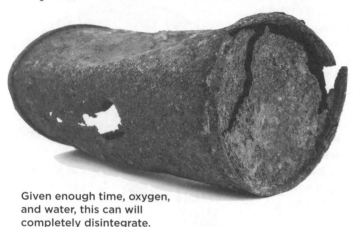

Given enough time, oxygen, and water, this can will completely disintegrate.

DIGGIN' DECOMPOSING

Rotting food is definitely icky. But you can turn all those fruit peels, eggshells, and vegetable bits into nutritious treats for your plants—this is called compost. Sure, compost sometimes looks slimy and can get a little smelly if you don't treat it right, but if you care for it, mix in the right ingredients, and wait long enough, you can add it to your garden and grow really happy and healthy plants. Who needs a pet when you can look after rotting food?

You know that when plants or animals die, they decompose. This means that little microorganisms, like bacteria or fungi, break them down into smaller parts. These parts become a rich, soil-like material that is full of really nutritious particles that other plants can use to grow strong and healthy. When you compost your leftover veggie scraps, you are recycling these nutrients back into the soil instead of trapping them in a landfill. You are

20 MINUTES
PLUS 3 DAYS OF OBSERVATION

ANTIGRAVITY RUST?

GO FETCH

- 4 empty, skinny see-through spice jars (or test tubes), lids not necessary
- Pen
- Tape and small pieces of paper or sticky notes
- Measuring spoon and measuring cup
- 3 small bowls
- Vegetable oil
- Steel wool
- Salt
- Water
- Flat, see-through container that's large enough to hold all the spice jars, such as a Pyrex baking pan or food storage container
- Food coloring (optional)

Want to see some rust in action? Don't worry, you don't need a junkyard or a giant bridge. In this experiment, you'll run a rust race with steel wool, and you'll see water "magically" defy the tug of gravity.

1. Think about a hypothesis. What will happen to the steel wool when it comes in contact with water, salt water, oil, or just air? Which one will cause the most rust?

2. Label your jars with the pen and tape (or a sticky note). They will be called *salt water*, *water*, *oil*, and *control*. Stick the labels about halfway up each jar.

3. In one bowl mix 1 teaspoon of salt with ½ cup of water, in the second bowl just add ½ cup of water, and in the third bowl add ¼ cup of vegetable oil.

4. Rip the steel wool into four pieces that are the

size of the width of your spice jars—about the size of a large cotton ball. You want the steel to fit so snuggly in the bottom of the jar that it won't fall out when you hold the jar upside down.

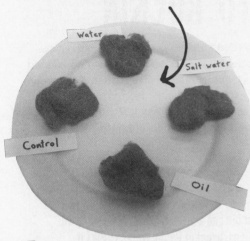

5. Take the first piece of steel wool and dunk it into the salt water. Squeeze out the excess water, stretch the wool out a bit, and then shove it down into the bottom of the jar labeled *salt water*.

6. Take the second piece of steel wool and dunk it into the oil, then squeeze out the excess oil. Stretch it out and then shove it into the bottom of the jar labeled *oil*.

7. Take the third piece of steel wool and dunk it into the plain water. Squeeze out the excess water, stretch it out, and shove it into the bottom of the jar labeled just plain *water*.

8. The fourth piece of steel wool

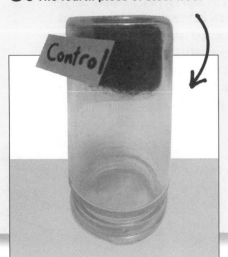

will stay dry. The cool science word for this piece is the *control*. A control is the part of an experiment that you don't do anything to. This enables you to compare your results to a piece of "normal" steel wool. Shove it into the bottom of your jar labeled *control*.

9. Place the jars upside down into the see-through container. (Remember, don't use their lids.)

10. Add about an inch of water to the container. Before you pour it in, you might want to add a few drops of food coloring to make the water level more visible. Notice how the water level inside the jars is lower than the water level of the container. This is because the air in the jars is preventing water from rising up inside the jars.

11. Pledge not to lift the jars out of the water for two to three days. Keep them safe from nosy relatives or pets with a strong interest in science. You don't want them to accidentally ruin your experiment.

12. Each day, check for rust forming on the steel wool. Equally important, keep your eye on the water level inside the jars as compared to the water level inside the container.

WHAT JUST HAPPENED?

Congratulations, you've grown your very own rust! Okay, that's not quite true; rust isn't alive, so it doesn't actually "grow." Rust (or iron oxide, as it's technically called) is simply two iron atoms connected to three oxygen atoms with water molecules attached, and it forms when iron is exposed to air and moisture. The steel wool is full of iron, but where did the oxygen come from? It came from the air inside the jar. Air is a mixture of different gases, but it's mostly made of two gases: nitrogen (78 percent) and oxygen (21 percent). So, there was plenty of oxygen just hanging around in the jar.

Was your hypothesis correct? The most rust probably formed on the steel wool that had been soaked in salt water, because salt helps speed up the rusting process. The oil-coated steel wool probably had the least rust, because the oil acts as a raincoat, keeping the water away from the steel wool. Iron needs water to rust.

Now, check the water level inside the jar with the most rust. We bet you'll see that it's higher than the water level of the control container. The water inside the jar seems to defy gravity! But it isn't magic—just air pressure. When you started the experiment, the air pressure in the room was equal to the air pressure in the jar. But after the oxygen in the jar combined with the iron in the steel wool, there was less oxygen gas available to push back against the water. It looks like the steel wool is sucking up water, but that's not what happened. The air pressure in the room pushed the water higher up into the jar, where there was less air pressure. Air can be SO pushy!

also reducing the amount of trash that goes into a landfill. That's a really good thing, because landfills take up a lot of space and are filling up fast. What would you rather have in your neighborhood: a giant pile of trash or a pretty garden full of flowers and veggies?

Finished compost can be used as mulch around trees and shrubs or mixed with soil to make your dirt healthier. What's really amazing about compost is that it produces HEAT! If you take a pitchfork and dig to the center of the pile, you will see steam rising as those mighty microorganisms do their work! You may even be able to feel the heat if you just stick your hand near the pile.

RAH! RAH! RECYCLING!

Most items we use today (plastic, metal, glass, paper, cardboard) can and should be recycled. Even food can be composted. But right now we are all getting a D in recycling. Recycling a single aluminum can saves enough energy to power a TV for three hours, but Americans throw away enough aluminum cans to build all the airplanes in our country's fleet. What a waste. And every hour, Americans toss over 2.5 MILLION empty water bottles in the trash. (Note to self: Buy a cool reusable water bottle or two and use them instead!)

DO YOUR PART!

Recycle, and the Earth (and these guys) will thank you.

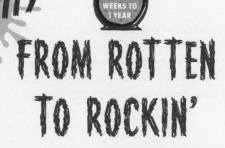

6 WEEKS TO 1 YEAR

FROM ROTTEN TO ROCKIN'

Composting food and paper scraps and yard waste can keep about 20 to 30 percent of your household waste out of a landfill, and put nice nutrients into your garden!

Making compost is easy. You just add the following ingredients and microorganisms will do

GO FETCH

A compost bin and a place to put it. Ask your town or city Department of Public Works (DPW) if backyard composting is allowed. If you don't have a yard, perhaps your teacher can get your school to offer up some space. Also ask the DPW if they provide inexpensive bins. You can also find plenty of bins for sale at hardware stores and online, or you can find instructions for how to build one out of wood and chicken wire. If you live in the country, you won't need a special bin.

Green and brown plant parts (more on that in the compost recipe)

Pitchfork (optional)

Water

Note: Flies, pesky rodents, or even larger animals can be a problem with some compost bins. Find out what critters live in your town. Some rats ate their way through our plastic compost bin (and made a cozy home underneath it!), so we got a pest-resistant rolling bin that sits above the ground on a metal stand that rats can't climb. No more rodents! You can also wrap your bin with a couple of layers of chicken wire so that animals can't get in.

The Compost Recipe

the rest! Adding the right ratios of ingredients helps to speed up the process and keep your compost from getting super stinky, but really, you can't go wrong.

1. Brown (carbon-rich) materials
Examples: dry leaves, corncob stalks, teabags (without the metal staple), paper (plates, coffee filters, napkins, towels, and tubes—rip them into small pieces to add to your compost), pine needles (in very small quantities because they are acidic and too many can be bad for the compost), sawdust, and straw.

2. Green (nitrogen-rich) materials
Examples: fruit and veggie peels and scraps (cutting them into smaller bits will make them decompose faster), coffee grounds, eggshells, grass clippings, fresh leaves, and fresh weeds.

Note: Your compost bin needs lots more brown than green. Aim for a 3:1 ratio (i.e. put three times the amount of brown materials in as you do green ones). It's tough for city dwellers to collect enough brown, so save all your newspapers and napkins and paper plates! You can even shred used white paper and use that as "brown." Or collect a bin of leaves in the fall and use it throughout the year. Always cover your green items with the brown items. After all, you don't want pests and flies to think you've opened a fast-food joint! A thick layer of brown will smother bad odors and help the food scraps break down faster.

3. Water
The compost should be as moist as a well-wrung sponge. If it's too dry, pour a little water in. Too wet, add more dry leaves or open a drain if your compost bin has one. If you collect the excess water, you

Three part compost bins allow you to have an "incoming" bin, a "working" bin, and a "finished" bin.

can pour this "compost tea," a dark brown stinky liquid, on your plants. They will love it! It's like a vitamin-and-mineral smoothie for them!

4. Oxygen
It is possible to compost *anaerobically* (an-uh-<u>row</u>-bick-lee)—without oxygen. Some people like it because it's a lot less work, but it takes a LOT longer than composting with oxygen and can get smelly. Basically it means just throwing stuff in a pile or a bin and waiting. Composting aerobically (with oxygen) means that you find ways to mix air into your pile. That means that you either turn your bin (if it's a rolling kind) or use a pitchfork to turn the pile. Turn the pile every 4–5 days, or every time you add new materials.

What NOT to compost:
meat scraps and animal fats, fish scraps, bones, dairy products, peanut butter, cooking oil, diseased plants, pet waste, plywood or pressure-treated wood, and anything that does not biodegrade (break down naturally),

including plastics. Nonbiodegradable stuff will contaminate your compost.

Add, mix, and wait:
Keep adding your food scraps and brown materials whenever you have them. Many people keep a little bucket on their kitchen counter to collect food scraps, and then dump them in the big compost pile every day or two. Every time you add new materials, mix the compost with a pitchfork if you can, or if you have a barrel, give it a roll. If you can't mix it, bury the food under leaves and grass clippings so animals don't think you're providing an all-you-can-eat rotten buffet. In warm weather, and with plenty of mixing, you could have usable compost in about 6 weeks. It takes a lot longer in cold weather or if you let your pile just sit there. You might have to wait for a whole year or even two that way. When it is done, your compost will be dark brown and crumbly, like soil. It will have a sweet or musty smell. It's ready to put in your garden or around your nearest tree! It went from ick to ick-cellent!

PAPER OR PLASTIC? CHOOSE NEITHER!

When a grocery store checkout clerk asks what kind of bag you want, consider this:

● More than a third of the waste Americans throw away is paper. About 14 million trees are cut down every year so folks can take their cornflakes and hamburger meat home from the market in a paper sack. Making paper also uses *lots* of energy and water. If you bring home a paper bag from the store, reuse it again and again the next time you go shopping, and recycle it when it starts falling apart. You can also use it to make silly costumes or wrapping paper, or turn it into a ball and use it to play with your cat!

● Is plastic any better? It takes 12 million barrels of oil to make the approximately 1 billion plastic bags Americans use each year—and many of these bags end up floating around in the air or in our oceans once we're done with them. In fact, because humans have tossed so much plastic over the last 50 years, no place in the ocean is free of plastic garbage. There are two huge floating "islands" of spinning plastic debris in the Pacific Ocean—one between Hawaii and California and the other near the coast of Japan. The plastics floated there and then got trapped by swirling ocean currents. Some plastic even looks like krill (a whale's go-to food), but not only is it not good to eat, it can actually kill sea creatures. So try to cut down on the amount of plastic you use, reuse it as much as possible, and dispose of it properly by recycling it.

So which is it? Paper? Plastic? NEITHER! Tell your grown-ups to always carry reusable shopping bags with them, and you do the same. Most bags fold up so small, they can easily fit inside a purse or backpack. Do your part to keep any more plastic from harming wildlife. So many things can be reused and recycled: Plastic, clean paper, glass, and metal can all be saved from a smelly, sodden end in a landfill!

Litter can get into the animal food chain, as you can see by what this Lysan albatross upchucked (obviously it didn't come back up all neatly organized like this!).

Now that you know the facts, you're going to start recycling (if you aren't already), right? RIGHT??? Check with your local recycling center to make sure you're recycling *everything* you can!

You are now a garbage expert.
Your banana peels and your wadded-up napkins have been composted. You have, of course, recycled your plastics, papers, cardboards, glass, and metals. If you're interested in waste disposal of all kinds, head over to POOP (page 182) to find out where your brown biscuits go after they leave your rump! But first, find out how your body turns food into those brown biscuits—GUTS, next!

Guts

You just polished off a bean-and-cheese burrito, guzzled a glass of milk, had a bite or two of broccoli to make your grown-ups happy, and topped it off with a chocolate bar. So what happens to all that food between the moment you put it in your mouth and the moment it comes out your butt hours later? It turns out that food has quite the adventure in our bodies, moving downward through a system of tubes and tunnels that connect your mouth to your butt's escape hatch. This whole system is known as your guts. Let's slither down along your digestive tract and take a closer look.

FROM BIG GULP TO FINAL FLUSH

Picture a long tube—a VERY, VERY long tube, close to 30 feet long. That's almost as long as a school bus! That's how long the segments of an adult's digestive system would be if they were stretched out in a straight line. This gooey, glorious tunnel system starts with your mouth and ends with your anus, but along the way it twists and turns and coils like a wild roller coaster, all the while breaking your food into much smaller bits that your body can use for energy, growth, and repair.

What happens if you stick that bean burrito into a blender? It turns into a nasty, mushy blob. Your mouth is a bit like your body's blender, with your teeth doing the tearing and grinding. After a few seconds of chewing, thanks to the addition of spit (see page 211 for more on that awesome stuff), your burrito bite will become a soupy slime. It will start to slide down your throat into the tube that hooks your mouth to your stomach. That stretchy 8-inch-long tube is called the *esophagus* (eh-<u>soff</u>-uh-gus), and its job is to squish and squeeze food down to your stomach.

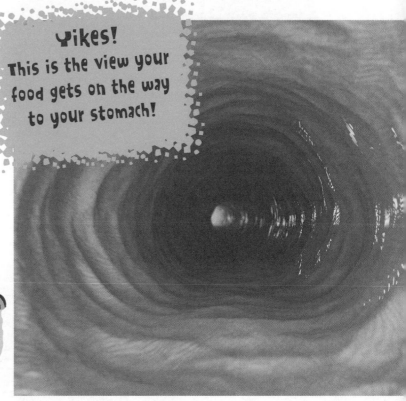

Yikes!
This is the view your food gets on the way to your stomach!

Slide down the inner esophagus!

MAJOR-LEAGUE STOMACHS

Make a closed fist. THAT is the size of your stomach with no food in it. Now picture a quart of milk (you know, those containers that hold about four glasses' worth of milk). That's how much a stomach can comfortably hold (more if you are at an all-you-can-eat dessert buffet). And just as there are superstars of basketball and Olympic snowboarders, there are also world-champion eaters. These people can pack their stomachs to the point of ridiculousness.

Major League Eating runs all sorts of eating competitions. Frozen yogurt, pastrami sandwiches, hard-boiled eggs—you name it! Speed and quantity go hand in hand here. Some recent record holders include the man who ate 34 beef brisket BBQ sandwiches in 10 minutes and a woman who downed 8.31 pounds of Vienna sausage, also in 10 minutes. Then there was the fellow who wolfed 7 quarter-pound sticks of butter in 5 minutes. These competitors weren't born with giant stomachs: They practiced a lot so that their stomachs could expand *way* beyond normal size. And they trained their brain not to want to upchuck all that food. Don't try this at home, kids! Emergency medical staff are always on hand at these competitions, and they warn that if your stomach gets too stretched, you may have to live with never-ending nausea and vomiting for the rest of your life. Not fun!

This squish-squeeze is called *peristalsis* (per-uh-<u>stall</u>-siss)—powerful wavelike contractions and relaxations of the muscles that line the esophagus. Peristalsis is so powerful that it enables you to drink water while standing on your head. You have no control over these muscles, and normally don't feel them at all. The only time you might become aware of them is if you swallow a chunk of food that is too big. Then you feel uncomfortable as your esophagus works hard to move that chunk down.

CAN YOU STOMACH THIS?

That blob of soupy burrito stew has made it to your stomach. For the next few hours, your food will all be churned together as your stomach muscles contract and the walls ooze out *hydrochloric* (hi-droh-<u>klor</u>-ick) acid. The same stuff that's found in toilet bowl cleaners and rust removers, it's 10 times more acidic than lemon juice. In your stomach, it's also known as *gastric* (<u>gas</u>-trick) acid, and it kills most bacteria and other microorganisms that you might have swallowed: either those on your food or those you accidentally licked off your unwashed fingers. (But don't leave it entirely up to your gut, friends. Wash your hands before you eat!) If you have ever had a mini-barf that burned your throat, you were tasting gastric acid. NOT delicious. Fortunately, you have a thick layer of mucus to protect your stomach lining from being dissolved by this acid stew. The mucus is replaced every few days with a fresh layer. Aren't bodies amazing?!

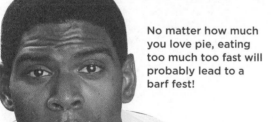

No matter how much you love pie, eating too much too fast will probably lead to a barf fest!

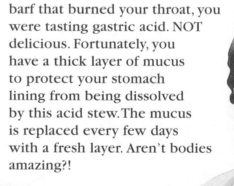

Your stomach muscles keep contracting and relaxing, mixing the acid with your food and breaking your food down into smaller parts. All this mixing turns your pretty meal into a nasty-looking half-liquid, half-solid, totally vile goop called *chyme*. Your stomach holds on to the chyme and releases blobs of it in a controlled way into your small intestine. This keeps the intestines from getting overwhelmed by the giant meal you just ate.

HOLE-Y COWS!

Speaking of stomachs, let's pause a moment and consider cows' awesome four-compartment tummies. The *rumen* (<u>roo</u>-min) is the first and largest part. It can hold up to 50 gallons—about as much as one of those big trash cans you haul to the curb. If you were a hungry cow, you would gobble lots of big mouthfuls of grass, chew it just a tiny bit, and swallow it into your rumen. There, digestive juices soften it, and billions of nice microorganisms (like bacteria, mold, and yeast) break down the grass into digestible parts. The grass would then make its way into the second chamber of your stomach, the *reticulum* (reh-<u>tik</u>-cue-lum). But you wouldn't be done.

The reticulum would squeeze the food, making you barf a soft ball of this partially digested grass (called *cud*) back up into your mouth. Since you're a cow, this is normal, not gross, and you spend 8 hours a day chewing and reswallowing these upchuck wads. Swallow and barf, swallow and barf. Again, and again, and AGAIN! All this chewing helps break the grass down into tiny bits, making it soft and easier for the friendly microorganisms in your stomach to do their work. Eventually the grass is digested enough to make its way through the other two remaining stomach chambers, where water and nutrients are absorbed into the cow's body. The fourth chamber—the equivalent of our human stomachs—digests anything that is still left.

Ed DePeters, a professor of animal science at the University of California, Davis, is fascinated by rumens and wanted to know more about how cows' digestive systems worked. He also wondered if there are things other than grass that can keep them well nourished, and if changing their diet can change how nutritious their milk is.

Hole-y cow! The opening in this cow's side allows scientists to study its digestion.

Here's what Dr. DePeters did. Using the bottom of a coffee can, he traced an outline in chalk on a cow's side and then painted the cow's skin with an anesthetic solution that made the next step pain-free. He then cut a hole through the skin and into the rumen, and fitted the hole with a plastic plug that could be opened to view what was going on inside as well as to insert and remove food. Fear not! The cows felt no pain! They were able to go back to eating right away, and received excellent treatment on the farms where they were studied.

These cows now had a *fistula* (<u>fist</u>-you-luh)—the scientific word for a small opening. Dr. DePeters's students called his test subjects "Hole-y cows"! The hole was perfect for getting the inside scoop on how the stomachs digested food. DePeters filled mesh bags with all sorts of odd food and nonfood bits, including prune pits, scrap paper, dryer lint, and lemon pulp. He lowered each mesh bag into the cow stomachs and then pulled it out at various intervals to see what was happening. Turns out a cow's amazing stomach can digest all sorts of interesting things! His research has helped dairy farmers know what kinds of foods to feed cows beyond just grass. This process of fistulation can actually help a sick cow, because the farmer can transfer healthy bacteria from another cow into the sick cow's stomach so the healthy bacteria can help them digest properly again.

DISGUSTING DIGESTION— ANIMAL STYLE

- Some sharks can turn their stomachs inside out, then push the inside-out organs through their mouths (like how you can turn your pockets inside out). It's their clever version of vomiting.

- Coiled-up horse intestines are almost 90 feet long. That's the distance from home plate to first base in Major League Baseball!

- Penguins have amazing stomachs. Since they often have to carry fish home to feed their babies, they swallow the fish, but their stomachs basically shut off and become moving shopping bags. The food's there but there is no churning, no acids released, nothing! When the parents return to the offspring, they upchuck the fish in much the same way your grown-ups unpack their grocery bags after a trip to the market.

- Tennis players, violinists, and surgeons all utilize intestines! Strings on tennis racquets and expensive stringed instruments, as well as the thin thread used to stitch up wounds, are made from catgut. But kitties everywhere can relax! Catgut is made from sheep or cow intestines that have been stretched, bathed, chilled, washed, and twisted. And these days metal, cotton, or plastic strings can often be used instead.

- Python snakes have the BEST esophagus! We are so jealous! Imagine really thick yet super-stretchy bubblegum. Together with its jaws, which separate both up and down and side to side, a python can swallow an entire kangaroo. Such a useful trait!

SMALL NAME—BIGGEST PART

The stomach is awesome. No doubt about it. But it's not the true star of the digestion show. That honor goes to the intestines.

A human without food is like a car without gas. It's not going anywhere. Food fuels your body, but first you have to break down that bean burrito into usable parts—proteins, fats, and carbohydrates. You need protein to build and repair muscles. You need carbohydrates to give you energy. And you need fats to build brain cells, to keep your skin healthy, and to keep your organs warm and protected. The mouth and stomach have started the job of breaking food down, but the small intestine is where the real digestive work gets done. Your food will spend about four hours here on average.

When that acidic blob of chyme exits your stomach and enters the first part of your small intestine, your pancreas injects substances called *digestive enzymes* that break down fats and proteins so our

Does the critter I just swallowed make me look fat?

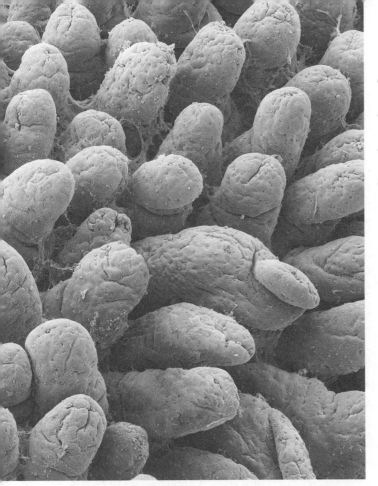

Who are these little cuties? Just some villi hanging out in the intestine.

No discussion of digestion is complete without a round of applause for the *sphincter* (<u>sfink</u>-tur) muscles. A sphincter is a circular muscle that controls the opening and closing of a (usually) tube-shaped organ. It can shut tight or be completely open, kind of like making a fist and then opening your hand. Here are the key sphincters at work in your digestive system.

Swallow: No one wants their burrito-and-saliva combo sliding back out of their mouths after they've taken a big gulp. The *upper* and *lower esophageal sphincters* take care of that. The upper sphincter slams shut after you swallow so your food doesn't go down your windpipe. The lower one (also called the cardiac sphincter) usually keeps the gnarly acid stew that is being digested in your stomach from escaping back up into the esophagus. Occasionally the acid does creep back up, and when it does, you will feel like a blowtorch has just roasted your chest. No wonder it's called heartburn!

Digest: The pulverized glop that was once your dinner is now ready to pass through the *pyloric sphincter*, at the lower end of the stomach, into the small intestine. The mushy remains of your meal will be further squished and squeezed before reaching the next gate—the *ileocecal* (ill-ee-oh-<u>see</u>-cul) *sphincter*, where the small and large intestines join.

Poop: Leaking doo-doo is a don't-don't! This is such an important gate that there are two "doors" to pass through. You can't control the *internal anal sphincter*, which leads from the large intestine into the rectum. But you definitely are in charge of the *external anal sphincter*, aka anus—all the better to have time to find something to read before you settle down to do your business.

bodies can absorb them. Your liver and gallbladder also make a big contribution to the slimy stew with the addition of a fluid called *bile*, which is used to dissolve fats. All of these fluids are bases, so the gastric acid is neutralized and doesn't hurt your small intestine. Old red blood cells are also added to the mix in the intestine, and it's the combination of bile and red blood cells that gives your poop that fudge brownie color.

The "small" intestine is actually a very long (over 20 feet in the average adult), surprisingly large bit of plumbing (though it's only 1½–2 inches wide). Take a small intestine and flatten it and you will have a surface area equal to a tennis court! That's because the inside of this tunnel is covered with zillions of lumpy folds called *rugae*. And what's more—each of *these* folds in the small intestine is covered with zillions of tiny fingerlike bumps called *villi*. And the villi have even tinier bumps on them called *microvilli*! All that surface area means your small intestine can absorb lots of nutrients from the thin, watery mix that your food has become. The outside of your intestines are covered with lots of tiny blood vessels. The microvilli work like little sponges, moving the nutrients out of the intestines and into those blood vessels, which carry the nutrients to your cells.

DIGESTION INSIDE OUT

30 MINUTES

Follow the progress of food from your mouth down to your pooping parts with a "working" model of the digestive system complete with a squishy brown "end product."

WARNING!!!

Add too much liquid, and things could get very, very messy. You might end up with the "runs" rather than a "solid" at the butt end of this experiment.

GO FETCH

2 cups cereal

Large bowl

Pestle or potato masher

¹/₂ cup water

¹/₂ cup yogurt

2 gallon-size ziplock bags

1 cup vinegar

Red and green food coloring (about 20 drops of each)

Nylon stockings (cut into 2 legs)

Scissors that can cut cloth

Sink

1. Put 2 cups of dry cereal in a large bowl. The bowl will represent your mouth. The cereal will represent, well, cereal.

2. Chewing is the first phase of digestion. Use a pestle or potato masher (or even a big spoon or the side of your fist) to smash the cereal into tiny pieces. You are simulating the destructive power of your teeth.

3. Saliva aids in this part of digestion. Your saliva contains a chemical called amylase that helps break down starchy foods like cereal, potatoes, and pasta. You can't go to the grocery store and buy a bottle of amylase, but yogurt contains other enzymes that are helpful for digestion, so we'll use that instead. Add ½ cup water and ½ cup of yogurt into the bowl to create your own fake saliva and continue mashing up the mixture. (Of course you could also spit a lot

into the bowl. See SPIT, page 211, for more on that.)

4. It's time to "swallow" that food and send it sliding down your esophagus and into your stomach. Transfer the mixture into a ziplock bag and add 1 cup of vinegar. The vinegar represents your stomach acid (although stomach acid is much stronger). Put that bag inside a second ziplock bag in case the first one leaks. Use your hands to mash the food and vinegar together,

creating a mushy paste. In your stomach, muscles squeeze and release to mix strong acids and enzymes into your food and really break it down. (Remember to close the bag tightly or things will spill out and you'll get "heartburn," which should really be called "esophagus burn" because it's when stomach acid accidentally gets pushed up into your esophagus.)

5. After your stomach churning is done, the food travels to your small intestine. Here, your liver releases green bile to help break down fats. Old red blood cells also get dumped into the intestine. Remember: The addition of bile happens in the small intestine, but since you want to get the color just right, it's much easier to do it in this clear plastic bag where you can see what's happening. So, add a few drops of green and red food coloring to finish your masterpiece. Experiment to achieve the desired hue for your make-believe poop. We ended up using 18 drops of green and 20 of red, mixing in a few of each at a time and then squishing for a while.

6. Your stomach is a sack, but your small and large intestines are long tubes. Cut a pair of stockings in half so that you have 2 long leg tubes. (You'll just use one in this experiment—the small and large intestines will be represented together.) First, cut a small hole (½ inch across) at the foot end. That's where the "poop" will come out. Over the sink or a large bowl, pour the mushy brown food into the larger end of that nylon stocking. Ask a friend to hold the foot end up in the air while you do this. It takes hours for food to move through your intestines, so you don't want this simulated poop to rush through. That would be similar to diarrhea, which is never a good thing! The food at this point might look disgusting to your eyeballs, but the rest of your body can't wait to absorb all those yummy nutrients.

7. Squeeze the food inside the stocking over the bowl or sink to simulate how the small intestine pulls the nutrients and water out of the food and into your body. In reality those nutrients aren't going into the sink, they're going into your bloodstream to be carried to your cells. Enjoy the icky feeling of squishing the liquids out. (If you start to gag, remember it's just cereal, yogurt, water, vinegar, and food coloring . . . not actual poop.)

8. After squeezing for a while, your food has now gone through the large intestines too, and the majority of water and nutrients has been removed and carried off into your bloodstream to feed your cells. Your body has no need for the leftover waste. Out it goes! The final part of the intestine is called the rectum, which is sealed shut by a sphincter known as the anus. Squeeze the pretend poo out of the stocking "anus" into a large bowl in your sink.

9. The appropriate final step? What else! Go flush your breakfast down the toilet!

WHAT JUST HAPPENED?

You just modeled how food moves through your digestive tract. Models are useful but don't always tell the whole story. This activity probably took you less than 30 minutes to do. In real life, food stays in your body anywhere from about 10 hours to several days, depending on your body, your gender (men's digestive systems tend to work faster than women's), and what you ate. Fruits and vegetables travel faster than meat. Although your body does a lot of hard work to get the nutrients out of the food, it doesn't work alone. If you've read about bacteria (see page 20), you know you have about 100 trillion of those critters in and on your body. Many of these bacteria spend their entire lives in your large intestine. They help digest food and keep your body healthy. But bacteria don't live forever. Dead bacteria, and some living ones, make up the bulk of your poop. No wonder everyone is always yelling at you to wash your hands after you wipe! Walking around with intestinal bacteria on your paws is disgusting!

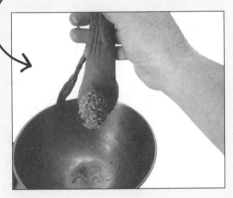

THE CHUBBY INTESTINE

So your very big *small* intestine has just sucked every useful nutrient imaginable from your lunch while strong rings of muscle squeezed to keep food moving along by peristalsis. Anything still left passes through a sphincter into your large intestine, which is thicker (about 3 inches around) than your small one but shorter (about 5 feet long in an adult).

What's left from your bean burrito by the time it gets here? Not a whole lot. Mostly water and bits of plant matter (called *fiber*) that your stomach and small intestine couldn't digest. Friendly bacteria that live in the large intestine think these leftovers are delish, and they will chow down, releasing useful vitamins (B and K) in the process. Most of the water and the vitamins are absorbed through the walls of the large intestine into the bloodstream, and all you're left with is a brown solid mass. You guessed it . . . poop! Most of that bulk is water and the friendly bacteria. There are also some dead cells that have been shed from your stomach, small intestine, and your blood, as well as any fiber, fat, and protein that wasn't digested. The cells that line your large intestine make lots of mucus, which helps your poop slip and slide on its way out.

The last bit of the digestive tract is called the *rectum* (<u>rek</u>-tum). It's a 4×6-inch-long tube where all the stuff your body couldn't use goes before being plopped into a nearby toilet. If poop could talk, it would bang on the rectum walls, screaming, "Let me out!" Instead it simply puts pressure against the walls of the rectum, giving you that feeling of gotta-go-right-now. Poop is the end of the line!

Of course butt brownies are super interesting, so head over to POOP on page 182. Or, turn the page for a HAIR-raising adventure!

Of course butt brownies are super interesting, so head over to POOP on page 182.

ICK-TIVITY
60–90 MINUTES

THE COIL CHALLENGE
GO FETCH →

- Small plastic bowl for mixing the petroleum jelly and food coloring
- Small jar of petroleum jelly
- Red and orange food coloring or paint
- A ruler or, better yet, a tape measure
- Roll of wax paper (at least 22 feet)
- Paintbrush (or fingers if you're a true slime lover)
- Clear tape
- Pair of scissors
- Pair of old nylon stockings
- Paper towels or old newspaper
- Small rubber band
- Red balloon (optional)
- An empty shoebox—try to find one about the size of your midsection
- Screwdriver or knife (optional)

Liver

Stomach

Pancreas

Gallbladder

Large Intestine

Small Intestine

Rectum

Your task: Make a life-size small intestine, attach it to a life-size large intestine, and then neatly fit it all back into a life-size abdominal cavity. It's not as easy as you might think, but it sure is fun to try. This is a good icktivity to do outside on a nice day.

1. In the plastic bowl, mix the petroleum jelly with the food coloring or paint.

2. Measure out 22 feet of wax paper and spread it out on the ground. Paint a big stripe of the colorful petroleum jelly right down the middle of the wax paper, the long way.

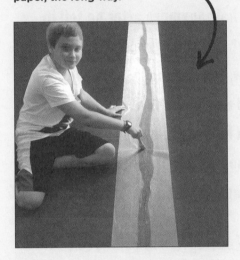

3. After it dries, roll it width-wise into a long snake, then twist your snake as if you were wringing out a towel to dry. Secure it with clear tape along the entire length. You have just made a small intestine!

4. Cut the legs off a pair of old stockings. Stuff each end of the stockings with paper towels or crumpled newspaper until the tube is about 3 inches wide. This is your large intestine. Knot the foot ends of each tube together. Combined, the tube should be about 5 feet long.

5. Use tape or a small rubber band to attach the large intestine to the small intestine.

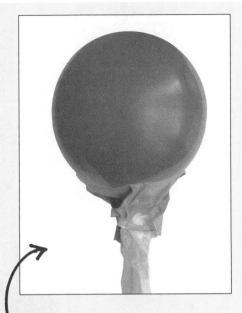

6. For extra fun, blow up a red balloon to about the size of a grown-up's fist. This is about the size of a stomach. Attach one end of the small intestine to the balloon end with pieces of tape.

7. Study the diagram on page 114. You didn't make a liver, pancreas, or gallbladder, but otherwise you will have all the parts. Position your stomach and guts inside the abdominal cavity (or in this case a shoebox).

8. For extra authenticity, get a grown-up to help you poke a hole in the bottom of your shoebox using a screwdriver tip or a knife. Pull the last little bit of large intestine (also known as the rectum) out of the box for a poop escape chute.

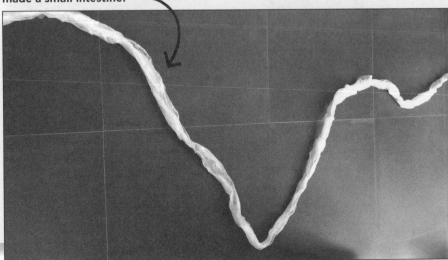

Hair Horrors

How would you feel about carrying around a 20-foot-long coil of hair sprouting from your head? Think of all the fun you could have with it! You could wear it as a muffler on cold days. Jump rope with it. Use it to lasso an ornery bull at a rodeo. On the other hand, your poor scalp and neck! Twenty feet of human hair is heavy—about 20 pounds! Still, that didn't stop Tran Van Hay, a Vietnamese gentleman, from deciding not to cut his hair anymore after he fell ill after a haircut. For the next 50 years his hair grew and grew, and for the last 11 years of his life it was too enormous to wash.

They call hair our crowning glory, so let's learn more about **YOUR** crown! Grab a comb and brush, and get ready for a hair safari.

YOU HAIRY THING!

It may not look like it, but we humans are COVERED in hair. It's *everywhere* on our skin except our lips, the soles of our feet, and the palms of our hands.

All our hair is genetically programmed to only grow to a certain length and then stop. You can easily see examples of that on your eyelashes, arms, and legs, but even your head hair will eventually stop growing—usually long before that of Tran Van Hay. (How weird would it be if your body hair just kept growing? Imagine having to push your eyelashes aside to read this book. Barbers and hairdressers would have a lot more work on their hands!) So what exactly IS that stuff sprouting all over you?

Hair so long you can cuddle with it! Tran Van Hay's locks were more than 20 feet in length.

STRETCHY STRANDS

GO FETCH →

Think hair is delicate? Think again! Here's a chance to play a game of hair tug-of-war.

1. Pluck two hairs from your head. (Ouch . . . sorry about that. At least you know you're feeling pain in the name of science!) If you have very short hair, go bother someone with long hair, and maybe bring along a cookie as a bribe.

2. Make sure the hairs are the same length and are between 4–8 inches long. Cut if you have to. Make a hypothesis about whether wet hair or dry hair will be stronger, and why.

3. Place one hair in a bowl of hot water for 15 minutes.

4. While you wait, tape one end of the dry piece of hair to the end of the ruler.

5. Ask your friend to keep one finger on the tape (to keep the hair from slipping out) while you stretch out the other end. Look at the ruler to see how far you are stretching it and jot down the number.

> 2 hair samples from your head, 4–8 inches long (or shorter)
>
> Bowl
>
> 2 cups hot water
>
> Piece of tape
>
> Ruler
>
> A friend

6. After 15 minutes, try the same experiment with the wet hair (dry it on a towel first or it may be too slippery to hold).

7. Compare your data. Which strand stretched farther? Why do you think that is? Was your hypothesis correct?

hair here

8. If you want to make this a truly fair experiment, you should do this with several sets of different-size hairs so that you can compare your results.

WHAT JUST HAPPENED?

We were able to stretch our dry piece of hair from 8 to 10 inches. The wet piece stretched from 8 to 11 inches but then broke. When you wet your hair, water molecules actually get in between the proteins of the cortex of your hair. That makes the hair stretchier but also weaker, because the proteins can't hang on to each other; there are now water molecules in the way. That's why wet hair breaks more easily. That's also why many people change the style of their hair when wet. You can put curlers in and let them dry to make your hair wavy, or you can straighten your curly hair by pulling it straight as you use a hair dryer. When the hair dries, the bonds between the proteins re-form and stay in that new shape. But when you wet your hair again, it goes back to the shape you started with.

ANATOMY OF A HAIR

How do you make a strand of hair? Take some sulfur, add carbon, swish in a little hydrogen, nitrogen, and oxygen, and ta-da! Okay, so it's not that easy. But your body manages to do it every day. Each hair grows from a tiny, saclike hole in your skin—kind of like a plant set in potting soil. But the hair that you see is not alive. The part of your hair that you shampoo

CHEWY HAIR?

Do you chew gum? Many brands contain lanolin, an oily secretion found in sheep wool. Every time you chew, you're chewing sheep hair oil. How tasty!

ICK-TIVITY HAIRBALL!

GO FETCH →

Why should cats have all the fun? Make a hairball all your own and gross out your grown-ups!

- Your own hair or a friend's hair
- Ziplock sandwich bag
- Lotion or shampoo

1. If you have long hair, you're in luck. If you don't, go find a friend or family member who does. What you need is a bunch of hair. Long hair tends to stick to your clothing and your hairbrush, so it's easier to collect. We spent a month collecting bunches of hair that fell out after combing or that were stuck in our hairbrush. Every day, we stuffed it in a sandwich bag, eagerly awaiting the day we would have enough to make a hairball.

2. Once you have filled the bag with hair (you want a small handful), it's time to roll it up. Remove it from the bag, and mash it and roll it between your hands until all the strands have tangled up into a ball. Add a dab of lotion or shampoo to get it to stick together a bit. You could add your own saliva, like cats do, but that might just be too gross!

3. Now comes the really fun part. Hide the hairball in your fist. Stand near the person you want to gross out and cough really violently, tossing the hairball out of your hand so it lands on the person.

4. With a straight face, say, "Oh, I must have just coughed up a hairball." Politely pick it up and walk out of the room. Then run to a safe place to laugh until your stomach hurts.

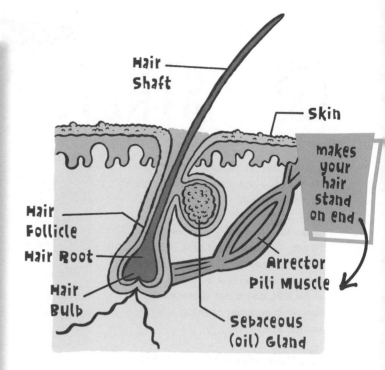

Hair Shaft

Skin

makes your hair stand on end

Hair Follicle
Hair Root
Hair Bulb

Arrector Pili Muscle

Sebaceous (oil) Gland

and comb is dead as dirt. Yes, dear reader—dead! This is a good thing, actually. If your hairs were alive, haircuts would be utter anguish. The only living part is that small sac where the hair sits, called a *follicle* (fol-ick-ul). Each follicle holds all the ingredients needed to make a hair strand. You have about 100,000 of these little sacs on the top of your head alone! When you were born, you were already covered with every follicle you'll ever have . . . about 5 million!

Picture a little cup filled with living cells. That's a follicle. The cells at the bottom (the root) of the follicle divide faster than any other cells in your body. The cells at the top of the sac get pressed together and pushed upward into what we call a "hair." By the time you can see a hair sprouting out of your skin, the cells in the hair have already died. The cells contain a protein called *keratin* (care-uh-tin). It's the same stuff that makes your fingernails hard, but fortunately the strands of keratin that form hair are soft and stretchy! As the hair is pushed up, little glands connected to the follicles release an oil called sebum (see page 59 in EARWAX), which keeps your hair from drying out. But too much sebum and you will be combing gross and greasy strands . . . Ew!

If you had a teeny-tiny pair of scissors and the world's steadiest hands, and you could somehow slice a human hair down the middle (or if you examine a hair under a microscope), you would see that a strand of hair has two to three parts. The outside—called the *cuticle* (<u>cue</u>-tih-kul)—is covered with overlapping flattened cells. Imagine lots of tiny roof tiles overlapping each other. Run your fingers in the direction your hair is growing. Now try the other direction—against the grain. Feel the difference? When you run your fingers against the grain (or up from the end of your hair toward where it attaches to your head) your fingers bump into those flattened cuticle cells. It feels rougher and may even squeak.

Next comes the inner layer—the *cortex*. (<u>cor</u>-teks). This part is made of long strands of protein that are twisted like an old-fashioned telephone cord or a super-small Slinky. That's why you can stretch a strand of hair. This is also where the pigments that give your hair color are located.

The innermost part is the *medulla* (meh-<u>dul</u>-loh, not to be confused with a chunk of your brain with the same name), which is made of soft, spongelike tissue. The medulla is present only in thicker, coarser hair, like the hair that sprouts from your head. Fine hairs, like those on your arm, don't usually have this part.

I CAN'T DO A THING WITH MY HAIR!

Red, brown, blond, black, gray (or white, in the case of your Great-Granny Franny). Curly, wavy, straight, frizzy. Hair comes in all kinds of colors and textures.

In the case of hair color, that slender stalk of dead keratin is a bit like a hollow straw filled with different combos of two types of melanin pigment. (Melanin also determines the color of your skin.) Depending on the amount of melanin and how these two varieties get mixed, your hair might be jet-black, flame-red, chestnut-brown, golden-blond, or something in between. If there is very little or no pigment being added to your cortex (pigment reduction happens as you age) you will have Great-Granny-Franny–colored hair—pure white.

When it comes to hair texture, blame your follicles if you want curly hair but have stick-straight strands or vice versa. A perfectly circular follicle will sprout straight hair. An oval one will make slightly asymmetrically shaped hair that will curl. The size of the follicle also contributes to thick hair (a big follicle) or thin (tinier ones).

You are lucky that each hair grows and falls out according to its own schedule. If all our hairs were on the same schedule, we'd *molt* (periodically shed all our hair, likes snakes shed their skin) and be bald at regular intervals. And speaking of bald—people with thinning hair, or NO hair, can blame follicles that have shut down.

DEAD HAIR LIVES ON

You—smart scientist that you are—know that everything decays. But human hair decays so slowly that if you dig up an ancient mummy, the hair will still be there. Our super-hair is even strong enough to survive encounters with many acids and corrosive chemicals. Just ask any plumber trying to clean a giant hair plug out of a bathroom drain!

HIDING IN HAIR

You are the proud owner of over 5 million hair follicles—about the same number as as a mountain gorilla, but your hair is much less thick. Why did humans evolve to have smaller and thinner hair than our primate cousins rather than becoming totally hair-free? The inquiring minds of two scientists at the University of Sheffield in England wondered if all those tiny little hairs could be an early-warning system to alert us to the presence of creepy crawlies.

To test this hypothesis, a group of 29 brave (or foolhardy) student volunteers—19 men and 10 women—each had an area on one arm shaved. The hairless area was outlined in marker and surrounded with a barrier of petroleum jelly. A similar-size area was marked off on the other, hairier arm. The volunteers closed their eyes tight while the two scientists dropped equal numbers of very hungry bedbugs on each marked patch. Whenever the subjects felt something crawling about on their arms, they pressed a button that linked to a machine that counted the number of crawls he or she felt.

Amazing! Bugs on the hairy arm were detected about every four seconds, but it took more than double the time on the hairless arm. This is because our hairs have nerves attached to them, so we can feel a bug clambering around, searching for a good place to bite. But biting was much more difficult for bugs on the hairy spots. It's hard to find a good meal while wandering around in a forest of hair. Then again, having too much hair, like a mountain gorilla, could provide places for bugs to hide, and we don't want that, either. So be grateful for your just-right follicles! They might keep you from becoming a snack for some hungry bugs! (Then again, ever-clever bugs know to look for hair-free areas, which is why ankles and wrists are some of their favorite spots!)

This unlucky lad suffered from hypertrichosis, which leads to long silky hair growing all over the face and body.

RAPUNZEL, RAPUNZEL... REALLY?

In the hair-raising fairy tale, our hairy heroine Rapunzel had locks of hair so long and strong that they could hoist a full-size hero up to the top of her tower prison. Could that even be possible? Let's start with the length of her tresses. The hair on a typical person's head grows about 6 inches a year. Rapunzel's was 70 feet long in the story. Hmm . . . Can you do that math? That would mean that she'd be at least 140 years old.

Based on the strength of real hair, a team of physics students at the University of Leicester in England calculated that Rapunzel's 70-foot-long locks could, in fact, hold more than 6,000 pounds (2,750 kg). That's the weight of two adult male hippos! So if she could grow hair that long (and her neck could support it), she'd have no problem at all hauling up any handsome princes who happened to be wandering by.

HAIR WEIGHT LIFTING!

30 MINUTES PLUS EXTRA TIME TO COLLECT HAIR

GO FETCH

How strong are your hairs? Does dyeing or bleaching hair make it more brittle? You're about to find out!

1. Collect hair samples from your own head (if it's long enough) as well as those of friends, relatives, and helpful teachers. (If you tell them it's in the name of science, they should be able to spare a few strands of hair!) Make sure all hair samples are at least 5 inches long. Place the hair into the small bags and label them as natural, dyed, or bleached.

2. Make a chart like this to record what happens:

TYPE OF HAIR	# OF PENNIES SUPPORTED
Natural #1	
Natural #2	
Natural #3	
Dyed #1	
Dyed #2	
Dyed #3	
Bleached #1	
Bleached #2	
Bleached #3	

3. Make a weight holder that you can hook on the hair: Bend the paper clip out so that it looks a little like a *C*. Push one end of the paper clip through the top of one side of the cup so that it goes all the way through. Then make a triangle hook on the other end of the paper clip. This basically is now a cup with a hook on it. You will hook this onto your hair and then be able to drop pennies in the cup to weigh it down.

4. Try the experiment first with an extra sample of hair. Tape each end of the hair to a separate surface. Make

- At least 10 hair samples that are at least 5 inches long: 4 natural, 3 dyed, 3 bleached
- 3 small bags (paper or plastic)
- Pen for labeling
- Large paper clip
- Small paper or plastic cup
- 30 inches of clear tape
- 2 smooth surfaces of similar height, like the backs of 2 chairs, or 2 nearby tables, or 2 boxes. We used 2 tall glass food storage containers.
- About 20 pennies

sure the hair is taut, but not too tight, and that no one bumps your testing surfaces. Also, only tape ½ inch of hair on each side so that most of the hair is hanging between the two surfaces.

5. Place the hook of your cup on the middle of the hair and add one penny at a time until the hair breaks. If the hair slips out of the tape, try it again and have a friend put a finger on top of each piece of tape. Write down the number of pennies the hair held.

6. Repeat this test for each hair

sample, writing down your results immediately so you don't forget!

WHAT JUST HAPPENED?

What did you find out? Which kind of hair is strongest? Which is weakest? The chemicals used in coloring or bleaching hair can damage the protein of the hair, making it more brittle, so it's likely that the bleached or colored hair broke first. Bleach penetrates into the hair and actually removes the pigment. Perms (chemical straightening or curling) break the bonds inside your hairs, and then re-form them in a new way. Both of these make your hair weaker. Highlights and coloring aren't quite as bad for your hair, but they still do some damage. Blow-drying, braiding, putting your hair in a ponytail when it's wet, adding heavy extensions, or even overbrushing can also hurt your hair. Remember: The shaft of your hair isn't alive, so it can't repair itself! The only real solution is to cut it off and wait for new, healthy hair to grow in. Then treat that hair more kindly!

If you want to do some more tests, try permed or chemically relaxed hair. (It's best to get these samples just after the hair has been treated.) You can also test wavy or curly hair versus straight as long as they are all natural or all chemically altered in the same way. Or you could test the wet hair versus dry hair from the Stretchy Strands ick-speriment (page 117). Or test red, blond, and brown hairs. If you were to braid three strands of hair together, is it three times stronger? If you tie a knot in the middle of a single hair, does that make it stronger or weaker?

Furry face, unfurry body!

Many folks blame dog fur for their allergies and try to get dogs with hair instead of fur. But the truth is, hair and fur (and wool!) are very similar, and the stuff that makes some people sneeze is actually a protein in the dog's saliva, skin flakes, and urine called *dander*. Some breeds, such as poodles, simply shed less, so the dander doesn't get released and the dogs don't trigger allergies to the same degree.

"I CAN'T SEE YOU . . . "

ICKY KITTY

Cats love to lick their furry selves clean, but their tongues are covered with small backward-facing hooks. Dead hairs get stuck on the hooks and swallowed. Some of the hair gets tangled together and smooshed into pieces that are too big to pass through the cat's digestive system. There is no way out but back the way it all came in. Hairball! And it comes with sound effects! Gagging and hacking noises are a sure sign that your floor is about to be graced with a lumpy thing about the size of a mouse that is a combo of fur and stomach acid. Yum!

ANIMAL HAIR

All mammals, from ferocious lions to sleek seals to humans, have hair. It's one of the things that makes them a mammal. (In case you're wondering, whales and dolphins start out their lives with hair—some lose it early on, and in others it's barely visible.) Even naked mole rats—tiny, shiny pink rodents that live underground—have whiskers and tiny hairs on their paws. Here are some fascinating tidbits about what sprouts where, and from whom.

Porcupine quills? Sharp enough to use as sewing needles, but they're actually just great big hairs.

Whiskers? Hair that is highly sensitive to touch. Whiskers actually help animals feel their way around in the dark by sensing tiny changes in the way the air is moving. They are also like tiny rulers, used to measure spaces before they try to enter. Never trim a cat's whiskers! It will really confuse it. Imagine trying to find your way around in the dark without the use of your hands and fingers!

Wool? Where would we be without warm sweaters and fuzzy pom-pom hats? Wool comes from the superfine, densely packed hair found on sheep, alpacas, and other similar animals. The wool often gets sheared off with clippers and spun into yarns for knitting and weaving.

Hairy bugs? Not hair! (Remember . . . only mammals have true hair.) A fuzzy caterpillar is an insect and is coated with things that look like hairs but are known as bristles, which are used for self-defense. Resist the temptation to tie little bows on its back or give it a Mohawk!

SOMETHING TO BE THANKFUL FOR

Before we move on to the next giant helping of ickiness, take a moment to be grateful that you don't have a condition called *black hairy tongue*. No need to shampoo this "hair." It's actually not really hair at all. Sometimes when dead skin cells pile up on the little bumps on your tongue, they can grow longer than usual and easily trap food or bacteria. Gross! Some people who smoke tobacco can end up with VERY black hairy-looking tongues. Double gross!

Enough about hair! Let's move on to bad breath, rotting teeth . . . it all awaits in HALITOSIS!

Halitosis

Did you brush your teeth this morning? REALLY? Or did you simply swipe a little toothpaste on your two front teeth while you ran the water? Sorry to give you a lecture, but if you take good care of your teeth, tongue, and gums, chances are you will have breath that smells fresh instead of like garbage. Bad breath stinks and makes people back away from you! (Plus, if you take care of your mouth, you'll be more likely to keep your teeth into old age—a good thing if you like chomping into foods like pizza and corn on the cob.)

TERRIBLE, HORRIBLE, NO GOOD, VERY BAD BREATH

Bad dental hygiene is one of the biggest culprits when it comes to a mouth that is *malodorous*. How's that for an "impress the grown-ups" word? It means foul-smelling. And even if you brush your teeth, your tongue can still be a real stink bomb. Bacteria are the culprits here. Tongues are anything but smooth, with so many tiny little lumps and grooves! They're a perfect place for bacteria and other small, pesky things like yeasts and viruses to hide, and these guys love to hop on over from your tongue to your freshly washed teeth! Chew on this fact: At this very second there may be as many as 20 billion bacteria living in your mouth. That's way more bacteria than the entire number of people who live on Earth—a mere 7 billion!

Go to a mirror and stick out your tongue. Is the back of it coated with a white, filmy paste? That's bacteria and their party guests, yeasts, all having a smelly good time! Then ask to inspect your grown-ups' tongues. Bet you will find some icky stuff growing on them too. In fact, an unclean tongue is the main cause of bad breath.

No one wants to hang with someone whose mouth smells like sheep dung.

ROTTEN TO THE ROOTS

15 MINUTES
PLUS A FEW DAYS FOR OBSERVATION

GO FETCH ➡

Your teeth are way too precious to experiment on. You've also probably noticed that they're stuck to your jaw, so it's hard to pick up your teeth and study them closely. In some ways, the enamel around your teeth is like the eggshell around an egg. Both are hard mineral layers of armor that protect the soft insides. Because enamel and eggshell are made of similar chemicals, we can study tooth decay by experimenting on eggshells. This is a whole lot less painful than surrendering your own pearly whites to science. The question you will answer: Which common drink causes the most damage to your teeth?

1. Gently wash all the eggs with soap and water to remove any potential salmonella bacteria. Wash your hands too. In fact, always wash your hands after dealing with eggs. (Learn more about eggs in YUCKY YOLKS, page 248.)

2. Place one egg in each bowl.

3. Pour a different liquid (water, vinegar, soda, and juice) into each bowl, until the egg is covered. The egg in plain water will be the control to which you will compare everything else.

At least 4 brown eggs

4 bowls

Water

Vinegar

Fizzy soda

Juice

Old toothbrush (it was time to replace yours anyway, right?)

---

4. Place the bowls in the refrigerator and wait a day.

5. Take the eggs out of the bowl one at a time and observe any changes in the shell. Compare each egg to the egg that was placed in the water.

6. Gently brush each egg with a toothbrush and see if anything comes off. Put the eggs back in their bowls.

7. Time for a fresh batch of liquids. Pour the liquids down the sink and then refill each bowl with the same type of liquid again. Return the bowls (with eggs back in them) to the refrigerator and wait one more day.

8. Very gently remove each egg from its bowl and observe any new changes in the shell.

WHAT JUST HAPPENED?

Eggshells contain a mineral called calcium carbonate, somewhat similar to a mineral in tooth enamel called calcium phosphate. These mineral crystals dissolve in the presence of strong acids. Vinegar, soda, and orange juice are all acidic, so that's why they ate away at the eggshells. These liquids can damage your teeth too, but luckily there are several things that help protect your teeth. First, you swallow instead of letting your teeth soak in a bath of cola or juice. Second, your saliva contains calcium and phosphate and replenishes the minerals your tooth enamel loses from acidic assaults. Finally, brushing teeth helps remove food particles that tooth-damaging bacteria like to munch on. Most toothpastes contain the mineral fluoride. Fluoride helps reinforce the layer of mineral armor that your saliva coats your teeth with. Bottom line: If you want to keep your teeth strong, avoid soda and other acidic drinks, and USE that toothbrush!

THE BACTERIA BADDIES

Sulfur is the chief cause of bad breath, but it's not the only culprit. Scientists have detected more than 600 different strains of bacteria that just LOVE human mouths. Depending on your personal bodily biome, it's likely there are about 50 different kinds of bacteria frolicking in your mouth at this very moment. Some bacteria give off sulfur smells, but depending on what we eat, other bacteria offer up these foul fragrances:

Cadaverine—The word *cadaver* refers to a dead body. So think of the way yucky rotten meat smells . . . Ahh . . . Cadaverine!

Putrescine—Ever unwrapped a raw steak or piece of chicken and realized that it smelled REALLY putrid? This chemical compound—closely related to cadaverine—is to blame.

Skatole—Smelly poop? Bet you know THAT odor. Blame this gas.

Isovaleric acid—After gym class, sniff your feet. You are smelling isovaleric acid, which also hangs out in your mouth.

Mix all of these together and hold your nose! Luckily our noses can't detect low amounts of these odors. So if you keep them under

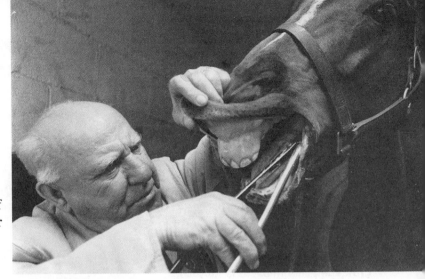

Open wide and say "neigh."

control by brushing your teeth and flossing, you'll avoid losing your friends.

A NOT-SO-GOOD MORNING SMOOCH

Ask your grown-ups if you can sniff their breath first thing in the morning, before they have brushed their teeth. While we sleep, our mouths dry out. Saliva is our very own mouth rinse. It kills some odor-causing bacteria, dilutes some of the smells, and rinses away many other bacteria and food bits, which we then swallow. Since we don't have as much saliva in our mouths overnight, conditions are perfect for those bacteria to have a major party (no saliva chaperones! YAY!) and create lots of foul gases.

Since saliva is mostly made of water, it's important to drink lots of water throughout the day so that you can keep producing this natural "mouthwash." But even saliva needs help. Brushing your tongue (especially in a side-to-side manner so you don't gag) is an important part of a healthy and fresh-smelling mouth.

Go ahead, we dare you! Take a good whiff of a dog's mouth. Or your hand after it has given you a slobbery lick!

15 MINUTES PLUS SEVERAL DAYS OBSERVATION

G-G-G-G-G-G-GARGLE!

GO FETCH

You should probably ask your dentist about the pros and cons of mouthwash before you start using it, but you can still test how effective it is against the bacteria in your mouth. In this experiment, you'll grow some mouth bacteria, so you'll need to make some bacteria hotels using the steps on page 21. Once you have the bacteria established in their hotels, you can analyze how well different types of mouthwash keep them under control.

1. First thing in the morning, before you've brushed your teeth, take a clean cotton swab and rub it around in your mouth (especially the back of your tongue), and then rub the swab on one of the bacteria hotels. Throw away the cotton swab. Put the bacteria hotel into a ziplock bag and label it *no mouthwash*; this will be the control that you compare your results to. Seal the bag. Promise to NEVER EVER OPEN IT!

NO MOUTHWASH

2. Take another clean cotton swab and rub it around in your mouth, and then rub the swab on a different bacteria hotel. Carefully pour a tiny splash of mouthwash over the middle of the gelatin. (It might be easier to pour a little into a spoon or into the cap first, then pour from that.) Seal the bag and label it with the type of mouthwash you used (alcohol, no alcohol, the brand name, etc.). Throw away the cotton swab.

- 6–12 of the bacteria hotels you made on page 21
- 6–12 cotton swabs
- 6–12 ziplock bags
- A few different kinds of mouthwash (preferably a brand with alcohol and a brand without alcohol)
- Several family members and their unbrushed mouths

3. Repeat step 2 with each different type of mouthwash you have. You'll probably have some leftover bacteria hotels, so have another person repeat steps 1 and 2 with their own mouth bacteria.

4. Zip the bags tightly shut. Promise to never open up the bags again: You might be growing some dangerous bacteria (called pathogens)! Seriously, say it out loud: "I will not open this bag again. I promise!" Pinky swear!

5. Store the bags in a warm, dark place in your home, out of reach of curious life-forms like your little brother or pet hermit crab.

6. In a few days, your mouth bacteria will probably have multiplied into visible colonies. Look carefully to see how well bacteria grew near the drops of mouthwash. This space is called the *kill zone*, and the better the mouthwash, the bigger the kill zone will be. AGAIN! NEVER EVER OPEN THE BAGS!

7. When you have finished examining your sealed bags, put the bacteria bags in the trash can.

WHAT JUST HAPPENED?

We hope you discovered that some mouthwashes worked better than others at killing or slowing the growth of the bacteria from your mouth. You may have noticed that some that claim to kill bacteria aren't very good at it. It's amazing how advertising can make you think something works when it actually doesn't! That's why science is so great: You can figure things out for yourself.

There are two types of mouthwashes: cosmetic and therapeutic. Cosmetic mouthwashes work by covering up the bad smells made by bacteria. It's kind of like spraying air freshener on a pile of garbage; the garbage might smell better, but it's still there. Therapeutic mouthwashes have antibacterial and antiseptic ingredients. Antibacterial ingredients can kill the foul bacteria by breaking them open or stop them from metabolizing food and reproducing. Antiseptics (such as alcohol and cetylpyridinium chloride) slow down the growth or reproduction of bacteria and lots of other microorganisms such as fungi or yeasts or viruses. The mouthwash that had the biggest kill zone in your experiment is probably a therapeutic mouthwash.

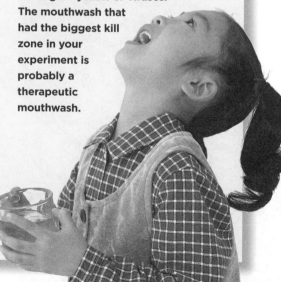

THE TROUBLE WITH TEETH

Our actual pearly whites can be another reason for icky breath. Food can play hide-and-seek in the spaces in between our teeth, and the longer it stays there, the worse it smells. The other culprit is *plaque* (plak), a gunky, clear, sticky film made of millions of bacteria that coats your teeth. These bacteria have a sweet tooth. As the sugar-loving bacteria happily gobble up the food items stuck between your teeth or the sugar that just washed through as you sucked on a candy or drank soda, they ooze acids that eat away at the hard enamel that protects your choppers.

Leave that acid slime on long enough without brushing (or eat lots of sugar), and it can eventually eat through the entire tooth until it crashes into the nerves and blood vessels that nourish your teeth! You now have a cavity. Trust us: You do not want this to happen. Cavities are no fun—having one will result in a dentist drilling for what feels like hours.

Without proper brushing and flossing, your gums can also get irritated by the acids that the bacteria leave behind. When your gums swell, the plaque can burrow down even deeper, making it even harder to clean. More bacteria equal more stink. It's a very vicious cycle.

So brush! And floss! AND brush your tongue! And yeah—nag, nag, nag, but you'll thank us years from now, and your friends will thank you today!

GARLIC AND ONIONS—GAK!

You can brush your choppers 24/7, but still smell like a sewer when you open your mouth. We can blame certain kinds of bad breath on some of the foods we eat. Garlic and onions are two culprits. Both of these plants give off sulfur gas—the delightful stench of rotten eggs—when they are broken down in our intestines. That gas enters our bloodstream, which eventually heads back to the lungs. Then we exhale it out as garlic breath! Ick!

FLOOR CLEANER FOR YOUR MOUTH?

Lots of people turn to mouthwash to zap bad breath. One of the best known of these is a concoction called Listerine. It was invented in 1879 and named in honor of a fellow named Joseph Lister, who knew a thing or two about bashing bacteria, but its original intent was to clean wounds as surgeons sliced patients open. It was also used to keep hospital floors clean and germ-free. It took more than 15 years for dentists to agree that it would be good for murky mouths.

In the 1920s a clever advertising agency had a bold idea—let's make people worry constantly about whether their breath smells bad! They ran magazine and newspaper ads warning of the dangers of *halitosis*—a word they plucked from ancient Latin that means "unpleasant breath." No friends? Unloved? It couldn't be because you were a big meanie. It HAD to be because of your breath!

Soon Listerine sales skyrocketed. It was also marketed as dandruff shampoo and a cure for smelly feet. It was even added to cigarettes or, as we like to call them, "cancer sticks." Seriously, those things are

Teeth so gunky they need a broom!

A Listerine ad from the 1920s

DO YOU HAVE HALITOSIS?

10 MINUTES

Since you can't stick your nose into your mouth, here's how to self-sniff.

1. Lick it! Give your wrist a good, juicy, slobbery lick, and count to ten as it dries. Now bury your nose on the spot and sniff. Smell anything? Maybe yes, maybe no. If you do smell something that reeks like dirty gym socks, run to the nearest toothbrush and give your tongue a good cleaning!

2. Tongue soup Grab a teaspoon and pretend you are going to eat some yummy ice cream. Now flip the spoon over and run it along the back part of your tongue, but be careful to not land too far back.

Ever hear the saying "gag me with a spoon"? That is exactly what you will end up doing if you go too far back down your tongue. Slowly scrape your tongue until the spoon fills with some gunk. It might be a thick, grayish goo, loaded with bacteria. Be brave. Take a sniff. We hope it's not too revolting, because that's what your friends are smelling!

3. Floss those pearly whites! Grab some floss and dig around in the space between your back teeth. Then smell the goop on the string. Now you know why you need to floss, because food and bacteria love to hide between your teeth!

not only terrible for your overall health and lungs, but they will give you the WORST breath.

Today mouthwash is still a very big business. But truth be told, some of the ingredients in mouthwash can make your mouth dry—a condition that can actually CAUSE bad breath. Before you start gargling, best to ask a dentist about using them, and which brands are best.

Next up, something you should definitely brush your teeth after eating: ICE CREAM!
Everyone's favorite frozen dessert—but with an icky twist, of course!

Icky Ice cream

WHAT'S THE MATTER?

In order to understand ice cream, first you have to get a grasp on the states of matter. Imagine a wily wizard has just turned you into a molecule of H_2O, and you and a few hundred thousand of your nearest and dearest water molecule friends are stuck together at the bottom of a drinking glass. Did you know that you have the power to change your form? You can even escape your glass prison! How? Matter—meaning anything that has mass and takes up space, including H_2O molecules—can take on three different forms (or "states") depending on the temperature. Let's see what happens to you and your pals as the temperature changes.

Solid—It's really, really cold—at or below 32°F (0°C). You and your H_2O friends are huddling together, trying to stay warm. You are lined up in very neat, very straight lines, shoulder to shoulder. You can wiggle a tiny bit, but not much. Together, you and your molecule buddies form an ice cube!

Liquid—It's a nice warm day. The temperature is above 32°F. You and your molecule buddies are hanging out, floating around in the drinking glass, just going with the flow. You all feel somewhat energetic, but mostly relaxed. Together you form a liquid.

Gas—It's really, really hot—above 212°F (100°C). You and your molecule BFFs have gone a little bonkers. You are bopping around like jumping beans on pogo sticks. Some of you have bounced clear out of the glass! Together you form a gas.

Okay, okay, we know what you're thinking. Ice cream isn't "Oh, ick!" In fact, it's "Oh, yum!" But we bet you didn't know that ice cream chemists use ingredients like seaweed. Or that octopus is an ice cream flavor in Japan. What else don't you know about your favorite dessert? Read on for some icky, lickable fun!

Let's face it. We ALL scream for ice cream.

So there you have it. The three states of matter all involve the same molecules, just in different forms. This is important, because matter's ability to change forms is what allows us to make certain tasty treats . . . like ice cream!

FEELING COLD, COLD, COLD

Not sure what you want to be when you're older? There are actually scientists who do nothing but study ice cream! How cool—er, cold—is that? Ice cream is one of the most complicated foods we eat. You may have an ice cream maker at home, or might see one at your local ice cream shop, but to a chemist, that ice cream maker is actually a *scraped surface-heat exchanger*. Pretty fancy, huh? It turns out that behind every lick of the cool creamy stuff, there is a whole lot of science going on.

To understand cold, first we need to understand heat. You experience "heat energy" every day. Think of those nice warm rays beaming down on us from the sun. Or sitting in front of a crackling fire. Now imagine taking a bowl of hot chicken soup and sticking it in a freezer. Your freezer doesn't add "cold" to your soup. There is no such thing as "cold energy." It's all about the heat—either you add heat

When ice cream cones were invented in the early 1900s, they were called "cornucopia cones."

GO FETCH

ICK-SPERIMENT

1½ HOURS
DEPENDING ON HOW MANY CHEMICALS YOU USE

THE REASON? FREEZIN'!

At least 2 identical mugs or cups

Measuring cup

6–10 ice cubes, or 2 per solute you want to test. Try to make them the same size. If your fridge doesn't have an ice maker, be sure you have 5 full ice trays' worth before you attempt this and the next ick-speriment or you might run out!

⅛ cup of the solutes you want to test: rock salt, table salt, sugar, dish soap, baking soda, sand, etc. (Make sure you test at least one of the salts.)

¼ cup water for each solute you want to test

Digital thermometer

Stopwatch or a clock with a second hand

Time	Control	Table Salt	Rock Salt	Sugar	Baking Soda	Dish Soap
30 seconds						
1 minute						
1.5 minutes						
2 minutes						
2.5 minutes						
3 minutes						
3.5 minutes						
4 minutes						
4.5 minutes						
5 minutes						
5.5 minutes						
6 minutes						
6.5 minutes						
7 minutes						
7.5 minutes						
8 minutes						

or you take heat away. Just like burning wood in a fireplace releases heat into a room, hot soup is actually releasing heat energy into the freezer box. The thermostat on your freezer notices the change

How can we turn liquid cream into ice cream without an electric ice cream machine or even a freezer? We need to surround the cream with something even colder than ice. What can we add to ice to make it as cold as possible? Rock salt? Table salt? Sugar? Kitty litter? Dirt? Baking soda? Your mission: Dissolve these items in water so they become *solutes* with the water as the *solvent*. These words are super-important in chemistry. And yes, melting and freezing (changes of states of matter) are definitely chemistry! Then you'll add ice to see which of the solutes makes water the coldest.

1. Make a chart like the one shown on the facing page, testing each solute at for least 8 minutes.

2. First let's test our control (the part of the experiment to which we will compare the rest of our results). This will be just ice and water. Make a water bath in a cup by popping in two ice cubes and ¼ cup water.

3. Use your thermometer to gently stir the water for 30 seconds. Then look at the temperature and write it down in your chart. It's best to record in Celsius when you are

being a master scientist. 0°C is the freezing point of pure water.

4. Make a temperature measurement every 30 seconds for 8 minutes. Keep gently stirring in between measurements. Then, rinse out your cup and let it sit and return to room temperature.

5. Using your second cup, repeat the above procedure, making a water bath of ¼ cup water and 2 ice cubes, but then add ⅛ cup of one of the solutes. Stir and take temperature readings every 30 seconds for 8 minutes. Then, rinse out your cup and let it sit and return to room temperature.

6. Test the rest of the solutes in this way, rinsing and alternating cups as you go. That way you'll always be starting with a room-temperature cup.

7. When you have collected all your data, draw a graph of temperature versus time (see chart below). How did the temperature change over time depending on the solute?

WHAT JUST HAPPENED?

You probably noticed that table salt and rock salt lowered the temperature of the water bath way below 0°C. Your other solutes may have lowered the temperature a bit (or even raised it), but they don't have the same impact as the salts. In order to melt, ice needs to absorb heat energy from the things around it. For example, when you hold the cup in your hands, your hands feel cold because heat is moving out of your hands and into the ice. When you add salt to the ice water bath, it actually lowers the freezing point of ice, so that even MORE energy must be absorbed from the surroundings to melt your ice cubes. This leaves the surrounding ice water colder than it was before. So even though the ice melted, the temperature of the salty ice water became colder than the freezing point of pure water! It seems like magic, but you have proof: your thermometer! Knowing this "cool" fact is about to lead to some very tasty science. Ice cream! Check out the next ick-speriment, Shake Your Booty, page 132.

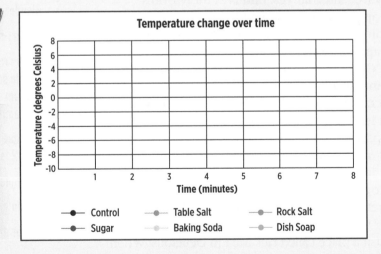

Temperature change over time

Temperature (degrees Celsius) vs. Time (minutes)

Legend:
- Control
- Sugar
- Table Salt
- Baking Soda
- Rock Salt
- Dish Soap

and turns on a compressor that pumps very cold "refrigerant" chemicals through coils on the back or underneath your freezer. The heat moves into those chemicals and is pumped away. The compressor will keep pumping those chemicals until there is no more heat to be pulled out of your soup. It's frozen! The same thing happens in your fridge, just not to the same degree.

EXTRA-CREDIT ENGINEERING

Can you design a container for the Shake Your Booty experiment that will hold your ice and salt [water], your cream mixture, AND help you shake it up all at the same time? You might use a large and a small coffee can. Or a big plastic bucket. How could you get the thing to shake without wearing out your arm? Could you and a friend toss it up in the air with a sheet? Or roll it back and forth on the ground? Think about what kind of materials would be best to use. The container between your cream and salty ice should conduct heat really well, so that the heat from your cream can escape to the ice. But the container that holds the ice should not conduct heat as well, or else all your ice will melt before it can freeze your ice cream. Draw your icy invention in your notebook and then give it a try.

WE ALL SCREAM FOR ICE CREAM

Just about everyone loves ice cream or its dairy-free alternatives. Vanilla is the world's most popular flavor, followed by chocolate. But depending on where you are on the globe, you can wrap your tongue around some pretty bizarre flavors. Go to Ice Cream City, a shop in Tokyo, and spoon into a scoop of cow tongue, octopus, or squid ice cream. In Ireland, you can lick smoked-salmon ice cream cones. Not to be outdone, an ice cream parlor in North Yorkshire in England offers minted mushy-pea flavor, or how about dinner and dessert in one lick with a scoop of battered-fish flavor, topped with a french fry?

Crack open the piggy bank and fork over 200 bucks if you want a cone of jellyfish ice cream in England at a place called Lick Me I'm Delicious! When your tongue touches it, it glows! Or try duck liver ice cream in France—it's quackingly good. Another flavor not to be missed is *mamushi* ice cream, also from Japan. It's made from one of the most venomous snakes in the country. Add a hint of garlic and almonds, top with sprinkles, and say a prayer!

ICK-SPERIMENT
SHAKE YOUR BOOTY

Now that we've got you licking your chops, it's time to get to work and make some ice cream! We're going to conduct an experiment to see how shaking the ice cream while it freezes affects the consistency. What's your hypothesis? Will shaking make it better, or worse?

GO FETCH ⟶

- 2 cups heavy cream (or whipping cream)
- I cup whole milk
- ¼ cup sugar
- Flavor of choice: I teaspoon vanilla extract or whatever flavor you want to add. If you want to go icky, then add ¼ cup mustard, ketchup, or fish oil. It's up to you!
- Blender
- 2 quart-size ziplock bags
- 2 cups rock salt (rock salt has larger crystals than table salt and will lower the temperature of the ice cream at a slower rate and make the ice cream, well, creamier)
- 2 gallon-size ziplock bags that close very well (or 2 large coffee cans or other containers)
- 5 pounds ice (at least 4 ice cube trays)
- A couple of small towels
- Winter gloves

Dairy-Free?

Here's a mix for those of you who can't have or don't want milk:
- 2 cans (13 ounces) full-fat coconut milk
- ¼ cup sugar (or coconut sugar)
- 2 teaspoons vanilla (or whatever flavor you want to add)

1. Pop your ice cream ingredients in the blender and whizz them up!

2. Divide your mixture into two quart-size ziplock bags and make sure they are sealed tightly and have no leaks.

3. Put 1 cup of rock salt in each gallon bag, and fill each bag with ice.

4. Put your cream bags inside the salty ice bags and zip the bags closed.

5. Set one bag aside, cover it in a towel, and just leave it alone. This will act as a control.

6. Put on your gloves and start shaking the other bag. Don't make the mistake we made by tipping it upside down. Keep it upright so that you won't have a dirty, salty mess all over the floor!

7. Shake, shake, shake your booty (and the bag) for 15 minutes. You'll build up an appetite.

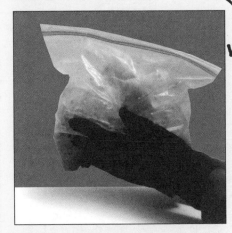

8. Open the gallon bag and take out your cream bag. Compare it to the bag you set aside. Is there a difference? Write down what you notice.

9. Once you've written down your observations, you can enlist your friend or sibling to shake the control bag too, so that you'll have more ice cream to eat. Once you've shaken each bag for 15 minutes, if it's still not frozen enough, close it up, pop it back in the ice-bath bag (perhaps with a few more cubes of ice), and shake some more! Or you can cheat and put the mostly frozen bag in the freezer for a while.

10. Finally, the yummy part! When it is frozen to perfection, rinse off the bag under some cool water (eating rock salt water in your ice cream is really icky!). Then scoop out the ice cream, add whatever toppings you like—mushy peas or squid bits—and lick away.

11. To clean up, you can pour the rock salt and water into a large glass pan and let the water evaporate over the next week. Then you can use the salt again! You can also strain the mixture over the sink and throw away the solid bits. Turn the bags inside out and wash in the sink. Then let them dry and reuse. If you've read GARBAGE (page 97), you know that plastics are already a huge problem, so reuse whenever you can!

WHAT JUST HAPPENED?

Was your hypothesis correct? When you compared shaken versus not shaken bags in step 8, we hope you noticed that the cream in your control (the bag that just sat there) wasn't really frozen. It might have had frozen bits in it, but they would be chunks of ice. . . not fun to eat. The one that you shook was oh-so-creamy. Shaking mixes up the little crystals of ice as they form and spreads them out evenly. Air gets mixed in too, and the fat in the cream is spread out as well. All of this gives it a deliciously smooth texture. *Mmmmm!!*

YUM!

SOMETHING SO COOL IT'S HOT!

GO FETCH

Want to do some REAL chemistry? Well, dear science wizard, today is your day. You're going to make sodium acetate, a really interesting chemical, and then get it to crystallize on your command. It's a super-cool "super-cooled" liquid! And all it takes is good ol' vinegar and baking soda, and a little bit of patience. Well, a LOT of patience. . . . This takes a long time to boil and may not even work the first time you try it. But persevere, and your labors will be rewarded with lots of hot-and-cold fun.

1. Pour the vinegar into a medium saucepan.

2. Add 1 tablespoon of baking soda at a time, letting the bubbles disappear before you add more. Enjoy the show each time!

3. Stir (once all 4 tablespoons have been added).

4. If you have a lot of patience, then you could just set this on a shelf and let it evaporate for 2 weeks. But if you want it sooner, then put the saucepan on the stove and turn on low heat. Leave the cover off. It will take between 1 to 2 hours to boil off all the water. The lower your heat, the less likely it is to turn yellow. (But since this book is about icky things, you might like making something that looks like yellow snow. If you don't mind, then you could boil it down in about a half hour.) Enjoy reading more of this book while you wait.

5. You want to boil off about 90 percent of the liquid. When the liquid level gets low, keep a close eye on it.

An adult to help with hot liquids

4 cups white vinegar

4 tablespoons baking soda

Medium saucepan (stainless steel, enamel, or glass. Don't use copper!)

Spoon

Container that can go in the fridge and microwave, like a plastic takeout dish or a coffee mug covered with plastic wrap

Refrigerator

Plate

Thermometer (optional)

You are looking for little crystals to form on the top, similar to the ice fronds that form on a cold window.

As soon as you see crystals, take the pan off the heat and cover it (this prevents more evaporation from happening). You now have *sodium acetate trihydrate*.

6. Pour the liquid into another container and cover with plastic wrap or another kind of cover. Scrape some crystals off the sides and bottom of

---

the pot to save for later. You can put those in a separate container or on a small plate. Don't wash out your saucepan yet. You might need it again if your first try doesn't work.

7. Chill your liquid in the refrigerator until it is cold to the touch. Or, if you are getting impatient, make an ice bath for your liquid by putting some ice cubes in a baking dish, and add some water. You could even throw a little rock salt into the ice bath because now you know that makes it even colder! Put your container of liquid in the ice bath, being careful to keep it covered.

8. Once your liquid feels cool to the touch, take the temperature with a clean thermometer. It will likely be 15–20°C (59–68°F).

9. Drop one of the crystals you set aside into the liquid. What happens? The liquid should turn into solid crystals really fast! And it should get surprisingly HOT! That's hot-AND-freezing! Amazing! If nothing happens, dump it back in the pot, add a little more vinegar, and boil it down again. Our first "failed" batch froze instantly when we added a teaspoon of vinegar, stirred, and poured it all back in our saucepan! (Another method to get the liquid to freeze is

---

to sprinkle a tiny bit of baking soda on it. This will contaminate the mix, so after it freezes, add a teaspoon of vinegar, mix, and boil it down a little.) If you get really frustrated, or are really into this ick-speriment, your friendly adult can purchase sodium acetate trihydrate online. It will make nice white crystals instead of these homegrown yellow ones.

10. Feel the "ice." What do you notice? If you have a thermometer, stick it in the "ice" and take the temperature. That's hot!

11. Want to play again? Melt the sodium acetate in your saucepan. Even easier, nuke it for 45 seconds in your microwave in a microwave-safe covered mug or plastic container. Swirl to make sure all the crystals melted. Then cover it and put it back in the fridge until it's cool. Always keep it covered once it's become liquid sodium acetate trihydrate. You can use it over and over again if you keep it clean.

12. Clean up your mess and wash everything with soap and water so that the dishes will be safe to use for food again.

WHAT JUST HAPPENED?

You made "hot ice"! Yes, it is really frozen, but don't use it to chill your drinks. It will actually warm them up! And though it's not toxic, it sure tastes nasty.

If you've already read about acids and bases (page 11), you know that when you mix vinegar and baking soda, you get a chemical reaction. Mixing those two produces carbon dioxide gas (which you saw bubbling up), water, and sodium acetate. That's three new products! When you boiled down the liquid, you made a special kind of product called sodium acetate trihydrate. Putting it in the fridge cooled it quickly to make a super-cooled liquid. Basically, super-cooled means you cooled it *below* the temperature at which it would usually freeze into a solid, but it didn't become solid.

Here's the really "cool" part. Super-cooled liquids will freeze really quickly, but they need a little kick-start. Add something like a piece of dust or another crystal, and the liquid will start to crystallize around the solid bit until it's all frozen! This happens in nature too. Freezing rain is an example of super-cooled water. It's liquid, but it freezes the second it hits the road or your car's windshield. Sliiiiippery!

But why did your "ice" get hot? Heat is released when molecules go from a less ordered state (moving around in the liquid) to a more ordered state (being stuck in a crystal). When they were in liquid form, the water molecules were actually zooming around with quite a bit of energy (not as much energy as they'd have in a gas, but more than in ice). When they were forced to sit still in ice—or mostly still; they still vibrate, kind of like kids trying to sit still in class—the energy they had was released into the surrounding air as heat. That's why

the ice felt hot! And that's the way many instant hand warmers work!

Want more fun? Try making hot towers! Put one of the tiny crystals from your pan on a small plate. Begin to pour the super-cooled liquid slowly onto your plate, right over the tiny crystal. The liquid should immediately start crystalizing, and you can make a tall ice tower.

Pick up one of those extra crystals you set aside with a small spoon and stick it in the super-cooled liquid. The liquid should form solid "ice" around the spoon. We don't recommend using your finger, as the liquid gets quite hot!

That's enough hot and cold ice cream for now. Time to move on to the world of INSECTS!

Insects

Your basic ant can definitely be annoying, but usually not too scary. When you see an ant, you normally don't run away screaming and flailing your arms. But the same is not true for, say, a swarm of bees, or a beetle that can snap a pencil in half with its mouth, or a gang of 10,000 cockroaches slobbering in your dog's dinner bowl. Those creepy-crawlers are a whole 'nother story!

BAD LITTLE BUGGERS

There are a lot of bugs we fear . . . and for good reason! Bedbugs! Stinkbugs! Bugs that sting! Bugs that suck your blood! Bugs with venomous bites! And think about this: What's the deadliest creature out there? Sharks, maybe? Crocodiles? Guess again! Sharks kill about 10 people a year and crocs about 1,000 unlucky folks. The winner of this deadly contest? Those very small, annoying, itchy little buzz kills, mosquitoes—murderers of over a million people a year. How? Mosquitoes can infect people with deadly diseases such as malaria, West Nile virus, and dengue fever.

Wouldn't it just be glorious if there were no bugs? Nothing to swat at. Nothing to step on. No insect-borne diseases. Sounds awesome! But think again. The truth is, a world without insects would be flat-out disgusting. For starters, we would be waist-high in poop and trash. Many insects are decomposers—they eat our garbage. It would be like the ultimate sanitation workers' strike, except that piled-up trash would be the least of our problems.

Think about all the planet's plants. Plants don't get married and have babies. Plants reproduce in a very different way, and they need insects to help them do it. Many insects are *pollinators* (paul-lin-ay-torz). Pollen is a key ingredient in the way plants make new plants, and insects are the mail delivery people for this oh-so-important stuff. Bees and butterflies are the superstars of pollination. Teeny pollen grains stick to their bodies like yellow dandruff as they suck sweet nectar. When they fly off to the next plant, the pollen comes with them and gets snagged by a sticky little "finger" in the flower called the *stigma*. The plant now has everything it needs to make seeds! Thank you, bees and butterflies!

Bet you didn't know that "wearing" bees is a sport. The world record, set in 2014, was the wearing of 637,000 bees—more than 100 pounds of pure buzz!

So, bottom line: no bees, butterflies, and other pollinators, no new flowering plants. That means no food for many species. Those species that eat plants and fruit would have nothing to munch on and *they* would soon die of hunger. The creatures that eat the plant eaters would also go hungry. Suddenly we would all be starving to death. To top it off, there would be less oxygen to breathe because so many plants—which take in carbon dioxide and release the oxygen that we need to survive—couldn't reproduce. So, maybe that world without insects isn't such a good idea after all?

Gotcha! This fellow is on a bug safari.

I WAS MYTH-INFORMED

Spiders are insects too, right? Wrong! Spiders belong to the class Arachnida, while insects belong to the class Insecta. A spider is as different from a beetle as a goldfish is from a giraffe. Check out ARACHNIDS (page 4) to learn more.

ICK-SPLORATION · **30 MINUTES**

INSECT SAFARI

GO FETCH →

Hunting for bugs is one of the easiest and most fun activities for anyone who loves creepy-crawlies. And with a million known species of insects in the world, you'll have a lot to discover. Who needs lions, zebras, or rhinos when you can get buggy?

1. Okay, so you're going on an insect hunt. Where should you start? Well, there's no wrong place to look, but here are five suggestions:

● Windowsills (the graveyard of so many flying insects)

● Under rocks and logs (almost always occupied)

● On plants, especially flowers (insects are big-time pollinators)

● Lights that are on at nighttime (irresistible to moths and other bugs)

● Ponds or streams (aquatic insects are signs of healthy ecosystems). Don't be afraid to lift up some rocks and look for larvae (baby insects).

2. Catch the critter! For slow-moving (or dead) insects, tweezers can be helpful. For faster ones, you might be able to capture them with a jar or net. Be smart: Leave stinging insects like bees and wasps alone, and while you're hunting, keep an eye out for spiders, snakes, and poison ivy or poison oak.

3. Look at your critter closely. Perhaps it looks familiar; perhaps you have no clue what

Besides your eyes and bare hands, you might find these useful:

Containers with lids

Magnifying glass

Tweezers

Butterfly net

Insect identification guide from your local bookstore, or search online for an "insect identification key"

it is. Under a magnifying glass, it probably looks entirely alien. But the million-dollar question is, "Is it an insect?"

WHAT JUST HAPPENED?

So how do you pick an insect out in a police lineup? Insects have three, and only three, pairs of legs. If your creepy-crawly has more than six legs, it's not an insect. Insects also have three major body sections: a head, a thorax, and an abdomen. Less or more? Not an insect! Most have wings, two eyes, and antennae. But that's not true for all insects. Keep in mind, these requirements only apply to the adults. Like a lot of things in life, the rules for kids are different. Many larvae don't have any legs. None have working wings, and most look nothing like they will when they grow up. Just ask the nearest maggot!

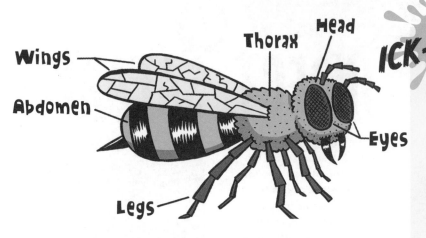

Wings
Abdomen
Thorax
Head
Eyes
Legs

EXOSKELETON EGG DROP CHALLENGE!

40 MINUTES

GO FETCH →

- 1 egg (3 if you want the ultimate challenge and a big mess)
- Household recyclables (milk carton or egg carton, newspaper, paper towel rolls, paper cups, etc.)
- Pipe cleaners, garbage twist ties, or straws (for insect legs and antennae)
- Scissors
- Miscellaneous supplies, depending on your design (paper, tape, string, stapler)
- Markers or pens (to give your insect some personality)
- Measuring tape or ruler
- Something to clean up a broken egg (if your first design doesn't succeed)

A FACE ONLY A MOTHER COULD LOVE

How to tell if the critter you're looking at is an insect or not? Peer at that buggy head. You should see eyes, a mouthpart, and antennae (depending on the insect, the antennae can be used for sensing touch, smell, and taste, as well as wind, heat, and if something is wet). The head is also insect command central—home of the insect's brain. But a bug brain doesn't have the same importance that yours does. An insect can survive headless for several days provided it hasn't lost a lot of "insect blood," which is actually called *hemolymph*. Since it breathes through holes in its body (called *spiracles*), it can still get air. But with no eyes to catch food or mouth to eat with, eventually it will starve.

Study the thorax. The thorax is the middle part that makes an insect mobile. If it has wings, they will be attached here. Its legs will be attached here too. On a grasshopper, you can look near the base of the middle leg for a small breathing hole called a *thoracic spiracle*. That's right, it's breathing through its leg! Look carefully at your bug's feet if you can. They might have little hooks, or sticky bits, or even small suckers. All the better to cling with, my dear.

Now examine the abdomen. You might be able to see breathing spiracles on the sides of each abdominal segment. The abdomen brings up the rear and digests the food, makes the female's eggs, holds a stinger if the insect has one, and produces buggy poop, which is called *frass*. It rhymes with *gas*. But several thrifty insects use their frass for food, defenses, and best yet—construction materials. Home, poopy home.

Have you ever brushed an ant off a picnic table and then watched it walk away unharmed? Have you thought about how amazing this is? The height of the picnic table is enormous compared to the size of the ant. It'd be like someone pushing you off a 60-story building and you walking away without a scratch. There are two reasons an insect can survive a death-defying fall: It has very little mass, and its body is surrounded by a handy exoskeleton (see page 140). Your task: Build a 3-D insect model that holds an egg, and then drop your megabug from 5 feet without breaking the egg.

1. Design and build your insect model. You only have a few rules to follow. Your insect needs to have a soft inside and a hard outside. Your insect needs to have three separate body parts (head, thorax, and abdomen). Your insect needs six legs. Finally, you have to put an egg inside it. No cheating: It can't be hard-boiled! Some hints: A wider and lighter design can help with air resistance. Also, think about what materials are used to cushion things you mail or delicate grocery store items—these materials might help protect the egg too. Note: *If you want an ultimate challenge, put an egg*

in each of the three sections of the insect's body.

2. Select a hard surface to drop your insect on. Be smart: Do this outside or in a place that you can easily clean up if the egg breaks. You might stand on a stepladder and drop it on the driveway or hold it up high and drop it in the bathtub.

3. It's time for "Parachutes away!" except without the parachutes. Make sure your insect is 5 feet in the air and then drop it.

4. Judgment time: Is your egg safe and sound, or is it now a Humpty Dumpty look-alike that was sacrificed in the name of entomological science?

WHAT JUST HAPPENED?

Hopefully your fake insect survived, but how do real insects survive falls that would be lethal to so many other animals? The first reason is that they aren't falling very quickly when they hit the ground. All falling objects speed up as they fall, but they eventually reach their own *terminal velocity* and stop accelerating. This is because there is another force at work:

air resistance. Air resistance, or drag, pushes up on a falling object, slowing it down. Terminal velocity is when the force of gravity (pulling down) and the air resistance (pushing up) become equal—and the object falls at a constant speed. Exactly when this happens is determined by the shape, size, and mass of the falling object. Insects are so small and have such little mass that their surface area creates a kind of parachute, which creates more air resistance and slows them down. An ant would hit the ground at only about 4 miles per hour (tiny ouch) even if it jumped out of an airplane; a human without a parachute would hit the ground at well over 100 miles per hour (big splat).

The exoskeleton is the second reason insects could be fearless trapeze artists. An exoskeleton is made primarily of *chitin*, a tough molecule also found in lobster shells. It's somewhat similar to our fingernails. An exoskeleton is like a car bumper: It's strong but flexible, designed to deform slightly in crashes to absorb impact. If your egg survived the drop, it was because something other than the egg absorbed the energy of impact. If it didn't survive, celebrate your failure (because we often learn the most from failing). Figure out what went wrong, and try, try again!

can you pick out the insects in this lineup?

It's molting time! This cicada has got himself a new exoskeleton.

WE'RE OUTNUMBERED!

Who's really the royalty of the living critters on planet Earth? Insects! They win the prize for the largest number of different species (more than one million have been found, and there may be 30 million more crawling out there, undiscovered!). They also top the charts for the greatest actual number of living bugs—about 10,000,000,000,000,000,000. Too long a number to read? That's 10^{19} or 10 quintillion for you lazy bugs. That means that for every one human being, there are more than 1 billion crawling, burrowing, and swarming bugs. Here's another way to look at it. Get the world's most ginormous scale and take all the elephants in Africa and weigh them. Now take all the teeny termites in Africa and pile them up on the same scale. Just that one species of insect alone would outweigh those massive pachyderms, and by a lot! (It's 445 million tons of termites to 2 million tons of elephants.)

Not only are there tons of insects everywhere, but they can survive under the most extreme conditions. Think of the most terrible location you can imagine—someplace so awful that nothing can live there. Surprise! There will be a bunch of critters that not only get by, but thrive. They can chill in the Arctic, so well adapted to the cold life that they will actually die of heat just by being held in a human palm. A type of fly can live in bubbling black crude oil pools, and others can survive the hottest desert. There's even a type of insect that can go without water for months and months, completely dry out, look totally dead, and then return to life when the rainy season begins. Amazing!

I'M MOLTING!

One reason for insects' world domination is the way they are made. You know how the Knights of the Round Table wore armor for protection? Insects do too, except theirs doesn't rust or weigh a ton! It's called an *exoskeleton*, and it is a hard, protective covering on the outside of an insect's body. There's even a thin layer of exoskeleton on its eyes. There's one wee problem with having a hard exoskeleton. It's hard to grow bigger if you are encased in a coat of armor.

Imagine if we humans didn't have skeletons. We'd basically be just like jellyfish—a collection of soft, squishy organs making a gloppy mess on the floor. Not only do our skeletons help us stand, they provide a scaffold for all our body parts to connect to one another. Most important, they protect all of our delicate innards.

In humans and other animals with skeletons on the inside, everything has room to grow because there are spaces between our bones. You may have noticed your own hands, feet, and legs have grown a lot since this time last year. Your inner organs—like the heart, liver, lungs, and brain—are growing too. But if you were an insect, your lengthening legs would bump into your exoskeleton and get trapped. So, as an insect grows to adulthood, every once in a while it must shed its protective armor and grow a new one. This can happen anywhere from a handful to a few dozen times in an insect's lifetime.

Just as you couldn't exist without a skeleton, neither can an insect, so

I'M NOT A TRUE BUG.

I WAS MYTH-INFORMED

Lots of people call insects, spiders, millipedes, and any creepy-crawly a "bug." But in fact, if you want to get technical, bugs are a particular type of insect. True bugs include bedbugs, stinkbugs, water striders, and other members of a group called Hemiptera. So, all bugs are insects, but not all insects are bugs.

when it grows it develops a larger (wrinkled-up) exoskeleton under its existing outer layer. When it's shedding time, the insect takes a deep breath (or swallows water), puffs up, and splits apart (or disconnects) from the old shell. The insect then crawls out of the shell in a new soft skin. The new layer will expand and harden as the bug fills out the space and—*ta-da*—this bigger, juicier bug is ready to crawl or fly about. Molting can be a dangerous time for an insect because it sits still while its new skeleton hardens, making it an easy target for birds and other predators. (Eighty-five percent of insect deaths occur during molting!)

TO SCREAM OR NOT TO SCREAM?

What are the biggest, heaviest, scariest, most dangerous insects out there, and what should you do if you see one? Here's a handy guide!

How would you like to smooch a stag beetle?

1. Asian Giant Hornets They're bigger than a grown-up's thumb and look like they're saying, "Don't mess with me, buddy." If you are a honeybee in Eastern Asia, be very, very afraid. One of these hornets can rip apart 40 bees in a minute. They destroy whole beehives because they like to feed honeybee larvae to their young. This hornet usually doesn't sting people, but if it does, it might sting again and again, with a particularly toxic venom that can destroy a person's kidneys. Other than that, they're adorable. . . . Just kidding. If you see one, SCREAM. (Or eat it. In Japan, they enjoy them deep-fried!)

2. Botflies You know how you have a favorite food? Botflies, which live in Africa and South America, are like that. But they like things like horse stomach and sheep nostril. Here's how they sneak onboard a living host. Let's say you are a horse. You're just standing around when a little bee look-alike fly starts to hover and dive-bomb you, laying its eggs on the hairs of your legs and other body parts. Later you happen to lick those hairs, and in your warm, moist mouth, the eggs start to hatch. The larvae then make themselves at home in your mouth, where they can create pus pockets and even loosen your teeth! Then you swallow them, and they get cozy in your stomach, where they cause you all sorts of digestive problems. When they are finally ready to move on to their final life stage, they take a ride out in a pile of poop, where they hang out for about two months before finally becoming adult flies. See a pile of horse manure with a horde of flies emerging? If you're a sheep or horse, SCREAM!

3. Giant Stick Insects

These residents of Borneo, an island that forms part of Malaysia, Brunei, and Indonesia, look like creeping tree branches—tree branches that can be up to 2 feet long and can walk! Plus, the sticks have nymphs (babies) with wings, which is unusual for insects. But DON'T SCREAM. They might be a little strange-looking, but they aren't dangerous.

4. Titan Beetles

How about a flying bug that's bigger than a hamster—one with jaws powerful enough to snap a pencil in half, and the ability to make a horrible hissing noise when it's feeling ornery? Actually, DON'T SCREAM. Titan beetles, which mainly live in the Amazon rain forest and are the largest species of beetle, are usually harmless to people, unless you step on one and have to figure out how to get it off the bottom of your shoe.

THE ANTS GO MARCHING TWO BY TWO . . .

How does one ant tell his buddies how to get to a really great all-you-can-eat buffet on the next street over? And then how does that ant get home again? They can't just open their mouths and speak, so most ants use smell as a road map. As they walk in search of food, they leave behind a scent trail. When it's time to head back home, they sniff the ground, find the trail, and march safely back to the nest.

That system works perfectly on firm and solid ground, like pavement or dirt. But what about ants that live in the desert, where it is sandy and windy? The scent an ant leaves behind can end up being blown in 10 different directions! Now how is the ant going to get home?

Scientists at the University of Ulm in Germany had an idea. They believed that desert ants counted the number of steps they took as they left their nests so they knew just how many steps to take to get back home. But how to test that idea?

The scientists gathered a group of desert ants, created a nest, and left a food source about 33 feet (10m) away. The ants marched out to the food, but just as they were about to eat, the scientists grabbed them and divided them into three groups.

One group was left unchanged. Phew! Lucky ants! The second group had rigid pig bristles superglued to their legs. Imagine ants on stilts! These ants' legs were now twice as long as they had been. The third group faced a different fate. Their legs were snipped off at the knees. (It's okay—desert ants' leg tips sometimes break off due to the extreme desert heat and age. Once ants molt again, they can grow their legs back.) Amazingly the ants could still walk after this, but since they had short, stubby little legs, they could only take baby steps.

All the ants were returned to the food source. When it was time to head back to the nest, something amazing happened. The lucky ants who had been untouched made it back home with no problems. But the super-tall ants, taking bigger, longer steps, walked right past their nest and then stopped—confused. The snipped stubby-legged ants, taking smaller, shorter steps, stopped well before reaching the nest. All three groups had taken the exact same number of steps!

The scientists placed the superglued and snipped ants back in the nest, curious to find out what would happen on the following day. The ants emerged to seek their chow. They all walked to the food source. And when it was time to head home, all the ants made it safely back. The altered ants had counted the number of steps it had taken with their new stride lengths. And all made it back to the nest with no trouble at all.

Professor James Gould, a bug specialist at Princeton University in New Jersey, explains what happened: "It's a matter of counting steps. And if you are taking giant steps, well, that's fine. It's now 10 giant steps to the food source and 10 back. And if you're taking baby steps, maybe it's 40 to the food source and 40 back. But the point is, because you're counting the steps, you know exactly how far to come back."

PICKY BUGS

GO FETCH →

15 MINUTES

PLUS OBSERVATIONS OVER SEVERAL HOURS

We know you're probably choosy about what you eat. Do you think ants or other insects are too? Let's find out what they like the most and what makes them gag. If you find things that repulse them, you can use it as insect repellent!

1. Make a prediction about which food (or nonfoods) the insects might like or dislike. Also predict what insects might come along.

2. Place a variety of foods on plates and set the plates near an anthill, or in another area where you know there are insects.

3. Wait for a few hours and keep checking back to see what's happening at your "neighborhood diner."

6 small plates

Tape and a permanent marker to label your plates

Foods (or nonfoods) to try, such as: Salt (mix it with some water) • Sugar (mix it with some water) • Vinegar • Orange peels and/ or orange slices • Doughnuts or cookies • Carrot or celery sticks • Apple slices • Spinach leaves • Vanilla • Cinnamon • Baby powder • Chalk dust • Borax powder (be careful handling this and wash your hands afterward) • Coffee grounds or old teabags • Hot pepper—either powder or an actual pepper (be careful with this and wash your hands before touching your eyes!)

Anthill or another insect-filled area where you can leave the plates

Camera (optional, but fun to record changes over time)

4. You might leave these overnight if your adult agrees. Then get out your notebook and jot down some observations the next day.

WHAT JUST HAPPENED?

You will likely see that ants and other insects go to certain plates and not to others. We noticed that our ant went over to the vinegar but practically bounced away when it got close. Once it found the sugar water, however, it couldn't get enough. Later there were swarms of ants around the sugar water and the orange (but not the orange peel), and just a few ants investigating and then walking away from the salt water and the vinegar. They know what they like. In fact, chalk, baby powder, cinnamon, coffee grounds, vinegar, and citrus peels are all known as ant repellents, and borax is used to kill closet moths. We love insects in the wild, but in our house? No, thanks! Many people try to keep their homes insect-free with these types of natural repellents. Ask your grown-up, and maybe you can too!

ORANGE PEELS ORANGE SLICE

Be Patient!! It may take a while for the insects to discover your plates. You can just go off and play for a while, returning every 10 minutes or even every hour, or you could sit nearby with a good book, and peek every few pages. You could also do what we did once when we got impatient: Catch an ant on a leaf and then drop it into a plate. Observe its behavior. Then convince it to walk onto the leaf again and then drop it on a different plate.

5. Tarantula Hawk If you've read about arachnids on page 4, you know that a tarantula is a pretty scary-looking creature. So an insect that preys on tarantulas has got to be *super* scary. Tarantula hawks aren't actually hawks—they're wasps with hooks on their legs that snare their eight-legged

victims and flip them over so they can sting them. If you are unlucky enough to somehow get mistaken for a tarantula, their super-sharp stinger can leave you in a world of pain. DEFINITELY SCREAM!

Bugs are pretty cool, huh? Did you know that some bugs like to hang out around volcano summits? And speaking of volcanoes . . . LAVA, up next!

Lava

When a fart erupts from deep within your body, it can be pretty noxious. It may even clear a room in seconds. But when the Earth erupts, the gaseous emissions are a whole lot more dangerous. Scaldingly stinky. Toxic-ly gassy. A big, bubbling, hot, oozing mess of deep Earth goo—otherwise known as *lava* (lah-vah).

WHEN THE EARTH FARTS

Volcanoes are named after Vulcan, the god of fire in Roman mythology. He was one scary character—hurling fireballs hither and yon. When volcanoes erupt, they kind of do the same thing—ash, gas, and liquid rock explode in a powerful burst of fire. Volcanoes are basically holes (or shafts) in our planet's surface that can appear as gently sloping domes or as mountains that rise up from deep within the Earth. Many are under the ocean! Most of these volcanic shafts are quiet and calm. But once in a while things get a little crazy beneath the Earth's surface, and all heck breaks loose. *Magma* (mag-muh)—a scalding stew of liquid and semi-liquid rocks mixed with poisonous gases—spews up to the surface. Once it erupts, it is renamed lava. In time this amazing river of molten inner-Earth goo will cool and harden, forming volcanic rock and volcanic glass.

What makes the Earth shoot off these mighty, often deadly, rock-and-gas farts? Well, our planet's surface is made of lots of very s-l-o-w-l-y moving giant chunks, kind of like huge puzzle pieces. At the places (or boundaries) where these pieces crash into one another or pull apart, cracks occur in the Earth's surface, giving the hot melted rock an escape route. These puzzle pieces of the Earth's surface are called *tectonic plates*. The official "impress the grown-ups" name for the theory of their movement is *plate tectonics*. Read more about it in QUAKES AND SINKHOLES on page 190, but here's a little hands-on crash course.

HUMPTY-DUMPTY EARTH

The next time someone is cooking eggs, ask if one can be spared (and soft-boiled, please) for an experiment. Let the egg cool for ten minutes, then put it on a few layers of paper towel and gently roll it around. Now press a little harder so that the shell starts to crack. Roll it and press down more firmly still. What do you notice?

The broken shell of the egg is a lot like the Earth's crust. It's cracked in a bunch of places. Each of those chips of eggshell represents one of the Earth's tectonic plates. When you pressed more urgently on your eggy Earth, the

Have you ever shaken

a can of soda and then opened it? The soda erupted because of a sudden release of pressure. Volcanoes work the same way—the pressure builds up and then, POW! Lava spews from the Earth.

"plates" started to move and spaces opened up between some of them. When you really pressed hard, stuff started to ooze out between the cracks. When that happens to our planet, instead of egg, you get molten magma seeping out, and no one wants to eat a magma omelet!

JOURNEY TO THE CENTER OF THE EARTH!

Hop right in! All aboard a giant heatproof elevator headed for the center of the Earth! On your trip down you'll pass through four layers.

Lava Scrub!

When a lot of gas spews out of a volcano, it can turn lava into a molten froth, and when this frothy lava cools, it forms amazingly light stones full of tiny holes, called pumice. They can even float on water! You can buy pumice stones at your nearest drugstore. They are perfect for sanding the dead skin off the soles of your feet!

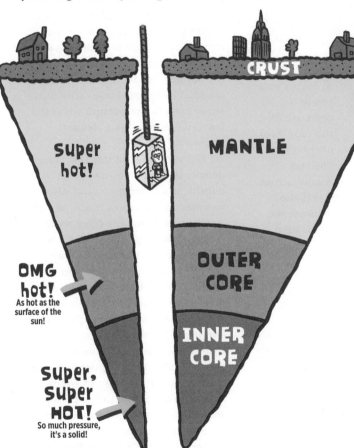

Super hot!

OMG hot!
As hot as the surface of the sun!

Super, super HOT!
So much pressure, it's a solid!

CRUST
MANTLE
OUTER CORE
INNER CORE

The Crust: That's the solid stuff we stand on, build our gardens and homes upon, and drill for oil through. It's the thinnest layer, averaging about 25 miles (40 km) thick on continents. Overall, it's *way* thinner than the cartoon above shows it to be. It's only about 5 miles (8 km) thick in oceans, but can be as thick as 62 miles (100 km) under some mountain ranges.

The Mantle: Next stop, Earth's thickest layer—the stuff the crust floats on. It's about 1,800 miles (2,900 km) thick. Are you sweating yet? It's getting pretty hot down here! Where the mantle meets the crust it's a balmy 1,830°F (1,000°C). As we hurtle deeper down, the temperature soars to a VERY steamy 6,690°F (3,700°C). For the most part, the mantle isn't molten. It's solid rock, but it still flows like a liquid. How can that be? Picture a ball of Silly Putty or oobleck (for an oobleck recipe, see page 208). If you let the putty or oobleck sit for a while, it begins to ooze very slowly. But if you hit it with a hammer, it shatters like a solid. The mantle is like that. While it's mostly solid rock, over the geological timescale of millions of years, it moves around and flows more like a liquid. Much of the magma that explodes from a volcano comes from this layer, when small areas of the mantle actually do melt and become liquid rock.

The Outer Core: Third stop on our journey to the center of the Earth. It's REALLY hot down here! This layer of Earth is about 1,360 miles (2,200 km) thick with temperatures ranging from 8,130°F (4,500°C) to a whopping 10,800°F (6,000°C) as you near the inner core. (That's as hot as the surface of the sun!) The outer core is mostly made of the metals iron and nickel. They are completely melted into a violently churning liquid metal mixture.

The Inner Core: Hot, hot, hot! You're in the last 770-mile (1,240 km) stretch. Although it's definitely hot enough to melt metal (about 9,400°F; 5,200°C), there's so much pressure from the rest of the Earth pressing on the metals here that they have actually turned *back* into a scalding, solid ball.

AN EARTH PARFAIT

20 MINUTES

GO FETCH →

Alas, there's no way to journey to the center of the Earth, so you can't see its layers. But if you do this ick-tivity, you'll get a good sense of how Earth's layers "float" on top of each other. It's a fun demonstration of density too.

1. Pour ½ cup of dish soap into the glass.

2. Mix ½ cup of water with 1 drop of blue food coloring in a measuring cup.

3. Gently tilt the glass and slowly pour the blue water down the side of the glass so that the water sits on top of the dish soap layer.

4. Gently tilt the glass again and slowly pour 1 cup of vegetable oil down the side and on top of the blue water layer.

5. Mix 1 tablespoon of rubbing alcohol with 4 drops of red food coloring in a measuring cup.

6. By now you're a pro at this: Gently tilt the glass and slowly pour the red alcohol on top of the vegetable oil. It's okay if the different liquids seem to mix a bit. If you let it sit for a while, the boundaries between the four layers in your glass will become more distinct as each liquid settles.

GO FETCH

- Tall clear glass
- Dish soap
- Water
- Food coloring (blue and red)
- Vegetable oil
- Rubbing (isopropyl) alcohol
- Measuring cup

WHAT JUST HAPPENED?

The four layers you see in the glass are like the four layers of the Earth. The red alcohol represents the Earth's crust; the vegetable oil represents the mantle; the blue water represents the outer core; and the dish soap

is the inner core. As you know, the Earth's layers aren't all liquid. But they do have different densities. And just like the liquids in the model you made, the Earth's layers are organized by density. The layer with the highest density (the core) is at the center of the Earth, and the least dense layer (the crust) is on the outer edge. This is because, as the Earth was forming and cooling 4.5 billion years ago, the more dense materials sank toward the center, and the lighter materials stayed closer to the surface. It's the same in your model. The densest layer (the dish soap) sank to the bottom while the least dense layer (red alcohol) floated on top.

Not sure what all this talk about density is about? You can think of density as a comparison between an object's mass (how much "stuff" is in it) and its volume (how much space it takes up). (The "stuff" we're talking about is particles of matter like atoms and molecules. And the math to calculate density is mass divided by volume.) Items that are more dense have more matter packed into them. Think of a cotton ball and a similar-size pebble. They are about the same size, but the pebble is much more dense. If you were to weigh a half a cup of each of this experiment's liquids, you would find that the dish soap weighs the most. It has more matter packed into it than the water, oil, and rubbing alcohol do. Hey, that sounds like a cool thing to try!

crust

mantle

outer core

inner core

The massive crater of Santa Ana, a composite volcano in El Salvador, which last erupted in 2005.

THAT VOLCANO IS JUST MY TYPE!

Think all volcanoes are cone-shaped mountains with a crater at the top? Uh-uh! Here are four different kinds for you to explore.

1. Cinder cones are the simplest and most common spewers. They're rather small compared to the other kinds. They're what you think of when you draw a picture of a volcano. Magma bubbles up

About three-quarters of the Earth's volcanoes are found in one area called the Ring of Fire. Well named! This area surrounds the Pacific Ocean in a region where the Earth's tectonic plates are moving quite a lot. (Well, a lot for rocks. They move on a timescale of millions of years. So don't even bother trying to watch.) Alaska and Hawaii are both part of this ring. When a volcano is having a deep, long snooze, we say it is dormant. When it's belching and farting a constant stream of molten lava, it's active. There are about 1,500 active volcanoes worldwide (not counting the ones on the ocean floor) and almost all the doozies are in the Ring. No need to bite your nails to nubbins worrying, though. Only about 500 have erupted, and most of them are just slowly simmering away like a saucepan on a low flame.

and erupts from a single vent. That eruption forms a pile of lava cinders that harden to form a hill, with a bowl-shaped crater in the middle.

2. Composite volcanoes, also called stratovolcanoes, are the big, the beautiful, and the famously fearsome ones like Mount St. Helens. Magma rises to the surface through many tunnels over and over again, as if the Earth cannot stop upchucking. They can explode violently, even from the sides, because tons of pressure builds up from the gases trapped inside. Layers of lava, cinders, and ash settle on slopes, building the mountain up higher and higher.

3. Shield volcanoes form in areas where thousands of cracks in the Earth's crust allow the slow flow of fluid lava to seep great distances over the land, forming a giant shield of black basalt rock. Very icky stuff until it cools. Then it can become a lush island. The islands of Hawaii are actually large shield volcanoes!

Tungurahua, a composite volcano, spews lava, ash, and stones in Ecuador.

LAVA-LICIOUS

GO FETCH →

30 MINUTES FOR PREP AND 4–12 HOURS TO WAIT

Were you expecting to make a vinegar-and-baking-soda volcano here? They're fun and look cool, but they have absolutely nothing to do with what really happens when lava lets loose. In those fake volcanoes, the bubbles foam up because of a chemical reaction between the vinegar and baking soda, which releases a lot of gas. That's not why a real volcano erupts, although lots of vile gases *do* get released during volcanic eruptions. Try this experiment for a real understanding of the ways magma escapes from the Earth. You're going to make a gelatin volcano and then inject it with "magma" until the lava gushes out the top!

1. Boil 1½ cups of water in a kettle or pot. Boiling water can be dangerous, so have an adult help you. Meanwhile, in a separate pot, sprinkle the packets of gelatin over ½ cup cold water. Let it sit for 1 minute. Then add the hot water to the gelatin mixture and stir until the gelatin completely dissolves.

2. Spray the inside of the mixing bowl with cooking spray or wipe it with some vegetable oil (this will prevent the gelatin from sticking to the bowl later on).

3. Have an adult pour the liquid gelatin into the bowl and allow it to cool for several hours in your refrigerator until it's solid. If it feels like you're waiting forever, just ask a real volcano how long *it* had to wait to form. Geological time moves as slow as dirt!

An adult to help with hot liquids and hole poking

2 cooking pots or one cooking pot and a kettle

2 packets of unflavored, powdered gelatin (equaling ½ ounce)

2¼ cups water

Vegetable oil or cooking spray

Large mixing spoon

Medium mixing bowl

Large piece of cardboard (about 1 square foot or big enough to cover the top of your mixing bowl)

Aluminum foil

Something with which you can punch a hole through the cardboard (like an awl, a skewer, or a thin screwdriver)

Cookie sheet or other large tray to catch drops of "magma"

4 tall glasses (of equal height)

Medicine syringe (without a needle) or toy syringe or turkey baster (check your local pharmacy or the grill section of the hardware store)

Red food coloring

Old towel

4. If you're feeling ambitious, repeat steps 1–3 with different-shaped containers (such as a bread

pan, Jell-O mold, or pie plate)—that way, you'll have more volcanoes to experiment with later.

5. Wrap the piece of cardboard with aluminum foil. This will prevent the cardboard from getting too mushy when you put your volcano on top of it.

6. With the help of a friendly adult, poke about four or five small holes near the center of the aluminum foil and cardboard using your awl, skewer, screwdriver, or even the tip of a knife.

7. Put the foil-covered cardboard on top of your cool gelatin-filled mixing bowl and then carefully flip both over so that the gelatin plops down onto the foil. (You may have to wait for the bowl to warm up for a few minutes.) You want the gelatin to cover all the small holes in the cardboard. Congratulations, you now have an aspiring volcano!

8. Get out your cookie sheet and put four glasses on top of it to make a stand for your volcano. This stand will allow you to reach underneath the volcano to the holes you've punched, and the cookie sheet will catch any drips. Rest the cardboard and gelatin on the stand.

9. Fill the syringe with a mixture of water and enough food coloring so you have a dark red liquid.

10. Have the towel handy to catch any drips or leaks. Stick the syringe underneath the cardboard and into one of the holes. Inject the "magma" into the middle of the gelatin volcano very slowly for your first attempt.

Watch as the magma searches for a way out of the ground. Is the magma moving horizontally or vertically through the volcano? Can you predict if and where it will break through the surface and turn into lava? Experiment by injecting more magma into the other holes. If your lava is just leaking out of the bottom of the gelatin, then try more forceful injections and/or poking some skinny holes in the top of the gelatin (to mimic the natural fractures that occur on the Earth). Does the location of the hole affect the way the magma moves? Try making some different gelatin volcanoes with different molds. Does the shape of the volcano affect the way the magma moves?

lava eruption!

WHAT JUST HAPPENED?

Maybe your "magma" slowly leaked out of your volcano, or maybe it gushed out. Your result depends on how your gelatin held together and how quickly you squirted in your magma. Magma is under a lot of pressure, from the Earth and the gases that surround it. When that pressure reaches its limit, the magma escapes through any cracks along the Earth's tectonic plates, erupting or oozing out to our planet's surface.

Magma either moves through existing holes and cracks in underground rocks or makes new cracks. In your transparent volcano, you could see this happening. When the magma finally did break through, it got a name change: lava. Over time, real lava cools and hardens into solid rock called basalt. As with all rocks, it gets weathered by water and wind over the years, and turns into soil. Luckily for all of us, plants love volcanic soil. In time, they will put down roots in this new real estate and turn the blackened ruins into a lush green oasis!

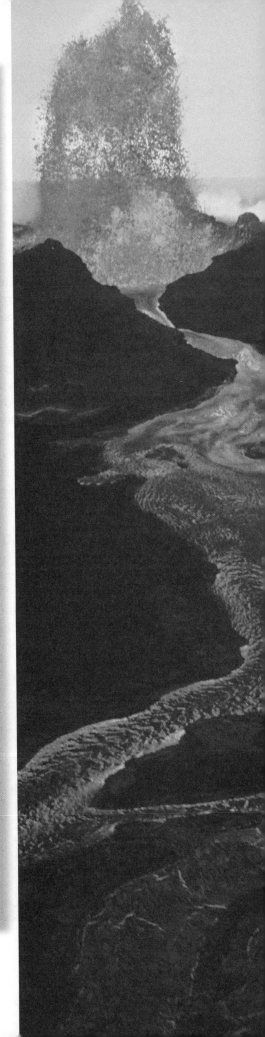

4. Lava domes are globlike bumps formed by lava that was just a bit too thick to flow very far. Instead it just gunkily piled up around the vents. They are smaller than other volcanoes, and often form on the sides of composite volcanoes.

HABLA LAVA? PARLEZ VOUS VOLCANO?

So lava is lava, right? It's all the same blackish, lumpy stuff dripping down a conelike volcano. Wrong! There are different types of lava, depending on the temperature, mineral content, and where the volcano erupts. Learn the different types of lava and become a lava linguist. . . .

A'a This lava is rough and jagged, and even a little spiny. It moves fast, plowing over things like a bulldozer, and it cools quickly, becoming brittle. It makes a cool clinking sound as you walk over it, but you wouldn't want to be barefoot unless you like having totally shredded feet. In fact the name comes from the Hawaiian word for "to burn" and is pronounced like the sound you would make if you walked on it . . . Ah . . . AAAH!!

Pahoehoe (puh-hoy-hoy) When it cools and hardens, this kind of lava can be flat like a parking lot, or look like coils of thick ropes or a gazillion tree roots all mushed together. It cools and moves more slowly than A'a. The name comes from the Hawaiian word *hoe*, for paddle, because it looks like the swirls a paddle makes in water.

Pillow lava On our planet, most volcanoes actually erupt under the sea. Underwater, lava can form something that looks like someplace fluffy to place your sleepy head—but alas, it's hard as a rock!

CELEBRITY VOLCANOES

Some volcanoes erupt and no one is there to applaud (or more likely, to evacuate before their house gets flattened). Other volcanoes become superstar stone blowers. Here are five rock stars.

Pompeii Bad Mount Vesuvius! The only active volcano on mainland Europe, this beast near Naples, Italy, blew its top almost 2,000 years ago in CE 79. People were literally smothered in ash and buried alive. You can still see their eerie remains in the area today. Vesuvius erupts every few decades now (but not since 1944), and with today's volcano warning systems, a disaster that big isn't likely to happen again.

The residents of Pompeii, including pets, died instantly. Casts were made from their remains.

A'a

Pahoehoe

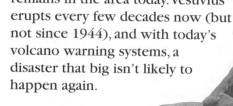

Pillow Lava

The explosions on Krakatoa in Indonesia threw so much debris into the sky that it affected sunsets as far away as New York.

Krakatoa Perhaps you've seen pictures of an atomic bomb exploding? Scary, right? Now, multiply that destructive power by about 13,000 and you will have the terrible force of this island monster, located in the infamous Ring of Fire. People three thousand miles away could hear the explosion in August of 1883, and 36,000 people were killed from the heat and from tsunamis (giant waves of water) that swept over nearby islands afterward. The explosion was so huge and so much lava shot out into the air that most of the island collapsed upon itself and was swallowed up by the sea.

Mount St. Helens This volcano in Washington State lay dormant for 120 years, until 1980, when it started making Earth fart noises. Scientists knew something was definitely up. But in a double whammy of bad geological news, a nearby earthquake weakened the walls of St. Helens and *BANG!* Hot stones exploded out the side and landed as far as 15 miles away, traveling at speeds over 300 miles per hour. A plume of ash soared over 15 miles skyward before falling to Earth and blanketing three states, covering people as far as 250 miles away with black rain.

Mount Tambora Something has to be THE WORST EVER. This volcano in Southeast Asia holds the title for the biggest volcanic eruption in recorded history—an eruption so enormous in 1815 that it totally messed with our planet's climate, making 1816 "the year without summer." So much ash darkened the skies that crops could not grow—even as far away as Europe and North America. People starved as a result.

Mauna Loa The state of Hawaii is comprised of a string of volcanic islands. Most of them are pretty quiet, with the exception of Mauna Loa, the world's largest active volcano. It's over 13,700 feet above sea level, many miles wide, and it has a serious Earth fart problem. It has let loose 33 times since 1843, when people started counting its eruptions.

In 1980, the US mainland had its own violent volcano eruption when Mount St. Helens literally blew its top.

So show a little respect, people. Volcanoes are no laughing matter, and they are awesomely powerful. They have fearsome friends too—earthquakes. If you want to know more now, head over to QUAKES AND SINKHOLES on page 190 and get ready to rumble! Or just turn the page and dive into the world of MUMMIES!

Mummies

Mm, mm, mm-mummies! So creepy! So mysterious! Unless you've been living in a tomb all these years, you've probably heard of those bandaged bodies that lurk in creepy coffins. What's their story? How did they get there? And why are they all wrapped up?

WHAT TO WEAR TO THE GREAT AFTERLIFE PARTY

Mummies might be a little spooky, but mummy making is actually very cool science—a way to preserve a once-living person or animal so it does not decay or crumble into dust. And when it comes to master mummy making, you have to head to ancient Egypt.

More than 5,000 years ago, along the fertile banks of the Nile River, the great Egyptian civilization began to rise. The Egyptians strongly believed in an afterlife—a place where after death a soul would be reunited with its body. Of course, no Egyptian wanted to hang around the afterlife with a rotting body. So Egyptians figured out ways to preserve dead bodies, giving the dearly departed a snazzy "new body" for the afterlife. Like all good scientists, they learned from their mistakes and developed better techniques over time.

It takes serious science smarts to stop the decay that begins the moment someone dies. The ancient Egyptians noticed that the inner organs were some of the first to start rotting in a dead body, so an important early step in the mummy-making process was to make an incision in the body and scoop out all of the wettest organs—like the lungs, intestines, liver, and stomach. This helped to slow the decaying process, because bacteria (which—if you've read BACTERIA, page 20— you know help decompose things) didn't have as much moisture to play in. Egyptian corpses were then bathed in wine, where alcohol zapped even more bacteria.

BRAIN STEW! EW!

The plucked-out organs were packed in salt and preserved in special little jars. Eye sockets were filled in with beeswax, or sometimes small onions for a truly eerie effect. What about the brain, the most vital of the vital organs? Well, the Egyptians didn't see it that way. They'd say, "Who needs a brain in the afterlife? What value could anything have that looks like spoiled gray mac and cheese?" Brains were often scooped out through the nose using a special little hooked spoon and fed to whatever animals were skulking around the mummification room. Some embalmers (the official name for people who prepare bodies for burial) used a slightly different technique. They used a special tool to stir the contents of the skull around and around until

What's more fun than a barrel of monkeys?
A tombful of mummies!

the brains began to liquefy, then let the liquefied brain flow out through the corpse's nose. You can just imagining them yelling, "Here, kitty, kitty, kitty!" and feeding the brain soup to some very happy cats. The heart was left untouched inside the body for a final weigh-in just before the deceased was allowed into the afterlife. The goal was to have such a happy and pure heart that it would weigh the same amount as a feather. Talk about lighthearted!

Early on, the ancient Egyptians noticed that bodies left in the sand dried out and didn't decay very quickly. In fact, the earliest mummies were created naturally, just by burying a body in the hot sands of the Saharan desert. The sand there is rich in a chemical called natron, a mixture of sodium carbonate, baking soda, and salt. Natron does a great job of absorbing moisture out of the body and preventing bacteria from speeding up the decay process.

So after the organ removal and wine bath, mummy makers put the deceased into a tub filled with natron. After leaving it there for almost six weeks (good mummies take time!), the super-salty, moisture-free body became a lot darker. It also

Brain drainers from ancient Egypt

MEET TOASTANKHAMUN

5 MINUTES
TO MAKE MUMMIES & 2 WEEKS TO OBSERVE

GO FETCH

- 2 pieces of plain white bread with no preservatives added
- 2 ziplock plastic bags
- Permanent marker

L et the mummy making begin! Let's start by asking, "Does the amount of moisture in something affect how it decays?"

1. For fun, use the permanent marker to draw on your bread and give each of your pharaohs a face. Place one slice of "pharaoh" in a ziplock bag and seal. Toast the other slice on medium-high until it is crispy. Let it cool completely and then place it in the second ziplock bag and seal. Don't open the bags!

2. What do you think will happen? Will there be differences between the two "pharaohs"? Make a hypothesis, stash the bags somewhere out of the way (and where they won't get tossed), and then check back in two to three weeks.

WHAT JUST HAPPENED?

Y ou probably noticed that the untoasted pharaoh developed many more moldy bits than our toasted king. Bacteria and fungi love moisture. The toasting removed much of Toastankhamun's moisture, so he didn't rot as quickly.

TOASTANKHAMUN (not toasted)

TOASTANKHAMUN (toasted)

MEET SALTANKHAMUN

15 MINUTES

TO MAKE THE MUMMIES & 1 WEEK TO OBSERVE

GO FETCH

A key step in mummy making involves drying out the dearly departed by packing the body in salt. What's the best preservative to keep a mummy unmoldy? Let's compare some different household chemicals and try to mummify some apple slices. What do you think will work best? Make a prediction, then get to work!

1. Label each plastic cup: *baking soda, Epsom salt, table salt,* and *control*.

2. Pour enough baking soda into the cup labeled *baking soda* to just cover the bottom. Place an apple slice in and add the rest of the baking soda so the apple is completely covered.

3. Repeat the procedure with Epsom salt, completely covering the apple.

4. Do it once more using table salt to completely cover the third slice.

5. Put the remaining apple slice in the control cup.

- 4 apple slices of about the same size
- 4 6-ounce clear plastic cups
- Permanent marker to label the cups
- ¾ cup baking soda
- ¾ cup Epsom salt (available at any drugstore)
- ¾ cup table salt

6. Park all four cups where they will be out of the way.

7. What's your hypothesis about what will happen to each slice? Write it down.

8. Wait a week, then take a peek. What happened? Which white sprinkly stuff did the best job at making an apple-mummy?

WHAT JUST HAPPENED?

Not all white powders are created equal. The baking powder was useless in preventing rot. That apple probably looked pretty similar to the control. Epsom salt with its large grains did a better job. But the table salt worked best at keeping Saltankhamun looking fresh as a daisy!

Salt has hygroscopic properties, meaning that it can attract and hold moisture. And, in fact, salt has been used to dry out food for centuries all over the world. In the days before fridges, it was the best way to preserve food. In ancient times salt was worth more than gold in some places! Salt can also draw water out of bacterial cells, which prevents them from reproducing. That stops them from decaying food . . . or mummies, for that matter. Epsom salt is actually not a salt. It is a compound of the elements magnesium and sulfate, but it forms saltlike grains and absorbs some moisture.

became smaller and skinnier, kind of like a deflated ball, so the body was plumped up with wads of cloth and sawdust through that convenient slit used to remove the organs. Oils rich with herbs were also rubbed on the body to make it smell good. Next came a painted-on layer of resin—a sticky sap from pine trees that hardens when exposed to air. Insects and other decomposers cannot snack their way through the rigid resins. It's like trying to eat concrete!

IT'S A WRAP!

The salty, oily, stuffed, and hardened body was now ready for the final touch! Gift wrapping! The ancient Egyptians wanted to keep the body looking as much like the once-alive person as they could. How else would previously dead friends and loved ones, already living in the afterlife, recognize the newcomer? Wrapping with thin, resin-soaked strips of linen helped keep the shape

This cow plopped down, expired where it sat, and became a "nature-made" mummy. It happened in South America in the Atacama Desert, one of the driest places on Earth. The Atacama gets about an inch of rain every 100 years! No moisture = no bacteria. No bacteria = no rot. No rot = a mooooovelous mummy, resting dryly in peace.

of the body and face. It's a lot like the papier-mâché that you might use in art class.

A football-field's worth of cotton or linen would be cut into strips and the wrap session began. Every finger, every toe, every body part was wrapped in layer upon layer of bandages with more resin and lots of good-luck charms stuck in between layers of fabric to ward off grave robbers. The tightly bandaged body was then topped off, either with paint or with a mask of the dead person, before placing the gift-wrapped guy or gal into a special coffin, called a *sarcophagus* (sar-<u>coff</u>-uh-gus).

But that's not all that got buried. If you were a really wealthy Egyptian, or better yet a *pharaoh* (<u>fare</u>-row)—an Egyptian king or queen—your burial goodies would be totally luxurious. Gold masks.

Jewels. Even furniture and boats. All your riches buried right alongside you!

Now it was time for the final step. The mummies were placed in their safe, sturdy sarcophagi, in secret tombs where grave robbers (hopefully) couldn't find them. (Guess how well THAT worked out! Almost every single Egyptian tomb has been ransacked. Grave robbers just do not respect the idea of *rest in peace*.)

MODERN MUMMIES

It's been more than a thousand years since the last Egyptian mummies were made, but some scientists are still obsessed with the process. Egyptologists at the University of York, in England, decided to run an advertisement looking for someone willing to be mummified upon death. A taxi driver named Alan Billis, who was dying of lung cancer, saw the ad. He'd led a pretty ordinary life. The mummification would give his grandchildren something to remember him by, so he decided to go for it. In January 2011, Mr. Billis passed away and the scientists got to work.

They had been experimenting for years to prepare for this moment. They had done over 200 mummification tests using pig parts, but they had never tried doing something with a real, live (ahem . . . well, make that dead) human. They began by making a slit in Mr. Billis's side and plucking out most of his internal organs, including all 28 feet of intestines. Most of the bacteria in our bodies live in our gut, so it definitely had to go! They left his heart

TUT TIME

The pharaoh *Tutankhamun* (<u>Too</u>-tank-ha-men), nicknamed King Tut, is one of the most famous mummies ever. His big claim to fame was that his tomb managed to remain intact for thousands of years. When it was finally located in the 1920s, the archaeologists who found it discovered all sorts of marvelous things inside the tomb, including an amazing solid gold death mask. Tut became the talk of the world! But a lot of folks went mummy crazy as stories of a terrible curse filled the newspapers when a handful of the folks who discovered his tomb died suddenly in the months and years after it was opened. Was it really an ancient curse? Not likely—most of the people who took part in the opening of the tomb went on to live long lives. More like a mummy's blessing!

and brain intact. The empty insides of Mr. Billis were then packed with small bags filled with linen to keep him from flattening out.

The incision was sealed shut with a layer of beeswax and Billis's body was slathered in a goopy mixture of sesame oil, resin, and beeswax. Then, based on mummies they had studied from the height of the Egyptian mummy years, his body was completely submerged in a natron bath for 35 days.

Now comes the gross part: On the 21st day, the super-salty water in the bath turned blood red. The salty fluid had dissolved the blood in all of Mr. Billis's remaining tissues and all that blood was now being "sweated out" into the tub. Finally, after this month-long bath, the body was removed. Next came the "desert" room—a very dry, very warm room, where the body was placed for another two weeks. This mimicked the hot conditions of the Egyptian desert.

By now, Mr. Billis's skin was a mottled gray-green color, but he definitely was not decaying. It was time to gift-wrap him! Each finger, toe, leg, and arm was individually and very carefully wrapped. Eventually his body was completely covered. Once again, Mr. Billis was left to "rest in peace," this time for six more weeks.

Did it work? Did Mr. Billis cease to decompose? The Billis mummy was placed in a CT scan machine that can see inside a body. And ta-da! Even in the deepest tissues remaining in the body, nothing was decaying. He had become a mummy! The scientists plan to keep studying Mr. Billis. Presumably, in a few years he will turn dark and leathery and will look just like the mummies from Ancient Egypt. As for Mrs. Billis, she sometimes goes to visit her mummy hubby, who is on display at the Gordon Museum in London. And her grandkids have been known to wrap themselves up in towels and play "granddad."

MORE MUMMIES, PLEASE!

Some mummies are man-made. Others happen by accident. A mummy is *any* body that has been preserved and has not decomposed. You've seen how heat and salt will dry out a body. Freezing cold is another way to preserve a corpse. A person who perishes in a place where the temperature is rarely or never above freezing will remain much like the food in your freezer—preserved for a *very* long time. How long? In 1991, two hikers high up in the mountain passes of the Italian Alps saw something

ICK-TIVITY

MEET FOODANKHAMUN!

1 HOUR FOR MUMMY MAKING AND 4 WEEKS FOR DRYING

GO FETCH

Make a full-body Egyptian-style mummy from start to finish.

1. Peel the apple with the veggie peeler. Be careful and do not peel your fingers! Now, poke out small dents for the eyes with the tip of the peeler, and scrape away apple bits to form a nose and lips. You are making the head of mighty King Foodankhamun!

2. Place a raisin in each eye spot.

- 1 apple
- Vegetable peeler
- 2 raisins
- 1 grapefruit
- Small plastic knife
- 1/2 cup rubbing alcohol
- Scissors
- An old pillowcase cut into strips about 1/2 inch wide by 12 inches long
- Several toothpicks or kitchen skewers snapped in half
- 2 hot dogs cut in half
- Cinnamon
- Cloves (optional)
- 1 large box of kosher salt (about 2 pounds)
- Brownie pan, about 9 inches x 12 inches

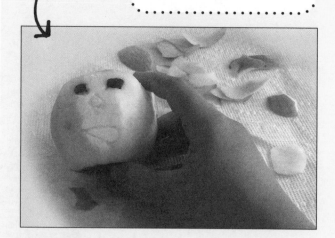

3. Next, get that grapefruit. Carefully cut (or ask your adult to help cut) a 3- to 4-inch slit in one side and, with your fingers, start to scoop out the "internal organs"—in this case, the fruit. Feel free to munch on the grapefruit sections you remove.

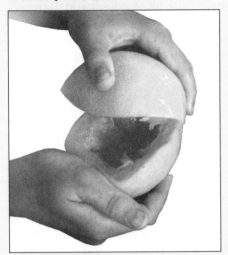

4. The Egyptians bathed the corpse in a bath of wine. Since kids and wine are a no-no, use ½ cup of rubbing alcohol to clean the inside of the "body" by pouring it into the slit you made. Swirl it around and then hold the grapefruit over the sink so it drains. Now stuff the grapefruit with some of the fabric strips to plump it up.

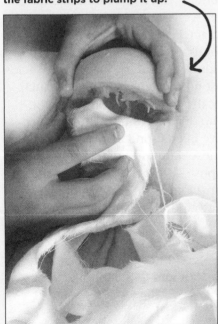

5. Attach the head to the hollowed-out grapefruit using a toothpick. Use toothpicks to attach hot dogs for the arms and legs.

6. No one likes a smelly pharaoh, so sprinkle the "body" with ground cinnamon and cloves, if you have them. These two spices also zap microbes! Think of them as deodorant for the dead.

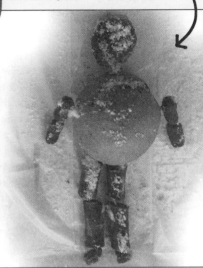

7. Arrange the body in the brownie pan and pour the entire 2-pound box of kosher salt over it until it is completely covered. Now comes the waiting part. It will take about four weeks for Foodankhamun to dry out.

8. After four weeks, place the pan on several sheets of newspaper or a plastic garbage bag and scrape away the salt into a nearby garbage can until your mummy can be moved onto a plate or brownie pan.

9. Observe what's happened to your dearly departed. Give him the sniff test.

10. If you are feeling ambitious, you can wrap the mummy in cloth strips, cut the long way from an old pillowcase. Every kid should have a pet pharaoh!

WHAT JUST HAPPENED?

Bacteria and fungi love moisture, so removing the squishy inner organs helped to eliminate a lot of the "wet" that leads to decay. Bathing the body cavity in alcohol was a second way to zap germs, since the alcohol kills most of them. The spices also helped to ward off microbes. And packing the mummy in salt drew out even more moisture, even from the mummy's hot dog arms and legs. Those moisture-loving microorganisms never stood a chance!

ICK-TIVITY

PLAY MUMMY MAYHEM

20 MINUTES

GO FETCH →

- 1 roll of toilet paper per mummy
- Scotch tape

You think it's easy wrapping a mummy? Grab a roll or two of toilet paper and a "willing victim" and start wrapping!

Begin with the toes on the right leg and GENTLY begin to wrap each toe, then move on to wrapping the foot. You want your mummy to resemble a person, not a box. Plus, a mummy's gotta move! For fun, grab two more friends and have a contest to see who can wrap the fastest, the neatest, and with the least ripping.

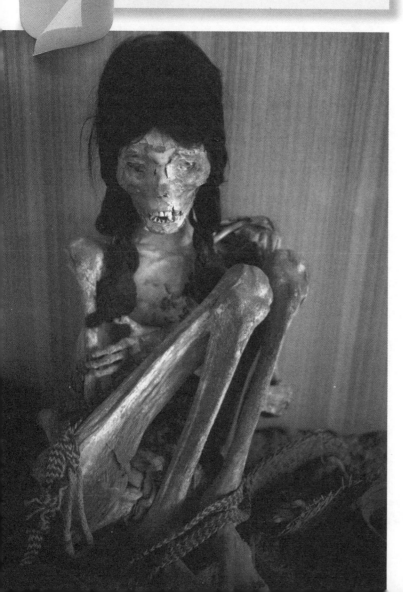

A Chinchorro mummy found in Peru.

gruesome frozen in a glacier. They thought it was some unlucky soul who had recently slipped, fallen, and died. Surprise! Turns out, the corpse—nicknamed Ötzi—had been there for around 5,000 years. Ötzi was so well preserved that the scientists who studied his body could even tell what he had eaten just before he died (a snack of ibex meat and some grains) and that he suffered from whipworm, an intestinal parasite. And, most ghoulishly, they even speculated that the poor fellow had been murdered. An arrow shaft in his shoulder and a bashed-in head are pretty compelling clues!

Ötzi was an accidental mummy, but there are other cultures besides the Egyptians that made mummies on purpose. Along the west coast of South America there is a vast desert called the Atacama where it is extremely dry. There, archaeologists—the people who dig and search for remains of past life—found mummies that had been made 7,000 years ago by the Chinchorro peoples—2,000 years before the Egyptians began their "wrap" sessions. The Chinchorros had several different ways of making their mummies. One popular way was to carefully remove all the skin, dry it in the desert sun, then make a clay-and-stick dummy and drape the dried human skin over it. Think of it as a dummy mummy.

MEET THE BOG-EEE MAN!

We've been talking about how drying preserves bodies, but some mummies have been found in very wet, slimy places called bogs. Peat bogs, to be exact. Peat is made from layers and layers of decomposed plants that get squished together. Certain kinds of peat are loaded with acids and there is almost no oxygen in the dense muck, so bacteria cannot thrive. By now you know the drill: no bacteria, no decomposition. Hundreds of bog mummies have been found in parts of northern Europe. Most of these mummies were likely not preserved on purpose—they fell or were pushed into the bog. Ooops! One even had stubble on his chin and a noose around his neck! Guess we know how he died. . . .

Peat chemicals are great for preserving skin and hair, but not so good for preserving bones. Bog mummy bones are soft and look a bit like glass

MAKE BOGGY BONES

1
HOUR

TO MAKE THE MUMMY BONE, PLUS 3 DAYS

GO FETCH

Compared to a brittle dried-out bone from an Egyptian mummy, a bog mummy bone is soft. Why? Bog water is very acidic, and acid removes calcium, the mineral that makes bones hard and strong. No calcium means rubbery bones! Let's see how acid removes calcium from a skeleton, or in our case, a chicken leg.

1. Eat the chicken, gnawing the drumsticks until they have no meat left on them. (If you are vegetarian, you can ask a meat-eating friend to do this for you.) Wash the bones off in the sink.

2. Make a hypothesis about what each of the bones will be like after being heated, soaked in acid, or just left to sit (that's our control bone). If you have extra bones you could compare a different acid, such as vinegar, or you could compare bones of different thicknesses.

3. Put one bone in a bowl and cover it completely with lemon juice. Lemon juice is an acid that is very much like the acids in a peat bog.

3 cooked chicken drumsticks of equal size

2 cups lemon juice

Bowl or old glass jar

Cookie or baking sheet

Plastic wrap

Plastic bag

4. Put the other chicken bone on a cookie sheet in the oven and bake it at 300°F for 45 minutes. Let it cool, then place it in a plastic bag.

5. Wrap the third bone in plastic wrap and let it sit on the counter.

6. After three days, gather your bones. Try to bend the control bone, then the baked bone. Now try to bend the lemon-soaked bone.

WHAT JUST HAPPENED?

The bones in your body are flexible yet strong because they contain both collagen (which makes bones flexible) and calcium (which makes them strong). You most likely noticed that the baked bone was much more brittle than the control bone. Baking removed moisture from the bone and broke down the collagen. Without collagen, bones become brittle and break easily.

The lemon-soaked bone should bend a bit. This is because the acid in the juice dissolved the calcium out of the bone, making it more rubbery. The acidic bog water does the same, though over a much longer period of time. Thus boggy bones!

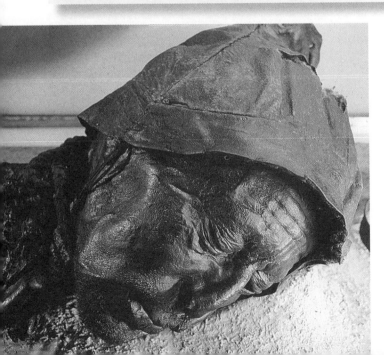

after a thousand years of stewing in the muck. Why does this happen? Make some boggy bones (see above) and find out for yourself.

Well, that's a wrap!

The ancient Egyptians knew so much about human anatomy from looking inside bodies, and you can learn more too! Head over to OFFAL on page 174 and check out a cow's kidney and a lamb's heart. Or just turn the page and be prepared to cover your ears learning about NOXIOUS NOISE.

A peat bog mummy.

Noxious Noises

SCREEEEECH!

Some sounds are lovely—a babbling brook, a sweet lullaby, a gentle breeze. But this isn't a book about anything babbling or sweet or gentle. We're talking shrill, annoying, teeth-rattling noise here! Some sounds are simply too loud, while others might just make your brain go bonkers. So get ready to cover your ears. But first, what exactly is *sound*?

Sound and air go hand in hand. Air is made of gazillions of tiny molecules of gases such as nitrogen and oxygen. They are constantly in motion—swirling all around you. You can't see molecules of air because they are so tiny, but you can feel air moving when you blow on your fingers. Sound causes air to move too, but in a different way. Blow air on your friend's face and many of the molecules of air that came out of your mouth will bump into their eyeballs. You will probably also annoy the heck out them. But hum or clap near someone and something different happens. The air molecules move back and forth in a special pattern. The molecules that eventually touch your pal's eardrums will not be the exact ones that you moved when you made the noise. Here's why.

Nails on a chalkboard. A baby screaming in the supermarket. The disgusting noise Great-Uncle Fergus makes when he clears a wad of phlegm from his throat— that *cccchhhhhhhhhkkkkk* sound that makes you want to hurl. Why do some noises make your ears go *"Aaaargh!"*?

THUNDER!!

It seems like you hear sounds at the exact moment they're made. If you drop a book, you hear the sound of the book hitting the floor at the same moment that you see it hit the floor. That's because your ear and brain work so quickly, and sound travels pretty fast too. But sound doesn't travel as fast as light. In fact, light travels about 900,000 times faster. Think about what happens during a thunderstorm. You see the lightning and then . . . wait. Wait . . . still waiting . . . *CRACK!! BOOM!* you hear the noise it made! Lightning heats up the air by thousands of degrees, causing it to vibrate and explode outward—this is what you hear as thunder. The reason for the delay between seeing the lightning and hearing the thunder is that it takes longer for the sound to travel to your ears than for the light to travel to your eyes.

COPYCAT BOTTLES

 5 MINUTES

GO FETCH →

> 2 identical glass or plastic bottles without caps

Copying is usually a no-no, right? No copying homework or test answers! But when it comes to the science of sound, copying is a lot of fun!

1. Hold the first bottle close to your mouth and blow across its top. Experiment with the angle and speed that you blow until the bottle produces a sound.

2. Now that you're an accomplished bottle musician, hold the second bottle next to your ear while blowing into the first bottle. Listen carefully to the second bottle. You should be able to hear a similar sound coming from the second bottle. You might have to play around with how you hold the bottle near your ear to get it to make the copycat sound.

WHAT JUST HAPPENED?

All objects have a *natural frequency*: the rate at which they tend to vibrate even if nothing is striking, strumming, plucking, or blowing on them. A musical instrument has a set of natural frequencies that sound rather lovely together (if you know how to play it!). Dragging your nails across a chalkboard has a set of natural frequencies that might make you squirm.

Because the bottles in our ick-tivity were identical, they shared the same natural frequency. When you blew across the first bottle's mouth, the air inside the bottle started to vibrate. The vibrations from this bottle traveled through the air and some of them happened to collide with the second bottle. The frequency of these vibrations was the same as the natural frequency of the second bottle, so the second bottle made a copycat sound. Scientists call this *sympathetic vibration* or *resonance*. Fortunately, sympathetic vibrations don't happen unless you have materials with the same natural frequency. Otherwise, every time you farted in class you'd have to endure a chorus of books, posters, and desks farting back at you!

Try experimenting with how far apart your bottles can be and still produce sympathetic vibrations. Have a friend hold the second bottle and stand really close together. When you blow on the first bottle, your friend should be able to hear a sound coming from the second bottle. Now, keep moving a little farther apart and see how far you can get before it no longer works.

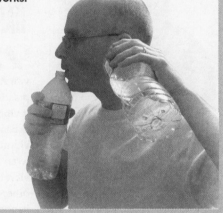

BUMP-BUMP-THUMP

Let's say you are hanging out on one side of the gym. Your best bud is on the other side, but there are a whole bunch of kids in between you. You want to get your pal's attention. Hmmmm ... how can you get a message across the room without the hassle of making your way through the crowd? You have a brilliant idea! You bump shoulders with the kid next to you and say, "Pass it on." That kid looks at you a little oddly, but passes on the shoulder bump to the next kid. The bump moves onward through the crowd from kid to kid, until it reaches your friend who looks a little surprised, then realizes it's from you, and jumps up high enough to grin and wave back! Hooray! You didn't have to move but the energy of your shoulder bump did.

That's kind of how sound travels through air molecules, though it travels out in all directions. When you pluck a guitar string, or sing, or yell at your little sister to stop pulling your hair, air molecules near you get bumped, and they bump into their neighbors, who bump into their neighbors, who bump into their neighbors, and on and on (like the shoulder bump) until the sound energy finally reaches someone's ear. What bumps the air molecules? Vibrations!

THE RICE DISCO

5 MINUTES

GO FETCH

Let's take a look at sound in action. *See* the vibrations that sounds make—and watch rice get its groove on!

1. Tightly stretch some plastic wrap over the bowl. Use a rubber band to keep the plastic wrap tight across the bowl.

2. Sprinkle about a dozen grains of uncooked rice on top of the plastic wrap.

3. Now make a lot of noise! Bang a drum or pot very close to the bowl (but *don't* bang the bowl itself). Or try singing really loudly. You should see the rice move and vibrate on the plastic wrap. A little rice dance party in your kitchen!

> Plastic wrap
> Bowl
> Rubber band
> Uncooked rice (or other small grains)
> Drum (or a pot and a wooden spoon)

WHAT JUST HAPPENED?

Your drumming made the air vibrate. Those vibrations reached the plastic wrap, making it vibrate, and this caused the rice to vibrate too. Plastic wrap is very thin, so it vibrates more easily than other materials. What happens when you put the bowl with the rice next to a big speaker? Does the rice respond more to bass notes or high notes? What kind of music does rice like to groove to?

FEEL THE VIBRATION

Grab a rubber band and stretch it between your thumb and index finger. Now pluck it with your other index finger. The rubber band will vibrate, which means it moves back and forth really quickly. That fast back-and-forth movement (aka vibration) squishes and then pulls apart the air molecules next to the rubber band. Squish–pull apart, squish–pull apart. It forms a pattern. Your vocal cords are like rubber bands too, vibrating whenever you talk. Don't believe it? Touch your throat gently and hum.

DOIN' THE WAVE

Ever been to the ocean or a water park and watched the waves? The energy from vibrations travels in waves too, and just like the ocean, there is a space between one wave and the next, and some waves are bigger than others. Getting walloped by a big wave that's crashed down on your head feels very different than just gently bobbing up and down on small waves, right?

I WAS MYTH-INFORMED

A VOICE THAT CAN SHATTER GLASS?

You've seen the cartoons. An opera singer opens her mouth, lets out a loooooong wail, and soon people's eyeglasses start shattering as the giant crystal chandelier on the ceiling of the opera house explodes. Can a human voice shatter glass? Yes and no. Bottom line: It's really, really hard to do. It has to be very thin glass—like an expensive wineglass, and that glass has to have some microscopic defect in it that will crack when the right vibrations hit it.

The Discovery Channel show *MythBusters* tested the idea with Jaime Vendera, a rock singer with a powerful voice. Twenty glasses into the experiment, he finally shattered one thanks to a vocal blast of 105 decibels. This was the first proof ever captured on video that a human voice can actually shatter glass.

What makes you want to plug your ears? Screeching sirens? Wailing toddlers?

ICK-TIVITY   CUT OUT THAT KAZOOING!

5 MINUTES

PLUS ENDLESS HOURS OF ANNOYING ENTERTAINMENT

Here's an easy-to-make yet very noxious noisemaker that will annoy the whole family. They'll likely be yelling the name of this ick-tivity in no time! Plus, you can use it in your next ick-speriment: Sick Sounds (page 166).

1. Flatten one end of a drinking straw with your fingers.

2. Use the scissors to cut the sides and the middle of that flat end into something that resembles a bird beak. The cuts might each be about half an inch (1 cm) long.

3. Put that bird beak in your mouth (be careful not to poke your tongue on the sharp points) so that the beak is behind your lips, actually in the cavern of your mouth.

GO FETCH

> Several drinking straws
>
> Scissors

4. Blow really hard through the straw. You may have to change the position a bit to get the most obnoxious noise. Or flatten it more or cut a little deeper. Or blow harder or less hard. We got a nice range of high-pitched squeaks and lower honks.

5. Now march around the house until someone yells, "Cut out that kazooing!"

6. Optional: Snip off the other end of the straw to make it shorter and see if you can get a differently pitched instrument. Pop several of different lengths in your mouth at the same time, and make a painfully pitched panpipe.

WHAT JUST HAPPENED?

The beak-shaped end of your straw is acting like the reed in woodwind instruments such as a saxophone or clarinet. When you blow, one side of the beak vibrates against the other side, creating sound waves. Unlike the pleasant saxophone or clarinet, your kazoo's sound wave patterns are more chaotic, so they just sound awful.

A longer straw will make longer sound waves. Longer sound waves have lower frequencies, and therefore lower pitches. When you snip your straw, you create a higher pitch. Instruments use the same principle, changing the length of piano or guitar strings, or the length of the air column inside a wind instrument, to create different notes.

MUSIC OR NOISE?

So, what's the difference between lovely music and noxious noise? Well, to put it simply, music is organized sound, sort of like kids peacefully marching down the hallway. There are specific frequencies arranged in a specific order, and they follow mathematical rules. Noise is sound that is disorderly, like a lunchroom gone wild. With noise, all the frequencies are random and chaotic.

SQUISHY SOUND

If you want to get all proper and scientific, you could inform your favorite grown-up that sound waves are a compression wave. That's because the air gets bunched up or compressed when a vibration passes through. A pattern is formed of compressed air and then air that is spread farther apart. Back to our gym example! All of us like to have a some personal space. If you get right in the face of a nearby kid, they will get uncomfortable and back up, and likely bump into the next kid, who will then back up and bump into the next kid, who will then back up, etc. A pattern of compressed

(and irritated) kids would pass through the crowd. But if you then back away, they can spread out again. Air molecules get moved in a similar way by sound, getting compressed and then decompressed over and over.

When a baby screams, sound waves move through the air until the air molecules right next

A GROSS GUIDE TO DREADFUL DECIBELS

Sound is measured on the *decibel* (<u>de</u>-sih-bull) scale. The lower the number, the softer the sound. Exposure to high-decibel sounds can damage your hearing. The extent of the damage depends on how long you are exposed to the sound. Remember those minuscule hairs we mentioned at the start of this section? Those are what get damaged and contribute to noise-induced hearing loss.

Your ears can handle eight hours of 85-decibel sound (like heavy city traffic or the school cafeteria) without damage, but only four hours at 88 decibels, and only one hour at 94 decibels (like a motorcycle). If there is a sound that is 105 decibels (like your headphones turned up all the way), your ears might start to get damaged after just four minutes. And you should really only be exposed to rock concert noise (115–120 decibels) for 30 seconds. So unless you want to constantly be saying, "What? Can you repeat that? Come again?" when you're older . . . be very mindful of the noises around you! And wear earplugs to rock concerts!

5 Decibels: A very small mouse pooping

27 Decibels: A stinky fart passed through clenched butt cheeks

38 Decibels: The sound of a pop quiz: pencils scribbling, papers shuffling, and students fidgeting

65 Decibels: Polite dinner conversation (not the kind where you and your siblings are driving your parents insane with squabbling)

78 Decibels: Ancient Uncle Leo snoring on the couch. Zzzzzzzzzzzz

105 Decibels: Your headphones turned up all the way on a loud song (so turn it down, silly, and save your ears!)

109 Decibels: World's loudest burp, delivered via the mouth of Paul Hunn, the world record holder. Louder than a Hell's Angels motorcycle dude revving his engine at a red light!

120 Decibels: An ambulance siren, or a rock concert, complete with screaming fans

128 Decibels: A jackhammer breaking up a sidewalk

140–165 Decibels: Fireworks on the Fourth of July (so watch them from a distance!)

to your ear get bumped, and then bump into your eardrum. Your eardrum then vibrates and in your inner ear, tiny bones, some liquid and miniscule hairs work together to change the vibration into an electrical signal. That signal travels along your auditory nerve to your brain. And your brain interprets it as sound, or "Could someone PLEASE make that baby stop screaming!!"

THAT "HERTZ" MY EARS!

You can measure the quietness or loudness of sound with the decibel scale, but you can also measure the frequency of sound thanks to Heinrich Hertz, a German physicist. You now know that sound travels in waves. *Frequency* (<u>free</u>-kwin-see) is the word we use to describe the number of waves that occur in a given time. *Hertz* is a unit for measuring sound frequency (like the way that meters and feet are units of length). One hertz equals one wave per second. Deep, low sounds, like the left-hand keys on a piano, have about 28 hertz. The high keys have more waves per second and reach about 4,200 hertz. We humans can hear sounds in the 20 hertz to 20,000 hertz range. Anything above 20,000 hertz (ultrasound) or below 20 hertz (infrasound) will fall on our deaf-to-it ears.

Some animals have extraordinary hearing. Cats can hear sounds as high as 64,000 hertz. Bats can tap their toes to sounds up to 110,000 hertz. And dolphins are the ultrasound prizewinners! They can hear sounds over 150,000 hertz—perfect for using their ears to find prey in dark, murky waters.

How can you use sound to find food? Both bats and dolphins emit high-pitched squeaks. Their sound waves travel out, hit a victim, and bounce back with an echo, which helps them target dinner. It's called *echolocation* (eck-oh-low-<u>kay</u>-shun).

At the other end of the sound spectrum are the low talkers. Take giraffes. Ever heard one of those guys talk? We didn't think so. They are actually quite chatty, but you can't hear them because they talk at a below-20-hertz frequency. Perfect for gossiping about the tourists gawking at them from minibuses on a safari!

THE TOP NASTY NOISES

When it comes to music, we don't all agree on what sounds awesome. One person might love heavy metal, and another might think that heavy metal musicians want to destroy the world's eardrums. But do you think most of us would agree on the worst noxious noises? Ever had a mosquito whine around your ear while you

ZOOM ZOOM, BOOM BOOM

Sound travels fast: In room-temperature air it can go 770 miles per hour, but it goes four times as fast through liquids and even faster through solids! (That's because the molecules are packed the tightest in solids, making the vibrations pass from one molecule to another at high speed. Put your ear to a desktop and have a friend tap one of the legs to test sound moving through a solid.) But here is something really cool: When jets fly at supersonic speeds (moving at speeds equal to or faster than sound) a startling phenomenon occurs. The jets pass through an invisible "wall" called the sound barrier, which leads to a huge noise that you can hear on the ground called a *sonic boom*—a big *whooomp!* that you can almost feel in your chest. The reason for this is that when the jet is flying at normal speeds, it creates a series of pressure waves all around it. These waves travel at the speed of sound, but when the jet goes supersonic, the waves are forced together (or compressed) behind it. When the plane passes through the waves it creates the sonic boom.

A vapor cone forms around this US Navy F/A-18 as it approaches the speed of sound.

20 MINUTES

SICK SOUNDS

GO FETCH

You probably know a lot of your family's and friends' favorite sounds. You know which aunt loves bird songs and which cousin adores Bieber. But what about their *least* favorite sounds? Don't take their word for it, because they might not even know yet. The only scientific way to find out what sounds make them beg for earplugs is to conduct an experiment.

1. Assemble your noise-making supplies and practice your technique in secret. Try sliding a butter knife, a fork, and a ruler across a glass bottle or dragging chalk or a nail along a mini chalkboard. Experiment with the angle that the objects rub against one another. If you have the equipment, you might have fun recording the sounds to play back later. Make a hypothesis about which ones will be the most excruciating to your test subjects.

2. Put all your supplies in the backpack or bag so they can't be seen.

3. Explain to a friend or family member that you want to conduct an experiment to uncover which sounds are most annoying. Remember to get their permission first, like any good scientist would!

This is only a suggested list of materials. Snoop around the house and try other objects too, until you find the most annoying sound ever.

Glass bottle

Nail

Butter knife

Fork

Mini chalkboard

Chalk

Backpack or large paper bag

4. Have your test subject close his or her eyes, and unleash a variety of awful noises. Ask your brave volunteer to rate each noise on a scale of 1 (pleasant) to 10 (unbearable). Record the results.

5. Repeat steps 3 and 4 with as many willing participants as you can.

6. After all the experiments are done, reveal what the sounds were and ask your test subjects to share why they found some sounds so unbearable. Was your hypothesis correct? Were they surprised to learn what was really making the sounds? What qualities make some sounds less tolerable than others?

WHAT JUST HAPPENED?

Scientists aren't sure why we find some sounds so painful. Surprisingly, the nastiest sounds tend to be within the range of human speech (150–5,000 Hz). The ones that make us want to jam our fingers in our ears are the high-pitched ones, similar to the frequency of a human or chimpanzee scream (2,000–4,000 Hz). Do these screechy sounds trick our brain into thinking someone is in danger? Maybe. A different theory is that the shape of the human ear makes some sounds physically more painful than others—like being poked with something sharp. Finally, some studies have revealed that if people expect a sound to be annoying, it will be. If you repeat your experiment but let people keep their eyes open, you might get different responses. Whatever the reason, we can all agree that some sounds are best left unheard!

tried to sleep? Ever covered both your ears as a police car or ambulance raced by with sirens blaring? Here are some of the winners of the most upsetting sounds to humans, according to a study done at Newcastle University in England, where volunteers listened to and rated some 74 annoying sounds to find the absolute worst!

* **Dragging a fork on a glass**
* **Chalk or fingernails on a blackboard**
* **Squealing brakes on a bicycle**
* **A baby crying**
* **An electric drill**

Give your ears a round of applause—they are pretty amazing! But there are plenty of other senses still waiting to be explored. Up next: ODIOUS ODORS. Time for your nose to have a chance to be revolted as well!

Odious Odors

Go ahead, we dare you. When you get home at the end of the day, pull off your shoes and socks and stick your nose between your toes. P.U.! But feet aren't the only nasal offenders. There are some pretty foul fragrances out there—take a whiff of rotting garbage, sweaty armpits, and dead fish, not to mention seriously scared skunks that have just lifted their tails.

SUPER NOSE TO THE RESCUE!

The nose is the unsung superhero of your body's senses. Your ears can identify an impressive half a million (500,000) different tones. That's nothing compared to the roughly ten million (10,000,000) different colors your eyes can distinguish. But the real champion is the nose— it can detect one trillion (1,000,000,000,000) different odors! This doesn't mean your nose can memorize all these smells, but it can probably tell the difference between an astronomically large number of scratch-and-sniff stickers.

But how do those smells reach your nose, anyway? Smells are the result of something— rotting garbage, hot cocoa, or tuna—releasing tiny bits of itself (its molecules) which drift off into the air. The tiny, smelly molecules (called volatile compounds) float through the air, moved about by breezes, and some are sucked up into your nose. Here, they get stuck to smell receptors, like a key fitting into a lock. A message is then sent through your nerves to your brain, and your brain perceives this message as a smell. Your brain organizes its library of smells alongside its library of memories. If you've ever been wowed by how certain smells can make you instantly recall certain places or events, you've experienced your brain thumbing through its scent encyclopedia.

THINK A FART SMELLS BAD?

Your nostrils sort of have a built-in ability to judge all of these odors, letting you know whether you should take a deeper inhale of something that smells mmm, mmm, good, like apple pie or fresh flowers, or if you should run away from the putrid pile of fresh dog poo nearby or, more important, a dangerous gas leak in your basement. Your nose can be a literal lifesaver, the ultimate warning system for getting you out of danger. But it has to act quickly. Say you encounter a terrible odor, like the stench-o-rama of hydrogen sulfide—rare in everyday life but a poisonous, flammable, and explosive gas that smells like rotten eggs. In high concentration, it can not only make your eyes water and your nostrils and throat burn, but it can cause your brain— sensing a terrible sensory attack—to shut down and temporarily lose its ability to smell. Meaning a stink bomb can neutralize your senses. In the presence of toxic chemicals, that can be a very bad thing, because even a few

THE NOSE KNOWS

GO FETCH →

Most people navigate through the world relying mainly on their senses of sight and hearing. But your sense of smell helps you understand your surroundings too. Grab a few noses (you'll find them attached to your friends' faces) and put them to the test to find out how much the nose knows.

1. Assemble your smell samples. Anything's fair game except toilet-bowl items. You might try different spices, slices of fruit, talcum powder, grass clippings, pencil shavings, a sliver of deodorant, a sweaty sock, or a rag that's been stuffed in your grown-up's stinkiest shoe for 30 minutes.

2. Put each object in a different bag. If you can't identify it by sight,

Armpit Rag + Tomato

Assortment of about 10 things with different smells

Ziplock bags

Marker

Someone with a nose

---

write what it is on the outside of the bag with a marker.

3. Round 1 of testing: Tell a friend to close his or her eyes and then hold an opened sample bag under his or her nose. Your friend should take a whiff and try to guess what's in the bag. Repeat this for all the other samples.

4. Round 2 of testing: Create some combination sample bags (for example, cinnamon and sliced tomato, pencil shavings and soap, or sweaty sock and a tea bag). See how well your friend can name all the contents of each bag. For a harder challenge, create a bag with three different items in it.

5. Your turn. Reverse the role of tester and sniffer so you can give your nose the same workout. How did you do?

WHAT JUST HAPPENED?

Your nose probably did a "nose-toriously" good job in Round 1, but even though your sniffer is amazing, it has its limits, as you probably saw in Round 2. And even the best smellers have difficulty identifying more than three odors from a mixture. The nose gets overloaded when there are multiple scents present, and some smells get drowned out by stronger odors. That's actually why some folks wear perfume or cologne, and why deodorants are scented. The powerful volatile compounds overwhelm any body odor so others don't notice it. Back before indoor toilets, when people dumped their waste in the streets, you would often see people holding hankies dabbed in pleasant-smelling oils over their noses to mask the bad smells.

---

deep breaths of strong hydrogen sulfide gas can lead to death. So, if you ever find yourself working in a waste-treatment plant or on a manure farm, pay heed if your nose ever encounters the smell and signals RED ALERT! GET OUT OF HERE! (Hydrogen sulfide is also made in tiny, nondangerous amounts by the bacteria in your intestines.)

That little sniffer of yours is the most sensitive sensing organ in your body. But before you get all puffed up and proud of *your* honker, know that humans are not the best sniffers in the animal kingdom. Some other animals can detect

smell a lot better than people. A bloodhound—sometimes called a nose with a dog attached—has a honker that can smell 1,000 times better than a human's. Bloodhounds can smell the microscopic bits of skin that people shed all day long. And since everyone's skin smells slightly different, the police often use bloodhounds to track a missing person or criminal. Very useful puppy! But bloodhounds STILL are not the best super sniffers of the animal realm. Let's heap some praise on the silvertip grizzly bear! These ferocious fur balls have a sense of smell seven

This pup smells a criminal!

ICK-TIVITY

THE STINK-O-SCALE

GO FETCH →

1 WEEK

Notebook and something to write with

If you read **I NOXIOUS NOISES** (page 160), you know about the decibel scale. Earthquakes have the Richter scale and hurricanes get measured by the Saffir-Simpson hurricane wind scale. Tornadoes have the Fujita scale. But alas, poor little smells have no scale of their own. Your job? Invent one.

On a scale of 1 to 10 with 1 being the most yummy smell imaginable, 5 being basically okay, and 10 being "I am going to hurl," create your very own Stink-o-Scale. In the days to come, rate the smells you encounter. Your great-uncle Igor's herring-and-cigar breath? Probably a solid 10!

times stronger than that of the bloodhound. They can sniff food from as far away as 18 miles. And a big bravo to the African elephant, which wins the prize for most smell receptors—almost 2,000! What else would you expect from a critter with a nose that size?

QUICK! HOLD YOUR NOSE!

Why do WE smell bad from time to time? Brilliant scientist that you are, you probably know that farts and poop and sweaty grown-ups' underarms reek because of bacteria. But how does this work? Let's find out!

You have between two and five million sweat glands, which fall into two categories:

DEODORANT TOURNAMENT

9-12 DAYS

GO FETCH →

You've got a lot to look forward to as you get older: getting your driver's license, voting in a presidential election, and developing ripe body odor for the rest of your life. Perhaps you've already noticed that your armpits have been getting a little stinkier than they used to be. Now, there's nothing wrong with a little BO, but some people go to great lengths to get rid of it. In this experiment, you'll test which deodorant keeps the bacteria in your volunteers' apocrine glands from making too much stink.

1. Make a hypothesis about which deodorant or antiperspirant will work the best, and record it in your notebook. Then choose one to start with and have your volunteers commit to using it for three days. Ask them to apply it once a day after they shower.

2. At the end of each day, do a smell test on each volunteer. Sniff those pits and rate the smell on a scale of 1 (smells nice) to 10 (OMG, my nose just exploded!). Record your results in your notebook. Jot down a few

3 or 4 different types of deodorant. Look for natural versus chemical ones, or scented versus unscented, or deodorant versus deodorant plus antiperspirant.

A few sets of armpits (you can use your own if they have started getting stinky, but you may have to ask a teenager or grown-up)

words describing what you smell. If you feel uncomfortable sniffing your volunteers' pits, they can sniff and rate themselves.

3. At the end of your three-day trial, give your volunteers a new deodorant and repeat the process. Do this for each type of deodorant.

4. Analyze your data. Does one deodorant seem superior? Are there reasons to question your results? For example, were your participants doing the same amount of physical activity each day?

WHAT JUST HAPPENED?

Deodorant and antiperspirants fight BO with three different game plans. Antiperspirants try to stop the sweat (no sweat = no food for bacteria). When an antiperspirant chemical comes in contact with the wetness of your skin, it creates a sort of glue that seals up the apocrine glands. The sweat is stuck under your skin and can't come out. This is just a temporary success, though, because the barrier will only last so long. You might win the battle, but the sweat always wins the war. The second plan of attack is to use alcohol or other antimicrobial weapons to blast the bacteria—no bacteria, no odor. The third strategy is to add a pretty smell—fresh flowers or yummy fruit—to cover up the stinky odors. And many products do all three things at the same time.

eccrine (<u>ek</u>-krin) glands and *apocrine* (<u>app</u>-uh-krin) glands. Eccrine glands are all over your skin. They stay active your whole life and are great for keeping you cool when you overheat from exercise or a fever. Very important! Apocrine glands are another story. As we grow to adulthood, certain glands in our body start to really work, especially the apocrine glands. They are found near hair follicles in your armpits, ears, nipples, and groin.

Feet actually have more sweat glands than your armpits. That's why your shoes can stink!

Bacteria find eccrine sweat too salty to eat but love to feast on apocrine sweat. Apocrine sweat contains a protein with a sugar coating. And just like you might, bacteria love sugar! As certain bacteria devour and digest this fetid "drink" for energy, they release smelly chemicals. That's why little kids don't smell super stinky after exercising; they don't have those hairs or working apocrine glands yet, and thus no stink-making bacteria. But if you're a teenager, WASH those stinky body parts and wash your clothes, especially your underwear and socks.

Feet can smell especially skunky because they actually have more sweat glands than your armpits! Shoes and socks trap the sweat so it can't evaporate. It's like a damp swamp down there, perfect for a bacteria party! That's why it's a good idea to change your socks every day. If you can, don't wear the same shoes day after day. Let them air out after an afternoon sprinting across the soccer field. That way your family won't gag every time you take off your shoes.

I SMELL A SKUNK (and Other Loathsome, Smelly Things)

The same Mother Nature that gave us roses and the aroma of baking cookies has also provided these nose-foulers!

King of the Stinkers

Skunk! Now here's a smell that just sticks to you and doesn't let go! What else can you expect from an oily liquid that has just been shot out of the anal glands located in the skunk's butt? The skunk does this to protect its furry black-and-white-striped self from attack by predators. The

GRUESOME SCIENCE

A FOR-REAL STINK BOMB

The US Department of Defense has an important job to do: protect all 317 million Americans (and counting) from harm. In 2001, it decided to build the world's foulest stink bomb—a weapon that wouldn't hurt people, but would make them run away! The government hired Dr. Pamela Dalton, a sensory psychologist at the Monell Chemical Senses Center in Philadelphia, and tasked her with creating the foulest smell on Earth. Dr. Dalton got to work, revved up her nose, and using her knowledge of the most dreadful scents on the planet, she stirred up something she affectionately labeled "stench soup." Was it the aroma of decaying fish? Portable toilets on a hot summer day? That not-quite-empty milk carton wedged under the seat in the car and forgotten for a month or two?

It turns out that there are two smells that humans everywhere are programmed to run away from, and for good reason. One is the smell of a decaying corpse. The other is human poop. Of course, Dr. Dalton didn't want to work with an actual rotting body or a real pile of doo-doo, so she figured out the chemistry of those two smells and whipped them up in her laboratory. But that STILL wasn't enough. While she was at it, she stirred in some eau de rotten egg for good measure and a few other despicable scents to put the finishing touches on her "bomb." Testing was difficult. Dr. Dalton had to round up volunteers to willingly smell the vile vials, but fortunately no one's nose was permanently damaged. Her stench soup hasn't been used yet, but it's certainly a "fragrant" use of science.

reason for the reek is something called a *thiol* (<u>thy</u>-ol)—the same chemical compound present in a pile of poo or rotting flesh. The oils in the skunk's butt blast make it cling to every surface instead of wafting away in the breeze.

What should you do if your dog gets sprayed? Everyone thinks a bath in tomato juice will do the trick, but this recipe works MUCH better on our noses: Using rubber gloves and with an adult's permission, mix 1 quart hydrogen peroxide with ¼ cup baking soda and 1 tablespoon of dish soap. After the fizzing settles down, pour it into a plastic spray bottle and lather up your pooch. Rinse and repeat! (Warning: Don't store this liquid in the bottle for too long or it might explode.)

Halitosis Hoatzins (aka Stinkbirds)!

You might want to bring along nose clips if you ever find yourself going to the Amazon rain forest. Why? Hoatzins! These birds look like a prettier version of a chicken with a brilliant blue face, spiky Mohawk, and long feathers, but they smell like a pile of fresh cow dung. Why? They digest their food in a pouch in the esophagus—at the base of their long necks. Instead of food making its way down through the stomach and then out

Hoatzins—so adorable, and so stinky!

You do NOT want a bouquet of the enormous *Amorphophallus titanum*, aka titan arum, which smells like a rotting animal.

through the little birdie poop chute, these fetid flyers ferment their food in their throats, where it basically rots. It's the equivalent of having a pile of moldy eggs just down the hill from your mouth. And with every exhalation . . . well, you can imagine!

Putrid Petals

Who says that all flowers smell good? That person has never stuck his or her schnoz in an *Amorphophallus titanum* or *Rafflesia arnoldii*, which share the fun nickname of corpse flowers. And that's what they smell like—something that has died and is rotting away. Of course, to a fly or other insect who likes to lay its eggs on something dead, this flower is like a luxury hotel. Mother Nature is tricky, though—these plants are "flesh eaters." As the insect goes to deposit its eggs, the plant simply closes its petals and has fly soup for dinner.

Vomiting Vultures
Barf is one of the THE worst smells around. The smell alone is enough to make people around the barfer want to blow chunks too. Vultures, those eaters of the dead, seem to instinctively know this; plus, their vomit happens to be super acidic. If they are attacked or threatened while they are scavenging, they can projectile vomit up to ten feet and burn a potential predator.

A little scientific knowledge goes a long way. Just ask two Cornell University computer-engineering students. For a class project, they built a machine that measures fart smells. The machine uses sensors to measure the three qualities needed to

unleash a world-class personal stink bomb—the actual aroma (hydrogen sulfide—one of the chemicals that makes farts reek), the temperature (a hot fart travels faster than a cold one), and (using a microphone) even the sound. Needless to say, the students got an A. And it's not just a silly class project. Their invention has attracted a lot of attention from dentists, who can diagnose diseases from mouth stink, and from veterinarians—doctors who deal with animals. Believe it or not, you can learn a lot about an animal's health by sniffing its farts! Better to let a machine do the sniffing than sticking your nose near a dog's butt.

Retching Roller Birds
Delicious newborn baby birds are many a predator's favorite food, so resourceful Eurasian roller bird fledglings have a trick up their tiny feathery sleeves. They puke all over themselves if they are attacked, thus repelling the would-be attackers with the revolting smell. When the parent birds come back, they smell that there has been a scary incident and can be on the lookout for returning baby-eaters.

Bad smells, nasty noises . . .
Feel like launching an attack on another one of your senses? Next up is OFFAL. Your mouth wants in on some of the AWFUL action!

Offal

AND

Other Awful Eats

WARNING!

The upcoming content may be alarming to vegetarians! Read at your own risk!

Cow stomach lining, ant larvae, corn fungus . . . When it comes to eating, just about anything goes. Chefs around the world have been known to chop up pig bladders and sheep udders, or stir in a few spoonfuls of cow urine to make a savory sauce. And let's not forget fried, crispy bug bits—a great source of protein!

But chew on this: What you might find icky, someone else might find delicious. It all comes down to culture—where you live and what you were raised eating. If you often dine on lamb lips or fried worms, instead of wanting to hurl at the sight, you will think, "Oh, goodie! Thanks, Mom!" And if you were raised without ever seeing a hot dog, you might say "Ewwww" the first time you encounter one at the ballpark. After all, a hot dog is made of leftover beef and/or pork bits that have been scraped off the bone, sometimes mixed with a pink goop of chicken parts that have been filtered through a metal screen, then topped with powdered preservatives and food coloring, before being squeezed into tubes of processed cow skin to be cooked. Maybe a crispy, quick-fried fresh cockroach isn't so bad after all?

RHYMES WITH AWFUL

If you ever order a plate of "variety meats" you are about to chow down on some *offal* (<u>awe</u>-ful). Offal refers to internal parts of animals other than the bones and muscles—this includes all those hardworking organs like animal lungs, stomach, intestines, brains, and kidneys. And even though it rhymes with *awful*, in many cultures, offal is considered awesome. Classic recipes all over the world depend on these body parts. Some sausages, for example, use hollowed-out intestines to hold the ground-up goodness of spicy meat inside. (Others have artificial casings.) And chitlins, a Southern US favorite, are made from pig (or sometimes cow) small intestines. (Hamburgers, steaks, chicken breast, chicken tenders, pork chops, bacon, and many of the

DISGUSTING!

Dr. Paul Rozin studies the emotion of "disgust" at the University of Pennsylvania. Now, we assume you are a pretty evolved person at this point. You know that eating dog poop is flat-out disgusting. The thought of putting an apple crawling with maggots into your mouth brings about a certain feeling of nausea in the pit of your stomach. But are we born with that feeling? Are we hardwired to gag when someone puts a plate of offal in front of us? Dr. Rozin performed an experiment with toddlers, who we all know will pretty much put *anything* in their mouths. Working with one-and-a-half- to two-year-olds, he fed them the following perfectly safe foods:

☆ **Fish eggs**

☆ **Cookies with ketchup**

☆ **Dissolved human hair**

☆ **Dead sterilized grasshoppers**

☆ **Something Dr. Rozin dubbed "dog doo,"** which was peanut butter mixed with a very stinky cheese

The only thing the babies didn't care for was dissolved human hair, which they mostly spat out. But astonishingly, 15 percent of the toddlers were willing to eat even that! To a very great degree, disgust at eating something vile is not something we are born with. We learn it from our culture. So maybe those sterilized grasshoppers really *are* tasty? Ask your favorite two-year-old.

other popular meats out there are mostly made of animal muscles, and for this simple reason don't belong to the offal club.)

Offal is often considered a delicacy. In other words, it's pretty fancy stuff, and you can end up paying an arm and a leg in an elite French restaurant for *cervelles au beurre noir*—"brains in black butter." Some Scots enjoy eating *haggis* (hag-iss), a dish made of oatmeal and the minced heart, liver, and lungs of a sheep, all cooked up in a sheep's stomach. In parts of Canada, jellied moose nose is a finger-lickin'-good delicacy, while in South Africa *smiley*—a sheep's head on a plate—is considered scrumptious. Raw caribou kidney and brain, seal heart, animal

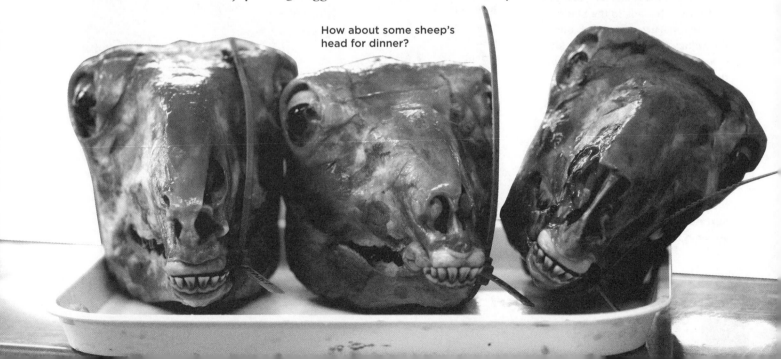
How about some sheep's head for dinner?

JUST KIDNEY-ING

GO FETCH

Exploring offal is a great way to get a head start on becoming a world-class surgeon. So before you try eating kidney, cut one up and have a look at the organ that filters our pee.

A beef kidney is really lumpy. Your kidneys are much smoother. But other than that, the inner structures are really similar.

1. You'll see some hard whitish and globby fat in the middle of the kidney. This part faces toward the spine in both a cow's and your body. In that fat, you should be able to find three tubes (called vessels) coming out of the middle of the kidney. They are the renal artery, the renal vein, and the ureter (which leads to the bladder).

The renal artery brings blood to the kidney to be filtered. Your kidney is basically a washing machine for all the blood in your body. It filters out the waste products and unfriendly chemicals from your blood.

The sparkling clean blood goes back to your body through the renal vein.

Once all that waste and some excess water have been filtered out by the structures inside the kidney, the mixture flows to your bladder via the ureter. It is now pee-pee time!

- A beef kidney (get one at a butcher shop, or ask at your local supermarket)
- Some toothpicks
- Sharp knife
- Cutting board
- A handy grown-up with a strong stomach
- Gloves if you want them, otherwise just be sure to wash your hands very well after handling the kidney
- Paper towels

Depending on how the butcher cut the kidney, it's likely the artery and vein will be together, while the ureter will be below them and longer.

2. Stick toothpicks into each of the vessels in the beef kidney. In our picture, the top one is the renal artery, the middle is the renal vein, and the bottom is the ureter.

3. Ask an adult to slice through the kidney down the whole length (It will be a little tricky to cut through the fatty parts). Compare yours to our picture and try to identify a few of the key structures. The *cortex* (<u>core</u>-teks) contains tiny tubes called nephrons, which is where the actual filtering of your blood happens. The *renal pyramids* (<u>ree</u>-nul <u>peer</u>-uh-mids) are easy to find, and they collect the urine (pee) from the nephrons. Then all that urine goes to the collecting ducts in the renal pelvis and into the ureter. From there it goes into your bladder, and soon it'll be exiting your body in that familiar yellow stream.

4. Take a close whiff of your kidney. You just might be able to smell a little cow tinkle. How lovely!

5. If you haven't lost your appetite yet, cook that kidney up! You can find lots of recipes online, including the British classic, steak and kidney pie.

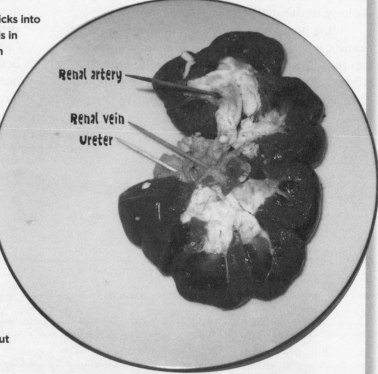

Renal artery
Renal vein
Ureter

eyes, reindeer stomach membrane . . . these are all delicacies among the Inuits in the far north of Canada. In the Arctic there is very little vegetation, mostly moss, which a human can't really eat. But if you eat an animal that DOES eat moss or lichen, maybe that reindeer stomach will provide your daily serving of fruits and veggies.

So go ahead! Be adventurous! If you're lucky enough to dine in a super-fancy restaurant, skip the steak and order sweetbreads (the thymus gland of a sheep). They're not sweet. They're not bread. But lots of folks swear that they are delish!

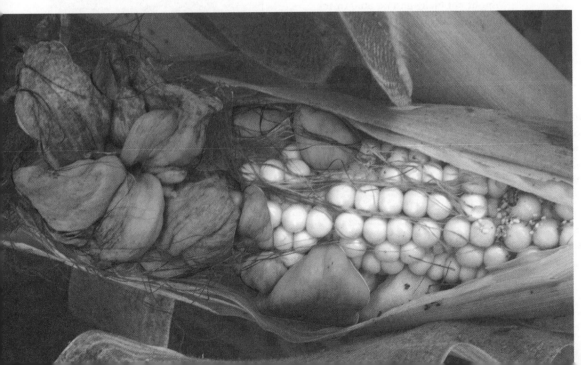

LARVAE AND FUNGI AND POISON FISH, OH, MY!

You learned all about creepy-crawlies in INSECTS—now how about popping a few in your mouth, along with a hearty side dish of fungi! If eating a heart or kidney wasn't your cup of tea, try some of these dishes that are beloved (or revolting) depending on where you live in the world. They aren't offal, but you still might find them pretty awful!

Escamoles—Venomous ants take center stage in this ancient Aztec delicacy, which you can still savor in Mexico. But not the actual ants—no! This dish contains the *larvae* (lar-vee) of these poisonous crawlers. To make *escamoles*, chefs scoop out the larvae from the *Liometopum*, big ants with nasty bites that burrow in the roots of the agave and maguey plants. The reward of this larvae harvest is a bowlful of a creamy, nutty, slightly slimy concoction with larvae the size of beans. Pan-fried with butter and spices, it's f-ANT-tastic . . . or so they say.

Huitlacoche—I'll have my corn covered with fungus, please. Corn can develop a disease called "corn smut"—a fungus that attacks the kernel and leads to the growth of yucky-looking gray "tumors" all over. It might look scary, but in Mexico, it's considered a great delicacy, and you can even buy it in cans. Its name is *huitlacoche* (weet-lah-koh-cheh), which actually means "sleeping excrement." Some people think it tastes like excrement too. But it turns out that the ancient Aztec farmers who treasured this "diseased" plant knew something: *Huitlacoche* is packed with all sorts of good-for-you nutrients and protein that turn ordinary corn into a superfood, strengthening bones, fighting infections, and keeping skin healthy.

The term *huitlacoche* comes from the Nahuatl words for "excrement" and "sleep."

YOU'RE IN MY HEART
(LITERALLY)

GO FETCH →

1 HOUR

Have you ever wanted to know what the inside of a heart looks like? Here's your chance to learn a little anatomy, and if you do it over a clean plate, you can even cook it up at the end. There are lots of big new words in this ick-sploration, but don't worry about memorizing them all. Just imagine that you are the world's greatest heart surgeon as you slice away!

1. If you're wondering where in the world to get a lamb's heart, we found one in the frozen meat section of our supermarket. You could also ask your local butcher. Or you can ask your parents to order one that is preserved for dissection from an online educational supply company, but don't eat that one!

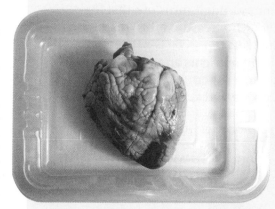

2. Dissecting a heart is no easy task, partly because it's hard to know which way you are holding it. So take a look at these photos to get oriented. A heart doesn't look much like those Valentine's Day hearts you made, does it? As you'll see, inside are four open spaces, or *chambers*, where blood enters and then gets pumped out every time your

- A lamb's heart
- An adult to help with the cutting
- Sharp knife or pair of kitchen scissors
- Large plate
- Paper towels
- Gloves if you want them, otherwise just be sure to wash your hands very well after handling the heart

heart beats, or *contracts*. Your heart is a pump, and without it your cells wouldn't be able to get the oxygen and nutrients they need.

3. Look for some tubelike things. Those are the blood vessels that come out of the top of the heart. It's fun to put your fingers in them and poke around. The largest one at the top is called the *aorta* (a-<u>ore</u>-tuh), and all the blood that gets pumped out to your body goes through it first. You might get lucky and be able to see some smaller arteries branching off

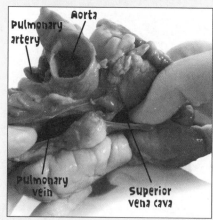

Pulmonary artery
Aorta
Pulmonary vein
Superior vena cava

the aorta (or they might have already been cut off). The other vessels are the *pulmonary arteries* (<u>pull</u>-mun-airy <u>are</u>-ter-ees), which send blood to the lungs to pick up oxygen; the *pulmonary veins*, which carry the freshly oxygenated blood back to the heart so it can be pumped out to the rest of the body; and the *inferior vena cava* and *superior vena cava* (vee-nah <u>cay</u>-vuh), which bring deoxygenated blood back to the heart after it has delivered oxygen to the body. In general, arteries take blood away from the heart and the veins bring it back.

4. While you're exploring the top of the heart, two other fun things to look for are the *auricles*. There is a right one and a left one, and they look like shriveled troll ears. In fact, their name

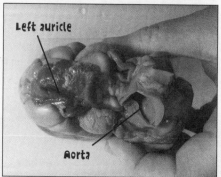

Left auricle
Aorta

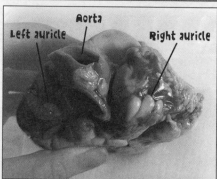

Aorta
Left auricle
Right auricle

comes from the Latin word *auricula*, for ear. These little "ears" cover two of the chambers of the heart, the left atrium and right atrium, collectively called the *atria* (<u>a</u>-tree-ah).

5. Now let's look at the bottom of the heart. It has a pointy end—the *apex* (<u>a</u>-pex)—that points over to the left in your body. That's why your doctor always puts the stethoscope on your left side to listen. (When you hold the heart in your hand and you're looking at the front, the apex will point to your right.)

FRONT OF HEART

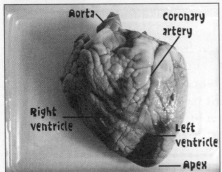

BACK OF HEART

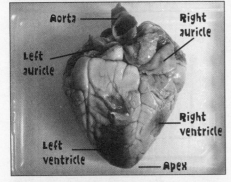

6. Looking at the front of the heart, search for some small blood vessels that look a bit like a branching river. These are some of the *coronary arteries*, and they supply blood to the heart itself. Your heart is made of muscle cells that need oxygen and nutrients just like all the other cells in your body. If these blood vessels become clogged from eating too much fat, cholesterol, and sugar in one's lifetime, it's bad news. So eat a healthy diet! Keep your heart healthy!

7. In the lower part of the heart there are two other important chambers known as the *ventricles* (<u>ven</u>-trick-uls). The right ventricle and the left ventricle are really strong muscle-y parts that contract and push your blood out to the lungs and all the other parts of the body.

8. Ask an adult to cut through the side of the left ventricle and go all the way to the other side of the heart. Stop just before you cut through the wall on the other side.

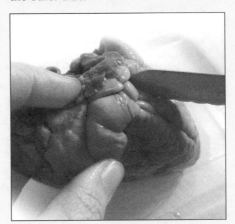

9. Spread the heart open and see if you can find the things we labeled in our photo. You might be surprised that the chambers (atria and ventricles) are pretty small. They're just big enough to hold the blood that pumps out to your body with each squeeze of the heart.

10. You may also notice some stringy things that connect the muscle to some clear tissue. These are parts of the valves of your heart. The valves open and close to make sure that blood goes in the right direction and doesn't flow backward. The stringy parts are called *chordae tendineae* (<u>core</u>-deh ten-<u>din</u>-ee-ah), though they're commonly known as heartstrings. They're made out of the same strong yet flexible stuff (collagen) as your tendons, which attach your muscles to your bones.

And if all that dissecting worked up an appetite, have a heart! For dinner! Just search for lamb's heart recipes online.

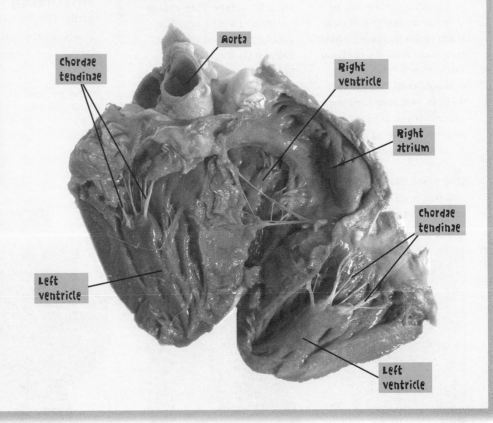

ICK-TIVITY

DRY-ROAST A CRICKET

1½ HOURS

You know how a lobster has to be cooked when it's alive? Just like a lobster, never eat a cricket that is already dead when you find it. Once they die, they begin to decompose and that means bacteria are getting to work.

GO FETCH

- About 15 live crickets (you can catch them yourself, or buy them at most pet stores)
- Cooking pot
- Water
- Salt
- Roasting pan
- An adult

1. Put your LIVE crickets in a plastic ziplock bag or storage container and pop them in the fridge for about two hours until it's roasting time. They'll "chill out" in the cold air, get really mellow, and stop jumping around. If you don't want to see them move at all, freeze them for an hour or two.

2. When they are good and still, grab a grown-up to help, and carefully put the crickets into a pot of boiling water (with a dash of salt) for two minutes or so.

3. Now, remove them from the water and arrange them on a roasting pan. Pop them into the oven and turn the heat to 200°F. You want to slowly roast them for about an hour or maybe just a bit longer. They should be dry and a little crumbly. Careful not to burn them! These bitty bugs are NOT tasty when burned. You can sprinkle your roasted friends with a little salt and chow down if you are starving. But they will be super yummy in your chirp cookies (see next page), so resist the temptation!

Casu Marzu—You have to be skeptical about something officially known as "rotten cheese" or "maggot cheese." But in Sardinia, Italy, the makers of *casu marzu* deliberately cut a hole in sheep's-milk cheese to let "cheese flies" enter and lay eggs. When they hatch, the larvae burrow around a bit and start eating the fat. Then they poop. When the cheese is crawling with thousands of maggots and maggot poop, you can take a bite. Oh, and as you eat it, the larvae jump around, some even as high as 6 inches! What does it taste like? To some, soggy baby diapers with a gruesome aftertaste. But to others, it's a bit like yummy soft Gorgonzola and black pepper! It just goes to show that what some people find icky, others find yummy.

Fugu—For eaters who like flirting with danger, nothing tops a meal of *fugu*, the Japanese name for pufferfish. *Fugu* fish guts contain a poison that is 1,200 times deadlier than cyanide. One drop the size of a head of a pin can kill a person. Chefs that serve it have to train for more than two years to learn how to remove all traces of poison from the fish, and a plate of it will cost at least $200.

Witchetty Grubs—Want to rustle up some grub? Rustle up some REAL grubs! Simply spear a witchetty grub or two. These wood-eating moth larvae are yummy raw, just plucked from a tree.

Bet you can't eat just one witchetty grub!

Or you can roast them over some hot coals. Aboriginal Australians adore these plump grubs that are loaded with protein and healthy fat. They say they taste like scrambled eggs.

BUGGY TREATS

If the thought of eating a baby bug seems creepy to you, consider this: You don't have to eat insects in their larval form. You can eat the adults too! In fact, about two BILLION people in the world eat bugs on a regular basis. Street vendors in China sell scorpions on a stick. In Cambodia, fried grasshoppers and tarantulas are popular snack foods. Beetles, crickets, giant water bugs—roasted, toasted, fried, boiled, or just plain raw—are all deemed yummy in many parts of the world. Might we "bee" missing out on something better than candy?

THREE REASONS TO BITE A BUG

1. So many choices! People munch on more than 1,900 different kinds of bugs. You could eat a different bug every day for more than five years.

2. Better than beef! Grasshoppers have almost as much protein per pound as a lean beef burger. Certain species of caterpillar are equal to turkey legs in the nutritional punch they pack.

3. Home, home, not on the range. Bugs don't need pastures to roam in or barnyards. As far as a bug is concerned, the cozier the space, the better. So raising bugs for food makes good ecological sense.

Eating organs and bugs not enough for you?

Want to REALLY test your stomach? Check out VOMIT on page 239. *Psssst:* You just might want to bring a barf bag! But first, find out what happens to your chocolate chirp cookies after you digest them—POOP is next!

ICK-TIVITY

CHOCOLATE CHIRP COOKIES
40 MINUTES

GO FETCH

Bet you've eaten your fair share of chocolate chip cookies. Now it's time to try a *chocolate chirp* cookie.

1. Preheat the oven to 375°F. Ask your adult to help with all the oven stuff.

2. Mix the butter, both sugars, and the vanilla. Beat until the mixture is smooth and creamy. Beat in the eggs and then slowly add the flour, baking soda, and salt. Stir in the crickets and chocolate chips.

3. Place rounded teaspoonfuls of the mixture onto a greased baking tray and pop them in the oven for 8 to 10 minutes.

- I cup unsalted butter, softened
- 3/4 cup superfine sugar
- 3/4 cup brown sugar
- I teaspoon vanilla
- 2 eggs
- 2 1/4 cups plain flour
- I teaspoon baking soda
- I teaspoon salt
- Your dry-roasted crickets (about 15)
- 12 ounces semisweet chocolate chips
- Mixing spoon
- Mixing bowl
- Baking tray
- Insect-loving adult

4. Let the cookies cool and then dig in! Careful not to rub your legs together afterward. You just might chirp!

POOP

The end of the line. The final farewell. Poop is the last step in a meal's journey to the light at the end of YOUR tunnel. Each and every day, the dark twisty tubes of your digestive system move all those plates of food you gorged on from your mouth to your butt. (See **GUTS** on page 107 for the juicy details on that long, squishy voyage.) Of that mass of yumminess you devoured, only a small amount ends up floating in your toilet. It's time to celebrate *feces* (<u>fee</u>-sees), also known as *dung, scat, stool*—or as we fondly call it, *number two*.

FROM FUDGE BROWNIE TO . . . WELL . . . FUDGE BROWNIE

Let's say that you had one or two brownies one afternoon. Now it's the next day and you are wondering, "What exactly is that brown stuff sinking to the bottom of the toilet bowl?" Well, about three-quarters of it is water and the other 25 percent, the solid part, includes undigested food, dead cells, body waste, and the mostly dead, mostly friendly bacteria that helped digest your food.

These bacteria are the ones we have to thank for the delightful fragrance wafting up from the bowl.

Your brown biscuits also contain some very *unfriendly* bacteria—bacteria that might still be alive. That's why grown-ups remind you to wash your hands *every* time you make a potty stop. (*Pssssst!* You ARE washing, right? RIGHT??) If you like to play video games during a long bathroom visit, give your phone or game console a wipe with some disinfectant. Studies have found that 16 percent of cell phones are covered with E. coli—some of which are *very* unfriendly bacteria.

What else lurks in your poop? There are also some dead cells that have been shed from your stomach, small intestine, and your blood. And there are lumpy leftovers—all the really junky bits of food that your body had no use for—stuff like tough, stringy vegetable fibers and undigested seeds. You might even find whole kernels of corn or other recognizable bits.

RAINBOW POOP

Wonder why your poop is brown? Say thanks to *bile* and *bilirubin*. Bile is a yellow-green-brown substance made in your liver and its job is to break down fats during digestion. Bilirubin is found in bile and is made of your no-longer-useful red blood cells. Parts of old red blood cells turn brown as they get broken down and—you guessed it—make your poop brown too!

But poop can also come in other hues. It might look greenish if it passes through you too quickly (the

FUN ANIMAL FECAL FACTS

- The biggest poop award goes to the biggest animal, the blue whale! They leave bright orange skid marks, the length of a school bus, in the sea.

- African elephants can poop around 300 pounds a day! That's the same weight as three or four kids.

- Can you shoot your poop 6 feet across the room? No? The tiny (inch-and-a-half-long) skipper caterpillar can!

- A goose typically poops once every 12 minutes (and yes, they can poop while flying).

- When you pick up a pet rat prepare to be pooped on. That's one way rats defend themselves, because an animal in the wild would be less likely to eat something that just dropped a stink bomb.

- Dung beetles are not only adorable, they love poop! They search out poop, roll it into balls (sometimes larger than the beetles themselves), and munch on the balls later or use them to lay their eggs inside. When the babies hatch, they can eat their cozy dung crib. Food and furniture all in one!

Twelve Ways to Say YOU GOTTA GO!!!

Say good-bye to Winnie the Poo

Serve up a Poo-Poo Platter

Gotta go boom boom

Code brown

Drop some friends off at the pool

Say good-bye to Mr. Brown

Tickets to the Super Bowl

Bake the brown biscuit

Do a doo-doo

Number 2

Go make brownies

Pinch a loaf

dreaded *diarrhea*) or if you eat a ton of green veggies. Is your poop yellow and a little shiny? That sometimes happens if you have eaten a deep-fried meal and your poop contains a lot of fat. It can also be a sign of a serious disease, so ask your doc if you see yellow. If your poop is bright red or black (and you haven't recently gorged on beets or red food coloring), go see a doctor right away. Blood in your poop is no joke. (Black poop means there is bleeding farther up in your intestines.)

BOWEL HABITS

How long does it take food to wend its way through your digestive system and come out the other end? You can find out for yourself. Corn kernels are very difficult for the human gut to break down. Figure out your body's "transit time" by munching some corn on the cob and then seeing how long it takes to come out the other end. One day? Two? Longer? Keep track of the doo-ings.

WHO POOPED THAT PILE?

GO FETCH →

Poop is everywhere! Go for a walk in nature and you just might see some interesting brown/black/grayish piles of scat. Knowing which animal did the deed could be a lifesaver. After all, you don't want to round a corner and see a grizzly, right?

A stick

Ruler

Camera

Disposable protective gloves (optional)

Hand sanitizer (optional)

1. First things first. Some important rules: Only look; never touch. If you do decide to poke a pile, use a stick.

Use your deductive powers to figure out who dunnit!

2. Go out and start exploring! When you encounter scat, take a picture. The poop you will find depends on where you live. If you live out in the country, you will find very different critters' poop than a city dweller will. Kids in Alaska will find different wildlife from what Florida kids find.

3. Ask yourself the following questions:

● How long is each "deposit"? How wide? Use your ruler to measure the poop's size (without actually touching the poop with the ruler or your hands).

● How many plops are there? Lots and lots, or just one or two?

● What is the shape? Round like a little ball? Like a tube, sort of a Tootsie Roll shape? Does it look twisted or braided like a thick rope, or smooth like a toilet paper roll?

● Study the ends of each bit of scat. Is one end flat and the other pointy or pinched, or are both ends the same?

● Can you see anything sticking out of the poop? Maybe seeds, berries, or a stray insect part?

● Is the scat fresh or has it started to dry out? What time of day is it? Could it have been left by a nocturnal critter?

● Are there any trees above the plop spot? Might the doo-doo have come from high above?

● Is there any white stuff in the poop? That's a clue! It means your pile of poop came from a bird, reptile, or frog, because their pee and poop end up coming out from the same hole, called a cloaca. In these creatures their pee (known as uric acid) comes out as a white paste. The black part is the poo.

4. Now use the handy "Key to the Scat Kingdom" chart to ID the poop!

Note: Were you able to identify the dog and deer poop in the photographs?

THE KEY TO THE SCAT KINGDOM

Here's how to identify the differently shaped butt gifts of our feathered, scaled, and furry friends.

SOLID SHAPE
Color: Black • Brown

SPLAT-SHAPED FLUID
Color: Whitish

About ¼". Small seed-shaped pellets
EEEK!! A MOUSE

Bigger than ½". Not seedlike

A dried liquid TRA-LA! **SONGBIRDS**

A dried powder **HISS!—REPTILES**

Round or oval shape

Tootsie Roll shape

Lots of roundish cylinders
DOE A DEER

Smooth and round
BUNNY-DO

Tube-shaped, less than 1" long

Tube-shaped, more than 1" long

Smooth. Round at both ends

Rough texture. Not round at both ends

Flattish threads
POP GOES THE WEASEL

Roundish-not-flat tubular shape

Woody fibers or nutty bits
IT'S A TREE SQUIRREL

No visible woody fibers
IT'S A GROUND SQUIRREL

Rounded at both ends

Pointy at one end
MEOW

Pointy at both ends
FOX TROTS!

Pinched ends. Rough texture but no visible bug-parts
OH, RATS!

One flat end, one pointy. Sparkly from insect bits
BATS, MAN!

Varies with food. Usually smooth. Insect parts sometimes
LET'S PLAY 'POSSUM

Has some hair in it. Not covered. Sort of smooth. Has twisty lines here and there
CANINE CACA

Covered by leaves. Grainy, loaf-shaped. Might have bits of nuts and berries sticking out
RACCOON

Not smooth. Covered by leaves. Might have insect bits but usually no plant parts. Dark color
I SMELL A SKUNK

And how often should you go? Humans have a pretty wide "normal range." Some folks poop three times a day. Some go once every three days. Everyone has a slightly different pattern, and that's okay, as long as you feel good and the pattern stays the same. If you have to go constantly or you can rarely go and you feel uncomfortable, it might be time to check with your friendly neighborhood doctor. Drinking plenty of water and eating lots of good veggies can keep your pooping parts happy.

EATING THE BROWN BISCUIT

For some animals, feces is actually a super-yummy treat. In fact, rats *need* to eat their own poop. Scientists discovered that young rats that didn't snack on their poopy pellets suffered from stunted growth. A rabbit is another animal that is big on

A rare and pricey treat—coffee beans pooped out by the palm civet.

coprophagia (cah-pruh-<u>fay</u>-gee-uh)—the official word for eating doo-doo. Why do they do it? As you may have noticed the last time you had corn on the cob for dinner, certain veggies and fruits are hard for us to digest. Eating poop gives critters another pass at the nutrients they might have missed the first time. Remember the cows who chewed and upchucked a mouthful of grass over and over, on page 109? That's a different approach to getting the most nutrients out of food.

Dogs are partial to poop-pops too. A new doggie mom will eat her puppies' poos to keep her den tidy. Some dogs like to munch on deer scat, which is rich in plant matter. Think of it as the salad course. However, if your dog eats its own poop, it might mean that you are not feeding it nutritious-enough food, or it might have a digestive problem. Time to see the vet!

What about us humans? We can't eat our own poop because it contains bacteria that would make us sick. And we don't eat any other animal's poop outright, but the world's rarest and most expensive coffee beans are plucked from the scat (another name for animal poop) of the palm civet—a mammal that looks like a big cat or a weasel. In Indonesia, civets eat the ripe coffee beans, and enzymes in their gut give the beans a unique and memorable flavor. The coffee is so good that it can sell for more than $600 a pound. Coming soon to a coffee shop near you? Likewise, over in Tanzania in East Africa, Hadza women harvest softened baobab tree seeds from baboon poop. They pick them out, carefully wash and dry them, then pound them into an extra-tasty flour.

PUTTING POOP TO WORK

Should all poop be flushed away? NO! Many kinds of poop can be used for fertilizer, and bat poop, called *guano*, was once used in the making of gunpowder. In parts of North Africa, folks used to utilize just-dropped horse or camel dung as a cure for dysentery, which is a sort of mega diarrhea, and some rural tribespeople still do. In Thailand,

Indonesian palm civets choose the ripest coffee beans.

FECAL TRANSPLANTS

You've heard of donating blood. Would you donate poop too? Perhaps you are asking, WHY would you do such a thing? Medical researchers have discovered that donated poop can actually help with illness! Here is one way: Some people have extremely bad problems with their digestion. This can be a dangerous side effect of taking antibiotics, which kill off the friendly, helpful-to-digestion bacteria in their intestines and allow bad bacteria called *Clostridium difficile* to move in. Those *C. diff* baddies make toxins that can harm the intestines, and that means terrible diarrhea and cramps, day after day, month after month. These people can't get the nutrients they need from their food. It's not something you'd ever want to experience! For years, doctors couldn't figure out a good treatment other than taking more antibiotics, but recently an experimental procedure seems to be working as well as one-poo-three!

Take feces from a healthy person, stir in some salty water, mix, and filter out any chunks, then inject it via a tube into the ill person's bum. The good bacteria in the poop can then take over again and kick out those *C. diff* bad guys. It definitely has a "yuck" factor but doctors who administer this treatment say it has an almost 95 percent cure rate. Researchers from MIT are also working on a fecal transplant pill. Perhaps other illnesses can be tackled with a nifty infusion of poop puree and poop pills!

elephant dung—which has a lot of long, stringy fibers in it—is collected, washed, dried, and pounded into beautiful writing paper.

Scientists and engineers are busy exploring all sorts of ways to turn feces into usable fuel. For many thousands of years people all over the world have burned animal dung as a heat source. Research is currently being done on using chicken poop, cow turds, and good old human doo-doo for electrical energy, to keep homes warm in the winter, and even to fuel cars. One way is to collect poop in special tanks. As microbes digest it they release methane gas, which can be burned for energy. In fact, there may be a cow-powered biogas facility near you that you could visit today! Another method uses solar energy to release hydrogen gas from the turds. Someday there just might be a pipe running straight from your toilet to a processing station in the family garage so you can power your car from your family's droppings.

TURD TASTIES

GO FETCH ➡

30 MINUTES

Unless you are a rat or a bunny, eating poop is totally disgusting. However, you can make something that *looks* like poop but is actually totally delicious. These cookies can be made to suit any dietary needs, as they are flour-free (and therefore gluten-free)—and can be dairy- and nut-free too.

1. Place the butter in the bottom of the saucepan and put the saucepan on the stove.

2. With an adult's help, turn on the burner to medium.

3. While the butter melts, measure your sugar, milk, and cocoa powder.

4. When the butter is melted, add the sugar, milk, and cocoa powder and stir until it is all mixed and comes to a boil.

5. Keep cooking for another minute, being sure to stir and watch the mixture so it doesn't boil over.

6. Turn off the stove and put your saucepan on a cool burner.

7. Add the peanut butter and vanilla and stir until well mixed.

8. Add the oats 1 cup at a time and stir. If it seems pretty thick after 3 cups (or if you want to add some of the "chunky" ingredients), you can stop adding oats. You want to be able to smoosh the dough into poopy shapes that won't break apart, so you don't want it too chunky.

9. Add any of the optional chunky ingredients as desired. Know that the more you add, the more likely it is that your "turd tasties" will fall apart.

I stick (¹/₂ cup) butter or vegetable spread

Saucepan

Wooden spoon or spatula

Stovetop

Adult

³/₄ cup granulated or brown sugar

¹/₂ cup milk or milk alternative

4 tablespoons dark cocoa powder

I cup crunchy peanut butter (or a non-nut butter)

I teaspoon vanilla extract

4 cups quick-cook oats

I cookie sheet or other plate

Wax or parchment paper

Unused roll of toilet paper

Optional: chocolate chips, dried coconut, flax or sunflower seeds, raisins or dried cranberries, rice cereal, dried orange peel, or candied ginger chunks

---

10. When the mixture has cooled enough to handle (test it carefully with the tip of your finger first), grab a handful and shape it into whatever form is most icky to you. You can roll the dough between your hands to make long logs and form them into the classic *S* shape. You could make little round deer or bunny poops. Another option is to roll it into round, flat "cow pies."

11. Place your tasty turds on a cookie sheet or plate covered with wax paper. Let them cool on the counter if it's not too hot in your house. You can also put them in the refrigerator to cool. If you don't warn your family, they are in for quite a surprise when they reach in for a snack!

ICKY SERVING SUGGESTIONS

Cover a plate with toilet paper from a BRAND-NEW roll (the one next to your toilet may be contaminated with bacteria). Arrange your poopy creations on the toilet paper. You could even place the rest of the roll near the plate, for extra icky effect. Or . . . get an aluminum baking pan that looks a bit like a kitty litter box. Fill it with any cereal that resembles kitty litter: crispy rice cereal would do, or anything with nuggets. Lay your poop cookies on top and watch your guests be really grossed out when you offer them a bite. You could even find a large spoon or spatula that can serve as the kitty litter scoop. Ewww!

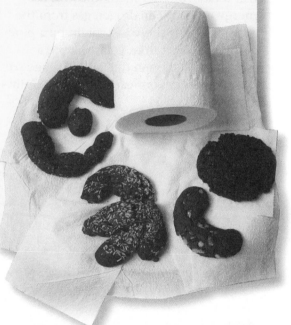

The Putrid Past

The place? China, a long, long time ago. The job? Inspector of the emperor's poop. It's true. A lucky fellow got to sniff and stir the imperial droppings every day to make sure that the emperor was being well nourished and kept in the best of health.

Over in France, back in the days when they still had kings running the show, lucky guests were invited to watch the king wake up in the morning. Part of the event involved the fun of watching the king going number two. One really lucky person was invited to wipe the royal butt. It was considered an honor. What would you do if you were asked? How fast can you run?

FUN WITH FECES!

Looking for a new sport? How about trying your hand at a turd-toss contest in Oklahoma? Turns out a cow plop makes a fine Frisbee, and the winning distance for a flying cow chip is more than half the length of a football field.

Don't want to actually touch, let alone toss, a turd? Play cow plop bingo instead. In places with lots of cows, like Vermont, a field is marked with a grid, and each square gets a number and a letter. On game day, you buy a square, then wait. A cow will be allowed to wander around for a while. A cow being a cow, it will definitely drop a bomb at some point during the contest (which are often fund-raisers). If you hold the winning number and letter combo, you win! Isn't poop fun?

And that's the scoop on poop! But where would Number Two be without its dear companion, Number One? Check out URINE on page 224 to become a world-class authority on the golden tinkle! And if the Earth shook the last time you took a big dump, you might like to read the next chapter—QUAKES AND SINKHOLES!

Take sports to a whole new level. Test your skills tossing cow chips at the Flint Hills Fest in Emporia, Kansas.

Quakes & Sinkholes

Y ou've probably figured out by now that you can't walk on water. Dirt, on the other hand, seems like pretty solid stuff—able to support your weight, even if you're an elephant. But in some places in the world a patch of solid earth can suddenly start to shake, rattle, and roll. It can split apart, and even swallow an entire house in a matter of seconds. So let's do some digging and learn how the earth beneath our feet sometimes has a mind of its own!

EARTHQUAKES, YIKES!

W hat's at the top of the natural-disaster-destruction chart? Earthquakes! Very powerful, very scary! What triggers a quake? Imagine a hot berry pie baking in the oven. Sometimes the pie crust cracks from the motion of those bubbling berries. The Earth is a bit like that pie. Underneath the Earth's crust there are large areas of molten rock—the same stuff that spews out of volcanoes (zip back to LAVA, page 144, for a refresher course if you need one). Huge areas of rock are always pushing together or pulling apart, causing the Earth's crust to break into enormous drifting pieces called *tectonic plates*. The places where these plates bump into one another are called *fault zones*, and that's where the trouble starts.

Imagine what would happen if you shoved two of your aunt Zelda's fine china plates into each other. Smithereens, right? But the movement of tectonic plates is slow ... slow ... slower than molasses: only 1 to 2 inches per year. But, even though the movement is super slow, when two plates meet, big changes occur, including rock-smashing, building-toppling, ground-wobbling earthquakes. Here's how: As two plates grind against each other, lots of tension builds up. (Try rubbing one sweaty hand across another ... Feel how the tension builds up before your palms slip past each other?) Earthquakes happen when the plates finally overcome the friction, releasing tons of energy very quickly and shaking the ground with *seismic* (<u>size</u>-mik) *waves*. Earthquakes can knock down buildings as easily as you can shake up an Etch A Sketch.

TOPPLING TOOTHPICK TOWERS

40 MINUTES

PLUS 4 HOURS OF JELL-O PREP & COOLING TIME

GO FETCH

- Jell-O or other gelatin-based dessert
- Water
- Bread pan or small casserole dish
- Trusty adult
- Cooking oil spray
- Cookie sheet
- Modeling clay, such as Play-Doh
- Toothpicks

Someday it could be your job to design and build structures that can handle earthquakes. But before you pursue your degree in architecture and engineering, you might want to get some hands-on practice. In this wobbly experiment, you'll investigate which types of designs can withstand earthquakes, and which are better to avoid.

1. First, create some shaky ground to build your towers on. Do this step at least four hours before you want to do the experiment. Make some gelatin in your pan or dish according to the directions on the box. This includes boiling water, so involve your trusty adult. Spraying your container with cooking oil first will help make the gelatin easy to remove after it cools. Make enough so your gelatin is at least an inch thick.

2. Once your gelatin has cooled for about four hours, flip it over and ease it out of its mold onto a cookie sheet.

3. Roll and squeeze pieces of your modeling clay into a few dozen blueberry-size balls or cubes.

4. Now it's time to build your toothpick towers! You can join toothpicks together by sticking their ends into the round pieces of modeling clay. It's okay to break toothpicks into smaller pieces if you want. Consider using four toothpicks and four clay balls to make a square, or three toothpicks and three clay balls to make a triangle. By combining these simple shapes, you can start to construct three-dimensional towers on top of the gelatin.

5. Time to test your tower. First, use your fist and bang on the bottom of the table underneath the gelatin. Congratulations if your tower survived this vertical force! And if it didn't, congratulations are still in order. You learned what design NOT to use.

6. Now, if it's still standing, give the side of your Jell-O some gentle whacks with your hand. If you wish, let your inner Godzilla out by being less gentle. How does your tower withstand a horizontal force?

7. Repeat Steps 3 to 6 with different designs. Experiment with what types of structures are the most earthquake-proof. Give yourself an engineering challenge: What is the tallest tower that you can build with only 15 or 25 toothpicks? Can you build a tower that can support a plastic plate or cup on top and still withstand vibrations? Does breaking the toothpicks into smaller pieces help?

WHAT JUST HAPPENED?

If you made a structure based on triangles, you probably just experienced the advantage of triangular bracing. A triangle may only have three sides, but it's sturdier than a square. Think about it: If you apply pressure sideways along the top of a square, you'll turn it into a squished rhombus, which is definitely not a good shape for a building. However, triangles are not as easy to deform. This is why builders use triangles in the frames of buildings (even though the triangles may be hidden behind walls).

Earthquakes make two basic types of waves: body waves, which travel through the inside (or body) of the Earth, and surface waves, which travel along the outside (or surface) of the Earth. When you banged on the bottom of the gelatin, you were simulating a body wave. When you shook the side of the gelatin, you were simulating a surface wave. Body waves move faster (they are the first sign of an earthquake), but surface waves cause much more destruction. Your toothpick tower was probably less damaged by thumping the bottom of the table and more damaged by shaking the sides.

San Andreas Fault

IT'S NOT MY FAULT!!!

Located in California, the world-famous San Andreas Fault is 810 miles of *strike slip fault*, the kind of fault where two tectonic plates slide in opposite directions alongside each other. Here, the Pacific plate and the North American plate are constantly moving very s-l-o-w-l-y. Each year they move approximately as far as your fingernails will grow in the same time period—about 2½ inches. Usually the plates simply slide past one another, but every once in a while they rub and get stuck. Imagine a metal spring getting pushed down and flattened. When the coil is released it springs back with a lot of force. That's kind of what happens to the stuck part of the plate. It releases with tremendous force to make *seismic waves*—the words we use to describe all that quivering earth. Because the San Andreas Fault happens to be in an area where a lot of people live, California now has laws that require buildings and bridges to be designed in a way that makes them sway in an earthquake, instead of crumbling.

ICK-SPERIMENT

SINKING CITIES

GO FETCH →

Some things are safest to observe in "pretend" mode instead of in real life, like hungry dinosaurs, the bubonic plague, or liquefaction from an earthquake. Unless they want to compete with the Leaning Tower of Pisa, architects have to pay close attention to the soil they are building on. In this experiment, you'll measure how well structures on different types of ground can resist earthquake-induced liquefaction (see page 194).

- 3 shoebox-size waterproof containers
- Enough sand to cover about 3 inches of the bottom of a container
- Similar amount of gravel
- Ditto for dirt
- Water
- City toys (see step 4 for details)
- Your fist or a mallet

1. Come up with your hypothesis on which type of material (sand, gravel, or dirt) will be most susceptible to liquefaction.

Tectonic plates move in 3 different ways

They move away from each other (which can cause valleys on land and trenches in the sea floor).

They move toward each other (the process that builds mountains over eons).

They move side by side (with one plate sliding in one direction, while the other slides in the opposite).

All of these movements can create earthquakes, but especially the last two. The reason California is so earthquake-prone is that it straddles the place where the Pacific plate slides against the North American plate.

2. Fill the first container with about 3 inches of sand, the second container with about 3 inches of gravel, and the third container with about 3 inches of dirt.

3. Slowly pour water into each container until the water rises almost to the top of the sand, gravel, or dirt.

4. Construction time. Build a miniature city on the surface of each container. Use LEGO bricks, buildings from a model train set, or anything your imagination comes up with to make some structures. Sprinkle some toy cars and action figures around too. Ideally each city will have a similar mix of

components. Whatever you add to your city, make sure they are pushed down about ¼ of an inch into the ground so they are stable.

5. Earthquake time! Use your mallet or fist and bang on the side of each container about 10 to 15 times.

6. Notice what happens to each city. Was your hypothesis correct?

WHAT JUST HAPPENED?

Your earthquakes probably created a lot of chaos in your cities. Structures may have sunk into the ground or tipped over, as the ground itself seemed to liquefy. The city on the sand undoubtedly was the greatest disaster, whereas the gravel and dirt cities probably fared better. This is because sand particles are rounder and more similar in size, which reduces the opportunity for friction and makes liquefaction more likely. All the particles of sand were perfectly happy to stay where they were until *somebody* started getting all earthquake-y on them. One slow big push would have squeezed the water out, but lots of quick impacts don't give the water enough time to get out of the way. So the water is trapped and doesn't let the soil particles pack closer together. The result is that the dirt has an identity crisis: The particles slide all over each other and behave more like a liquid than a solid.

How can you avoid liquefaction? Experiment with different types of soil, such as mixing gravel with sand. Ground that has a variety of small and large particles, is densely packed, and has angular (and not round) particles is less susceptible to becoming soupy when it's Earth crunch time.

STUCK IN QUICKSAND? THINK QUICK!

The Earth has some other soil tricks up its dirty sleeves. Maybe you've seen a movie where someone steps into quicksand and a few horrifying moments later, nothing but a finger or two are sticking up before one final *glug-glug-glug* and some sad music. Well—HOGWASH! Quicksand isn't so deadly, so you can stop freaking out!

Unlike beach sand, where the grains are packed tightly together with just a little water and air around the grains, quicksand can be up to 70 percent water and air, with the grains of sand suspended in between. So it looks like solid ground but is really a big wet blob.

What happens if you step in quicksand? It's not a pleasant feeling to be sure, but it's also not a death sentence! So how DO you get out? For starters do NOT start thrashing around. Quicksand will only get harder the more you thrash. It's a non-Newtonian fluid, so it behaves more like a solid than a liquid when you move quickly. (Learn MUCH more about that in SLIME, page 204.) And don't ask a friend to pull you out . . . you might pull them in! Instead S-L-O-W-L-Y wriggle your legs apart as much as you can and get them up toward the surface. This creates space for water to seep in, loosening the sand around your limbs. Lie back, spreading your body out flat on the surface of the sand, then roll over and slowly crawl to safer soil. You'll get dirty, but you will get out!

LIQUID EARTH

During an earthquake, solid ground sometimes acts like a liquid, which makes it really hard for buildings and people to remain standing. You probably know that much of the ground beneath our feet is pretty wet with groundwater (that's why people drill holes to make wells). An earthquake's violent shaking can cause the water-saturated soil particles to lose contact with one another. Those sloshy soil particles that were once a solid start to act like a liquid and flow. This process is called *liquefaction* (lick-wi-<u>fack</u>-shun) for all you budding geologists. You can probably imagine what will happen to anything

Stuck in quicksand, this car is going nowhere fast.

resting on top of liquefying earth. As the ground begins to flow, it can't support any weight. Down come any buildings atop it!

When the shaking stops, the soil particles will once again become terra firma—solid earth—but the damage has already been done.

THAT SINKING FEELING

One minute everything was calm and quiet at the National Corvette Museum in Bowling Green, Kentucky. The next, an enormous hole, 40 feet wide by 60 feet long, opened up and swallowed an entire roomful of classic cars. One otherwise normal Sunday afternoon in Guatemala City in 2010, the ground suddenly gave way, sucking a small factory into a chasm about 300 feet deep.

Certain places on Earth are prone to *sinkholes*—places where the layer under the topsoil is made of limestone. Limestone is a type of rock that dissolves easily in acidic water, and sometimes, pockets of water underground—called groundwater—can be really acidic. Over time, groundwater seeps up through the limestone, eating away at it and hollowing out a cavern. The cavern is unnoticeable to folks walking around above because it is still covered by the topsoil. However, if limestone is constantly eroded by the

Now THAT'S a big sinkhole!

This round sinkhole in Guatemala City is 30 stories deep.

acid-laced water, it can reach a point when the weight on top of the cavern finally becomes too much. Crash! The roof of the cavern (which may also be the ground you are standing on), collapses into the empty cavity below.

Sinkholes can accidentally be made by human activity. Some soil layers that rest above groundwater supplies are slightly supported by the water pressure underneath it. When people pump water out of the ground, it removes the structural support that the water was providing to the top layer of soil. UH-OH! Sinkhole! In other words, both the presence *and* absence of water can create sinkholes. Either way, sometimes things get sunk!

These prized sports cars went on an unexpected road trip when a sinkhole opened in the Corvette Museum in Bowling Green, Kentucky, in 2014.

SINKHOLE ROULETTE

20 MINUTES

GO FETCH

There are certain things you take for granted—like the ground not swallowing you up. But even though the odds of this happening are staggeringly low, it's interesting to experiment with how sinkholes appear. Grab a friend and a few simple supplies to test your luck at avoiding these unpredictable geological pitfalls.

1. Cut a strip of aluminum foil about 2 inches wide and 14 inches long. Tape the ends of the foil strip together to form a circular ring. Place the ring in the casserole dish.

2. Curl and tape each piece of paper into a short tube that is 2 inches high. These represent limestone chambers, which exist in some soils.

3. Don't let your friend watch the next five steps. Stand the tubes in different locations in the ring.

4. Fill up the ring with sand almost to the top, but try to keep sand from going into the tubes (a little is okay). It's easiest if you try to stand up the

Aluminum foil

Scissors

Tape

Casserole dish

3 pieces of paper,
   2 inches wide x 4 inches long

Sand

Funnel

Sugar

Several tiny toy houses (like hotels in Monopoly or LEGO bricks)

Water

tubes with one hand while pouring in some sand with the other.

5. Use a funnel to fill each tube almost to the top with sugar, which represents limestone. You want the sugar level to be as high as the sand.

6. Pull the paper tubes out, leaving the columns of sugar in the sand.

7. To conceal your sugary limestone deposits, lightly sprinkle just enough sand on top to cover them up.

8. Invite your friend back and have them place the toy houses on top of the sand.

9. Slowly pour water into the casserole dish until it's about an inch below the top of the sand. This "groundwater" will immediately start to infiltrate your chunk of land. Soon, you'll see the sand turn wet as it gets saturated with the water. And then, your sinkholes will start to appear. Oops! Did one of your houses get dragged down?

WHAT JUST HAPPENED?

Sugar and limestone have something in common: They both dissolve in water. As the water seeped through the sand, it dissolved the sugar and created weak spots that couldn't hold the thin layer of sand on top. If a house happened to be there, down it went! Of course, limestone dissolves at a MUCH slower rate than sugar. The Earth is in no rush to produce sinkholes, but it has a big head start on you, being about 4.5 billion years old.

Scabs AND Stitches

What is it about a scab that makes it so tempting to play with? Why do we have the urge to pick and then flick those hard, crusty blood blobs that form on our knees or elbows after we take a tumble? They are totally irresistible, but what exactly *are* they?

Think of them as bike helmets for boo-boos. Just as a helmet protects your skull and brain from a close encounter with the pavement, a scab keeps your insides safe from attacks by dangerous germs. So, let's explore how they form and what lurks beneath that lovely crust. Plus, you'll even get to make some model "scabs" you can pick to your heart's content!

IT'S IN THE BAG

When you go to the grocery store, someone probably puts your purchases in a bag. After all, it would be really hard to walk out clutching a bunch of loose cans, cereal boxes, lots of fruit, and a dozen eggs. Like your shopping bag, your skin is basically a big body bag that holds your internal parts—organs, blood vessels, bones, and all the other bits that make you tick. If your grocery bag breaks, your items will roll all over the floor. We can't have that happening with our insides, can we? So our bodies have a way to repair tears and leaks in our skin almost instantly.

P.U., PUS!

What's happening under that crust of dried blood? Well, for one thing, there are a whole lot of dead germs still lying around. A few live ones too. That's a recipe for *pus*—a kind of stew made from bacteria and special white blood cells known as *phagocytes* (fa-guh-sites), including macrophages. Phagocytes' favorite food is dead body cells and dirt with a side of bacteria. That creamy whitish, yellowish ooze that forms is mostly made up of stuffed-to-death phagocytes, dead bacteria, and skin cells. Pus is a sign that your immune system is working to fight off an infection, but it looks pretty gross. Bet you don't want to touch that scab now!

SUPERHERO CELLS TO THE RESCUE!

Let's pretend you just tried to do an old-school kick flip on your skateboard (what were you thinking?). Instead of sticking the landing you went *splat* on the pavement and ended up with road rash, complete with little trickles of blood. Your blood is full of materials that are helpful when you get a wound. Tiny *platelets* (plait-lets) start clinging to blood vessels like a zillion little Post-it notes. They also stick to each other to plug up the wound with a clot, kind of like a cork or a cap on a bottle. This clotting process where blood turns from a liquid to a gel is called *coagulation* (co-agg-u-lay-shon). Add some *fibrin* (fy-brin) strands—elastic bands of protein—that lay themselves atop the platelet plug, and you have the start of a scab.

Once the scab has formed, your immune system can really get to work. White blood cells come rushing toward the wound through the bloodstream, even squeezing through tiny spaces in your blood vessels to get there faster. Some white blood cells—called *macrophages* (mack-row-fay-jiz)—are there to "eat" and destroy any bacteria that don't belong. Their name means "big eater" in Greek, and they form a blob around a bacterium and digest it! Attack of the killer blob! Macrophages can also send out messages, asking other cells, like *B cells*, to come help. B cells are a bit like jailers for bacteria (and viruses). They surround the bad guys by building prison walls made of special proteins called *antibodies* until more macrophages arrive on the scene to finish the job. Meanwhile, more red blood cells arrive, bringing oxygen and nutrients to help the cells that are at work repairing the wound. No wonder your wound gets puffy—all these cells and fluids take up space!

HOUSE OF SCABS

Humans aren't the only living things that make scabs. Other animals heal that way too. But some go beyond just patching *their own* boo-boos. One species of aphids—tiny sap-sucking bugs that wreak havoc in gardens—live in teensy little "houses" called galls. Galls are hollow ball-like growths that form on the plants that aphids (and other insects) have invaded. The gall provides food for the aphids and protects them from bad weather and predators. If a gall gets damaged, out come the aphid repairmen to patch the hole. But this particular type of aphids asks a lot of their handymen. These little guys are known as "suicide plasterers" because they repair the galls by oozing their own bodily fluids over the damaged walls, stirring that ooze with their legs, and then smooshing the goop over the hole to form a scab on the gall wall. That scab hardens in an hour, helping to protect the aphid's territory. It's similar to what happens under your own scabs. But what do these special aphids get for all this heroism? Robbed of all their bodily fluids, they sadly expire!

ICK-TIVITY

SPAGHETTI SCAB DINNER

GO FETCH →

20 MINUTES

Here's a cool way to understand what happens as a cut starts to heal, without the pain of actually getting a cut! This activity about blood clotting and scab formation has the extra bonus of being totally edible—if you can stomach it, that is.

1. Have an adult help you boil the lasagna and spaghetti. It's okay to cook both types of pasta together. The lasagna takes a little longer to cook, so drop it in a few minutes before the spaghetti. When all the pasta is cooked, drain out the water in a colander and pour a little cold water on the pasta so it doesn't stick. Then pop it back in the pot to keep it warm.

2. Heat up your tomato sauce in a pot on the stove or in the microwave.

3. Place the lasagna flat on the plate—this pasta strip will represent the inside wall of a blood vessel close to your skin. The plate beneath the lasagna is the outside world. In a perfect world, the blood would never see the light of day (or in this case, the plate). But unfortunately you don't live in a perfect world because . . .

4. OUCH! You've just ridden your bike into a tree. The impact tore a hole in your skin and blood vessels. Represent this by using the knife (with a grown-up's help) to cut a long sliver in the lasagna. Pour a little tomato sauce on the lasagna to represent the blood leaking out from your wound.

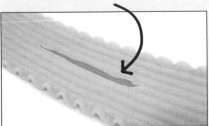

An adult

1 piece of cooked lasagna pasta (wide and flat)

About 10 to 15 strands of cooked spaghetti pasta

Colander

1/4 cup tomato sauce of your choice

Dinner plate

Knife (and an adult to help)

1/8 cup mozzarella cheese, cut into small raisin-size pieces

5 to 8 cherry tomatoes

5. Your body senses that there's been a tear. The first responders are your platelets, which gush toward the hole and link together to try to plug it up. Place the pieces of mozzarella in the lasagna opening, and squeeze them together until they stick. In the same way that the pieces of cheese bond to each other, your platelets connect together too.

6. Platelets alone will do the job if it's a tiny cut, but you've got a big gash. You need something that can hold everything together. Now your body calls in fibrin, long elastic chains of sticky proteins that form a net over the platelets. Cover the cheese with

the spaghetti to represent the weblike fibrin that strengthens the clot.

7. Blood still continues to flow past the wound, and some red blood cells get stuck in the net, making the scab even stronger. Drop the cherry tomatoes (aka red blood cells) on top of the spaghetti to represent this.

WHAT JUST HAPPENED?

You have stopped the bleeding and made a delicious scab that you can eat rather than pick. MUCH tastier than a real scab.

A cool thing about fibrin is that it starts out long and elastic but hardens and contracts over time. This is important because it helps pull the torn skin together to seal up the wound. Your cooked spaghetti can do the same thing. Instead of eating all of your spaghetti scab dinner, leave a little bit of it out overnight and observe how the spaghetti shrinks and tightens its web as it dries out.

A SCAB YOU CAN PICK!

20 MINUTES

GO FETCH →

Since it's a bad idea to pick at a real scab, take a scratch at this instead. You can also use it to see if you can fool your folks into thinking you scraped your knee or elbow (or whatever body part you want).

1. Pour the gelatin into the saucepan.

2. Add the cold water and stir to dissolve.

3. Ask your friendly adult to help you put the mixture on the stove over low heat and stir until the mixture is clear.

4. Take it off the stove and let it cool.

5. While you wait, pour the corn syrup into a small bowl and dip a paintbrush in. Paint a few dabs on your arm or leg, in the size and shape of scabs.

6. Take a pinch of cornmeal or polenta and sprinkle it over your corn-syrup scab. This will give it a nice scabby texture.

7. Wait a few minutes and then gently blow off any excess cornstarch.

8. In another bowl, mix a couple pinches of cocoa or ground coffee with a drop or two of red food coloring and a little bit of corn syrup to color the scab the appropriate scabby color.

9. Test the gelatin carefully with a fingertip to be sure it's cool enough to paint on your skin. It will be thick but still liquid.

10. Gently paint a thin layer of gelatin on top to secure the scab.

11. See if you can fool your adults or friends with the scab. Then pick away to your heart's content!

Materials

- 1 envelope of unflavored gelatin
- Small saucepan
- 1/4 cup cold water
- Mixing spoon
- An adult
- 1 tablespoon corn syrup
- 2 small bowls
- 2 paintbrushes
- 1 tablespoon rough-cut cornmeal or polenta
- Cocoa or ground coffee
- Red food coloring

The Putrid Past

No one likes to get stiches, but be glad you live in the 21st century! In the past, catgut, pig bristles, and kangaroo tendons were used to sew wounds together. And in South America, people used ants to keep the edges of a cut closed. The ant would be placed in a way that its mouth could chomp down on both sides of the wound at once, closing the wound up. Then the ant's body would be twisted off, leaving the dead head stuck in the patient like a clamp. Pretty ingenious, really. Sad for the ant, though!

CREEPING SKIN

Once a scab has formed, your own skin cells start to swell and replicate themselves underneath the scab. They even MOVE themselves over the wound using *pseudopods* (<u>soo</u>-doe-pods)—a bit like little blobby feet. If it weren't so awesomely cool, it might be a little creepy. Soon there is a whole layer of nice new skin under that scab. The scab keeps those new skin cells safe as they grow. So even though it might be itchy, don't pick it or else you'll make your skin and blood cells have to start the healing process all over! Plus you could infect it with whatever lurks under your fingernails. The scab will fall off by itself after a week or two, so be patient.

TWINKLE, TWINKLE, LITTLE SCAR

You might end up with a lifelong reminder of your failed kick flip on your skateboard—a scar. Any injury (including popping a zit) to the deep layer of your skin called the *dermis* (<u>der</u>-miss) can leave white, pink, brown, or silvery permanent marks. Scars are created from layers of a naturally occurring protein called *collagen* (<u>call</u>-uh-gin) that forms underneath the new skin to repair the wound. It's known as scar tissue and it's tough but not as flexible as your original skin. Some scars are flat, and some are bumpy. Some can be quite itchy.

If you are trying to avoid a scar: Don't pick the scab, keep the wound covered with a Band-Aid or other bandage, and ask your doctor if there are ointments you can use to speed up the healing process. You can also ask about clean, moist dressings that may prevent a crusty scab and therefore a scar. Many scars fade over time, and there are even treatments to help them go away. But many folks are proud of their scars and tell tall tales about how they got them. "It was just me and my skateboard—the Olympic gold medal on the line—when I went for that 720 gazelle flip and had a major wipeout! That's how I got this scar, dude!"

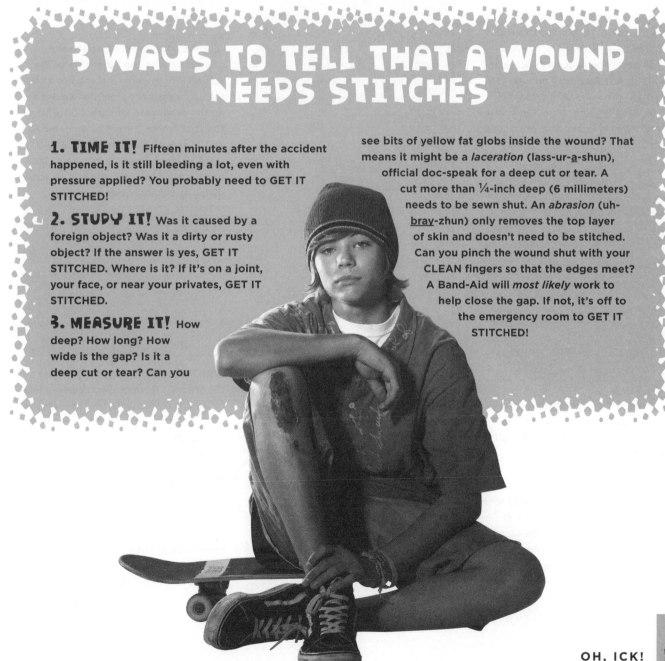

3 WAYS TO TELL THAT A WOUND NEEDS STITCHES

1. TIME IT! Fifteen minutes after the accident happened, is it still bleeding a lot, even with pressure applied? You probably need to GET IT STITCHED!

2. STUDY IT! Was it caused by a foreign object? Was it a dirty or rusty object? If the answer is yes, GET IT STITCHED. Where is it? If it's on a joint, your face, or near your privates, GET IT STITCHED.

3. MEASURE IT! How deep? How long? How wide is the gap? Is it a deep cut or tear? Can you see bits of yellow fat globs inside the wound? That means it might be a *laceration* (lass-ur-<u>a</u>-shun), official doc-speak for a deep cut or tear. A cut more than ¼-inch deep (6 millimeters) needs to be sewn shut. An *abrasion* (uh-<u>bray</u>-zhun) only removes the top layer of skin and doesn't need to be stitched. Can you pinch the wound shut with your CLEAN fingers so that the edges meet? A Band-Aid will *most likely* work to help close the gap. If not, it's off to the emergency room to GET IT STITCHED!

FRANKEN-ORANGE

GO FETCH

1 HOUR

You know Frankenstein didn't sew himself together, right? It takes mad skills to put in that many stitches. Doctors in training need to practice making sutures, but no person would want to be their first guinea pig because they'd end up looking like Frankenstein. So medical students sometimes practice on oranges! You can too.

1. Clumsy orange! It never looks where it's going! Now it has tripped and fallen on a sharp piece of metal. With an adult's help, cut a 2-inch-long slice in the skin, just deep enough to go through the skin but not very far into the flesh of the orange. Cut a little sliver of the skin out so that the wound is open.

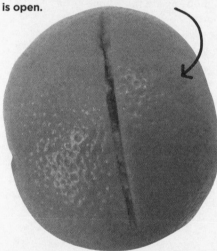

2. To keep the orange from rolling around as you stitch it, slice off a piece on the back of the fruit so that it will sit flat on a plate.

3. To mimic what a doctor would do, "irrigate" the inside of the wound with water. You can use a toy syringe or just hold the orange under the faucet in the sink. Doctors often irrigate a wound with saline solution, which is sterile water and salt, to blast bacteria.

I orange or grapefruit with thick skin

Knife

Plate

I adult to help with the cutting of the orange

Water

Toy syringe (optional)

Towel

I rubbing alcohol wipe from a first-aid kit, or just use water on a cotton ball and pretend it's the real deal

Scissors

Sewing needle (a curved embroidery needle is more like the curved needles that surgeons use)

3 feet of thread. Black is the traditional stitch color, though any color will do.

---

4. Dry the orange by dabbing with a clean towel. You can also pretend to clean the outside of the wound with a rubbing alcohol wipe (or a cotton ball dipped in water as pretend antiseptic).

5. Cut about 12 inches of thread and feed it through the eye of your needle.

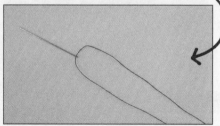

Ask an adult if you don't know how. Pull the thread through until one end is about twice as long as the other, but don't tie a knot.

6. Begin in the middle of the wound, and put your needle through on one end of the cut. It should go through the skin of the orange about ¼ to ½ inch away from the cut. Be careful not to prick your finger with the needle.

7. Push the needle through the orange flesh to the other side of the wound. Try to make it come out about the same distance from the wound as on the other side, directly opposite the spot where it went in. Depending on the size of your needle, you may need to mess around a bit to get the needle to go in and come out an equal distance on either side of the cut.

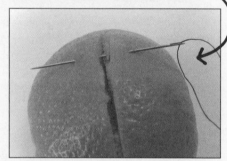

With real skin, doctors need to put the stitches through two upper levels of skin: the epidermis and the dermis. Just remember, you're practicing on an orange, not a human. It's okay to make mistakes.

8. Pull the needle and thread almost all the way through. Leave about 2 to 3 inches sticking out of one side of the orange. Cut the thread on the other side, leaving about 2 to 3 inches sticking out from the orange. Set the needle and remaining thread aside.

9. Pick up the two ends of the thread and start to tie it the same way you would tie your shoelaces. Tie it twice to make a knot. Make it as tight and flat on the orange as you can.

10. Trim the ends close to the knot and admire the stitch you made! It may be a bit loose, but that's okay! With practice, you'll get it flat and tight. You can always cut out this stitch and try again in the same spot. You can make more stitches, each about ¼ inch apart, to close the whole wound.

11. Enjoy your Franken-orange! Observe it over the next few days as it shrivels and dries up. A real wound similarly contracts after about 10 to 15 days of healing, though it doesn't rot like your orange will. If you want to really freak someone out, you could peel off the orange flesh, being careful not to break the stitches. Borrow some makeup to make the orange's skin look like yours, place it on your own arm, and wrap some gauze around it to secure it, being sure the freaky stitches show. Now you can gross out your friends with gory stories of your abduction by aliens.

WHAT JUST HAPPENED?

Congratulations! You made a stitch that resembles a "simple suture"—the most basic of all the stitching techniques. It's hard to make it tight and flat, huh? Surgeons have to practice a lot to become skilled and fast. There are plenty of other stitches that are fancier and—once you are good at it—take less time. Surgeons use special tools instead of fingers to hold the thread. They wear gloves and work with skin slippery with blood, which makes it really tough to hold and tie a string. They use tweezerlike *forceps* (<u>four</u>-seps) and a special "needle holder" that looks like a pair of pliers or scissors. If you have tweezers and pliers lying around, try using them to make a stitch!

Hey, congrats on getting an A+ in sutures from Ickster Medical School. You're well on your way to adding I.D. (Icky Doctor) after your name.

A STITCH IN TIME

Sometimes a wound is so big that it cannot repair itself without help. The sides of the wound are too far apart for a good scab to cover it, and it keeps pulling apart and bleeding. When that happens, off we trot to a nearby doctor who will sew the wound shut. You might think that having someone put a needle through your skin over and over is worse and more painful than your original wound, but luckily the doctor can numb your nerve endings so that getting stitches only hurts a little bit. It's important to get stitches for certain wounds, or else you could get a big scar, or, worse, harmful bacteria could enter at the wound site. There are three different ways to close a big, bloody cut.

Sutures (<u>soo</u>-churz) are special surgical threads that can be made of silk, cotton, steel, or nylon. Doctors use sutures to close a wound with a curved needle. There are also threads that dissolve over a period of time, which saves having to go back and have your stitches taken out.

Staples are another way to close a wound. They often work better than sutures because they can be put in faster and removed more easily once the wound is healed. However, do NOT try this at home. That school stapler of yours will NOT do the trick! Medical staples are made of titanium or surgical stainless steel.

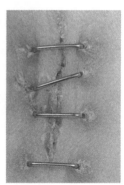

Glue It's true! Docs often stop the bleeding with—believe it or not—the medical equivalent of Krazy Glue. Its official lab name is *cyanoacrylate* (sy-uh-no-ack-ri-late), and this super-sticky stuff is being used more and more these days. It's quick, it's easy to use, and it works well. But, pinky-swear that you'll leave using it to docs!

S is such a lovely letter.
Besides scabs, so many other delicious, oozing things start with it, like SLIME and SPIT, up ahead!

Slime

Quick! Think of five things that are slimy. One dictionary definition of slime is: a moist, soft, and slippery substance, often considered disgusting. So what are your five things? Maybe snot? Why not? And slugs, for sure—those crawling mucuslike blobs that come out in rainy weather. Snails too— they leave a trail of slime everywhere they go. Oysters, sucked raw out of the shell, would make the list. And raw eggs. Definitely gooey! So what is it about slimy things that make us go *Ewwww?*

SLIME TIME

An official science word you could use to describe slime is *viscous* (<u>vis</u>-cuss)—a word that even sounds slimy. *Viscosity* (vis-<u>coss</u>-uh-tee) is how we measure a fluid's resistance to flowing. Think of it as thickness (or laziness if you'd like). Honey, molasses, and snot are thicker than water, which means they have a higher viscosity. High viscosity makes a fluid flow really s-l-o-w-l-y. Low viscosity means it flows quickly.

A liquid can become more or less viscous depending on its temperature. Think about what happens when you spread peanut butter on hot toast. In just a few moments, that once highly viscous blob will begin dripping onto your chin and dropping onto your lap! It has become less viscous. But pop that peanut butter into the fridge, and good luck even licking it off the spoon! Very viscous!

SOLID? LIQUID? WHAT THE . . . ???

Slime is awesome. But some slime and other gloppy goops are extra special. They can behave like a solid AND a liquid. As you know, a solid keeps its shape, while a liquid can flow and take on the shape of its container. But there are certain fluids that can flow like a liquid AND become a stiff solid in the blink of an eye. They are known as non-Newtonian fluids.

Think about ketchup, yogurt, and toothpaste. They have earned the name *non-Newtonian* because they don't behave in a way that fits the classic definition of how a fluid should act. Why non-Newtonian? Remember Sir Isaac Newton? He was a brilliant physicist and mathematician—the guy who, the story goes, got bonked on the head by a falling apple in 1666 and figured out the rules of gravity. (NO—he didn't actually get hit on the head by an apple, but he probably did get the inspiration from watching an apple fall off a tree.)

Not distracted by video games or TV since those didn't exist back then, Sir Isaac had plenty of time to think and discover amazing things. His work on gravity, calculus, light, and the three laws of motion were his biggies, but he was also fascinated by fluids (which include liquids *and* gases). He noticed that the viscosity of a fluid stayed the same no matter what external forces were applied to it. Take a glass of water and poke your finger in it, stir it, shake it. It doesn't get any more or less viscous. It will not pour out any faster if you blow bubbles in it with a straw first. It totally follows Newton's rules for fluids. Many oils do the same. Temperature changes can affect their viscosity, but external forces—like you swirling a carrot stick in a bowl of olive oil—can't.

But non-Newtonian fluids! Oh, my! Things like quicksand, ketchup, blood, paint, and shampoo are law breakers because their viscosity DOES change due to external forces. For example, when you touch some of them, they suddenly act like a solid! Others, like ketchup, actually flow faster when you smack the bottle. How strange! So, what's happening here?

It's all about something called *shear stress*, and it happens when you hit, stir, or squeeze a non-Newtonian fluid. Ketchup's viscous ability is called shear thinning. When you start spanking the bottom of the bottle because you are tired of holding it over your rapidly cooling fries, the ketchup actually thins a bit, becomes less viscous, and finally *plop-plops* out. Mayonnaise, mustard, and glue act the same way. If you stir or shake them, they act thinner.

Other non-Newtonian fluids do the opposite—shear thickening. They get *more* viscous when hit or moved quickly.

SLIMY ARMOR

In the Middle Ages, knights wore metal armor. Nowadays, many soldiers and police officers wear body armor made of a material called Kevlar. It's awesome stuff, but it's heavy, stiff, and hot. Kevlar can stop a bullet, but it can't stop a pointy spike or anything with a sharp tip, because it is basically "woven" of threads made from a very special type of plastic. Armies and police forces have been hoping for something better, so they are super-stoked about research on a new kind of non-Newtonian slime. This new substance instantly becomes rock-solid if it is hit by a bullet or stabbed. It can be added to a thin layer of Kevlar so that until that moment of forceful impact, this new kind of protective armor is soft and flexible. Armor from slime!

If you thrash around in quicksand, it will just feel like you are encased in brick. But you can escape by moving very slowly (for more on quicksand, see page 194). Even your body has non-Newtonian fluids. Your joints have shear-thickening fluids in them called synovial fluid. It is all nice and squishy most of the time, but if you get hit by a soccer ball, the fluid gets thicker, which helps to protect your joints! Who knew that you had gloppy, rule-breaking fluids in your knees and elbows!

THE WORLD'S LONGEST EXPERIMENT?

Scientists have to master a lot of skills—including patience! Tar pitch is a super-viscous substance that looks and acts like a solid (at room temperature, it can be shattered with a hammer). A form of petroleum, it's the star of an experiment on viscosity that began in 1927 in Australia and is still going today. The black pitch in this bell jar drips at the ridiculously s-l-o-o-o-w rate of about one drop every 10 years; scientists used this information to calculate that the pitch is over 200 billion times thicker than water. Bet you wouldn't want to be the person assigned to watch and wait for the next drop, unless you've got 10 years to spare!

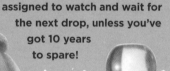

30 MINUTES

ICK-SPERIMENT
THE OOZE OLYMPICS

If your parents claim that you are moving "slower than molasses going uphill in January," then now's the time to see just how fast molasses—and other slimy substances—actually can move. Grab a bunch of viscous liquids, and challenge them to a race.

GO FETCH

3 or more household liquids such as the following:
- Molasses
- Milk
- Cooking oil
- Corn syrup
- Juice
- Ketchup
- Mustard
- Dish soap
- Shampoo or body wash
- Honey
- Measuring cup

I cup for each liquid you are testing

Enough friends to each hold a cup or two

A smooth 2- to 3-foot-long surface to serve as the testing track, such as a long cutting board, a long poster board, or one side of a large box. It has to be something you can place at an angle, and wide enough to test a few liquids at a time. A small table set on its side could work too.

An old towel

Stopwatch or clock that counts seconds

Pencil or washable marker

Tape measure or yardstick

1. Measure ¼ cup of each liquid, and put one liquid in each cup. It's important that you use the same amount of each liquid or else this will not be a fair test.

2. Since you now know that viscosity is affected by temperature, you want to be sure all the liquids are at the same temperature. So let them all sit at room temperature until they feel equally warm. Or put them ALL in the fridge for an hour. (Actually, that could make for another interesting experiment . . . testing and comparing the same liquid at different temperatures.)

3. Come up with a hypothesis about which liquid will be most viscous (slow to flow) and why.

4. Tilt your testing track so that it is at a 45-degree angle. Rest it against something that will hold it steady. Either tape it there or have a friend hold it. Make sure to keep the tilt angle the same for all tests.

5. Rest the bottom of the track on top of your old towel. That should keep

the mess contained and will also stop the board from slipping.

6. Decide who will hold the cups and who will keep track of time.

7. Hold the cups just at the top edge of your testing track, with some space between the cups. When everyone is ready, start your timer and yell, "Dump!!" Pour the contents of the cups on the racetrack.

8. After 10 seconds have passed, use a pencil or washable marker to mark where your liquids were at that point.

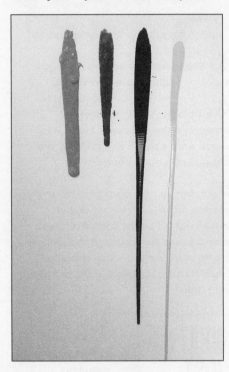

9. Use the measuring tape or yardstick to see which liquid had the highest and lowest viscosity . . . In other words, which one flowed the shortest distance in that 10 seconds, and which one flowed the farthest.

10. Wipe down your testing track and try some more, or clean up well!

WHAT JUST HAPPENED?

Was your hypothesis correct? You probably noticed that even though it was slow, the molasses did make some progress down the track. It obeyed the law of gravity just like everything else, just s . . . l . . . o . . . w . . . l . . . y. A material's viscosity depends mostly on the shape and size of the molecules it's made of and how they interact. If the molecules rub against each other a lot, it will create friction. Friction slows motion and flow.

Ever tried to move through a big crowd of people holding umbrellas on a rainy day? People keep poking into one another, which slows things down. If all those people were shaped like small, round, bouncy balls, it would be so much easier to flow past one another. Water molecules are small and compact, so they flow easily. Sugary molasses or oil molecules have large, lumpy shapes— kind of like that rainy-day crowd with their outstretched, umbrella-holding arms. That's why honey, corn syrup, molasses, and olive oil are more viscous and, therefore, flow more slowly than water. Their molecules keep bumping into one another! Traffic jam!

Did you compare the same liquid at different temperatures? When you heat a liquid, the molecules move faster, so even when they bump into a neighbor they bounce away quickly and keep flowing. When it's colder, the molecules slow down and have a harder time flowing past each other. That's why people joke about being "slower than molasses going uphill in January." That would be REALLY slow. So, the next time your parents complain about how slow you are, you can say, "Actually, I believe I am moving at the pace of refrigerated ketchup flowing at a 45-degree angle."

LIQUID? SOLID? SLIMY SNOT

GO FETCH →

2 MINUTES

PLUS DAYS OF OOZY AMAZEMENT

Liquid or solid? Check out this awesome non-Newtonian slime. Some very silly scientists have even filled entire swimming pools with this stuff just to experiment and play with it. You can actually run across these special fluids, but only if you move fast enough. Slow down and you will sink into a giant pool of goo!

1. Mix cornstarch and ¼ cup of water in a bowl with a spoon, or with your hands for an ickier feel. Save those last 2 to 3 tablespoons of water and add them one by one, stirring as you go, until all the cornstarch powder is wet. It should feel hard when you try to mix it, but then get gooey when you let go.

2. Squeeze it through your hands and enjoy. Notice what happens when you squeeze quickly versus when you just let it ooze. Take a spoon and jab it into the bowl. Or scrape the flat end across the surface. Use the flat of the spoon to hammer down on the ooze. Try punching it with your fist. What happened? Now try lifting it out with your fingers, letting it ooze between them. Now jab your fingers back down in the bowl. What happens?

3/4 cup cornstarch

¼ cup water plus 2 to 3 tablespoons more water

Small bowl

Spoon or your hands

Yellow or green food coloring (optional)

Tissues

3. Experiment by adding more water, or adding more cornstarch.

4. Color it yellow or green or whatever color suits your fancy. Pop a glob onto a tissue and pretend you just picked a giant booger!

5. When you are done playing and need to dispose of this slime, put it in the trash or on the compost. If you pour it down the drain and then follow it with more water . . . that pressure could turn it back into a solid and plug your drain!

WHAT JUST HAPPENED?

This slime (often called oobleck) behaves like both a solid and a liquid. Not only is it a non-Newtonian fluid, but it is also known as a *colloidal suspension* and a polymer. The cornstarch molecules don't dissolve in the water. They simply hang out—suspended throughout the water. As they hang there, they're all feeling a little antisocial (technically they "repel" each other). If they could talk, they'd be saying, "Hey, man, give me some space." But when they feel the pressure of a tap from your hands, the cornstarch molecules in the water join together and briefly act like a solid wall. When you don't apply pressure and simply hold some in your open palm, there is enough water to allow the cornstarch molecules to glide past one another as a liquid would, and they go back to hanging out in their own personal space.

Think of the cornstarch molecules as being a big bunch of fuzzy gorillas all hanging around, eating bananas. If you run straight at them, screaming and flailing your arms, you'll run right into a big hairy wall of angry primates who want to stop you from ruining their fun. (In the cornstarch, your hand gets stuck because you didn't give the molecules time to get out of the way.) But if you crawl very slowly and quietly toward the gorillas, you just might be able to slip past them without being noticed. In a similar way, your fingers will slip through the cornstarch molecules when you move very slowly.

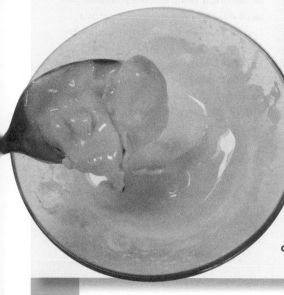

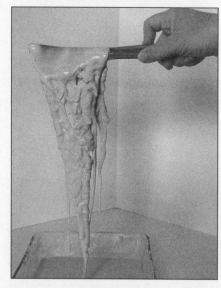

NATURE'S SLIMEBALLS

Making slime in the lab is fun, but depending on where you live, you may be able to simply open your door and find some quivering in your backyard! Back in 1973, a Dallas, Texas, resident discovered a foot-long, jellylike glob pulsating on his lawn. It was disgusting. Scientists were called in to investigate and they went nuts with excitement! This thing could ooze across the lawn. As it moved it ate dead leaves, bacteria, fungi, and even other slime. The THING was a slime mold.

Slime molds are *protists* (<u>pro</u>-tists), which are mostly single-celled organisms. They are tiny but can join together to form a linked network of thousands, creating a superslime as big as 10 to 13 feet across. There are more than 900 different slime mold species. They come in all sorts of colors—bright red, vivid blue, neon orange, brown, black, white, or a hue scientists call dog vomit yellow. And even though they have no brains and no nervous system, when slime molds mass together they have proven their ability to make their way through a lab maze and go straight to food with no wrong turns. Clever slime!

There are other slick slime-sters crawling about outside. Take slugs and snails, for example. They both have a muscular "foot" that helps them drag themselves along the ground. This muscle oozes out viscous mucus—slippery when wet. It's like ice-skating on snot and helps them glide across whatever surface they are traversing. Early in the morning you may notice their slime trails crisscrossing your garden or walkway. Or check a leaf for some trail marks!

Many animals coat themselves with slime for protection. Fish have a slimy coating. Eels too. Being slippery makes it hard for predators (big or small) to grab them. If you are a hungry parasite trying to latch on to a critter covered in slippery goo, good luck holding on! And a hagfish can stop a predator with a shot of slime in less than half a second! As a defense weapon, this goo (squirted out of the hagfish) gums up the gills of its attackers, thereby suffocating them. Talk about a meal that takes your breath away.

Slime also means less friction. All the better to swim really fast! Frogs and salamanders don a coat of slime for that same reason. Plus, it helps them stay moist. And it helps them slip away from kids like you trying to catch them!

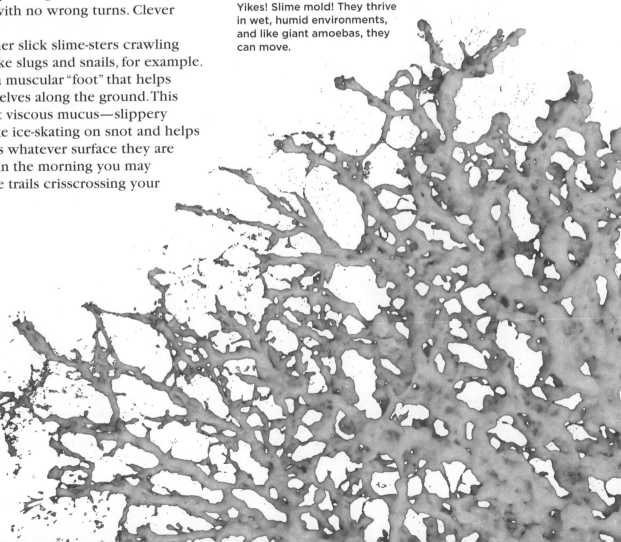

Yikes! Slime mold! They thrive in wet, humid environments, and like giant amoebas, they can move.

SEE-THROUGH SLIME SLUG

5 MINUTES

PLUS A LIFETIME OF ENJOYMENT

GO FETCH

Did you make the Farting Slime Bag in FARTS (page 79)? This ick-tivity is similar but kicks it up a notch! You're going to make a see-through slime that resembles the ooze left behind by a slug, which is basically a creeping ribbon of mucus-y ooze. And we know you have been longing to have a slime buddy to share your deepest secrets with!

1. Combine ½ cup glue with ½ cup warm water in the bowl and stir well with a spoon.

2. In the cup, mix 1 teaspoon borax powder with ¾ cup warm water.

3. Slowly pour the water and borax mixture into the watery glue, stirring as you pour. When the mixture gets really gooey and harder to stir, use your hands to mix everything together until it feels like a ball of slime. You may have some leftover water in the bowl, and you might not use all of the watery borax. If you have some borax left over in the cup, you can use it in your next load of laundry.

Measuring cup

Elmer's School GEL Glue

Warm water

Bowl

Spoon

Cup

Borax powder (available near the laundry detergent in your supermarket)

Food coloring (neon food coloring will make your slime glow in the dark)

Ziplock bag

4. Remove your slime from the bowl. Rinse it off, and be sure to rinse your hands too, as the borax can sometimes irritate your skin. Just in case you were wondering, your slime is NOT edible, but it's totally safe to play with once it's rinsed off. Enjoy the sheer pleasure of your gooey creation.

5. To prevent your new slimeball friend from drying out, store it in

a ziplock bag. If you let your slime rest for a while, it may become even more fun. Try to mush it into a ball, and then bounce it on the table!

WHAT JUST HAPPENED**?**

Curious about the chemistry of your slime? This activity used borax, which is a mineral that is dug up from the ground. The glue is a chemical called a *polymer*. A polymer is a very large molecule with many parts (*poly* is an ancient Greek work for "many") all linked together in a chain. In other words, polymers are really, really long chemical chains. Some polymers (like PVC piping) are strong and stiff; others (like the polymers in your slimeball) are rubbery and elastic. Your body has natural polymers in it: DNA, starch, and some proteins (like hair and nails). Plastic, paint, and nylon are polymers too. When you swirled the glue in the borax, all the chains of the glue polymer joined together to make even bigger, more complicated and tangled chains. These chains have a hard time flowing over each other, so the resulting blob is highly viscous, but it still can flow if you let it sit. It's also really flexible, which means it can be stretched, squished, and played with over and over. Who knew a slimeball could be such a good pet!

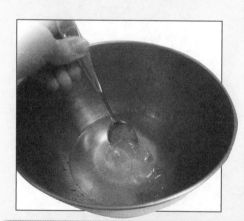

Viscosity! Non-Newtonian fluids!

Wow—your brain must be the size of a watermelon by now, and there's still more vileness ahead. Do you have enough room in there for more? If so, read on and find out about that slippery stuff brewing in your mouth, SPIT.

Spit

One of the flat-out grossest sights imaginable is watching someone hock a loogie—ejecting a flying wad of phlegm from mouth to ground. But that revolting glob of flying mucus and spit holds one of the keys to your survival. No spit? Well—good luck eating anything solid, including your next plate of french fries!

Morning Mouth? While you sleep, the amount of saliva your mouth produces goes way down, so the bacteria don't get washed away as much. More bacteria = more stink. That's why you have dragon breath when you wake up! Easy solution: Brush your teeth!

Male camel mating ritual: drooling and blowing bubbles in order to impress females.

GO ON! SPIT IT OUT!

Spit, also known as *saliva* (suh-<u>live</u>-uh), is a must-have in your mouth. Without it you wouldn't be able to swallow a single bite of that crispy fried-potato spear! In fact, you wouldn't be able to swallow anything except watery soups. The main job of saliva is to lubricate food for easy swallowing so it can slide down your esophagus. But spit does so much more! It helps your mouth stay clean by washing away bits of food and acidic drinks; plus, it brings food into contact with your taste buds (yum!), kicks off the digestion process, and helps protect your mouth and teeth from funky fungi and bacteria. Spit is pretty important—and pretty awesome!

But what exactly is saliva? Well, it's mostly water mixed with mucus (the same stuff that makes up your snot!) and electrolytes, such as salt and other minerals, that help your cells function properly. It's also packed with hardworking *enzymes* (<u>en</u>-zimes)! More on those in a minute. The average person produces 1 to 2 liters of spit a day! It's mainly produced in the salivary glands that sit between your cheeks and ears, and it squirts out when you get a whiff of hot pizza or just-baked chocolate-chip brownies. These glands are always gently oozing saliva even when you're not eating, but they really get to work once something is actually in your mouth. It doesn't matter how delicious (or disgusting) the thing you're chewing is: You could chew on a cotton ball and those ever-eager glands would still do their thing.

THE DROOLIEST DOGS IN TOWN

Hanging around certain dogs practically guarantees that you'll get an unwanted saliva shower. These breeds should only be petted while wearing a poncho!

Mastiff • Bloodhound
Saint Bernard • Newfoundland
Bulldog • Basset Hound

One shake of their big furry heads and drool is splashed on the floor, walls, and, if you're unlucky, your clothes. Why all the slobber? These dogs have deep, large jowls, short snouts, and big loose lips. Because of their anatomy it's more difficult for them to swallow their excess saliva—something you do all day without even noticing. Drooly dogs slobber all the time, but *all* dogs drool when they smell food. Pups also drop drool when they get stressed, kind of like how you might feel when your teacher springs a pop quiz on you. Good thing you usually just sweat instead of leaving a puddle of saliva on your desk.

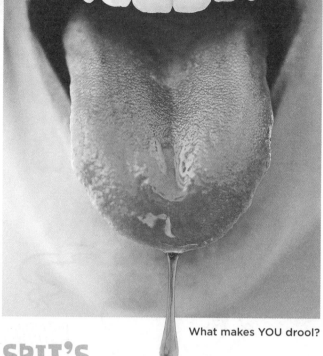

What makes YOU drool?

SPIT'S JOBS

Get ready to swallow—Last time you took a bite of food, your teeth, tongue, lips, cheeks, and saliva all worked to make a bolus—a ball of saliva-laced food. Spit's crucial role is to moisten and bind food into a nice slimy glob that won't harm your esophagus as you gulp it down.

Dilute acid—Do you like lemonade or orange juice? Some of our favorite drinks (and some foods) are chock-full of acid. When we take a big gulp of OJ, saliva rushes in to dilute the acid. If you did not produce saliva, your teeth would just soak in that acid bath. Bye-bye, tooth enamel, hello, cavities and major tooth pain!

Make things scrumptious—Saliva also helps food taste good! We're not saying saliva itself tastes good. Instead, the saliva moistens and starts to dissolve the food molecules. Flavors can't be detected until the tiny food bits are broken down by enzymes in the saliva. Only then can the food molecules touch your taste buds. Taste buds are your sensory organ buddies (get it?) that cover your tongue and send messages about savory, sweet, salty, sour, and bitter tastes to your brain. Without them, everything you eat would taste blah and boring!

Kick-start digestion—Remember those enzymes—molecules that help make chemical reactions happen? Enzymes in spit start breaking down food so your stomach and intestines don't

SPIT STRENGTH OLYMPICS

GO FETCH

Y ou and your friends have probably boasted about who can run the fastest, jump the farthest, or do the most push-ups. But whose spit is the strongest? You won't break a sweat participating in these Olympics, but you *will* get to judge how well your saliva does its digestive job.

1. Take one glass and label it *Control A*. Remember, a control is the part of the experiment that you compare your results with. Stir 2 teaspoons of water and 2 drops of iodine into Control A. Place the glass on the white paper so you can see the color clearly. This mixture should look brownish yellow.

2. Take a peanut-size piece of cracker and mash it inside a piece of folded paper. Pour the pulverized cracker into another glass and label it *Control B*. Stir in 2 teaspoons of water and 2 drops of iodine; this mixture should look much darker.

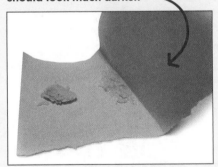

3. Each person participating in the Spit Olympics should now mash a peanut-size piece of cracker inside a piece of folded paper and pour it into their own separate glass.

- Clear drinking glasses or test tubes (you'll need 2, plus 1 for each participant)
- Marker
- Measuring teaspoons
- Water
- Tincture of iodine (an antiseptic available at drugstores)
- A few pieces of white paper
- Crackers
- Spit (available in your mouth, or at spit stores everywhere)

4. Let the games begin! Each person needs to collect 2 teaspoons of saliva and add it to their glass. Remember, your salivary glands crank out 1 to 2 liters of spit every day, so this should be easy. Some baseball players spit on TV, but you're a polite scientist right now, so you will be *expectorating* (the fancy word for spitting).

5. Mix 2 drops of iodine into each person's glass. Each person's mixture should get darker, like Control B.

6. Wait about 10 minutes and observe any changes in color in the mixtures, especially compared to Control B.

WHAT JUST HAPPENED?

A s you discovered, iodine has the cool ability to change from light brownish yellow (Control A) to dark blackish blue when it's around starch (Control B). (It also can be used to disinfect wounds and purify drinking water.) Crackers are full of *starch*, a tasteless substance produced by plants to store energy. Foods made from wheat, rice, and potatoes have loads of this complex carbohydrate. The iodine should have turned much darker when it was added to the glasses with crackers because it was reacting with the starch.

Saliva contains the digestive chemical (technically an enzyme) *amylase*. The job of amylase is to tear a molecule of starch into smaller pieces of glucose, a sugar, which is easier for our bodies to digest. Iodine turns dark in the presence of starch, but it gets lighter again when the starch is broken down. Whoever had the most amylase in their spit will end up with the lightest-colored mixture. Compare your glass to Control B. Whose spit was strongest? Now those are some bragging rights!

have to do all the work (check out GUTS on page 107 for LOTS more juicy details). One kind of enzyme, *amylase*, breaks apart the bonds in starchy foods like bread and potatoes so we can get to the useful bits. Another enzyme, *lipase*, tackles fats. In fact, some high-end laundry and dishwashing detergents use the same enzymes found in spit to get clothes and dishes clean.

SPIT SWEETENERS

GO FETCH →

5 MINUTES

A starchy but otherwise flavorless food such as an unsalted plain cracker or plain bread

Drool (now appearing in your mouth!)

Some kids would pay good money to be able to magically make food taste sweeter. Well, thanks to your spit, you actually do have that amazing power!

1. Remove any visible salt from the food so your taste buds won't get distracted by it.

2. Put the food in your mouth and start chewing, but don't swallow. Notice the flavor isn't particularly sweet.

3. Keep chewing, but don't swallow. The longer you are willing to chew before swallowing, the better your results will be. The mush in your mouth should start to taste a little sweeter.

4. Swallow!

WHAT JUST HAPPENED?

If you already did the Spit Olympics experiment, you know that spit has digestive properties, thanks to that helpful enzyme amylase. Starch is a long stringy chemical made up of lots of tinier pieces of the sugar glucose chained together. Amylase breaks this chain apart into bits of glucose, which our bodies use for energy. Glucose is not as sweet as other sugars, such as fructose (found in fruit) or sucrose (table sugar), but your tongue should be sensitive enough to detect the slightly sweeter flavor. Because sugar is an energy-rich food, humans have evolved to be dynamite at detecting it and are biologically driven to crave it. Now that you've demonstrated the sweetening power of your saliva, perhaps your next entrepreneurial venture will be a spit stand instead of a lemonade stand. Actually, never mind—that sounds disgusting!

GRUESOME SCIENCE

PAVLOV'S DOGS

One of the most famous experiments of all time involved a Russian doc named Ivan Pavlov and a bunch of dogs. Back in the late 1800s and early 1900s, Pavlov was busy studying the importance of saliva in digestion when quite by accident he made an important discovery. You may have heard of his renowned experiment—that dogs could be trained to start salivating at the sound of a tone. But in order to gather his data, he did a very gross thing.

Pavlov's pups were kept in small chambers and had collection tubes surgically attached to their salivary glands. As they were offered a savory snack of meat powder, the saliva would start to pool in the test tube hanging from their faces. Pavlov soon noticed that the saliva would start gushing whenever the meat-powder *waiter* entered the room. Just the click of the door opening was like turning on a frothy faucet! So Pavlov finessed this experiment by using a metronome to signal dinner time. Before long a little noise, even with no meaty treat in sight, would lead to a slobber fest. He had trained the dogs to super-salivate even when there was no food around. He had taken a basic physical response and made it a mental one!

HOW DRY I AM!

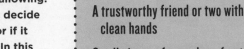
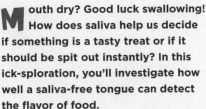

15 MINUTES

Mouth dry? Good luck swallowing! How does saliva help us decide if something is a tasty treat or if it should be spit out instantly? In this ick-sploration, you'll investigate how well a saliva-free tongue can detect the flavor of food.

1. Wash your hands with soap and make sure your friends do too (witness the act!). Dry them well.

2. Break or tear the foods into small bite-size pieces.

3. Decide who will be the first taste tester and who will be the food dispenser.

4. The taste tester should lick his or her towel until their tongue feels super dry, then close their eyes, open their mouth, and stick out their tongue.

5. The food dispenser should carefully place a small piece of food on the taste tester's tongue. Without

GO FETCH

A trustworthy friend or two with clean hands

Small pieces of a number of wet foods (like fruit) and dry foods (like cereal or cookies)

1 clean towel per person

moving the tongue around, the taste tester should try to detect which food has been deposited on the tongue.

6. The taste tester can now eat the food or just spit it out. A drink of water will help rinse out the taste.

7. Repeat steps 4, 5, and 6 with several different foods, both wet and dry. Always dry off your tongue in between tastings.

8. Switch the roles of taste tester and food dispenser. The new taste tester should use a clean towel.

WHAT JUST HAPPENED?

You probably found it much harder (or even impossible) to taste the dry foods but had decent success with the wet foods. This is because taste buds need water to work. The bumps you see on your tongue are actually called *papillae* (puh-<u>pill</u>-ee), and each one contains up to several hundred microscopic taste buds. Taste buds have super-tiny hairlike extensions called *microvilli* (my-crow-<u>vil</u>-eye) that detect different flavors, but these hairs really only work if the flavor has been dissolved in a liquid. Saliva is about 99 percent water, and it does a great job of dissolving food particles so they can be detected by your taste buds. The wet foods came with their own water, so you could more easily sense their flavors, but the dry foods didn't have water to activate the taste buds.

THE SPIT POLICE

People have known for centuries that spit is your gut's first defense against germs. One colonial medical pamphlet advised using human spit to cure sores. In fact, spit contains an enzyme called lysozyme that destroys bacteria.

In ancient China, saliva was considered a good antidote for smelly armpits. Bet the hard part of that one was finding someone willing to lick a loved one's armpits! But think about this: Mouth wounds DO heal much faster than skin wounds, and even dogs and cats lick their wounds to

quicken the healing. Scientists have pinpointed a compound, called *histatin*, in saliva that greatly speeds wound healing. Someday in the not-too-distant future, you just might be able to buy a tube of histatin at your local drugstore!

Chew on This!

Now you know what happens inside your mouth when that french fry hits your tongue. Now find out where french fries go when they make their exit into a TOILET!

Toilets

There's room for the whole family to go at the same time at these ancient Greek toilets found at Ephesus in Turkey.

You need a bathroom RIGHT THIS SECOND! One more instant and you'll be needing a change of clothes! Imagine if indoor toilets hadn't been invented. You might have to ask your teacher for a latrine pass to the pit out behind the playground. If the call of nature came in the dark of night, you might be doing your business in a clay pot that's otherwise stowed under your bed. And let's not forget outhouses. Long before Porta-Potties were invented, folks braved rain, blizzards, heat, and dangling spiders just to go number one or two! These were your toilet choices in the not-so-distant past.

WHEN YOU "HAD TO GO," LONG AGO

Indoor plumbing! A most luxurious thing! About 5,000 years ago some folks up in northern Scotland (a rain-almost-every-day kind of place) devised a sort of chute that carried poop and pee from their cottages to a pit somewhere outside their home. No need to brave the elements to visit the outhouse on a dreary day.

The first actual flush toilet made its appearance about 3,700 years ago in Greece at the home of royalty. It had a proper seat, a pan beneath it, and lots of drains and pipes that led away from the palace. Water was poured down the pipes to "flush" the deposits far away. Ta-da! The first royal flush! For ancient Greeks and Romans with money, this system was the height of luxury, but when Rome's civilization crumbled in the late 400s and the Dark Ages fell over Europe, the indoor toilet disappeared. Back to pooping in pits and peeing behind bushes or dumping pots of ick out the window.

Until about the year 1600 the state of the potty was pretty grim. Happily, around this time a clever inventor named John

30 MINUTES

THE CASE OF THE CLOGGED TOILETS

GO FETCH →

It's a slow day in your private investigator's office when suddenly the phone starts ringing like crazy. People are complaining about their toilets becoming clogged, others about their septic systems backing up. But why? You suspect that their toilet paper is to blame, and decide to conduct an experiment to figure out which brand of toilet paper breaks apart best in water and is least likely to clog.

1. In each bowl, put five sheets of only one type of toilet paper. Label each bowl to help you keep track of which brand of toilet paper is in which bowl. Make a hypothesis about which brand will disintegrate the best and why.

A bowl for each type of toilet paper you have

5 sheets each from at least 3 different brands of toilet paper. Be creative with your choices: superthick, recycled, septic-safe. Collect it from your school bathroom, friends, or relatives.

Marker

Water

Spoon

2. Fill each bowl with water.

3. Gently stir the toilet paper in each bowl for 15 seconds.

4. Wait 15 minutes, then use the spoon to scoop up and inspect each wad of toilet paper. Compare how much of each sample has deteriorated.

WHAT JUST HAPPENED?

Toilet paper engineers—and YES, that IS a job—have several goals. They need to design toilet paper that is soft and comfy to use. You wouldn't want to wipe with cardboard, would you? They also have to create something that absorbs moisture and will hold together long enough to wipe away waste. But the paper also needs to easily fall apart in water to avoid clogging up bathroom plumbing.

Your results will be different from ours depending on the brands you used, but you probably found that toilet paper made from recycled paper dissolves the best. Consider this one more reason to "go green" when going brown. Americans have become obsessed with using ultrasoft toilet paper, which is made by cutting down millions of trees. Dr. Allen Hershkowitz, a waste expert scientist, has said, "No forest of any kind should be used to make toilet paper." We agree! Recycled paper is the better way to go. The bottom line about your bottom's wipers: Every day 27,000 trees go "TIMBER!" to be turned into toilet paper. You can help make this zero trees if you buy toilet paper made from 100-percent-recycled paper next time you stock up.

SORRY!

Keep some reading material handy for toilet time.

Harington built one of the first modern toilets, which his godmother, Queen Elizabeth I, just adored. A throne fit for a queen! His design had a lot in common with the modern toilet: a tank with a valve at the bottom and a way for the water to flow into the bowl. Still, flush toilets were slow to catch on until Thomas Crapper spiffed potties up about 300 years later with some extra plumbing parts, such as the floating ball-shaped gizmo that sits atop the water in your tank and regulates the water level. Thanks to these two guys, saying you've got to use "the John" or "the Crapper" are now two ways to say "I gotta go!"

WORLDWIDE POTTY STOPS: The Good, the Bad, and the Furry

When you travel around the globe, be prepared to pee and poop in some toilets that may be different from what you're used to. It's guaranteed to be a bathroom adventure!

Catholes—Dig a hole in the ground, but make sure you can stand over it easily. You won't have a place to sit so just squat and hope your aim is good. Otherwise you might need an extra pair of shoes! If you are using the squat method in the Amazon, keep an eye out for fuzzy two-toed sloths.

I FEEL FLUSH!

The toilet is the unsung hero of any household. It dutifully does its job every day—a job no other item in your house would volunteer to do. But how does a flush toilet actually work? Here are instructions to build your very own model. It will probably require a stop at the hardware store for tubing, but if you want to master the fine art of toiletry, it's well worth the trip.

GO FETCH

- Empty plastic gallon milk jug, rinsed clean
- Scissors
- Duct tape
- About 3 feet of ¹/₂-inch-diameter plastic tubing
- Glue gun (optional)
- Modeling clay, such as Play-Doh (optional)
- Petroleum jelly
- 2 large stands to put your toilet bowl on (this can simply be 2 cups or jars upside down)
- Large bowl
- Food coloring
- Water

1. Cut off the top of the milk jug so it's easier to pour water into it.

2. Cut a ½-inch-diameter hole in the center of the bottom of the jug.

3. Time to leak-proof your toilet: Use strips of duct tape to attach one end of your tubing to the hole in the bottom of the milk jug. Be patient and thorough; the more time you spend on this, the less likely you are to have leaks. To make it super-leak-proof, get your favorite grown-up to seal it with a glue gun.

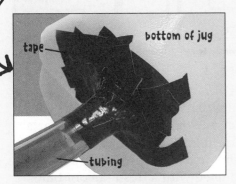

Sticking some modeling clay and petroleum jelly on the inside of the milk jug where it connects to the tubing will also help prevent a leaky connection.

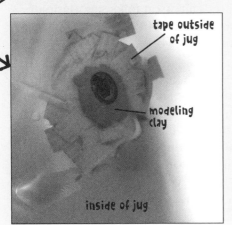

4. Rest the milk jug on the stands and have the end of the tubing drain into the large bowl. It's important that the tubing is positioned so that there is a bend in it about an inch higher than the bottom of the milk jug. In other words, when water eventually drains out of the jug, you want it to flow down, then up, and then down again.

The large bowl will be the sewage system that your toilet drains into; you might find it helpful to duct tape the end of the tubing onto the inside of the large bowl to help make a bend. You can also eliminate the bowl and have your "toilet" drain directly into the sink.

5. Add several drops of food coloring to the milk jug and then slowly add some water (the food coloring makes the water more visible). Some water will drain into the tubing. Keep adding water into the jug until the water level in the tube is barely as high as the bend. Congrats: Your mini toilet is now operational!

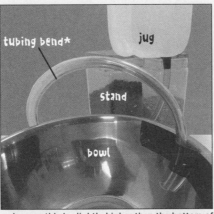

*make sure this is slightly higher than the bottom of the milk jug!

6. If you *slowly* add more water into the milk jug, the water level in the jug never changes. Can you figure out why? Ah—the magic of toilet plumbing.

7. Time for a major flush. This toilet lacks the tank of water mounted above the bowl that real toilets have. Instead, dump several cups of water quickly into the milk jug. This will cause your toilet to flush its contents through the tubing and into the bowl!

WHAT JUST HAPPENED?

When you added a small amount of liquid to your model toilet, the water level in the jug rose slightly before settling back to its original level. The excess liquid spilled over the top of the raised bend in the tubing and drained out to the bowl. When you flushed, you dumped a much larger amount of water into the jug, completely flooding the raised bend. The water pressure upstream of the bend became greater than the water pressure downstream of the bend. This pressure difference pushed water up and over the bend and then down the tube. The simple toilet you built, and most American toilets, are examples of *siphons* (si-funs), devices that move water without a pump.

Siphons are cool because although most of the water is moving downhill, some of the water also moves uphill. The siphoning will continue until the toilet bowl has drained out and air enters the plumbing tube, stopping the process. More important, air makes that funny and familiar toilet gurgling sound, and your fake toilet might too! Toilets use siphons to do our dirty work. After all, taking advantage of water pressure differences is much more appealing than emptying out a chamber pot with a bucket and shovel!

They have developed a taste for human poop, and you are like a human soft-serve poop machine. You don't want to hunker down only to find a furry face looking up at you!

Squat Toilets—To people who live in many parts of Asia, the thought of putting your butt down on a place someone else has just put his or her butt down is considered GROSS! A squat toilet has running water to wash waste away, like a flush toilet, but no sitting down on the job!

So many ways to go!

Place feet here! Squat to do your business.

Porta-Potties—We've all seen those rows of green or blue plastic "booths" with private doors—beloved by visitors to outdoor rock concerts, county fairs, and other crowd-gathering events. Too bad a Porta-Potty is not beloved by noses! When you "go" in a Porta-Potty (sarcastically named "honey buckets"), your "goings-on" land in a tank filled with a combo of chemicals that attempt to mask any odors while starting to break down the um . . . er . . . contents. When the fair or concert is over, the sloshing sewage will be extracted from each tank

by a giant vacuum that sucks it into a truck for transport to a sewage-treatment plant. The Porta-Potty will be picked up and carted away, and the actual "throne" will be scrubbed, disinfected, deodorized, and filled with a fresh tank of blue-goo disinfectant, ready for the next event.

Pig Potties—In some parts of rural China, squat toilets once had a chute that led directly to a pig pen. There is a reason folks say "Happier than a pig in poop"—pigs will eat ANYTHING, including your number two.

Pay Potties—Gotta go while out sightseeing? Drop a few coins in the slot, then pop into one of these pay toilets located on some street corners. Do your thing. In some European cities, when you open the door to leave, spray disinfectants will poof out from vents in the wall to sanitize it, so if you sneak in for free as someone else is leaving, prepare to get showered with chemical cleansers.

Who needs a bathroom in the middle of nowhere?

Composting Toilets—Very little to no water is used in this type of potty, and the waste is converted into valuable compost that can actually be used to help plants grow bigger and stronger. The US National Park Service uses these in many places.

German Toilets—No cheerful plopping noise as your poop hits the water with this type of potty. And no nasty splash-back. The German-style toilet has an above-the-water shelf for your poo to land on. All the better to inspect your daily offering for interesting bits before a swish of water washes it off the shelf and down the drain!

Japanese Toilets—Perhaps the most heavenly toilets on the planet: Heated seats. Pretty music to hide your sometimes not-so-pretty bathroom noises. Warm water that squirts up and gives your butt a little bath, followed by a gentle stream of warm air to dry you. When you are done, the seat cover conveniently flops down all by itself. The only thing it doesn't do is pull up your pants.

Airplane Toilets—Technology at its finest. Since you can't have a bowl full of water sloshing about at 35,000 feet in the air, you need another way to suck waste away. Airplane toilets use a vacuum system, similar to the one your grown-ups use to suck up dirt and house dust, only an airplane's sucks away poo and pee. Add a little slosh of blue liquid to sanitize the bowl, and you have quite a neat and tidy system. The waste is stored in a holding tank until landing, then the tanks are carted away to sewage-treatment plants.

FUTURE FLUSHING

Here's a holiday to add to your calendar: World Toilet Day, November 19. It was organized by the United Nations General Assembly because of one terrible fact: Almost two and half BILLION people do not have access to safe, clean potties. That's one in three people in the world. Scary, huh? Lots of germs and diseases spread when there's no place for people to go when they have to go.

Did you also know that we are wasting our waste products? There's valuable stuff in our poo—stuff that can enrich the soil for growing plants. And in places with water shortages, why let the water in our pee get flushed away? Let's put that stuff to use, team!

Luckily, engineers all over the world are busy working on new designs to replace the classic white throne. Some of these collect and treat our number one and two deposits and recycle them into usable items like compost, energy, and clean water. And who knows? Maybe one day, in the not-so-distant future, you just might drink a nice cool glass of recycled pee, straight from your family's toilet treatment center!

All this talk about toilets and flushing and potty paper has us doing a little "I gotta go" dance. URINE (also known as pee) awaits on the next page. Maybe you should take a bathroom break before you start reading!

Urine

Do you have to pee, piddle, wee-wee, or whizz? Need to powder your nose, take a leak, or sprinkle some tinkle? That warm stream of yellow liquid that gets squirted into a toilet near you every few hours is actually supercool. You'll be amazed at how it's made and all the ways it's useful.

Belgians are very proud of their famous "peeing boy" statue fountain, made in the 1660s.

In parts of the world where water is in short supply, you might see a sign in a restroom that says: *In this land of fun and sun, we do not flush for number one.* In the name of science, try doing the same. As long as all anyone is doing is peeing (no stray number two floaters, please), do not flush after you pee. Put the lid down after each use. After about three or four "deposits," lift the lid and take a whiff! GAH!!!! Urine has a pretty distinctive aroma. Some of that smell comes from ammonia, which is what urea breaks down into. Other additions to the smell come from bacteria reproducing in the bowl. But it's never a bad idea to save water wherever you live, so talk to your family about flushing less. Just flush when the toilet begins to get stinky or filled with TP!

UR-INE THE KNOW

Urine (<u>yer</u>-in)—the official sci-speak name for pee—is the end product of your hardworking kidneys. These two bean-shaped organs, each about four inches long and weighing about ¼ pound (5 ounces) in an adult, are nestled on the left and right sides of the body, against the back muscles and below the lungs. Think of them as tiny washing machines for your body's blood. Remember how you filtered dirty water in DIRT, page 50? The water went in filthy and came out clean? Your kidneys do the same thing, constantly filtering the 1.5 gallons of blood that is pumping through your body, over and over, day after day.

I KIDNEY YOU NOT!

Your blood carries nutrients to all the cells of your body. The cells break down those nutrients and use the bits they need to function.

Then the cells release waste products back into the blood. A quick trip through the kidneys will wash away any of the gunk your body does not need or want. Without your kidneys, waste and toxins would build up in your blood, like an overflowing trash can.

Every day about 50 gallons of blood pass through your dynamic-duo kidneys. How much blood is that? Picture 50 of the big gallon milk jugs filled with blood or a small bathtub filled to the top! And speaking of tubs, you know what bathwater looks like after you take a bath? Well, just as the soap/dirt/dead skin grayish sludge gets sucked down the tub drain after your bath, the leftovers after your blood has been cleansed go out a different kind of drain— your body's pee-ing parts.

I WAS MYTH-INFORMED

Does urine make a great antidote for a jellyfish sting? Nuh-uh! The pH of urine is close to water, so peeing on your sting won't help. Better to mix vinegar (more acidic pH) with plain water and pour it on the sting, then ice the sting.

DOWN THE HATCH!

Where does the urine go after the kidneys? Two long tubes, called *ureters* (your-ee-ters), carry it from your kidneys into a muscular, stretchy bag— your bladder. Pee gathers there until the bag gets full enough to press down on some sensitive nerve endings and you start to feel the need to dash to the nearest restroom. Once safely at the toilet (we hope), your bladder muscles contract and the pee is pushed out of your body through another tube called your *urethra* (yur-ree-thruh).

But if urine is made up of all those waste products from the blood, why does it look like yellow water? Well, there aren't any red blood cells in your pee to make it red (if there is blood in your urine, time to see a doc!). Pee is mostly water— more than 95 percent in fact. Some of the water

GOLD!!!! A lot of people wanted it and there wasn't enough to go around. It was (still is) pretty rare, as a matter of fact. Back in the 1600s in Europe, gold fever was at an all-time high. As a result, a group of people kept trying to turn a collection of random bits of this and that into gold. They were called *alchemists* (al-kuh-mists). All over Europe, alchemists frantically stirred and boiled odd assortments of ingredients. One of their brilliant ideas was this: Gold is yellow. Pee is yellow. Maybe if I add some of this and a little of that to pee . . . ? Soon urine became an alchemist's go-to ingredient.

Now off we go to Hamburg, Germany. It's a dark night in 1669. Down in the damp workshop of an alchemist named Hennig Brandt, something really freaky was happening. Brandt had taken 121 gallons (YES, GALLONS!) of urine and boiled it down in a special glass globe until he was left with a very thick syrup. He then mixed the syrupy pee with sand. Next came heat—high heat, and lots and lots of it. A chemical reaction took place, and Brandt's equipment began to glow in the dark. Was it liquid gold, perhaps?

Turns out he had discovered the element *phosphorus* (fos-for-us). Not gold, but still very valuable. We now use it (minus the pee) to coat match heads so they will burst into flame when dragged across a rough surface. Phosphorus also helps LEDs light up. And to think all it took to find it was 121 gallons of boiling urine!

What's in the flask? Take a wild guess!

Any spot looks like a good spot to a dog who needs to pee!

you drink every day gets absorbed into your body, but some gets mixed with the waste and forms urine. Drink more water, and you'll be headed for the potty a lot more often. The average kid goes about six times a day. How do you measure up? Keep a tally of how much you drink and how much you pee for a day or two to see.

As well as filtering your blood, your kidneys help your body retain just the right amount of fluid, and the color of your urine gives you clues about whether you are drinking enough water. If your pee is light yellow, good job—you are well hydrated! If your pee is dark yellow, it means you need to drink more water—your kidneys have held back some water from the pee because you don't have enough in your body. (Sometimes your first tinkle of the day is darker because you went several hours without water while you slept.)

In addition to water, there are a lot of other interesting things in your pee, including salts, proteins, hormones, and even a small amount of bacteria. The most plentiful ingredient is something called *urea* (u-<u>ree</u>-ah). Urea is a useful little substance. Picture each drop of urea as a teeny little trash can that carries old, broken-down *nitrogen* (<u>nye</u>-tro-jin) out of your body and dumps it on the curb—aka the toilet.

Eating food that contains nitrogen is a bit like sprinkling fertilizer on the inside of your body. We need nitrogen to build muscles and

grow hair and nails, but we don't need a whole lot. Protein-rich foods like meat and cheese are loaded with nitrogen. To get your daily requirement of it, a 100-pound kid only needs about 1.25 ounces of protein, which is about the weight of a cookie (but NO, you won't get much protein from a cookie!). Most of us eat way more protein each day than we need, so your body (your liver, if you must know) breaks down the protein, takes all the extra nitrogen, and combines it with other elements (such as hydrogen, carbon, and oxygen) to form urea. The kidneys then filter the urea out of the blood, and soon it's tinkle, tinkle, tinkle time.

UR-INE THE MONEY!

Think urine is just a waste product? In the past, people in England and France would pat pee on their faces to zap unwanted zits. Bakers once used urine to help make fluffier bread. And spies in ancient Rome wrote secret messages in urine. Until the object with the message was heated, the writing was invisible. These days people are thinking about reusing the water from pee in very dry locations, or even using it as a natural fertilizer for gardens.

Turns out the urea in urine is actually VALUABLE! Companies manufacture tons and tons of it on purpose (no, not from people's pee . . . they just replicate the chemistry of it). Here are just some of the places you will find it!

1. Fertilizer—Want leafier lettuce or juicier apples? Spray urea on your fields and watch the crops grow.

2. Explosives—Some things that go boom need urea to explode.

3. Car Engines—When urea gets mixed into diesel fuel, engines make a lot less pollution.

4. Beauty Products—Urea is an ingredient in many moisturizers and some bath oils. Urea bubble baths can leave you with softer skin!

5. Pretzels—Who wants to eat a pale beige pretzel? Some pretzel makers add urea to get that lovely dark brown color people are used to seeing.

6. Animal Feed—Farmers sprinkle urea on cow chow to speed the growth of small moo-ers.

7. Plywood—What holds all those little scrappy chunks of wood together? Yup! You guessed it— glue made with urea.

MASTER BLASTERS

In the animal world, pee can be used for air-conditioning, as a love note, and even as a kind of stinky GPS. Here are a few pee-masters!

Feeling Hot?—A camel can drink about 30 gallons of water in a mere 13 minutes. Unlike you, a camel does not take that long thirsty drink and start the process of turning water into urine. Instead, its body keeps all that water flowing through its blood vessels, while the kidneys and intestines hold on to water like sponges. As for those humps—they are filled with fat, not water! When a camel finally does pee, its urine comes out as a thick syrup that is twice as salty as ocean water. Camels also pee all over their legs to help keep them cool. Handy in places where the temperatures can hit 130 degrees Fahrenheit!

Asparagus pee gives new meaning to the word *pee-yew*!

OVER THE RAINBOW 2–4 DAYS

Did you know that you can change the smell or the color of your urine just by eating certain foods? Let's see how your pee reacts when you eat these interesting items.

1. On each day, eat one of these foods (along with your regular diet).

GO FETCH →

> Asparagus
> Beets
> Blackberries
> Fava beans
> Rhubarb
> Multivitamins (if your family says it's okay)

2. Throughout the next few hours to a day, notice the smell or appearance of your pee. Does it smell different? Has the color changed?

3. The next day try one of the other foods and record what happens.

4. Enjoy making changes to your pee just through what you eat!

WHAT JUST HAPPENED?

When you ate the asparagus, chances are your pee reeked. But why? The asparagus itself didn't smell stinky, it smelled like a vegetable. It turns out that in your body those slender green spears break down into compounds containing sulfur—the same gas that makes farts smell and skunks stink. A cool thing about asparagus pee is that not everyone can smell it. Some lucky folks have noses that can't detect this nasty odor. But plenty of us CAN smell it and think it's icky!

Is pee always yellow? No! Different foods can change your pee's color. Beets can turn pee reddish. Blackberries can tint it pink. You can tinkle neon yellow if you take a lot of B vitamins, and people who take a certain drug to fight malaria (a scary mosquito-borne disease) can actually pee green. And let's not forget fava beans or rhubarb just in case you want to deposit dark brown or even blackish urine the next time you go number one. Whether or not your pee will change color from eating any of these foods depends on the acidity of your stomach and what else you've eaten. In other words, the conditions have to be just right, otherwise you're stuck with boring, everyday yellow urine.

This camel knows how important it is to stay hydrated!

Stay Out!—Cats have some of the most stinky pee—especially grown-up male cats. They produce a substance called *felinine*, another chemical with a sulfurish stink. Cat wee-wee comes in very handy as a way to mark territory. "My street! My house!" Dogs are also pros at using pee in this way. Instead of writing your name on your math notebook, imagine peeing on it so no one else takes it! Ick! But on second thought, it probably *would* work. Would *you* want to touch someone else's pee-protected stuff?

My tree! This cheetah is staking his territory with a spray of urine.

Love Messages—When male billy goats are in the mood for love, they don't send flowers. Instead, they spray their pee all over their bodies, and female billy goats go gaga for the smell. They are not the only animals with an odd way to attract a mate. Male porcupines send up a smelly spray of pee in all directions, and when the porcupine of his dreams comes trotting by, he will pee all over her to show his affection! Ah, sweet, stinky love.

Male giraffes taste a female's pee before deciding on her as a mate.

Weapons of War—Nothing like a squirt of urine to settle a fight. A lobster has two urine releasing "nozzles" right under the eyes. All the better for a male to squirt urine straight in the face of a rival male lobster. The urine contains chemicals that tell the other lobster to back off.

Where Am I?—A trail of urine makes a great road map for some types of rodents. One South American critter, the degu, has pee that reflects ultraviolet light, which their eyes can see, so their pee trails literally glow for them. They will always find the way home!

ICK-TIVITY

YOU'RE THE PEE DOC!

GO FETCH →

30 MINUTES

If you've never peed into a cup when visiting the doctor, then you've got something to look forward to! Doctors and nurses can actually figure out what's going on inside your body by analyzing what comes *out* of your body. Get ready to test the chemistry of some fake pee just like lab techs in doctors' offices do.

1. First create your urine samples. Keep your pants on; you're making *fake* wee-wee. Fill up the four cups with warm tap water. Then, add a pinch of salt to all the cups (urine is salty!) and stir in a drop or two of yellow food coloring so it looks like real pee.

2. Stir a teaspoon of sugar into one cup. Then, have your assistant or friendly adult rearrange the cups so you no longer know which one has the sugar in it, but your assistant does. Smell the cups. Can your nose detect the sugar cup? Now take a sip of each cup (relax, it's not really pee!). Do you have a new guess for which one has the sugar? Once you guess correctly, dump the sugar water down the drain.

3. Now, *promise*—NO MORE DRINKING fake urine during the rest of this experiment. With a new spoon, mix in ½ teaspoon of window cleaner into one of the remaining sugar-free cups. Again, have your assistant rearrange the cups. Smell the cups. Can your nose detect the cleaner? Remember—DON'T do the taste test! Dump that water down the drain.

4. Carefully crack open an egg over a bowl and separate the egg white from the yellow yolk. Add about 1 teaspoon of egg white to one of the remaining two cups and stir with a clean spoon. Have your assistant shuffle the cups. Can you tell which one has the egg white in it?

An adult (boiling water is involved)

4 clear cups or glasses

Warm water

Yellow food coloring

Salt

Measuring spoons

Sugar

3 stirring spoons

Window cleaner

Egg

2 cooking pots

5. Pour each cup of fake pee into a separate pot and ask your adult to help you bring each pot to a boil. Let them boil for about 5 minutes. What do you see happen to the pee that had the egg white?

WHAT JUST HAPPENED?

Studying a patient's pee to make a diagnosis has been happening for thousands of years. It was originally called *uroscopy* (yu-<u>ros</u>-cuh-pee), and yes, some healers would actually drink the pee sample being studied. Fortunately, nowadays there are ways to examine urine without sticking your tongue in a sample! So what do docs look for when they do a modern-day *urinalysis*?

Glucose is a type of sugar that the cells in your body need for energy. But urine is not supposed to contain glucose. Sweet-smelling pee can be a sign that someone has diabetes, a medical condition where the body's glucose levels get out of whack and extra glucose ends up in the urine. Instead of relying on a nose or tongue, nurses and lab techs test urine with dipsticks containing chemicals that change color if there is glucose present. Ask to see one next time you are at the doctor's office!

There are a number of reasons why urine might smell like ammonia (represented by window cleaner in this experiment). It usually means you have a lot of urea in your pee, which breaks down into ammonia. Maybe you recently ate a lot of protein, which fuels your body's production of urea. Maybe you haven't been drinking enough water, so the urea in your urine is more concentrated (and more smelly!).

Your urine normally contains some proteins. The sample with the egg white represents urine with too much protein. Egg whites are loaded with proteins that are clear at room temperature, but heat makes them change shape and become white.

Fake urine test complete!

TINKLE, TINKLE, LITTLE STAR

You wake up in the middle of the night and you have to pee RIGHT THIS SECOND. But there's one problem. You are an astronaut on the International Space Station. Before you can answer the call of nature you will first have to float over to the toilet, then strap on your leg restraints and thigh bars so you stay put while you go. You'll also have to find your own personal pee funnel, because you sure as heck don't want to use someone else's. And where's the hose adapter so you can attach the funnel to the tube that sucks the pee into a wastewater tank? A potty stop sure can be complicated if you are orbiting the Earth.

Some space missions take a VERY long time. In the future, some may take several years as we explore planets farther away from Earth. How can the astronauts possibly carry enough water to stay hydrated that whole time? Even today, up in the International Space Station, where water is more precious than gold, every drop of H_2O needs to be recycled and reused. Sweat and breath vapor is collected from the air inside the space station and reused as water. Since more water is needed for long missions, the crew's pee is collected, saved, and put through a filtering system to make it completely drinkable. Cheers! But before you go "gack!" know this: The space station's recycled drinking water is cleaner than the water a lot of people on Earth drink.

POUR THIS ON YOUR CEREAL!

A glass of milk is a typical breakfast beverage in the Western world. But milk isn't the only drink that comes from cows, at least not in India. A cow in India is beloved. Adored. Revered. A cow is literally a "holy cow." There is a tradition among some Indians to drink cow urine, since they believe that drinking fresh pee is good for one's health. So folks at one of India's largest Hindu cultural groups have an awesome product: *gau jal*—which means "cow water." Sounds better than "cow urine." The company that makes this "refreshing" drink hopes that people will skip the Coke or Pepsi and order a Gau!

There's nothing quite like cow pee for a quick pick-me-up.

RAN OUT OF BATTERIES? JUST PEE!

Plain old urine is clearly pretty awesome stuff. Too bad it usually gets flushed away. Surely there is SOMETHING it can be used for? Four teenage girls from Nigeria read about the work of an American engineer who had figured out a way to take pee and convert it into electricity by extracting the hydrogen from it. Think about it! Pee-powered batteries! So these clever teen inventors took this knowledge to the next step: They designed a urine-powered generator that could produce six hours of electricity from one liter of tinkle. Is it a "world-changing breakthrough" as one newspaper suggested? Time will tell. This invention is one to watch!

We're done with urine—time to flush! What rhymes with pee? The letter *V*. Next up, some tiny troublemakers that can make you sick—VIRUSES!

Vile Viruses

What does a nose dripping with slime-green snot have in common with a raccoon with a foamy mouth and crazy eyes? How is an illness named after a cluck-clucking chicken related to the flu? They're all caused by a minute missile of misery—the virus.

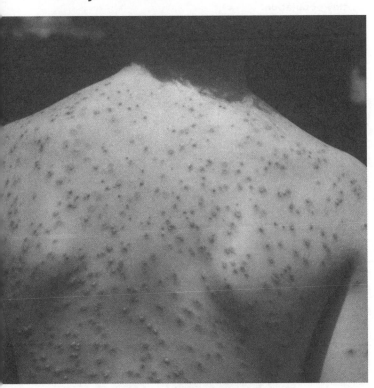

A nasty case of chicken pox. Don't scratch!

VIRUS? BACTERIA? WHAT'S THE DIFFERENCE?

Viruses and bacteria are both teeny-tiny, though viruses are much, much smaller. Viruses are very simple: just genetic material surrounded by a little coat, kind of like an M&M's candy, with the chocolate representing the genetic material inside. They're not even considered truly alive because they can't reproduce by themselves. They need the help of a living creature's cells for that. (Viruses aren't exactly dead either, though. Freaky, huh?)

Bacteria are living cells and are more complex than a virus. They can reproduce without any help.

Both viruses and bacteria can make you sick. Viruses hijack healthy cells and use them to make more viruses. This usually kills the cell. Antibiotics won't work on viruses, but antiviral medicines will. Bacteria can also kill cells and release horrible toxins, but antibiotics will usually stop them.

Surprisingly, many viruses and bacteria can be helpful, though so far, we humans know a lot more about good bacteria than we do about good viruses. We have a lot to learn! One example of a good virus is a kind called a *phage* (feyj) that lives in our mucus and can attack and kill mean ol' bacteria trying to infect us! So next time you pick your nose, say thank you to all those nice phages in your boogers.

A CHICK-CHICK HERE AND A POX-POX THERE

Uh-oh! Small red spotty blobs! They're multiplying and getting bigger! Each one is now a small blister, topped with a tiny dewdrop of fluid. These can fill with pus and leave deep scars called pockmarks. Diseases that do this are called poxes. Think of the bumps as little cupcakes of disease. But don't lick the "frosting," because it's filled with millions of microscopic alien invaders called viruses. In this case, chicken pox (*varicella*) viruses.

IT'S (NOT REALLY) ALIVE!

A virus is not exactly a living thing. It doesn't breathe. It doesn't eat. It cannot grow taller or gain weight. It can't even reproduce (make more of itself) without help! To do so it must find a host cell, perhaps one of *your* cells. But once it's found a cozy home in a host cell, it starts to make lots and *lots* of new viruses. Imagine a copy machine: You put a drawing of an alien space monster on the glass, select 5,000 copies, and push Start. Soon you will have 5,000 identical drawings. Now imagine a cell in your body that acts a bit like a wee copy machine. A virus sneaks into a healthy cell, turns on the "copy machine," and soon starts making endless copies of itself. Eventually, there are so many viruses inside your cell that it bursts apart and dies (a process called *lysis* (<u>lie</u>-sis). Viruses spew out and head off to infect other cells.

How does this viral reign of terror end? Your body has a top-notch police force: your white blood cells! These enforcers are always on the lookout for bad guys, gobbling up and destroying viruses. And even though viruses kill some of your cells, you DO have about 30 trillion other cells in your body, give or take a few trillion. Plus, your dead and injured cells are constantly being replaced with new, healthy cells. You can afford to lose a few battles, knowing that you'll probably win the viral war in the end.

HITCHING A RIDE ON THE SNOT TRAIN

A catchy tune is fun. A catchy disease is not. Viruses travel in all sorts of devious ways. They can snag a ride on spit and snot droplets ejected during a sneeze or cough (chicken pox is passed along this way—as well as from contact with the fluid in the poxes). Viruses can also hitchhike from person to person aboard a tossed ball or a borrowed book (so wash those paws after playing with other kids' toys, and especially after sneezing, coughing, blowing or picking your nose, or going number one or number two). And watch out for that innocent little kiss on

ICK-SPLORATION

FOLLOW THE FLU

20 MINUTES

GO FETCH

Viruses on the move? Science to the rescue! Some people actually volunteer to catch a cold for the sake of science (and often get paid cash to do so) so that the way viruses spread can be studied. If just the thought of doing that makes you sneeze, you'll find this experiment less risky and a lot more fun. You'll create a community of cup "people" and safely observe how the dreaded "vinegar virus" can spread through your tiny population.

- 16 identical cups (can be paper, glass, or plastic, but they must be identical)
- Pen or pencil
- Masking tape (optional)
- Lab assistant
- White vinegar
- Water
- Spoon
- Baking soda

HACK!

1. Each cup will be a person. Take a few minutes to give them some personality by writing the name of a person on the bottom of each cup. You don't want the names to be visible when the cups are standing up. If your cups are see-through, stick a piece of masking tape on the bottom and then write the name on the tape. It might be fun to name them after real people (yourself, friends, and family) and/or your favorite book or movie characters. Make sure that you can't actually identify any cup except by lifting it and looking on the bottom.

2. Leave the room for a moment. While you are gone, your lab assistant should pour vinegar into one cup (fill it a little less than ½ full) and remember that cup's name. Then, the rest of the cups should all be filled with water (the same amount: slightly less than ½ full). The 15 cups with water represent healthy people. The one cup with vinegar represents a person with the flu (but who isn't showing symptoms yet). All 16 cups represent the village of Cupville. Your lab assistant should keep the flu bearer, "patient zero" (the vinegar cup), a secret from you. Patient zero is the medical term for the first person in a community to get sick with a particular disease.

3. Before you come back, your lab assistant should randomly pair each cup next to another cup. Cupville is a very friendly town; everybody gets a buddy. Once this is done you can return to the scene.

4. Now that you're back in the room, your job is to make sure that everyone in Cupville comes in close contact with someone else. Cups shaking hands! Cups sneezing near other cups! Cups playing basketball! Since Cupvillians don't have hands to shake or noses to sneeze with, you'll model these meetings differently. Take a set of two cups and pour all of the liquid from one cup into the other, so it's almost full. Then pour half of it back into the empty cup.

5. Repeat this for all eight pairs of cups. Only mix one pair at a time, and once two cups have swapped germs, set them aside and move on to the next pair. Whoever had the "vinegar flu virus" has just infected someone else.

6. Ask your lab assistant to look away or leave the room. Now rearrange the cups in random places. This way neither you nor your assistant knows which Cupvillians might be "infected" with vinegar.

7. The residents of Cupville are still in a party mood. They like to hang out with their buddies. Let your lab assistant randomly arrange the cups into pairs again.

8. Now let those pairs "shake hands" by mixing their liquids. Do the same as in step 4: For each pair of cups, pour all of the liquid into one cup and then pour half of it back into the empty cup. Then set that pair aside. Keep going until all pairs have "shaken hands."

9. The Cupvillians are such a talkative bunch. Your lab assistant should do one more random sort of the cups while you look away. Then pair them up and mix their liquids. This is their third meeting.

10. Are your Cupvillians showing any flu symptoms yet? Cups with runny noses? Aches and chills? You can now check which cups got infected. While holding each cup over a sink, dump in about a teaspoon of baking soda. If the water fizzes and makes tiny bubbles (carbon dioxide gas is created when baking soda and vinegar mix), then this Cupvillian has been exposed to the vinegar flu virus. If the baking soda simply drops to the bottom of the cup, then your Cupvillian is healthy. Repeat this with the rest of the cups. How many Cupvillians got the flu?

11. Ask your assistant who "patient zero" was, and discover the identities of the sick Cupvillians by looking at the names on the bottom of the cups.

WHAT JUST HAPPENED? Were you surprised how many Cupvillians were infected? Our Cupvillians swapped germs three separate times. In only these few interactions it was possible for half of Cupville to become infected from just one virus carrier! Luckily, because someone with the flu might have been socializing with someone who was already infected, there's a good chance you had fewer than eight sick Cupvillians.

In the real world, people tend to hang out with the same people in the same place day after day (like at school or work), which sadly means they will infect each other, but it also means viruses can't quickly hit everyone on the planet. Also, you don't always catch a cold or the flu from someone who has it, because your body's immune system often kills the viral invader on arrival. Practicing good hygiene by washing your hands (you do wash your hands, right?) and not licking doorknobs (PLEASE tell us you don't lick doorknobs!) also helps prevent you from catching a disease. People get bombarded with viruses all the time, but even if they catch the illness, the good news is that most people get better, and that's nothing to sneeze at!

the forehead from sweet but snotty Aunt Edith. Once a virus is onboard a human it can be hard to stop it from hijacking your cells and making endless copies of itself. Some viruses, such as the ones that cause the common cold, are simply annoying. We all catch these viruses from time to time. But many others are cold-blooded killers.

A POX ON YOU!

Poxes are a nasty family of viruses, and one of the more nefarious is smallpox. There's nothing "small" about what it could do to a person. The smallpox virus was a curse that sent chills down a person's spine in bygone times. First the victim felt under the weather and achy. Then red spots appeared on the face, arms, and hands, and later, the torso—these turned into horrible pus-filled pocks. If the patient was lucky, scabs formed and then fell off, leaving deep scars. And for the not so lucky, their time on the planet was over. For thousands of years all people could do was hope that they would survive a pox attack. Between 1900 and 1977 (when smallpox was finally declared defeated), more than 300 million people perished from the disease. Another 600 million were infected and many had scars for the rest of their lives (in fact, smallpox scars have been found on ancient Egyptian mummies). Given that smallpox had probably been around since 10,000 BCE, you can see what a plague to humanity a pox can be. No wonder it was called the Speckled Monster!

I SMELL SOME SMALLPOX!

The first smallpox vaccine—in fact, the first vaccine ever—wasn't developed until 1796, but people were trying to come up with some way to stop smallpox and other diseases long before then. One thing they noticed was that if you somehow survived smallpox, then you would

SMALL BEATS BIG

What does a virus look like? Some look a lot like golf balls. Others look like science fiction spaceships! But they are all TINY. You are enormous by comparison. You have trillions and trillions of cells in your body. They are so tiny, you can't even see them without a microscope. But if one healthy cell in your body were equal to the size of your favorite football star, then one bacterium would equal the size of a football. And one smallpox virus (which is a large virus) would be the size of an AA battery. One polio virus (which is a "little" virus, but just as harmful as a big virus) would be the size of an aspirin! Think about that! Athlete to aspirin. That's the difference in size between your cells and a virus.

never get it again. You were *immune* (ih-<u>myoon</u>) to it. So people wondered, "How can we get people to get slightly sick but not sick enough to die?" Ever sniffed a fragrant flower with a deep breath? One technique to protect a person from the deadly pox was to have them take a deep inhale or two of a powder made of dried smallpox scabs from someone who had survived a mild case of the disease. The kid who had to inhale the poxy dust hopefully got a mild case too, and then he was forever immune.

Before the late 18th century, the most effective method of achieving immunity involved pricking a pus-filled pock with a sharp pin, then depositing the contents of that pinhead into the skin of a healthy person by making scratch marks on their skin. The person who was pox-scratched would develop smallpox, but usually a very mild case. There was always a risk that they could die or start an epidemic, but a mini-attack of smallpox was better than developing a full-blown and potentially deadly case of the dreaded disease. This procedure—called *inoculation* (inn-ock-you-<u>lay</u>-shun)—clearly helped. For a few hundred years, this was the best way to avoid smallpox.

COWABUNGA!

Let's time-travel to England in the mid-1700s. Eight-year-old Edward Jenner is squirming as live smallpox is scratched into his arm. He feels "blah" for a bit but soon recovers. He is now immune to smallpox! When Jenner is 13 years old, he is apprenticed to a doctor. While working there he overhears a woman who milks cows bragging, "I shall never have smallpox for I have had cowpox. I shall never have an ugly pockmarked face." Hmmmm, he thought. Interesting.

Jenner had an idea. Cowpox was not nearly as dangerous as smallpox. Would injecting a bit of cowpox stop a person from getting smallpox? It seemed less dangerous than being scraped with live smallpox fluid. In May 1796, Jenner met a young dairymaid named Sarah Nelms with fresh cowpox blisters on her hands and arms. A few days later he injected the pus from her blisters into the arm of an eight-year-old lad named James Phipps. The boy developed a mild fever and a few chills but quickly recovered. Two months later, Jenner grabbed a syringe full of smallpox and injected the boy with it. One can only wonder how James's parents felt about that! Or James himself, for that matter! Luckily, the child

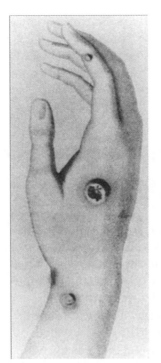

It looks ugly, but cowpox saved lives! It was the key to stopping the more dangerous smallpox.

was absolutely fine. No smallpox!

Jenner decided to honor the mooing marvels that had made this all possible. The Latin word for cow is *vacca*. The medical term for cowpox is *vaccinia*. So, Jenner named his new procedure *vaccination* (vack-sin-a-shun). It took quite a while, but eventually the idea caught on. Over the years more and more people got smallpox vaccines, and in 1980 (almost two hundred years later) the World Health Organization declared the world smallpox-free.

Today, vaccination is very common. Bet you've been to the doctor a time or two and cringed at the sight of syringes with needles nestled on a nearby tray, all aimed for *your* arm. Those shots deliver *vaccines* (vack-<u>seens</u>) into your body. Each slender vial is filled with bits of a weakened or dead virus, which alert your body into thinking it is under attack by an alien invader. Your immune system springs into action as it would for any other invasion— after all, its job is to protect you. It makes antibodies to attack the virus, and because the virus is weak, your body can handle it, no problem. But here's the best part: Even long after it "fought off" the vaccine, your immune system

Edward Jenner had the brilliant idea that led to the smallpox vaccine.

WANTED
DEAD OR ALIVE

VIRUS
REWARD

remembers these enemies. If you ever meet that virus again, even if it's much stronger, it's as if your body has seen the virus on a WANTED DEAD OR ALIVE poster and knows to immediately make antibodies to go on the attack. The virus's hostile takeover is thwarted before it can even begin.

THE TOP VIRAL TROUBLEMAKERS

Chicken pox: Another formerly common kid's disease, chicken pox causes itchy blisters all over your skin. The tricky thing about this virus is that if you have had chicken pox once, it hangs around in your body—dormant, like a sleeping volcano. It can erupt again in older folks if their immune systems start to falter. This leads to a pox called *shingles* that causes a rash some say feels like a blowtorch aimed right at you. Fortunately, there is now a chicken pox vaccine.

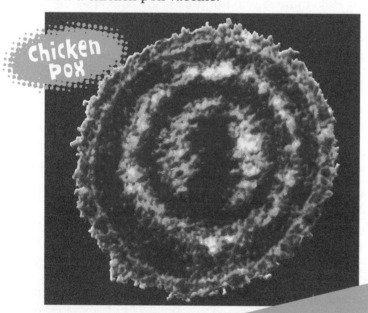

chicken pox

Who Knew? Our immune system (remember those white blood cells?) at work is what makes us feel sick (rather than the virus itself). Fever, headache, rash—all these symptoms mean your immune system is on the job.

ICK-TIVITY

MY PET VIRUS

GO FETCH

30 MINUTES

Modeling clay or Play-Doh in several different colors. (If you don't have any lying around, make some yourself using the recipe for conductive dough on page 263.)

Pipe cleaners of various colors. Each model will take 2 or 3 pipe cleaners, cut into 1-inch pieces (toothpicks or small sticks will work just fine too).

Scissors

Here's a chance to hold a virus, and even give it to someone else, without anyone actually getting sick! Let's make a model of one of the many viruses that cause the common cold. This particular one is called an *adenovirus* (ad-den-oh-<u>vi</u>-rus). It can make you cough and sneeze, but it can also bring on diarrhea, fever, and pink eye! Like all viruses, it consists of genetic material (DNA or RNA—in this case, DNA) surrounded by a protective protein coat, which has "spikes" that allow it to attach to and invade cells.

You'll probably want to make several of these little baddies for your friends and family. You could even hang one as a holiday decoration! You can make them as big or as small as you want, but these instructions are for cuddly little viruses that fit in the palm of your hand.

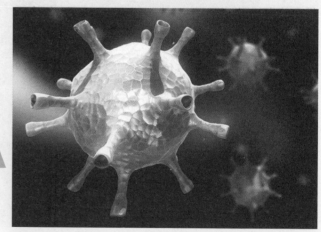

This is a drawing of what an adenovirus looks like.

1. For each virus, take a thumb-size piece of clay and roll it until it looks like a little snake. Then make another one and coil them together in a double helix shape. That will represent the virus's genetic material—its DNA or RNA (for more on DNA, see page 42).

4. Now grab your 1-inch pieces of pipe cleaner. These will represent "spikes" that allow the virus to attach to one of your cells. Stick them all over the ball. The ones on the bottom may get a little squashed, but you can adjust them as your virus dries.

(for more on DNA, see page 42)

WHAT JUST HAPPENED?

Just as you easily gave this pet virus to your friends and family, so is it easy to pass on the real adenovirus too. It travels in the air from coughs or sneezes, or hangs around on people's hands. It can also spread via poop. That's one reason why grown-ups keep reminding you to wash after you wipe, and why they tell you to cough or sneeze into your elbow, not your hands. AND . . . if you touch surfaces that other sick people might have touched, be sure not to touch your nose, eyes, mouth, or food until after you've washed your hands. AND, AND, AND . . . bottom line? Viruses lurk wherever sick humans have been, so be smart. Protect yourself! If you DO get a cold or the flu, protect others by staying home.

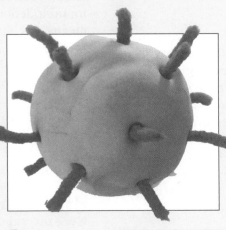

2. Now take a handful of a different color of clay. Roll it into a ball. This will represent the protein coat. More about that in a bit.

3. Use your thumb to make a hole in the side of the ball, and pop your double snake of genetic material inside.

5. For extra viral beauty, you can add some little clay knobs on the top of each fiber, to make them look more like the real viruses do under a microscope.

6. Make a few more models, for each friend or family member to whom you intend to give this little "gift that keeps on giving."

7. Let your pet viruses dry overnight. Then walk up to your friend and say, "I've got a present for you . . . hold out your hand!" When they do, you can tell them it's their very own "pet virus"!

Those little balls on the end of your pipe cleaner "fibers" are like a key that fits into a "lock" (called a receptor) on your cells. The virus sits itself down, puts the key in the lock, and then it's as if a little door opens to let the virus inside your cell! (Other viruses work by cutting holes in the wall of one of your cells and then injecting their genetic information, a bit like how a doctor or nurse gives you a shot.) The genetic instructions on the viral RNA or DNA (the stuff you twisted and placed inside your virus) take over your cell and force it to make many, many, MANY more copies of the virus. It's as if someone walked into a shoe factory and then used all the machines inside to make evil clones of themselves instead.

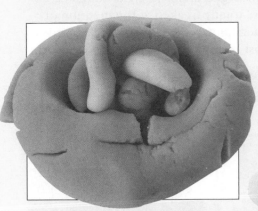

Then use a little more "protein coat"—colored clay to cover up the hole. Now the genetic material is inside where it belongs. Pinch the clay together so that it sticks, and roll it around in your hand until it is ball-shaped again.

What's super cool is that scientists are actually figuring out how to use adenoviruses as a way to get vaccines for other really bad viruses, such as HIV, directly into your cells. It's like turning a supervillain into a superhero!

The common cold: Oh, the sneezing! And that oozing nose! So far, it's been difficult to make a vaccine for the common cold because there are so many different viruses (more than 200!), each with a slightly different shape. It's kind of like a criminal wearing lots of different disguises. Luckily your immune system usually stops the invaders after a couple of days.

Ebola: Very dangerous! These viruses weaken blood vessels, so folks start with flulike symptoms but can develop oozing gums, bleeding from the eyes, bloody poop, and other horrible symptoms. This disease is currently concentrated in parts of West Africa, and is passed through direct contact with an infected person's bodily fluids. Many of the areas where ebola exists have poor health care, but the world's medical community has learned a lot about how to contain and treat the disease and is trying to put an end to it.

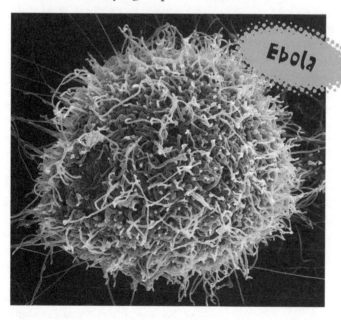

Ebola

The flu: So much misery wrapped up in a tiny package. Aches and pains and fevers, oh, my! This crafty virus changes from year to year, but we can often stop it with a new vaccine that is given annually. Each year, virologists try to determine which flu viruses will be the most widespread, and they create a vaccine for all those strains so, hopefully, fewer people will get sick.

Hepatitis: Love liver? This virus certainly does. It goes straight for that very much needed organ in our bodies and irritates it in a major way, preventing it from doing its many jobs. There are several kinds of hepatitis, but Hep A is the one that a kid is most likely to get. It's transmitted in the poop of infected people. Yet another reason to wash your paws after visiting a bathroom! There's a vaccine for it too.

HIV: These letters stand for this: Human Immunodeficiency Virus. H = *Human*. This means this virus is a people-only virus. I = *Immunodeficiency*. The virus attacks the *immune system*. A "*deficient*" immune system will not be able to fight off enemy germ invasions. V = *Virus*. And you know what those can do by now. The final stage of HIV brings AIDS (Acquired Immune Deficieny Syndrome). Not everyone with HIV will develop AIDS, and new drugs seem to be helpful in stopping the progress of HIV.

Measles and mumps: Back before vaccines were invented, having these two diseases was a rite of passage for most kids. One brought red spots, the other chipmunk cheeks from swollen salivary glands. Now there are vaccines for both.

Polio: This virus lodges primarily in the spinal cord nerves that control our muscles and can cause *paralysis* (meaning you can't move parts of your body). The polio epidemic hit its peak in the early 1950s and targeted kids in great numbers, so parents were totally freaked at the mention of it. Happily, a vaccine was developed in 1955 and polio has almost been eliminated around the world.

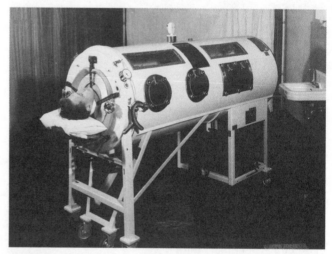

Polio affected the muscles that controlled breathing, so some folks had to use an "iron lung" contraption until they got better and could breathe on their own.

WHY DID CHICKENS GET THE BLAME?

Chicken pox is just one of several itchy, gross-looking ailments that can make life miserable. But why do these poor poultry get blamed for those ugly pustules that itch like the dickens, when the virus doesn't come from chickens at all? "Why me?" they cluck. Well, there are three theories for how the chicken pox got its name:

1. Those barnyard egg-droppers have a reputation for being wimpy—as in "You are SUCH A CHICKEN for not riding the 20,000-foot vertical drop Tornado of Doom roller coaster." Chicken pox, as far as poxes go, is usually not life-threatening, as compared to some other really terrible poxes. A wimpy pox.

2. An Old English word—giccan—sounds like chicken (ah, but does it TASTE like chicken?). It means "itchy."

3. The red, itchy rash looks like a chicken pecked your skin.

While we're on the subject, do chickens get chicken pox? Nope. But they DO get something called fowlpox, which is—no surprise—pretty foul! Other species have their own special poxes. There's monkeypox, canarypox, and even fruit can get ill! Poor plums with plum pox!

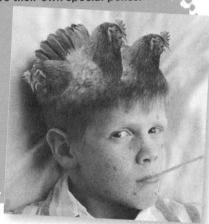

These days chicken pox is rare, thanks to vaccines!

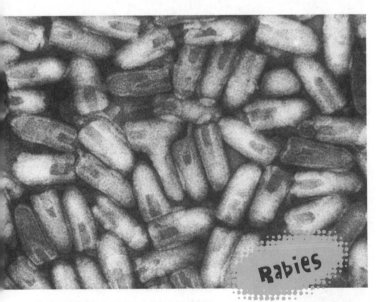

Rabies

Rabies: Here's a word to impress the grown-ups in your life: *zoonosis* (zoo-<u>no</u>-sis)—a disease that travels from animals to people. This type of virus spreads from the bite of an infected dog, raccoon, or other animal and ends up lodged in the unlucky person's brain. It can be fatal. Luckily there is a series of shots that will stop the rabies virus from destroying the bitten person's gray matter.

Bottom line here? Show a lot of respect for the power of these cell hijackers!

THE GREAT PLAGUE DEBATE

Perhaps you have heard of something called the Black Death? This awful plague wiped out between a third and a half of the population of Europe between 1347 and 1352. No tiny poxes here: This plague brought giant egg-shaped swellings that oozed blood and pus. Soon after infection, the victim's internal organs basically turned to Jell-O, followed by a swift and terrible death. For centuries, historians have blamed flea-infested rats that arrived on ships from Asia, carrying a dangerous bacterium. But now many scientists and historians are beginning to point a finger at another culprit—viruses! It makes sense. Up to HALF the population of Europe would have had to be bitten by fleas. And the plague raged all through the winter, a time when

BUILD A PLAGUE LAUNCHER, MIDDLE AGES-STYLE

30 MINUTES

GO FETCH →

We are quite sure that you are much nicer and more civilized than those marauding, plague-propelling armies of the Middle Ages. But you can still have some fun flinging things with your own mini catapult!

- 6 rubber bands
- 8 Popsicle sticks
- Scissors
- Spoon
- Several dangerous viruses (just kidding—several mini marshmallows or small pompoms to represent viruses)

1. Rubber-band six Popsicle sticks at both ends to make a stack. Then rubber-band two other Popsicle sticks at one end.

2. Slide the stack of six bound sticks in between the two sticks. Cut two rubber bands and tie each tightly around all the sticks so that they hold the stack of six sticks firmly in place near the spot where the two sticks are held together.

3. Rubber-band a spoon to the top stick.

4. Ready to launch! Load your "virus" into the spoon. With one hand, hold the catapult firmly down by pressing on both ends of the six-stack-sticks.

5. Now with your other hand, press down firmly on the spot where the spoon is banded to the launch stick.

6. Ready, aim, release!

fleas generally lie low. A virus, which spreads easily from person to person, would seem to make more sense.

Either way, one thing is for sure: A plague victim's body could be used as a weapon if you wanted to infect your enemies and wipe them out. But how? In those days, most big towns were surrounded by thick, high walls—some even had moats for protection. So soldiers turned to a handy-dandy invention called the *catapult* (<u>cat</u>-uh-pult) or its bigger brother, a *trebuchet* (tre-boo-<u>shay</u>). Tip a giant spoon back, load in a plague-ridden body, and let go—your projectile will travel a great distance without a lot of effort. Fast too! Perfect for diabolical and dastardly plague-spreading among your enemies. How awful! Humans aren't always the nicest creatures, are they?

16th-century plague victims.

Going Viral. Now that you understand how viruses can go "viral" faster than a YouTube video of a cat playing "Jingle Bells" on a grand piano, it's time to move onto something equally vile. Starts with *V*. Rhymes with comet. And it's upchucking now.

→

Plague doctors in the 17th century wore beak-like masks filled with scented plants to "filter the bad air."

Vomit

Considering what a disgusting thing it is to **DO**, there certainly are a lot of fun ways to say it: upchuck, hurl, blow chunks, spew, barf, toss your cookies, do the Technicolor yawn, ralph, and a lot more. Too bad the actual *act* of vomiting isn't so fun.

BARFING BASICS

Most of us will, at some point in our lives, puke. It's a part of life. Humans do it. Cats and dogs too. And even though it's nasty, a lot of the time vomiting helps get something harmful out of our stomach before it can go any further and make things even worse.

Hurling is as easy as 1-2-3. It usually starts with a cold sweat, then you get hit with *nausea*—an icky, queasy feeling, much like an early-warning siren before a storm hits. Feeling nauseous can be your body's way of saying STOP DOING WHATEVER YOU ARE DOING RIGHT THIS SECOND UNLESS YOU WANT TO BARF! And then, there's the main event: *emesis* (<u>em</u>-uh-siss). That's the official doctor word for barfing. Upchucking occurs when your tummy

muscles contract to push anything in your stomach up, up, and away.

Considering that the contents of your stomach come shooting out of your mouth, it might surprise you to learn that the real mastermind is your brain. Your stomach tells your brain that it's irritated, then your brain sends the signal to your diaphragm and abdominal muscles to contract and push out everything. This can happen for a variety of reasons.

1. You've eaten something vile and disgusting
—something with a toxin that you need to get out of your system ASAP, so your brain sends "get-it-outta-here-NOW" messages to your abdominal muscles. This is also known as food poisoning—barf-o-rama!

2. You have eaten something fabulous
but you have gobbled WAY too much, way too fast. Your stomach says to your brain, "Eating four servings of Aunt Gertie's lasagna was a bad idea and it's pressing too hard on my walls! So that I don't explode, please get it out!" Back out it comes!

3. You have picked up a stomach bug
—a flock of nasty intruder viruses that irritate your stomach lining. Your stomach sends an SOS to your brain, which gives the command—time to upchuck!

Quick! Run! Someone's gonna blow!

RIDING THE TILT-A-HURL

5 MINUTES

GO FETCH →

- A plastic cup half filled with water
- Yourself or a willing victim or two (er—we mean friends)

You've just staggered off a twisty amusement park ride called the Dizzy Dinosaur. You are not a dinosaur, but you sure are dizzy, and you're an inch away from barfing. Why? Try this ick-sploration to find out. No hurling necessary!

1. Fill a clear plastic cup about half full of water. Holding it at the edges of the top rim, gently swirl it around and around several times, then stop. Notice what happens to the water.

2. Put the cup down and spin around in circles, as fast as you can, about ten times. Then stop.

3. Take a minute or two to recover from your spin cycle and observe how you feel.

4. Now spin ten times in one direction, but instead of coming to a complete stop, change direction immediately and spin ten times in the other direction. Now how do you feel?

WHAT JUST HAPPENED?

When you stopped swirling the water in the glass, it kept spinning. The same thing happens to the fluid in your inner ear, called *endolymph* (<u>en</u>-doe-limf). As you spin, this fluid spins in the same direction as you do, but when you stop, the fluid keeps spinning for a little while longer. Until it settles down, you will feel dizzy, and your brain may send out the order to upchuck. But, when you spun yourself in one direction then quickly did the exact opposite, the counter motion canceled out the spinning and allowed the endolymph to come to rest, so you should not have experienced as much dizziness.

4. You've just ridden the Tilt-A-Whirl three times in a row. Or you have been playing video games in the backseat of the car while the driver navigates down winding roads. Wonder why you're sweating, feeling nauseous, and looking for a barf bag? When it comes to "motion sickness," your stomach isn't the problem. It's your ears, eyes, sense

THEME-PARK PUKE

Have you ever gotten a case of the "icks" at an amusement park? If you see a mop and a bucket near the exit of a park ride you might want to think twice about getting on it. Here are some rides that ought to come with a sick sack under the seat!

The Tilt-A-Whirl Spinning round and round while moving up and down? A recipe for ralphing.

Spinning teacups The cups are going in circles, and the FLOOR is also spinning in a different direction. Perhaps you would like some tossed cookies to go with your tea?

Any giant roller coaster Big, bigger, biggest—there's nothing like the feeling of hurtling over the edge of a 20-story-high building as you wonder where you left your stomach.

The Vekoma Waikiki Wave Super Flip Generally regarded as the barf king of all rides! This ride at a theme park in Mexico flips you quickly, spins you head over heels, and sloshes you from side to side. Up, down, left, right, all the while spinning. It's not uncommon for a guest on this ride to blow chunks in the midst of all that flinging. You can only hope someone's chunks do not fly onto you.

ICK-TIVITY

APRIL FOOL'S SURPRISE

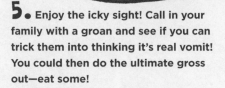

10 MINUTES

PLUS JUMPING UP AND DOWN SAYING, "GROOOSSS!!"

GO FETCH

½ cup yogurt, any flavor

Bowl

½ cup chunky salsa

Spoon

Paper towels for clean up

When you vomit, you get rid of the contents of your stomach, including stomach acid, some of the mucus that protects your stomach lining, and—of course—food in various stages of digestion. Because most people aren't patient enough to chew their food to a pulp, the food that gets swallowed often contains chunks of food. So, to "blow chunks" is actually quite an accurate name!

What vomit looks like really depends on what you've eaten, so there are plenty of ingredients that will work. Generally you need to mix a creamy, slimy thing with something that has good-size chunks of food in it. But we've also discovered that the way you display the vomit is the key. And that key, dear reader, is to drop your fake upchuck from a height of at least two feet, because the splat is the thing that makes it gross. So make a batch of this fake vomit, and make sure it lands with a nice thud. Then call over friends or family and see if they believe that you just blew chunks!

1. Put the yogurt in the bowl.

2. Add salsa a few spoonfuls at a time until you get the color and consistency you want. You might not add the full ½ cup.

3. Take your bowl of fake upchuck to a place where you can drop it from a height. This will be messy, so make sure it's a place that's easy to clean up, like outside or a tiled floor. Avoid rugs and furniture!

4. Lift some up with a spoon and let it splat down.

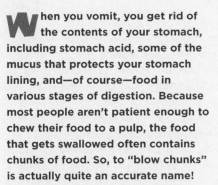

5. Enjoy the icky sight! Call in your family with a groan and see if you can trick them into thinking it's real vomit! You could then do the ultimate gross out—eat some!

WHAT JUST HAPPENED?

Did you notice the ingredients in this recipe are not gross at all? They're quite tasty alone or even mixed together. You might even enjoy tasting the mixture if you hadn't decided to call it fake vomit. Somehow, though, just NAMING it "fake vomit" makes it almost impossible to force yourself to taste. That's how strong your brain can be in protecting you against something that might be bad for you, even if you really know it's okay.

To make good fake vomit, you need something liquid to represent stomach acid, something slightly slimy to be the mucus, and something somewhat chunky to look like your food. The yogurt and salsa provide all of these characteristics. Feel free to experiment with other foods too. And a reminder: You need to clean up your April Fool's Surprise! Remember, you made the mess, so don't leave it there or ask someone else to clean it up! Failure to do so will result in your being kicked out of the AWESOME SCIENTISTS' CLUB.

of touch, and of course—control central—your brain.

Usually your brain knows where it is by sucking up info from all your senses. Every time you move, an area of your inner ear, called the *vestibular system*, is using its tiny, supersensitive hairlike sensors and its special fluid to determine which way your head is pointed and alert your brain. On a theme-park ride there are so many changes of direction that the hairs and fluid are going everywhere and your brain has no idea which end is up. In the car, your brain gets very different

Astronauts train on the KC-135, aka the Vomit Comet.

messages from all your senses. Your body is swaying in all directions, while your eyes, glued to a video screen or book, tell your brain you are not moving at all. All that conflicting info makes your brain decide that all is not well, so it thinks, "Well, might as well clear out the stomach in case the problem is there!" And now it's pull-over-and-puke time!

5. You've watched someone else barf.

Sometimes just seeing or smelling someone else's contributions to the Wide World of Vomit is enough to make you gag and then hurl too. Why do some of us "sympathy vomit"? Some scientists say that it's a survival instinct from way back when, still etched in our brains from cave-dweller days when people shared communal food. If barfing Bob ate bad bison, you probably did too, so you'll survive better if you get it out of your system before it can do serious harm!

FEELING THE BURN

You know how your throat feels like it's on fire after your puke? Blame your lovely stomach acid, which can also harm your teeth as it spews out during an upchuck fest. But your amazing body has a plan for protecting your pearly whites—just before you blow chunks, your mouth starts filling with a tidal wave of saliva to coat your teeth and keep them safer during the oncoming vomit storm.

What about gagging? Ever brushed your tongue, but stuck the brush a little too far back? Ever eaten some peanut butter and had it stick to

THE VOMIT COMET

Being an astronaut is supercool. But getting used to living in weightlessness can actually cause nausea and vomiting because an astronaut's senses send conflicting messages to his or her brain. They don't know which end is up or down because there is no up or down in zero gravity! A person blowing chunks all over the International Space Station is NOT a good thing. To get used to weightlessness and thus be less likely to upchuck, soon-to-be space dwellers train aboard a plane with the official name of KC-135. This plane is like a roller coaster. It flies almost straight up, then plunges down—over and over again. It its downward lunge, the lucky folks onboard will get to experience about 25 seconds of weightlessness. They will do this over and over and over again. Hopefully, eventually, their inner ears and brain will begin to recognize the experience and not freak out when they experience weightlessness in outer space! In spite of the training aboard the "vomit comet," once up in the International Space Station, new arrivals sometimes feel the need to let loose with a "liquid scream." Thank goodness there are seriously hard-core barf bags onboard.

the roof of your mouth? These things may trigger your gag reflex, causing the nerves in the back of your throat to send an urgent message to the brain saying, "I'm about to choke on something, help!" Your brain sends a message to your throat muscles and causes them to contract, which helps move things away from the back of the throat. Gag. Gag. GAH! All that gagging just might trigger vomiting. Some people have more sensitive gag reflexes than others, but not sword swallowers: They've learned to completely stop their gag reflex!

Barf. Poop. Pee. Farts. Burps. We have ick-splored so many fun things. Could there possibly be anything nasty left? Of course there is! Slither on over to WORMS!

Worms

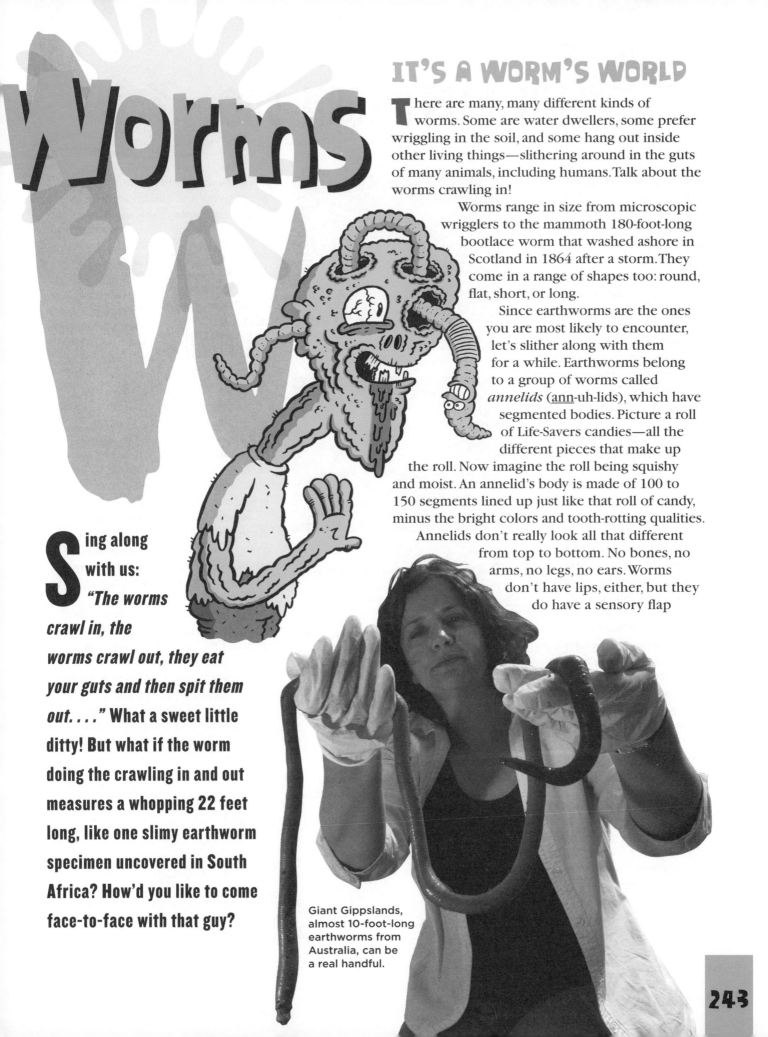

Sing along with us: *"The worms crawl in, the worms crawl out, they eat your guts and then spit them out. . . ."* What a sweet little ditty! But what if the worm doing the crawling in and out measures a whopping 22 feet long, like one slimy earthworm specimen uncovered in South Africa? How'd you like to come face-to-face with that guy?

IT'S A WORM'S WORLD

There are many, many different kinds of worms. Some are water dwellers, some prefer wriggling in the soil, and some hang out inside other living things—slithering around in the guts of many animals, including humans. Talk about the worms crawling in!

Worms range in size from microscopic wrigglers to the mammoth 180-foot-long bootlace worm that washed ashore in Scotland in 1864 after a storm. They come in a range of shapes too: round, flat, short, or long.

Since earthworms are the ones you are most likely to encounter, let's slither along with them for a while. Earthworms belong to a group of worms called *annelids* (<u>ann</u>-uh-lids), which have segmented bodies. Picture a roll of Life-Savers candies—all the different pieces that make up the roll. Now imagine the roll being squishy and moist. An annelid's body is made of 100 to 150 segments lined up just like that roll of candy, minus the bright colors and tooth-rotting qualities. Annelids don't really look all that different from top to bottom. No bones, no arms, no legs, no ears. Worms don't have lips, either, but they do have a sensory flap

Giant Gippslands, almost 10-foot-long earthworms from Australia, can be a real handful.

THE EARTHWORM DOC

10 MINUTES

ONCE YOU'VE CAUGHT YOUR SQUIRMY PATIENT

It'll take you about four years of graduate school after college to become a vet. Can't wait? We'll have you playing worm doctor in just a few minutes.

1. You first have to find a patient. Earthworms are notorious for avoiding doctors, so you're going to have to make a "house call." Find some ground and start digging around. With a bit of luck, you'll find an earthworm in no time. No luck or no accessible dirt? Go to a bait shop or pet store and pick one up.

2. Put a moist paper towel in the cup and then gently drop in your worm so it can get ready for its checkup. You want to keep it moist because the worm will die if it dries out.

3. First, oral health. A worm doesn't have teeth, but it does have a mouth. If you're looking at the wrong end, then you're looking at the worm's anus. (Hey, how about a little privacy please?) Worms are made of many body segments. The thickest segment (called the clitellum, which is used for storing worm eggs) will be closer to the mouth end (called the anterior) of the worm. Use your magnifying glass to take a closer look. . . . Unfortunately, we don't know how to say "Open up and say aah!" in worm-speak. Do you?

4. Next up, water reflexes. Run water over another paper towel so only half of it is wet. Lay the worm across it so half of it is resting on the wet side and half of it is on the dry side. Now let go and observe which side the worm moves toward.

GO FETCH

Shovel or trowel

Earthworm

Paper towels

Clear cup or glass

Water

Magnifying glass

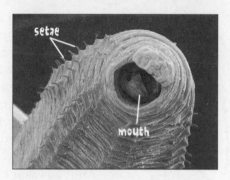

setae

mouth

5. Moisten your fingers and slide them back and forth along the body of the worm. You should be able to feel tiny bristles called *setae* that stick out of its body. These little "hairs" work with the worm's muscles to give it better traction to squirm.

6. Blood pressure. Use your magnifying glass and look near the anterior (front) end for the contracting pulses of its circulatory system. You should be able to see the movement associated with blood being pumped.

7. Time for dismissal. Now that your patient has a clean (or dirty?)

bill of health, gently return the worm to the soil outside, or pop it in a worm condo in the next ick-tivity.

WHAT JUST HAPPENED?

What interesting things did your worm do? Were you able to really get a close look at the segments and feel the setae? Those bristly setae you felt also explain why a worm doesn't just slip out of the ground when you pull on it. All those tiny little extensions act like living Velcro and anchor the worm in the ground (making it harder for you or a predator to yank it out).

Which side of the paper towel did your worm head toward? Worms don't breathe through their mouth but instead absorb oxygen through their skin, but only if they are wet. This is why your worm probably preferred the moist paper towel over the dry paper towel. It will suffocate if it's dry for too long, so make sure you keep it moist. Did you see the circulatory system pumping? A worm doesn't have a heart like yours. It has five tiny "aortic arches" that pump the blood around. Hmmm . . . Does that mean a worm falls in love five times as often?

clitellum

WORM INVADERS

Earthworms are cool, but some other worms are pretty freaky—they torment humans and pets by taking up residence inside a person or animal. The grossest worm-invader award probably goes to the *pinworm*. These are whitish and about ½ inch long. Their home of choice—the human intestines! The adult females lay their eggs around your butthole. Super itchy! *Tapeworms* are another misery maker. These critters sneak aboard a body in undercooked meat and have hooks and suckers that latch on to the intestines. Some tapeworms can grow to be 50 feet long and have enormous appetites. *Roundworms* seem to

have a preference for life aboard a dog, but many can infect humans too. If you have a pet, check its poop every once in a while. If you see something that looks like moving spaghetti, get your puppy to a vet quickly! How to avoid letting any of these creatures hop onboard? Wash your hands after using the bathroom and make sure your meat is thoroughly cooked.

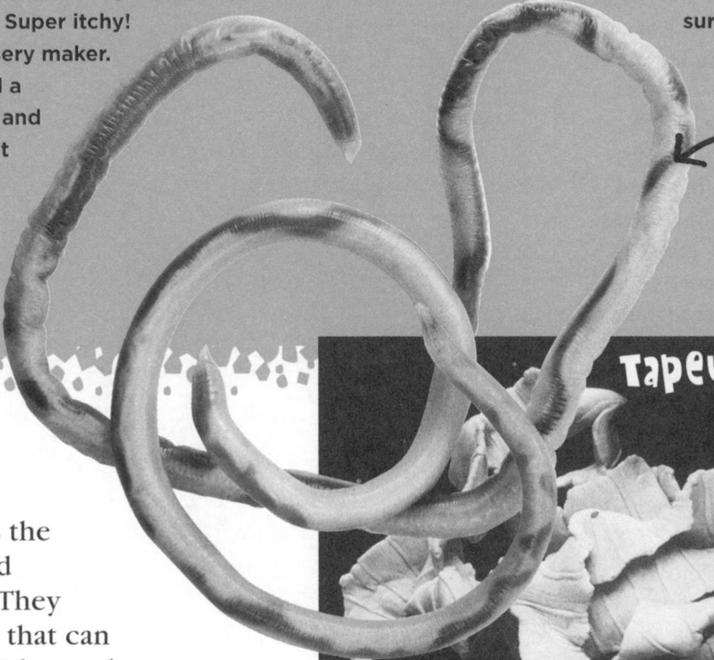

Roundworm

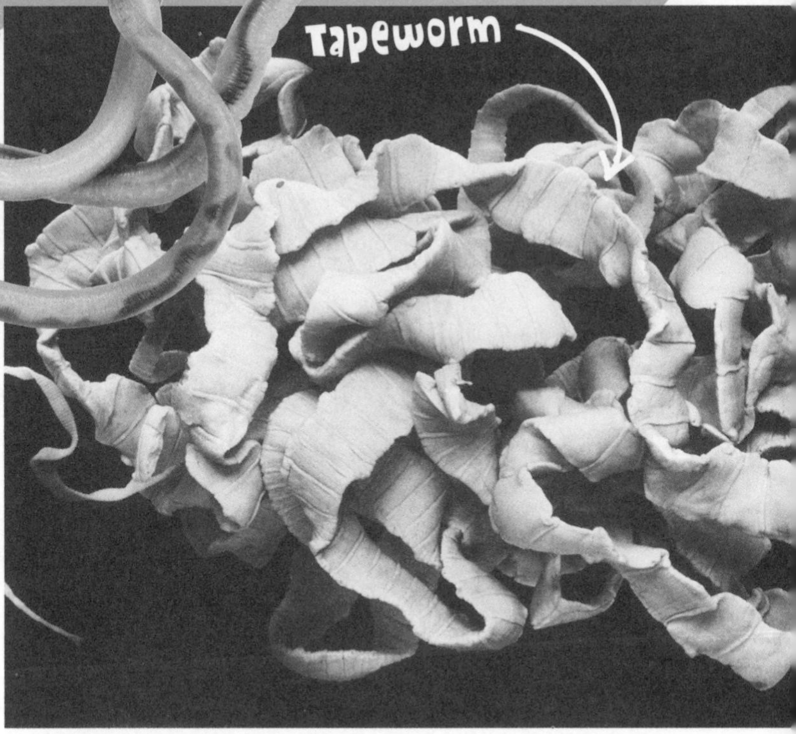

Tapeworm

around the top of the mouth (called a *prostomium*—proh-<u>stow</u>-me-um) that helps the worm feel its way around and pushes food into the mouth. They don't have eyes—just organs that can sense light, so all those annelids out there won't be able to read this book. When you look at a worm, you could easily think that their "butt end" and their "face end" look remarkably alike, but you can actually tell where an adult earthworm's "head" is, because you'll see a bigger band, kind of like a collar, called the *clitellum* (kly-<u>tel</u>-um) nearby. An earthworm DOES have a small mouth on its face end—perfect for eating dead leaves, animal poop, bacteria, and fungi. But it doesn't have teeth. Instead its food is broken down by its *gizzard* (<u>gih</u>-zurd), which contains hard stones and muscles to grind up what it consumes.

Worms might look slimy and bald, but they actually have little bristles called *setae* (see-tee) that help them move. Kind of like little stiff, hairy oars, the hairs row the worm forward or backward. By wriggling its segments, aided by the setae, a worm can scrunch and unscrunch along quite gracefully.

WORM CONDOS

45 MINUTES

PLUS I WEEK OF OBSERVATION

Dracula isn't the only dude who enjoys the dark. Most worms like nothing better than to wriggle around in pitch black. It's their happy place. So why don't you build them a cool, dark worm condo and then spy on the little wrigglers? It's the perfect place to dump your worms after their checkups!

1. Wrap the smaller jar or bottle with the dark construction paper or a black garbage bag cut to the right height and secure it with a few pieces of tape. Worms like it dark! Make sure the cap is on. Pour about an inch of sand into the bottom of the large bottle and nestle the smaller jar into the sand. You want to make it impossible for the worms to hang out deep inside the dirt where you cannot see them.

2. Now start making layers of soil and sand in the space between the smaller bottle and the walls of the larger bottle. Begin by adding a

I clean, empty 2-liter soda bottle with the wrapper removed and the top cut off. (A nearby grown-up is needed to do that, please!) No cap necessary. Save the cut-off top to use as a funnel.

A small jar or bottle that will fit inside a larger one. An empty 16-ounce plastic water bottle will work nicely. This one needs its cap.

Piece of black construction paper or a bit of a black garbage bag

Small pieces of clear tape

Scissors

Soil (dig it up or buy potting soil at the supermarket)

Light-colored sand

Soup spoon

Funnel (the cut-off top of the 2-liter bottle works perfectly) or a piece of paper rolled into a cone shape with a small opening

Water, preferably in a spray bottle

Worm snacks, like fallen leaves; potato, apple, and carrot peels; lettuce scraps; celery; banana peels; and crushed eggshells. But no meat, please—rotting meat will stink up your house!

I pair of old panty hose or a piece of cheesecloth

Strong rubber band or two

And of course the star of our show: EARTHWORMS! You can dig them up yourself (superfun) or buy them at any bait and tackle store. They're even sold on the Internet!

layer of soil about 1 inch thick and then add a layer of sand of about ½ inch.

3. Sprinkle the soil and sand with a little water as you go along. It should be damp but not muddy.

4. Worms need to eat. Layer in a little food.

5. Drop in your worms from time to time. Five to eight wrigglers make for a fine worm block party!

6. Repeat the process. Another layer of soil, then sand, then water, then snacks, then maybe a worm or two.

7. When your condo is full of sand and soil and worms, cover the larger bottle with a piece of panty hose or cheesecloth, held tight with

a rubber band or two. You do not want escapees slithering around in your home, but they DO need air.

8. Place your worm condo in a dark place. A closet works well. Earthworms love to party in the dark. Wait a day or two for the worms to do their thing. NOW you can peek. What's wrigglin' in your condo? Check it every day for the next week to see what's going on.

9. When you are done peeking at your pet dirt-stirrers, release them in a nearby park or garden and bid them a fond farewell! They need to roam and won't be happy or healthy staying in a tiny condo for much longer.

WHAT JUST HAPPENED?

Did you see how the worms moved the soil, sand, and snacks around? Those neat layers are not so neat anymore! Earthworms are born tunnel diggers. They may live deep down in the soil, but they still need air and water. Every tunnel they dig stirs up the soil and gives oxygen a way to get to the worm's skin. This tunneling is good for the earthworm but even better for the soil. All that stirring and churning and digging and eating and pooping helps to break down decaying bits of plant and animal matter.

If you really liked your worm friends and want to keep them longer, you can investigate using a worm bin to compost the leftovers from your house! There are lots of books and Internet sites on the subject, so have fun exploring the wide world of worm waste condos!

THREE WEIRD THINGS YOU COULD DO IF YOU WERE AN EARTHWORM

1. You could regrow your body! You don't want to hurt an earthworm on purpose, but if, while gardening, you happen to spear one, its wriggly life might not be over. Earthworms have been known to regrow both heads and tails!

2. You could eat the equivalent of a third of your weight every day. If you weigh a hundred pounds, you could eat 33 pounds of food in 24 hours!

3. You could breathe through your skin! Worms will suffocate if they dry out. The reason worms come aboveground at night is because it's likely to be damp thanks to the dew. Our wriggly friends just have to be careful to return to the dirt before the sun comes out and dries up all the dew (and their skin).

DWELLERS IN THE DIRT

There are thousands of different species of annelids out there. Some hang out on the surface. Some burrow down a little deeper, and there are those that love to dive deep below the surface. If you could dig up a football field of land you would find, on average, anywhere between 50,000 and half a million earthworms busy eating rotting matter. These worms are SUPER useful. In fact, as worms work their way through the soil, eating as they go, they help to mix up the soil and recycle dead and living things into it. Their poop (or "castings"—look for tiny clumps of dirt piled together) makes the soil richer by returning nitrogen and other nutrients from the food they ate to the soil. Plus, the tunnels they dig allow air and water to move through the soil, keeping it loose and moist—just right for new plants to grow. Healthy soil equals happy plants. Thanks, worms!

What's slimy, gooey, and smells like rotten eggs?
Why, rotten eggs, of course! Next up—YUCKY YOLKS! And we're not talking just chicken eggs here. Tarantula egg omelet, anyone?

Yucky Yolks

Let's admit it: Cooked eggs are tasty but raw eggs gross a lot of us out. For starters, they're really slimy. Plus, how about those blobby bits that are stuck in the oozy gel of the egg white? Or the blood clots you sometimes see on the yolk when you crack an egg open? And let's not forget the vile stench of rotten eggs. GAH! So let's get cracking and scramble up some egg-citing information.

THE YOLK'S ON YOU!

We may think of eggs as either scrambled or fried, but the point of eggs is not to make breakfast, it's to make new chickens—or turtles, or snakes, or cows, or people. Cow eggs? People eggs? Yup, we all come from eggs, it's just that mammal eggs don't have hard shells around them and they are no longer called eggs once they've been fertilized inside the mother. *Fertilization* (fer-tuh-liz-a-shun) happens when the male's DNA reaches the female's egg and combines with the DNA found there. Rooster and hen, bull and cow, man and woman, turtle and, um . . . turtle: The two sets of DNA mix, and suddenly all the instructions needed to build a new living, breathing, creeping, crawling, crying, or clucking creature exist. The amazing work of creating a new being is under way, and it all started with an egg!

EGG ASSEMBLY LINE

The whole egg-laying process for chickens starts when bright light (either sunshine or lightbulbs in factory farms) enters the chicken coop. It's kind of like an alarm clock for poultry. In this case, as the light hits a gland in the hen's eyes, it flicks the on switch for egg production. Keep a chicken in the dark and nary an egg will roll out.

The glands in the eye release a special chemical that travels to the hen's *ovary* (oh-vuh-ree)—basically a little area inside a chicken that stores thousands of immature eggs—and gets the ball rolling. One mature ovum (egg) and yolk will be

LET'S EGG-SPLORE

25 MINUTES

GO FETCH

Let's see what's actually inside that amazing shell. Time to explore all the crunchy and slimy bits.

1. Wash the egg with soap and water in case there are any harmful bacteria lurking on the shell.

2. Gently bang the side of the egg on a hard, flat surface like the edge of the bowl to crack the shell. Holding the shell over the bowl, use your thumbs to pull it apart and let the gooey bits plop out. Try not to let any shell bits drop in the bowl. It takes practice!

3. Look closely at the inside and outside of the shell. Tug on the thin skinlike parts that line the eggshell. They are called membranes. Surprisingly strong, huh?

4. Look at the wider end of the egg. Can you see how the membrane doesn't attach to the shell perfectly here? There is a space called an "air cell" between the inner and outer membrane.

5. Now the gooey bits—the egg whites. They should be called "egg clears." Not a lot of white there (not yet, at least)! The parts of the egg white nearest the yolk are squishy. The outer white is more watery and spreads around the bowl.

6. See a few whitish blobs in the egg white? Together they are called *chalazae* (kuh-<u>ley</u>-zee). (One blob is called a chalaza.)

I fresh egg
Bowl
Butter or cooking oil
Cooking pan

7. Now for the yolk. It's surrounded by a thin membrane, which holds everything in. What happens if you break that membrane? Give it a try!

8. Now put a little butter or oil in your pan, then pop the egg in and have your adult fry it on medium heat! Observe what happens. Then enjoy the egg on toast!

WHAT JUST HAPPENED?

Did you notice that the shell is a little bumpy? That's because it is full of little holes called pores—about 17,000 of them! The pores allow moisture and air to pass through and reach the egg. Did you tug on the membranes next to the shell? These membranes are strong because they are partly made of keratin, a protein that's in your hair! Actually, there are two membranes, but it's hard to see both. The "air cell" space forms between the two membranes as the egg cools after it is laid. You'll learn more about that in the Elderly Eggs ick-speriment!

Egg whites have 40 different kinds of protein but are mostly water and turn white when cooked. Each chalaza blob that you saw is a spiral band of tissue that acts like a tiny anchor to hold the yolk in the center of the egg. The yolk contains less protein than the white, but most of the vitamins and minerals. Depending on what the hen ate, the yolk can be pale yellow to sunset orange! When it's fully cooked, taste the difference between yolk and white. Which do you prefer?

air cell
Membrane
Inner egg white
chalazae
Outer egg white
Yolk

TO LAY OR NOT TO LAY

Living things that reproduce by "egg" can be sorted into two groups—egg-layers and live-bearers. In egg layers, the baby develops *inside* the egg but *outside* the mom. Babies that are live-birthed develop inside the mother until they are ready to be born.

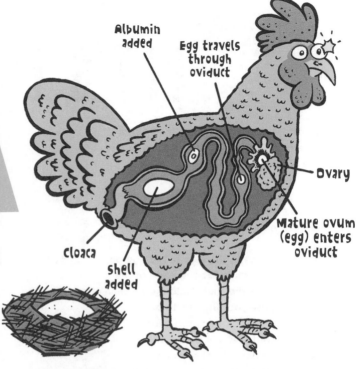

Albumin added
Egg travels through oviduct
Ovary
Mature ovum (egg) enters oviduct
Shell added
Cloaca

GROUP	EGG-LAYERS	LIVE-BEARERS
Mammals	Only two primitive egg-laying mammal types exist—echidnas (spiny anteaters) and the duck-billed platypus. They all live in Australia and New Guinea.	Nearly all mammals, including mice, humans, cats, dogs, bears, kangaroos, whales, and dolphins
Birds	All birds	None
Reptiles	All crocodillians (including crocodiles, alligators, and caimans) and turtles. Many snakes, such as cobras and pythons.	Some lizards and snakes, including garter snakes, boas, and rattlesnakes
Amphibians	Nearly all frogs, toads, and salamanders	A few species of frogs, toads, and salamanders
Fish	Most fish	Two percent of fish, including sharks and guppies

released and travel down a tube called the *oviduct*. That's where it starts to grow bigger and a layer of "egg white," officially known as *albumen* (all-<u>bue</u>-men), is added. Further along the egg-y tunnel, a little skin, called a membrane, forms around the egg white. Salt and water are added, and then calcium, which hardens into a nice protective shell. The final step is a coating called *bloom*, which seals all the tiny little pores in the shell. Bacteria stay out, while the delicious egg-iness stays safely inside. And all this happens in about 25 hours—just a little more than a day!

If the hen and the rooster have mated and the egg has been fertilized, it has to be *brooded*—that's the part where the hen sits on the nest. Brooding involves proper temperature, humidity, and a little bit of egg-turning on the hen's part. In about three weeks the teeny chick pecks its way through its protective shell and emerges into the world.

Hens and all other egg-making female animals keep releasing eggs, even if there are no males around to fertilize them. In fact, the average hard-working hen produces a couple hundred eggs a year.

Does it hurt the chicken to lay an egg, or is it as easy as pooping after eating a dozen prunes? Some chicken farmers say that laying a big one has *got* to be uncomfortable. Egg-sperts say that medium eggs are less stressful for the chickens, plus they taste better than large and jumbo eggs. Tell your grown-ups that with eggs, bigger isn't always better.

ELDERLY EGGS

GO FETCH

2 MINUTES
PLUS 3 WEEKS, SO YOUR EGGS CAN AGE

Did you know you can tell the age of an egg by watching what it does when placed in water? Try it yourself and see!

1. First make a hypothesis. Will a fresh egg float or sink in a bowl of water? Will this change as it ages?

2. Fill the bowl with water and gently place your egg in it. Once you've observed and taken a photograph or drawn a sketch in your notebook, remove the water from the bowl. Place the egg and bowl back in the fridge for another week, labeled *ick-speriment in progress* so no one eats the egg by accident.

3. A week later, take your egg out and repeat the water test, again recording the results and returning the egg to the fridge.

4. Dump the water and let the egg sit for 2 more weeks. Check once a week for several more weeks.

Bowl

A fresh egg (check the date on the carton or get one from a local farm)

Water

Camera or pencil and notebook

BEFORE

AFTER

WHAT JUST HAPPENED?

Why did the egg float more over time? As eggs age, air slowly enters the shell through tiny pores, and moisture slowly leaves. Over time, a bigger and bigger air bubble will form (usually at the larger end of the egg). A fresh egg will sink to the bottom and most likely lie on its side because it doesn't have much air inside it. An egg that is about one week old will also stay on the bottom, but it will move around a bit and possibly stick up at one end because of a small air bubble. A three-week-old egg will most likely balance on its pointy end with the large end up, because there is now a large air bubble there. Egg afloat? The air bubble is very large, and your egg is too old. Trash it! Unless you like the smell of rotting eggs.

I WAS MYTH-INFORMED

EGGS AND THE EQUINOX

On or about March 21 and September 21 of every year, day and night are exactly the same length. Legend has it that on that day you can stand an egg on one end and it won't fall over. Good luck with that particular bit of mythology! Depending on the shape of the egg, you just might be able to do it ANY day of the year.

THE FANCIEST EGGS

Hungry for eggs? Why not venture beyond chicken eggs. You could scramble up some duck eggs. Or how about ostrich eggs? Just one of those suckers can weigh up to five pounds and feed about 10 people! Just want a wee nibble? A quail egg is about a quarter of the size of your typical breakfast egg. But there's no need to stop at bird eggs.

How does a heaping spoonful of raw fish eggs sound to you? Not delicious? It's some people's all-time favorite food. Certain kinds of fish eggs,

A TRULY fancy feast! Caviar can cost thousands of dollars a pound.

like caviar, are considered a great delicacy and are VERY expensive. In fact, the fanciest caviar costs more than $30,000 for one measly pound, so you'd better start saving your birthday bucks right now. Why so pricey? "Real" caviar comes from just one kind of fish, the wild sturgeon that lives in Russia. Female fish begin the process of reproduction by squirting out masses of eggs to be fertilized by the males, but before they do, all those little unlaid eggs are safely nestled inside the mother fish's reproductive organs. If you can scoop the unlaid eggs from a fish you just caught you will have something called *roe* (row). Add a little salt and you can serve these dandy egg dots, now dubbed caviar, on toast with raw onions!

Caviar is not the only edible egg. You can eat almost any just-laid fish egg, snake egg, frog egg, snail egg, or alligator egg—although good luck getting THOSE away from Mama!

THREE MORE "INTERESTING" EGG DISHES

Red ant egg soup Official name: *Gaeng Kai Mot Daeng*, just in case you want to order it in Laos, a country in Southeast Asia. The recipe? Start with lots of ant eggs and partially developed ant embryos. Toss in a few tomatoes, onions, spices, and generous handfuls of baby ants for a nice tang. Heat and enjoy!

Tarantula omelets The Piaroa Indians of the Amazon just drool at the thought of tucking into a hearty tarantula-egg breakfast. Of course you have to get the eggs OUT of the tarantula first, but the Piaroa have the know-how. They wrap their hands in leaves to keep from getting stuck with the tiny tarantula barbs and squeeze the eggs out, wrap them in a leaf, and grill them over a fire.

One-hundred-year-old egg Some lucky fellow long ago found an old egg lying in a salty puddle, ate it, and thought, "Not bad!" Ever since, folks in China have sought to re-create this remarkable morsel. It's pretty simple: Take an egg, cover it in clay, ashes, and salt, bury it in the backyard, and leave it there for a few months. The salt actually preserves the egg instead of letting it rot, but the yolk still turns dark green and smells like a rotten egg. Nothing like the stench of sulfur to spark an appetite!

SQUISHY EGGS!

GO FETCH

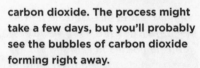
Here's how to get rid of an egg's shell without cracking up!

1. Wash your eggs with some dish soap. This will remove any bad salmonella bacteria from the shell and your hands.

2. Fill your container with vinegar. Leave an inch of space at the top.

3. Carefully place the eggs in the container one by one so that the shells don't crack.

4. Add more vinegar if necessary to cover all the eggs.

5. Look carefully. Can you see anything interesting happening to the eggs?

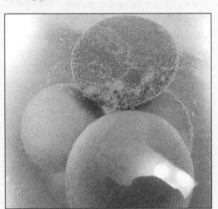

6. Place the jar in your fridge.

7. Come back a few times every day for several days and take notes on what is happening.

---

3 to 6 raw chicken eggs or however many you have left in your fridge

Dish soap

1 glass or see-through plastic container, large enough to contain your eggs and the vinegar

3 to 4 cups white vinegar (enough to cover your eggs)

---

8. 2 DAYS LATER: Touch the eggs. Are they squishy? Pick one up and gently hold it in your hand. What happened to the shells?

WHAT JUST HAPPENED?

Eggshells are made of calcium carbonate, a chemical that hardens into a solid. When you add an acid, in this case vinegar, the calcium carbonate separates into calcium and carbonate. The calcium floats free, but the carbon bonds with oxygen to form carbon dioxide. The process might take a few days, but you'll probably see the bubbles of carbon dioxide forming right away.

If there are bits of the old shell still clinging to the egg after a few days, you could put the eggs in a new container of vinegar for another day to remove the shell completely.

Why don't the eggs become leaking blobs? If you've ever peeled a hard-boiled egg you know that eggs have a thin membrane just under the shell. If an egg is fertilized and sat upon by a mother hen, this membrane is important because it (along with the pores in the shell) allows air to reach the developing chick. If an egg is unfertilized, as yours probably are, then the membrane just holds all the gooey bits together, even when the shell is gone. Try the next ick-speriment to see how water really can sneak through this membrane! Let's make some eggs from Mars (see page 254)!

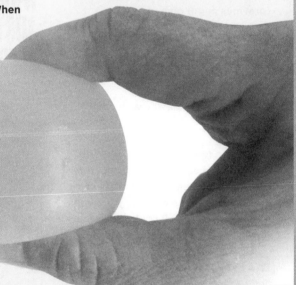

CALLING ALL EGGHEADS!

Want to be an egg-spert on all things eggy? Here are some more egg tidbits.

Free range or not? Egg sellers have lots of pretty words splashed across their egg cartons, but some commercial egg raisers treat their hens miserably. Others try to give their hens a happier

ICK-SPERIMENT

EGGS FROM MARS!

30 MINUTES
PLUS SEVERAL DAYS OF OBSERVATION

GO FETCH

Water and nutrients can move through the semipermeable membrane of an egg in a process called *osmosis* (aws-<u>mo</u>-sis). (Semipermeable means that some things can get through but others can't. The membrane is like a picky gatekeeper, only letting the good stuff in.) Let's see osmosis in action, and make some freaky alien eggs at the same time!

1. Make a hypothesis about what will happen when you put your squishy eggs in some corn syrup. Will they explode? Will they shrink? Will they just sit there and do nothing?

2. Use a spoon to carefully place your eggs from "Squishy Eggs!" (previous page) on a plate.

3. Dump the vinegar into the sink; rinse out and dry the jar with a dish towel.

4. Fill the jar halfway with corn syrup.

5. Add a few drops of your favorite color of food coloring. Red is good for Mars, the red planet. Green is good for making little green alien's eggs. If you have another jar, you could make some of each color or any color you like.

6. Put your eggs in the jar and add more corn syrup if they are not completely covered yet. Then stick them in the refrigerator.

Spoon

3 eggs and jar from "Squishy Eggs!"

1 pint corn syrup

Dish towel

Food coloring

7. After a day or two, scoop them out with a spoon, rinse them off, and hold them in your hand or put them on a plate. Aren't they weird!?? Go freak out your grown-ups for a few minutes.

WHAT JUST HAPPENED?

What made your eggs shrivel? Remember, the membrane around the egg allows water and gases to pass through, but they don't just pass willy-nilly. Osmosis happens when there are different amounts of water and other substances on either side of the membrane. Corn syrup has lots of sugar in it but very little water. The egg has more water and very little sugar in it. Put them together and you have a *concentration gradient*, a fancy way of saying there's more "stuff" (in our example, sugar) in the corn syrup's water than in the egg's water. That "stuff" is called a *solute* (<u>sawl</u>-yoot) In nature, and water and solutes (such as sugar) tend to balance out. The water flows from an area of low solute concentration (inside the egg) to an area of high solute concentration (the syrup) until the amount of water and solute in each is balanced. This leaves behind a shriveled egg with not much water left in it. The food coloring can also travel through the membranes, so both the egg and the corn syrup end up colored.

What would happen if you let the eggs sit in corn syrup for a while longer? We forgot one of ours in the fridge for three weeks! Talk about shriveled! What would happen if you put the eggs back in a jar full of plain water? Try it and see!

life, so look for these words: cage-free, free-range, and certified organic. Best of all would be eggs from pasture-raised hens on a local farm. That way, you might be able to get to know the mama hens personally!

Is it raw or cooked?
Just give it a spin to find out. A hard-boiled egg will easily spin. All those sloshy liquids in a raw egg make it very wobbly.

Brown eggs or white?
It's all the same thing! Different breeds of chickens lay different-colored shells. It's that simple.

Blood on the yolk?
Is this a crime scene? Nope, just a rupture of a small blood vessel as the egg was being formed. It's perfectly safe to eat. If the blood spot grosses you out, pluck it away.

NESTING INSTINCT

Where there is an egg in the wild, there is usually a nest. But since we are celebrating all things yucky, let's forget all about cute little circles made of neatly woven bits of grass or branch. Instead, let's go curl up inside a nest made from torn-apart ant corpses. That's where spider wasps lay *their* eggs. And what fun it would be to hang out in a nest made entirely of dried bird spit! These spit cradles, made by a type of bird called a swiftlet, are a major ingredient in a beloved delicacy in Southeast Asia called bird's nest soup.

Some animals don't even bother with nests. Monarch butterflies lay their eggs right onto leaves, usually on the undersides of milkweed. The jawfish requires a soon-to-be daddy fish cart a few thousand eggs around in his open mouth for more than a week.

BABY ON BOARD

If you were not shocked enough by all the vileness in YUCKY YOLKS, prepared to be literally shocked in the next entry! It's guaranteed to make your hair stand straight up.

GEORGE WASHINGTON'S BREAKFAST

What does the American Revolution have to do with eggs? Spies used eggs to send secret messages! *Steganography* (steg-uh-<u>nog</u>-ruh-fee) is the art of writing ghost messages—messages that cannot be easily seen. In a tale told about George Washington's spies, a message was written on a hardboiled eggshell using a combination of chemicals that seeped through the shell and could only be seen when the egg was peeled. With British soldiers everywhere, getting a secret message through in a box of groceries, or a lunch sack, became one way to get information past British checkpoints. Who would suspect a dozen eggs contained top-secret information!

Steganography has been around for thousands of years. The ancient Greeks knew about plants whose juices would dry to be invisible until exposed to heat. The ancient Chinese had an even better trick up their sleeves. They wrote notes on tiny pieces of silk, rolled them into little balls and coated them in wax. Then, a lucky messenger would swallow the wax balls, travel off to see the intended recipient, and then poop the message out upon arrival, pluck out the wax ball, and hand it over with a flourish. But poking around in a pile of poop to find a secret message? Surely there was an easier way. So George Washington's spies used egg writing!

Zaps

Think about all the ways you use electricity in your day-to-day life. Could you live in an unplugged world? No TV! No computer! No video games! No lights! No fridge! And no cheating—**NO** batteries either! All you electricity guzzlers who take the flick of an on/off switch for granted, prepare to be **SHOCKED**, surprised, and en-"light"-ened.

KA-BOOM!

You just heard the rumble of thunder. Moments before that there were white zigzags of light shooting through the sky. Lightning! What's going on? A huge amount of static electricity—the very same thing that makes socks stick to your shirt when you unload a clothes dryer in the dead of winter—has just been unleashed into the atmosphere. You think a 100°F summer day is hot? These bolts can reach more than 50,000°F—some are hotter than the surface of the sun. And big? You betcha! The biggest bolt of lightning can reach lengths of over 100 miles. And all this is happening about 25 million times a year in the United States alone.

Lightning is definitely dangerous stuff, but electricity—capturing it and putting it to work— is zappingly awesome!

THE ZAP DUO

There are two types of electricity that we deal with on a day-to-day basis. There's the kind that makes your hair stand up—static electricity—and there's the kind that keeps your fridge working. That type is called current electricity. Lightning is the result of a gigantic amount of static electricity suddenly being converted into a short burst of current electricity. Now, small amounts of static electricity are all around you all the time. But to fully understand what static electricity is and why your mom's pink-and-purple sock stays stuck to the back of your sweater all day, we need to take a peek inside atoms.

UP AND "ATOM"!

You remember atoms, right? The tiniest bits of elements, which make up everything in the universe? (If you need a zap in the brain to remember, go back to page 12.) But even atoms are made of something. Let's shrink down to microscopic size and check it out. Zap—you are now atomic particle–size. Wait! Where'd you go?

Positively centered—As you walk into the center of an atom you can see that there's a blob in the middle. That's the *nucleus* (<u>new</u>-klee-us) and it holds two of the three components you'll find in atoms. The first are *protons* (<u>pro</u>-tonz). The number of protons in an atom gives each type of atom its identity. For example, if an atom has only one proton, then it's hydrogen. Eight protons makes

FOOTBALL STADIUM ATOMS

Imagine the impossible: a gigantic atom the size of a Super Bowl stadium. Now place a pea in the center of the field. That would be the size of the atom's nucleus, and it would hold all of the atom's protons and neutrons. And the electrons? They would be the size of grains of salt and typically could be found bopping around in the last row of seats, as far from the playing field as possible. Atoms are mostly empty space! It's a bit like our solar system: An enormous sun (which is like the nucleus) in the center, and then these tiny planets (like electrons) moving around it from far, far away (though electrons don't follow predictable orbits like the planets do). Now shrink that whole football stadium down in your mind to a teeny-tiny speck so small it cannot be seen even with powerful microscopes, and you are looking at an atom. Just imagine how tiny the electrons really are!

it oxygen. And a whopping 79 protons? That's gold, baby! Protons carry a positive charge. Positive charges don't like to hang out with other positive charges. In fact, they want to get as far away from each other as possible. So something has to keep them together . . .

Just hanging around—The second part of an atom—also found in the nucleus—is the *neutrons* (<u>new</u>-tronz). Neutrons are similar to protons except they have no charge. We say they're neutral. Some might call them the boring, unimportant part of an atom. Wrong! Neutrons act like glue to help keep all those protons from flying away from each other. Think of them as cowhands rounding up ornery cattle.

Can't sit still—The third part of the atom—those wild and crazy *electrons*. An electron is much smaller and lighter than a proton or neutron, and this wee thing simply cannot stay put. Electrons, which have a negative charge, are

STATIC ELECTRICITY HIGH JUMP

15 MINUTES

GO FETCH

Protons and electrons have opposite charges: positive and negative. In nature, opposites attract. Kinda like peanut butter and jelly, they want to be near each other. In this ick-sploration, you will use this attraction to build a static charge and make bits of paper jump without even touching them!

1. Cut some of the paper into tiny pieces (it's okay if some are a little bigger or smaller). It's easiest if you make several skinny cuts in one direction, and then cut across these hairlike slivers. Put the pieces on a table in a cluster. Don't worry if some of the pieces are on top of or touching one another.

2. Rub the wooden pencil vigorously against the cotton shirt for about 20 seconds.

3. Hold the pencil about 6 inches above the pieces of paper and then slowly lower it until it's almost touching the paper. What happened? Anything?

4. Try another combination: Rub the pencil in your hair for about 20 seconds, and then repeat step 3.

5. Time to switch materials. Rub one of the balloons against the cotton shirt for about 20 seconds.

6. Hold the balloon about 6 inches above the pieces of paper and then slowly lower it until it's almost touching the paper. Observe what happens.

Paper

Scissors

Wooden pencil

Cotton shirt

Head of hair (if you're bald, borrow a human who isn't)

2 inflated balloons

7. Try another combination: Rub the balloon in your hair for about 20 seconds and then repeat step 6.

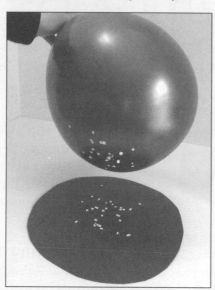

8. Now take the two inflated balloons, rub them both on your hair, and then hold them by the tied end. Do they stick together? Or do they repel (push away) each other?

WHAT JUST HAPPENED?

How cool were those jumping paper athletes when you rubbed the balloon on your hair? Bet some of the other combinations were a little blah, though. Wood and cotton are not great conductors of electrons, but hair tends to give away electrons, and latex—the stuff that balloons are made of—picks up electrons. After you rubbed the balloon on your hair, the balloon had tons of extra electrons—way more electrons than protons. That's all static electricity is: an imbalance of positive and negative. Just like opposite magnet ends snap together, so too do negative electrons and positive protons. When you lowered the balloon over the paper, the protons in the paper were attracted to the balloon's extra electrons. The attraction was so strong that it caused the paper bits to overcome gravity and jump up off the table!

Now for your two balloons: Remember that the balloons pick up electrons from your hair, so now they are both negatively charged. Just as opposites attract, two things that are the same repel each other. Think of trying to put the like ends of two magnets together. Can't do it! In a similar way, the balloons keep their distance. Keep on reading to find out why your hairs stood on end after you rubbed the balloons on them!

This dude's hair is full of protons.

always zipping about, orbiting the nucleus, like bugs dive-bombing around a hot lightbulb on a summer's eve. The job of electrons is to balance out the positive charge of the protons and allow different atoms to bond to each other.

HIP-HOPPIN' IN THE 'HOOD

While protons and neutrons normally stay inside the nucleus all day and don't play with any other atoms, electrons love to run around and explore other "neighborhoods." Sometimes electrons even jump from one atom to another atom. In fact, current electricity, the kind that powers up our TVs and computers, is exactly that. It's the flow of electrons from one atom to another along a metal wire. Anything you plug in or that runs on batteries (washing machine, cell phone, remote control) operates on current electricity.

When too many or too few electrons hang out in one place, then you get "static electricity." The electrons aren't moving in a specific direction, so the electricity doesn't flow. But bring them close enough to an opposite charge or even to something neutral, and electrons jump through the air! And then it's sparks-when-you-touch-a-doorknob time—or lightning!

HOW SHOCKING

Ever pull off a winter hat only to have your hair go straight up? Normally your hair has an equal number of electrons and protons and your hair strands are electrically balanced and happy (although you might still have bed head, dandruff, or lice, but that's another story). But a wool or fleece hat steals electrons from your hair, leaving your hair with too many protons. Your hair is now positively charged. Remember: Opposite charges come together and similar charges push away. Each strand of charged hair now wants to get away from the other strands. This electric repulsion is strong enough to push each hair away from its neighboring hair, making your hairs stand straight up. Instant electric hair, no crimping or gel required!

And then there's the joy of getting shocked by a doorknob or car door in winter. Here's a play-by-play of what happens. Picture yourself walking across a carpet in socks. As your feet rubbed the carpet, they pulled some electrons from it. The electrons started building up on your feet and then all over your body, transforming you into a walking, talking electron storage bin. Electrons are always looking for adventure—a quick getaway. That metal doorknob was just the ticket. As you touched the metal, all the electrons rushed out, releasing the static electricity from your body so quickly and with so many electrons that it created a shock. You might have even been able to see the minuscule lightning bolt!

Lightning bolts in the sky happen the same way, just on a ginormous scale. Of course clouds

LET THERE BE LIGHTNING!

GO FETCH

In Greek mythology, the god Zeus would throw lightning bolts at his enemies. Wish you could make your own lightning bolts? Go for it! Create safe sparks to battle hydras, demigods, and Titans.

1. Make the room as dark as possible (lower the window shades and turn off the lights).

2. Put on the rubber glove and hold the balloon with the same hand.

3. Vigorously rub the balloon against your hair (or fur or wool) for about a minute. Be careful not to let the balloon touch anything else until you are ready for the next step . . .

4. Move the part of the balloon that you just rubbed close to a metal object. Position yourself so you can see the moment of impact (you don't want the balloon to block your view). As the balloon gets really close to the metal, you should see and hear a mini lightning bolt!

Experiment with how to make the best zaps. Which type of material (hair, fur, or wool) seems to make the most impressive shocks? How close do you have to get to the metal object for the static discharge to take place? What types of metals give you the best results?

- Dark room
- Rubber glove (like one you'd use to do dishes)
- Inflated balloon
- A head full of lots of hair, or a piece of fur or wool
- Metal object (an iron skillet or a stainless-steel pan works well)

WHAT JUST HAPPENED?

When you rubbed the balloon against the hair, fur, or wool, the balloon stole electrons from the other material. This imbalance created static electricity on the balloon (too many electrons were now in one place, like on a cloud during a storm). These electrons were stuck there, and—because rubber does not conduct electricity—your rubber glove kept them from escaping into you. When you moved the balloon close to metal, the electrons were able to jump through the air, creating visible sparks—really mini lightning bolts.

This exploration won't work well if it's very humid in your house. Why not? Water is a good conductor of electricity, which is why you should NEVER go swimming during a thunderstorm. Warm, humid air contains more water vapor than dry, cool air. If it's humid, the electrons hitchhike off the balloon and onto the water droplets in the air instead of collecting on the balloon and building up enough static electricity to make a spark.

Zap!

STRUCK BY LIGHTNING!

Getting struck by lightning is rare (your chances are about 1 in 3,000 in a lifetime), but every year hundreds of people end up six feet under because of the awesome power of these bolts of sizzling electricity. Some people survive only to get struck again, like unlucky US park ranger Roy Sullivan, who earned the title "Human Lightning Rod" by being struck by lightning seven different times over a period of 35 years. If only he had followed these rules . . .

1. Go inside! And that means inside a closed building or a car. A porch, picnic shed, or tent will not protect you.

2. Stay inside! Wait 30 minutes after you hear the last thunderclap before poking your nose outside.

3. Don't take a bath or Shower in the middle of a violent storm. Water conducts electricity and it could travel through water pipes and end up shocking you.

What if you're outside and there's no place to hide?

1. Crouch down, preferably in a small ditch. You never want to be the tallest object in a storm.

2. Stay away from trees! Never hunker down under a single tree. Lightning will usually reach for the tallest objects in the area.

3. Stand clear of metal fences. Like water, metal is also a great conductor of electricity.

4. Get out of the water! If you are swimming or boating, get out of the water pronto!

don't contain tiny wool socks that rub against a carpet, but they do contain zillions of supercooled water droplets rubbing against zillions of ice crystals. No one knows exactly why, but that rubbing can cause a massive number of electrons to get stuck on the bottom of a cloud. We're talking a *gigantic* amount of static electricity. The cloud is negatively charged, but the ground is not! At first the air acts like a wall, keeping the positive and negative charges apart, but eventually the electrons make a beeline for the ground. As the electrons leap down, a positive charge rises up from the Earth. When the two meet, a return stroke zaps back up into the sky. That's the part you see. The energy that is released heats up the air to such tremendous temperatures that it glows. Lightning!

ZAPPED!

How cool would it be to shoot electricity out of your fingers? Well, if you were an electric eel (and . . . um . . . had fingers) you could. Of course you'd be grayish-green and slimy, and technically not even an eel (actually a kind of huge 7-foot-long knifefish, a relative to a catfish) but, hey! With up to 600 volts (enough to knock a horse to the ground) streaming from your slithery body, bet no one would mess with you! But what exactly IS a volt? Let's explore using a silly, furry analogy.

Current electricity is the movement or flow of electrons. Usually this flow happens through a metal wire because metal conducts electricity really well. But for now, let's think of those wild and crazy electrons as a bunch of furry, freaked-out lemurs that accidentally made their way from Madagascar and ended up at your school. They are bouncing around like wild things, trying to get into your classroom, which is at the far end of a long corridor. This flow of lemurs down the hallway is like the flow of electrons through a wire. So remember: flowing lemurs = flowing electrons. Got it?

High-voltage eels do NOT make good pets.

The Lemurs Are Coming: Current

You're standing at the door of your classroom watching the lemurs approaching. How many lemurs are coming down the hall and how fast are they moving? The rate of electron (or lemur) flow is called *current*. Is one lemur strolling down the hallway and entering your classroom every minute or are 20 rushing toward you every second? Can you imagine why large amounts of current are dangerous? If 500 lemurs came crashing into you every second, they'd flatten you! It's the same with current. Strong electrical current is dangerous. By the way, we measure current in units called *amps*.

The Lemurs Are Jumping: Voltage

Oh, those lemurs (ahem … electrons)! They're bouncing around the room. What would impact you more—a lemur that accidentally bumped into you? Or one that climbed onto a desk and flung itself down on you? What if you were outside and a lemur jumped on you from the roof, which was nine floors up? Major ouch! It's the same when talking about electricity. *Voltage* (measured in *volts*,

or V for short) is how hard the electrons are pushing, and higher voltages are pushing and shoving a lot more. That lemur leaping down you from nine floors up is going to flatten you! In electricity, the higher the voltage, the worse the zap.

Check out the batteries you use and look for their voltage. You might notice 1.5V written on AA batteries. Not many volts at all! Our Squishy Circuits ick-tivity uses a battery with 9V. It's still not a very high voltage, but it's strong enough. If you've ever seen a sign saying DANGER! HIGH VOLTAGE! pay attention—it's no joke. Higher voltage means more current flowing. Touching a high-voltage power line would be like having 50,000 lemurs all falling on your head at once. Game over for you.

Stop the Lemurs! Resistance

You have had enough of those reckless lemurs. Before you get totally "burnt out," you decide to shut your classroom door. You are now "resisting" the flow of lemurs. Official Zap Talk word: *resistance*. Some materials, such as rubber or plastic, resist the flow of electricity better than others. Just like the shut door that stopped those pesky lemurs from coming into the classroom, rubber and plastic have high resistance and are good insulators. Metal wires, on the other hand, have low resistance: Like a wide-open door, they are good conductors. You can also have medium amounts of resistance, as if you opened the door a tiny amount so that only a few lemurs (or electrons) could squeeze by at a time. Resistance is measured in something called *ohms* (oh-mmms).

So now that you are a lemur whiz (whoops—we meant electricity whiz), let's get zapping.

Real-life lemurs jump too.

SQUISHY CIRCUITS

45 MINUTES

A lot of people think of electricity as only flowing through wires, but electricity can travel through other things, such as water or even air, like lightning. It can travel through squishy things too, like the dough in this very squishy electrical circuit! This dough contains a lot of salt, which allows the electricity to flow through it. You'll also make some dough that won't conduct electricity, then hook it all together into a circuit and "let there be light!" The recipes and the idea for squishy circuits come from awesome people at the University of St. Thomas School of Engineering.

PART 1: CONDUCTIVE DOUGH
20 minutes

GO FETCH

- A helpful adult
- Medium-size cooking pot
- Mixing spoon or spatula
- 1¹/2 cups flour
- 1 cup water
- ¹/4 cup salt
- 3 tablespoons cream of tartar (or 9 tablespoons lemon juice)
- 1 tablespoon vegetable oil
- Cutting board or surface for kneading dough
- Food coloring of any color

1. In a medium-size pot, mix 1 cup of the flour and all the water, salt, cream of tartar (or lemon), and vegetable oil.

2. Cook over medium-low heat, stirring the whole time until the mixture starts to get thick and chunky, about 3 to 5 minutes. Keep scraping the bottom of the pan.

3. When the mixture forms a ball in the center of the pot, turn off the heat. Let the dough cool in the pot for 5 minutes.

4. Sprinkle the extra ¹/2 cup of flour on your cutting board or other surface.

5. Once the dough is cool enough to handle, dump it on the floured surface and start kneading it, squishing the flour into the dough. Keep rolling it in the flour until all the flour is kneaded in.

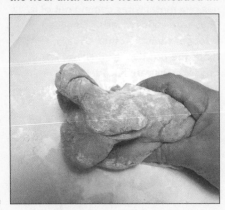

6. Divide up the dough into several pieces and add a few drops of food coloring of your choice to each. Knead in the color.

Store each color of dough in a bag (or airtight container) of its own. Some condensation might appear, but you can just knead that into the dough when you want to use it. Kept refrigerated, the dough should last several weeks or more.

PART 2: INSULATING DOUGH
10 minutes

GO FETCH

- 1¹/2 cups flour
- ¹/2 cup white sugar
- 3 tablespoons vegetable oil
- ¹/2 cup water

1. Mix 1 cup of flour with the sugar and oil in a bowl. Add the water a few teaspoons at a time, mixing as you go. Keep adding water until you have formed a sticky dough. You may not use all the water, or you might need a little extra.

continued on next page →

SQUISHY CIRCUITS
(CONTINUED)

2. Sprinkle some of the extra ½ cup of flour on the sticky dough and mix with your hands until all the flour is mixed in and the dough is not so sticky anymore.

3. Save it in a plastic bag in the refrigerator until you are ready to use it.

PART 3: SQUISHY CIRCUITS
15 minutes

GO FETCH →

- A handful of conductive dough
- A handful of insulating dough
- 1 or more 3- or 5-mm LEDs (light-emitting diodes) of any color (from a local electronics shop or order them online)
- 1 9-volt (9V) battery
- 1 battery snap for a 9V battery (from a local electronics shop or order it online) or a battery pack that holds 3 AA batteries as long as it has a positive and negative wire coming from it. It may be possible to salvage such a pack from an old toy.

Have you ever noticed that the word *circuit*, as in electrical circuit, sounds very similar to the word *circle*? That's not a coincidence. In order to make a working light circuit, you need to make a circle of electricity that flows from one end of a battery through a wire to a lightbulb and back through a different wire to the battery. But instead of wires, let's use squishy blobs of dough! READ THE SAFETY NOTES, then let's get started.

1. Grab some of your conductive dough and roll it into 2 blobs.

2. Now find your LED. Look at it closely. You should notice that it has two metal wires coming out of it. These are called "leads." One lead is longer than the other. Usually, that's the positive lead. The other one is the negative lead. LEDs are picky. They only work when electricity goes through in one direction and not the other. So you'll need to experiment to see which way it will work.

SAFETY NOTES

When the battery is plugged into the battery snap, DO NOT let the ends of the two wires touch. This will create a short circuit, and the battery will get dangerously hot. Always unplug the battery from the snap when you are not using it. If your grown-ups have some pliers, they can cut one wire shorter than the other and strip a bit of the insulation off to expose the wires underneath. At different lengths, the positive and negative wires will be less likely to touch by accident.

DO NOT attach the LED directly to the 9V battery or to the ends of the snap when it is plugged into the battery. The electricity that comes from the battery is too strong and will burn out your bulb immediately. However, the dough has enough resistance to slow down the electricity so that the LED will light up but not blow out.

3. Bend the leads so they look like the LED below.

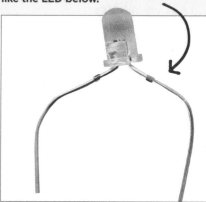

4. "Plug" the LED into the blobs by putting one lead in one blob and the other lead in the other blob. Don't let the blobs touch.

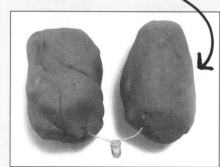

5. Snap the 9V battery into the battery snap. (This can be the hardest part, so ask a grown-up if you need help. Match up the big bump on the battery to the small bump on the snap.)

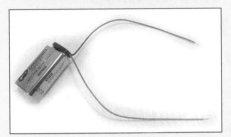

6. Now "plug in" your battery to the other side of the blobs, one wire for each blob. If the LED doesn't light up, switch which blob each wire goes into. (Hint: The red wire should go into the same blob as the positive lead of your LED. And the negative wire should be connected to the other blob, where the negative lead of the LED is inserted. Think "positive to positive, negative to negative.")

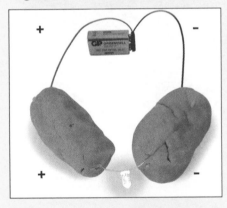

7. Congratulations! You just made a simple circuit! Woo-hoo!

8. If your blobs happen to touch, you will have created a short circuit. The electricity won't go through the light anymore, it will go straight back to the battery and make it hot and run it down. So to make a safer circuit, place a blob of insulating dough in between your two conductive blobs. Place your LED like a bridge over the insulating dough.

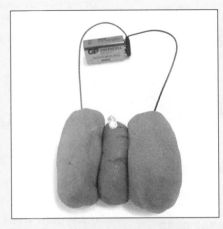

9. And now you can get really fancy and make a parallel circuit by placing several LEDs in a row, like three separate bridges! Be sure you put your LED leads into the conductive dough. And be sure the positive leads of the LEDs plug into the blob connected to the red positive wire from the battery.

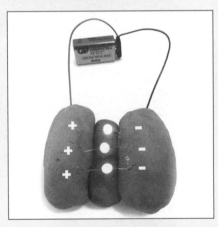

10. You can also make a series circuit by connecting the LEDs in a straight line across a repeating pattern of conductive-insulating-conductive-insulating-conductive dough. Look at the picture to see how to place your LEDs.

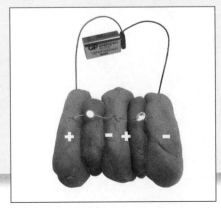

WHAT JUST HAPPENED?

If your lightbulb lit up, then you made a working squishy circuit! All the salt in the conductive dough allowed electrons to flow through it so the blob acted like a wire. It has low resistance. The sugar in the insulating dough resisted or blocked the electrons. It has high resistance.

LED stands for light-emitting diode. That means it gives off (or emits) light when electricity flows through it. But as you noticed, LEDs are picky. They only light up when electricity flows through them in one particular direction and not the other! If your bulb doesn't light up, all you have to do is turn it around (or reverse how the battery is connected—see step 6 in Part 3).

If you make a parallel circuit, each LED forms its own separate circle with the battery. Each one is independent and burns brightly, so if you remove one or it burns out, the others will still stay lit.

If you made a series circuit, you probably noticed that the LEDs dimmed as they went along. There wasn't enough power to make them all bright. Also, if you remove one of the LEDs (or if it burns out) all the lights go out. This is the kind of circuit used in many holiday lights, leading to long, frustrated hunts for the broken bulb.

Did you notice that if you try several different colors at once, some colors don't light? This is because each color of LED uses a different amount of energy. Red is the lowest energy and blue (and white) LEDs are the highest. So if you plug in a red and a blue, the energy goes to the lowest bidder . . . the red! The blue won't light up!

Hopefully you enjoyed this hair-raising adventure!
Next up, something you might wish you could zap—ZITS!

Zits

Forget Godzilla or Frankenstein. You want true horror? Wake up one morning with a giant pimple on the tip of your nose. GAAAHHHH!! You look like Rudolph the red-nosed reindeer! All you need is a sleigh! How can you ever emerge from your bedroom again?? But take heart, dear readers, it even happens to movie stars and politicians. And there are ways to zap zits!

ZITS ARE THE PITS

Pimples are stealthy little buggers. They sort of sneak up on you. One week you have silky-smooth skin, and the next you look like you have a scoop of rocky road ice cream for a forehead. Pimples are the most common skin condition in the world. An amazing 80 percent of Americans, at some point, will enjoy the unwanted presence of blackheads, whiteheads, and full-blown zits on their formerly smooth faces. Why, oh, why do we break out?

NOT BY THE HAIRS ON YOUR SKINNY-SKIN-SKIN!

First, a little basic biology review. You are a hairy little thing! We all are. Human skin has as many hair follicles as a great ape does. The only difference between *your* pelt and that of a gorilla is that your hairs are, for the most part, very, very fine. There is hair covering *all* of your external body with the exception of the palms of your

EEWWWW !!!

Luckily there are lots of pimple-blasters out there to save this teen's nose!

Relax! You may think a zit is the size of a melon, but it's not.

hands, the soles of your feet, your lips, and your eyeballs. Every tiny hair on your body hangs out in a little hair home called a *follicle* (foll-uh-kul).

Think of the follicle as a tiny cup. Picture a hair growing at the bottom of the cup. Skin cells line the whole thing. At the top of the cup (the surface of the skin) there is a small opening called a *pore*. Off to the side of the follicle is a *sebaceous* (see-bay-shus) gland that releases an oily, waxy substance called *sebum* (see-bum) into the follicle. Sebum nourishes the hair shaft and helps to keep your skin stretchy, soft, and waterproof. Otherwise you might look like an alligator! But too much sebum can clog your pores. Guess when your body starts making too much sebum? Hello, teen years!

Every day your skin is busy shedding old, dead cells to make room for new ones. The cells are quite tiny so you don't see them falling off. More than 30,000 little bits of your skin are flaking off every hour! Don't believe us? You know all that dust that settles on and under your furniture? It's mostly dead skin from you and your loved ones! Yes, you can say *"ICK!"* now! The average person sheds about eight pounds of skin cells every year. How lucky for us all that there are hungry dust mites lurking in our upholstery and pillows—creatures that LOVE dead skin and will gobble it up.

Anyway, now that you've just frantically vacuumed every surface in your entire house, let's get back to discussing your hair follicles: When too much gooey sebum gets stuck there, it traps the dead cells that are waiting to be shed. The cells start piling up, like too much dirty laundry in a hamper, and form a plug, blocking the pore. It's like fireplace smoke that can't escape via a blocked chimney and gets backed up inside the house. That pileup of dead skin and clumpy oil is what makes those wretched bumps on your face. But wait! It gets worse!

The dead-skin-and-sebum plug also traps bacteria. One of the culprits is called *Propionibacterium acne*, or *P. acne* for short. These teeny critters live naturally on the surface of our skin, and one of their favorite snacks is . . . yup . . . sebum! Normally they are friendly guests, but with lots of their favorite food around, they can make more and more and MORE of themselves. And when they get stuck in a clogged pore, your body senses an invasion. Call in the troops! Mount an attack! Soon your body's "armed forces"—the white blood cells—have started to swarm to the spot to make a mound of pus to devour and kill the bacteria. All this causes inflammation: redness, pain, and swelling. A pimple is born.

BLACK DOT, WHITE DOT, 1, 2, 3

So now you know how zits form, but let's dig deeper into pimple personalities. Some just look annoying. Others get swollen and painful.

If there aren't enough bacteria under the plug for your immune system to freak and make it all red and puffy, you have a *comedo*. Just a little bump. Nothing to fret over. There are two types: blackheads and whiteheads.

If a chunk of sebum gunk manages to get to the surface of your skin and is exposed to air, a pigment in it called melanin may darken. Congratulations! You have a *blackhead*.

If a thin layer of skin covers the gunky plug, lucky you! The skin keeps oxygen from the gunk, keeping it the normal color of sebum: white or yellowish. You have a *whitehead*!

Just like a huge traffic jam, dead skin is trapped on a highway of sticky sebum with no escape in sight. A bump forms. Hungry bacteria, attracted by the yumminess of all that dead skin and oil, are reproducing like crazy, so white blood cells swarm in to stop them. A big, red, painful, pus-filled bump emerges. Say hello to a *pimple*!

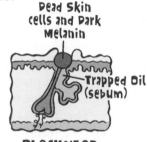

NORMAL HAIR FOLLICLE

Follicle · oil · Sebaceous Gland

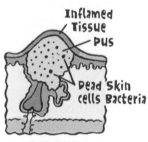

Dead Skin cells and Dark Melanin

Trapped Oil (sebum)

BLACKHEAD

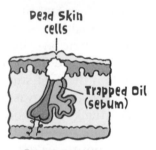

Dead Skin cells

Trapped Oil (sebum)

WHITEHEAD

Inflamed Tissue · PUS

Dead Skin cells · Bacteria

PIMPLE

It might be tempting, but there's no need to put a paper bag over your head if you get a pimple! We all get zits from time to time.

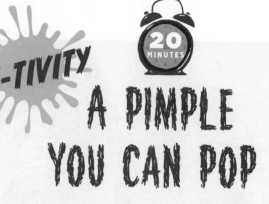

A PIMPLE YOU CAN POP

Most skin doctors recommend that pimples be left alone. Picking at a pimple can actually make the pimple worse or cause new infections. But we understand: There's something about a pimple that's so irresistible. It's like an unbearable itch that's dying to be scratched! Here's a way to make a giant, pus-filled pimple that you can safely let fly. Just don't get any on your bathroom mirror!

GO FETCH

2 golf ball–size pieces of modeling dough or clay (store-bought kid's brands, or make your own using our conductive dough recipe—see page 263). Dye it with food coloring to match the skin color of your choice. You can mix all the colors for darker skin tones. Use pink and yellow for lighter ones.

Bowl

Vegetable oil (e.g., olive oil or canola oil)

White toothpaste

Ground black pepper

Spoon

Red food coloring

Skewer or chopstick

1. As you know, a pimple is basically a plug of dead skin cells, sebum, bacteria, and white blood cells trapped under the surface of your skin. Use about half of your clay to create the hair follicle. Mold it so it resembles a volcano's crater—in other words, it should be a lump of clay with a hole in the middle.

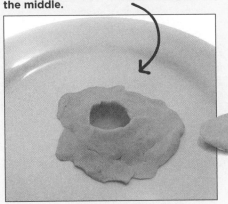

2. Now it's time to make your sebum/dead skin cell/bacteria/white blood cell pus mix. Oh, so delightful! In a bowl, create a thick mixture that's half vegetable oil and half toothpaste. You'll want to make enough of this goo to fill your pimple volcano's crater. The vegetable oil will represent the sebum. Toothpaste will represent the white blood cells and dead skin cells. Add a sprinkle of black pepper to represent the bacteria. Mix with a spoon until it is puslike and creamy.

3. Spoon the pus mix into the follicle.

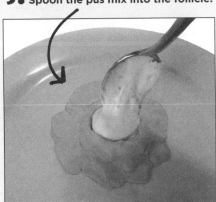

4. Flatten the rest of your clay into a thin layer that will represent the skin that covers the pimple. In the center, add a drop of red food coloring to indicate the irritation caused by pimples.

5. Put the skin layer on top of the pimple crater and squeeze that layer around the crater's edge so the pus is under some pressure and bulges up.

6. Okay, you've been very patient. Time to pop that pimple! Holding the skewer parallel to the ground and near the top of the pimple, push it through the clay until it comes out the other side.

Next, while the skewer is still embedded in the clay, slowly and gently force it up, further tearing the pimple's sack.

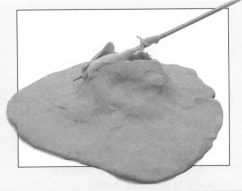

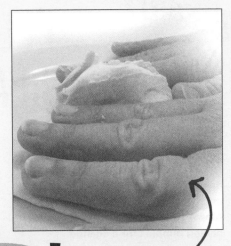

7. Use your hands to squeeze the sides to force the pus out of your pimple. If you have one, use your third hand to cover your mouth to prevent gagging.

WHAT JUST HAPPENED?

You just popped a King Kong–size zit using a gigantic "needle." The "skin" that was torn was a layer of dead skin cells, and, therefore, impervious to pain. But remember: Leave your own zits alone. Your skin is your armor; leave it intact or risk introducing more infections and/or creating permanent scars. Those of us with darker skin might be even more likely to get a scar from popping a pimple.

Many pimples disappear after about a week, but some can stay longer than that. Leave them alone, and if the urge to pop is too great, just repeat this ick-tivity!

I'LL HAVE A BITE OF BLACKHEAD, PLEASE!

30 MINUTES

PLUS 20–40 MINUTES FOR ICING

GO FETCH →

Sure, you can make a dull old cupcake with plain frosting and maybe some sprinkles, OR you can make whitehead, blackhead, and full-blown zit cupcake models and *enjoy* having pimples for a change.

1. With adult help, cook up a batch of cupcakes by following your family's recipe or the directions on the box. Allow to cool completely.

2. Study the drawing of the three different kinds of skin eruptions on page 268.

3. For every whitehead you want to make, use a butter knife to cut a small circular hole in the center of the cupcake. Cut down almost to the bottom. Scoop out a bit of the insides. You have just made a "hair follicle."

Your favorite cake recipe or cake mix (plus ingredients and utensils as noted on the package). You can choose chocolate (or add a little bit of it) to make a skin color to match your own, or choose a different color. Do aliens get zits? Probably—try green food coloring!

Cupcake pan and liners (baking cups)

Butter knife

Black string licorice or chocolate taffy candy

Scissors

2 small sandwich bags (if you happen to own an icing bag, then use that)

Container of vanilla frosting

1 piece of Fruit Roll-Ups or fruit-leather strip for every cupcake zit you plan to make (preferably red and yellow)

A few teaspoons cocoa powder

2 small bowls

2 teaspoons

4. Drop a "hair" into the bottom: Cut a piece of string licorice or pull a bit of taffy into a hair shape. The hairs on your face might be very fine and hard to see, but in our example we made the "hair" very visible.

5. Now, cut off one corner of a plastic bag to make a very small hole. Scoop 1 teaspoon of vanilla frosting into the large opening in the bag. Squeeze the frosting down toward the little corner hole until it starts to squirt out. Place it in the "hair follicle" in your cupcake and squeeze and squeeze until it fills up the hole! This represents too much sebum.

6. Open up a yellow Fruit Roll-Up. Stretch it out a little bit so that it will cover the whole top of the cupcake. Now carefully drape it over the top. Trim around the edges with your scissors. This represents the very top layer of your skin. In a whitehead the sebum plug does not reach the air, so it stays whitish-yellow. For a spectrum of skin tones, sprinkle cocoa powder and spread it around until you find a tone that matches yours!

7. For a red, swollen pimple, follow the directions for whiteheads above, but keep squirting the frosting until you have a big mound on top of the cupcake. Now the frosting represents pus—the sebum and bacteria and white blood cells arriving via the blood vessels in your skin to kill the bacteria. Stretch out a red Fruit Roll-Up or two and place it over the pus. The hair and pus will be hidden underneath the red, swollen "skin."

8. For blackheads, begin the same way as a whitehead, including dropping in a "hair."

For each blackhead, mix 1 teaspoon dark brown frosting (add ½ teaspoon of dark cocoa powder to the vanilla frosting and stir, or mix all the colors of the food coloring together to make brown). Then load the frosting in another bag with a corner cut off and squeeze it in the "hair follicle." This represents a pocket of sebum that has reached the air and turned dark brown.

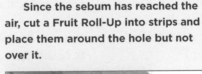

Since the sebum has reached the air, cut a Fruit Roll-Up into strips and place them around the hole but not over it.

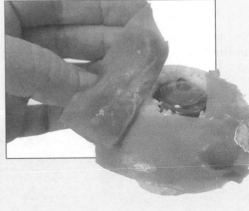

9. If you like, cut a couple of the cupcakes in half to show a cross-section. (Gently roll your zit-cakes onto one side and cut up toward the Fruit Roll-Up or else your whole cupcake may get squished.) See photos below.

Will your family or friends dare to "pop" the pimples in their mouth? What kind will you choose?

Blackhead

Swollen Pimple

Whitehead

HOW TO ZAP A ZIT

So you've read about zits, "eaten" one, and popped another, but what can you do if *your* gorgeous face gets hijacked by some sticky sebum and *P. acne* bacteria and you actually get a pimple? First of all, know that it is not your fault. It's not because you ate oily foods, and it's not from not washing your face enough. It's mostly because of your genes and those gnarly hormones that go haywire in the teen years. Some things that might make it worse are rubbing your face, stress, foods that you might be sensitive to, and dirty air. But happy news! There ARE treatments for it. If it bothers you, the doc to see is a dermatologist. He or she will know exactly what medicine will work for your specific skin type. You can also try some drugstore medicines or—much more fun—you can experiment! Ask your grown-ups if you can try the following home remedies, and, like the fabulous scientist you are, make notes about what happens. How quickly did the pimple dry up and disappear with each treatment?

ICE: Bacteria like to be warm. Ice is definitely not! Will icing it for 10 minutes (using the backside of a soupspoon left in the freezer for an hour) help conquer Mount Zit?

Raw potato: Slice a spud and place it on your pimple for 10 minutes or so.

Raw honey: A little dab might just do the trick. Raw honey is a hardworking bacteria-zapper. Just stay away from Winnie-the-Pooh and other honey-loving bears!

Toothpaste: Another test-worthy item. Some of the ingredients in toothpaste can zap germs. A small dab is enough, plus your pimple will have fresh breath!

Sea salt: Salt is a like a SWAT team for swelling. Just mix the salt crystals with a drop or two of water to make a paste, and perhaps soon your pimple will be lost at sea!

African black soap: This ancient soap is made from the ashes of palm and shea trees as well as tamarind extract and plantain peel. It has been used for centuries to treat a number of skin issues. It is said to soothe irritation and get rid of extra oil. Does less oil mean fewer pimples? Find out!

Bottom line: When you think about it, a pimple is really a golden opportunity to do some ick-sperimenting! And, know that as with all things in life, "This too will pass," so someday you'll be all grown up and mostly done with your pimply stage. Just remember to treat your face with tender loving care.

YOU MADE IT TO THE VERY END!

Well, stuffed-brain reader. There you have it—an A to Z of pure ickiness.
What was your favorite ick-tivity? What topic made you go "Eewwwwwww!" the loudest?
Can you burp the alphabet now? Cross your eyes? Mummify toast? Such useful skills—now all yours.

Promise us this: Keep exploring our weird, wild, beautiful, crazy, vile, amazing world.
Ask lots of questions! Experiment! Get outside and dig in the dirt!
It's all yours to squish, sniff, and explore! And most important—have fun!

Photo Credits

Experiment credits

Thanks for the inspiration!

Most of the activities in this book come from our 30 plus years of combined teaching experience. The experiments listed below, however, were adapted from certain resources. Any mistakes are unintentional and purely ours.

"Rockin' Rockets" and "Do We Have Liftoff?" were inspired by "Build a Bubble-Powered Rocket!" from NASA (spaceplace.nasa.gov/pop-rocket/en).

"The Reason? Freezin'!" and "Shake Your Booty" were adapted from activities developed for an MIT summer camp by Jessica Garrett (while working at the MIT Edgerton Center) and Ellen Dickenson (then of Lemelson-MIT). Imagine the tasty yet sticky mess a whole class can make!

"Lava-Licious" was adapted from an experiment created by Hawai'i Space Grant Consortium, Hawai'i Institute of Geophysics and Planetology, University of Hawai'i, 1996 (spacegrant.hawaii.edu/class_acts/GelVolTe.html).

"Bacteria Brew" was created by mad scientist Todd Rider of MIT, who generously shared it with us.

"The Great DNA Robbery" was adapted from the protocol developed by the genetics department at the University of Utah (learn.genetics.utah.edu/content/labs/extraction/howto).

"Seeing Upside Down" was adapted from Arvind Gupta's website, where you can find lots of other fun activities (arvindguptatoys.com).

"Fast Fossil Factory" was adapted from an activity on the National Park Service's website (nps.gov/brca/learn/education/paleoact3.htm).

"Foamy Fungi" was inspired by many similar experiments we've seen over the years. For more explosive fun and videos of what happens when you use higher concentrations of hydrogen peroxide, check out Science Bob's and Steve Spangler's versions called Elephant's Toothpaste or Kid-Friendly Exploding Toothpaste. Their websites have lots of other cool science experiments to explore, too (sciencebob.com, stevespanglerscience.com).

Thanks to the University of St. Thomas School of Engineering for sharing the "Squishy Circuits" experiment. Go to their website for even more electrifying ideas (ourseweb.stthomas.edu/apthomas/squishycircuits).

Index